School Counselor Accountability

A MEASURE of Student Success

Carolyn B. Stone
University of North Florida

Carol A. Dahir
New York Institute of Technology

Upper Saddle River, New Jersey
Columbus, Ohio

Vice President and Executive Publisher: Jeffery W. Johnston
Publisher: Kevin M. Davis
Editorial Assistant: Amanda King
Production Editor: Mary Harlan
Design Coordinator: Diane C. Lorenzo
Cover Design: Jeff Vanik
Cover Image: Comstock
Production Manager: Laura Messerly
Director of Marketing: Ann Castel Davis
Marketing Manager: Autumn Purdy
Marketing Coordinator: Tyra Poole

This book was printed and bound by Courier Kendallville, Inc. The cover was printed by The Lehigh Press, Inc.

Pearson Education Ltd.
Pearson Education Singapore Pte. Ltd.
Pearson Education Canada, Ltd.
Pearson Education–Japan
Pearson Education Australia Pty. Limited
Pearson Education North Asia Ltd.
Pearson Educación de Mexico, S.A. de C.V.
Pearson Education Malaysia Pte. Ltd.

10 9 8 7 6 5 4 3
ISBN: 0-13-147543-6

This book is dedicated to Elsie and Silas Bishop, Laura and Mitchell Dahir, and John Douglas Stone, because of the people they are.

Preface

A group of school counseling professionals (see Appendix A) through the initiation of Patricia Martin and Stephanie Robinson of the Education Trust met in 2001 to discuss an accountability plan for school counselors. These professionals collectively emphasized the need to develop a measurable process that provides school counselors with a way to align their work with the accountability requirements of No Child Left Behind (2001).

This book introduces MEASURE, a strategy for designing and implementing accountability as a cornerstone of a school counseling program. This approach provides methods for school counselors connect to the mission of their schools, demonstrate that students benefit from the counselors' work, and MEASURE success. We hope that *School Counselor Accountability: A MEASURE of Student Success* will:

- Demonstrate a simple step-by-step process for school counselors to connect their work with the expectations of school improvement and accountability.
- Encourage school counselors to implement a data-driven school counseling program and engage in data-driven decision-making.
- Prompt school counselors to participate in action research.
- Directly connect school counseling to the instructional program and student achievement
- Promote school counselor leadership, advocacy, collaboration, use of data, and technology.
- Help administrators, teachers, and others understand how the work of school counselors contributes to school improvement and systemic change.
- Motivate school counselors to align their work with the SSCA National Standards and the ASCA National Model.

Carolyn Stone and Carol Dahir

This book provides strategies for designing and implementing accountability as a cornerstone of a school counseling program. The approach presented provides school counselors with methods to connect to the mission of schools and MEASURE the school counselors' contributions to student success.

Acknowledgments

We would like to thank the thousands of school counselors across this country whose dedication and perseverance to improve the school experience for their students inspired and encouraged us to write MEASURE. A special note of appreciation goes to the contributing school counselors who generously gave hours for meetings, phone calls, data collecting, and editing. These counselors understand the importance of accountability and, by their actions, we can better MEASURE school counselors' contributions to student academic success:

Joan Apellaniz, Chelsea Career and Technical Education High School, New York, NY
Mary Ann Dyal, Alimacani Elementary School, Jacksonville, FL
Laura Lee Kinard, Bryceville Elementary, Bryceville, FL
Jim MacGregor, Pike High School, Indianapolis, IN
Linda Miller, District Supervisor of Guidance, Louisville, KY
Sejal Parikh, S. A. Hull Elementary School, Jacksonville, FL
Bob Turba, Stanton College Preparatory High School, Jacksonville, FL.
Edith Vanderhoek, Darnell-Cookman Middle School, Jacksonville, FL.
Dorothy Youngs, Ph.D., Assistant Director for Counseling K–12, Piscataway, NJ

In addition, we wish to express thanks to Kevin Davis, our editor, for believing in our vision of delivering a tool to school counselors to help with accountability; Autumn Crisp Benson, then editorial assistant; Karl G. Ruling, editorial review; David M. Luke, graphic design; Sharin Malecki Mitsis, typing and proofing; and Eileen FitzGerald Sudler, Esq. for editorial assistance.

We would like to recognize Karen Huffman, West Virginia Department of Education; Dawn Kay, Utah Department of Education; Joanne Miro, Delaware Department of Education; Mary Simmons, Tennessee Department of Education; and Robert Tyra, Los Angeles County Education Office for their critique and comments that strengthened this project. Finally we wish to thank Norman Gysbers, Curly Johnson, Patricia Martin, and Robert Myrick, trailblazers in the field of school counseling, whose contributions provided solid pathways to a bright future.

About the Authors

Carolyn Stone, Ed.D., is an associate professor at the University of North Florida (UNF) where she teaches and researches in the area of legal and ethical issues for school counselors and school counselors in the accountability climate. Prior to becoming a counselor educator, Stone spent 22 years with the Duval County Public Schools in Jacksonville, Florida where she served as Supervisor of Guidance, an elementary and high school counselor, and a teacher. Dr. Stone currently serves as ASCA's Ethics Chair, and is Past-President of the Florida Counseling Association and the Florida Association of Administrators and Supervisors. Stone has delivered several hundred workshops to practicing school counselors on legal and ethical issues and school counselors working in a climate of accountability and has written extensively on these two subjects in textbooks, journal articles, and other professional publications.

Stone can be contacted at UNF, COEHS, 4567 St. Johns Bluff Road South, Jacksonville, FL 32224, (904) 620-1828, or by e-mail at cstone@unf.edu.

Carol A. Dahir, Ed.D., is an assistant professor in counselor education at New York Institute of Technology (NYIT) . Dahir's career path includes working as a teacher, school counselor, and supervisor of school counseling programs and student support services. Dahir works extensively with numerous state departments of education, school systems, school counselor associations, and national organizations on excellence, accountability, and continuous improvement for school counselors. Dahir was the project director for the American School Counselor Association's National Standards for School Counseling Programs and Planning for Life (student career planning) She is the co-author of ASCA's best selling *Sharing the Vision: The National Standards for School Counseling Programs* and *Vision Into Action: Implementing the National Standards,* and writes extensively about school counseling improvement in textbooks, journals, and professional publications.

Dahir can be contacted at NYIT, School of Education, 21 West 60th St. New York, NY 10023, (516) 686-7777, or by e-mail at caroldahir@aol.com.

Contents

CHAPTER 1

The Accountability Imperative for School Counselors

"We need to know more than what your time-on-task numbers show. Tell us how your school counseling programs impacted student success in your schools. Test scores are down, attendance is not improving, postsecondary enrollment rates are stagnant, and the end of year failure rate for students in grades 4, 8, and 9 is over 35%. We appreciate our school counselors and understand that they work very hard. The numbers I have here in my hand are impressive. You delivered 2300 classroom guidance lessons, conducted 180 groups, and made innumerable individual contacts with student and parents. We face a dire budget next year. We want to help you, but where is the justification for continuing to fund school counselors when other educators who have shown their impact on student achievement are losing their jobs? We applaud your efforts, but in these fiscally dismal times we are forced to make tough choices. How do you know you made a difference in student achievement? Where is the data to show that your efforts have made a difference in student learning?"

- A school board member responding to the Supervisor of Guidance about tough decisions made while balancing a tight budget.

Accountability: Every Educator's Challenge

This all-too-real challenge from the district school board is a wake-up call for school counselors to rethink their traditional methods of demonstrating accountability. School board members, administrators, and others who are charged with making tough decisions about spending may not understand the relationship between the work of school counselors and student achievement. School counselors have not been held to the same accountability standards as other educators and have rarely been included in the conversations about how their contributions positively affect every student's academic life. Teachers and administrators have to show that they are making a positive difference in the critical data elements that school boards, legislators, parents, educators, and other community members consider to be vitally important such as test scores, attendance, retention, drop-out rates, grades, and success in rigorous academics. School counselors are just now beginning to understand how they too must be part of the discussion of how their contributions impact critical data elements.

Counting Is No Longer Enough

Time-on-task data, needs assessments, and the reporting of totals for the different types of activities are traditional school counselor demonstrations of accountability (Gysbers & Henderson, 2000). Is it possible to draw a direct line from counting services to academic outcomes for student achievement? Just totaling the number of student contacts made, group sessions held, and classroom guidance lessons delivered is "so what" data in the eyes of legislators, school board members, and other critical stakeholders. In other words, what do these totals really mean in the final analysis if students are being left out of the academic success picture and their future opportunities are adversely stratified? This traditional practice of counting will not demonstrate to our colleagues and community stakeholders that we are powerful contributors in our schools. More than likely your counselor instincts are starting to tell you that numbers of students seen, classroom surveys, or needs assessments are no longer acceptable yardsticks in a climate of school improvement.

Results-Based Accountability

Let's explore a familiar situation such as conducting a small group session for students experiencing a separation or divorce in their family. School counselors know that emotional stress can interfere with a student's academic success. By supporting a student's personal and emotional needs during the stress of divorce, we can help the student find a way to focus and succeed academically. If we evaluate the group from a results-based approach you might say that each group participant can identify at least three conflict resolution techniques. Results-based evaluation of school counseling strategies was developed by Johnson and Johnson (1991) and monitors student acquisition of competencies that are needed to succeed in school and to transition to postsecondary education to the work force. Results-based data documents outcomes. But the questions are quickly changing to, "Were the children in the divorce group suffering academically? If so, how did the group counseling session positively impact these children's academic achievement? Were you able to reduce their absenteeism, raise their test scores, or ensure promotion?"

Student Outcome Data

Which of these approaches will resonate with school board members and legislators who are looking for positive movement in school report card data? These scenarios offer three ways of demonstrating accountability.

- Counselor 1: Time-on-task. A school counselor may report time-on-task information such as 20% of every day is spent in career and academic advising, which includes helping students understand financial aid information for postsecondary education.

- Counselor 2: Results-based. A second counselor may take it a step further and report results-based data that stated that 60% of the student population can identify financial resources for postsecondary education.

- Counselor 3: Student Outcome Data. A third school counselor reported that 48% of the senior class completed and filed the Free Application for Federal Student Aid (FAFSA), which was an increase of 15% over last year and accompanied by a 3% bump in the postsecondary going-rate, an important school improvement goal.

Stakeholders understand the significant difference between reporting how the time is spent and reporting the direct benefit on students and their futures. The results of the third counselor's work showed that more students were willing to take a step forward toward continuing their education after high school. Each year the school counselors would raise the baseline so that the next year the goal might be to move from 33% (last year) to 48%, to the next year's goal of 58% for the number of students completing the FAFSA, to be accompanied by a proportionate rise in postsecondary going rates.

The same thinking can be applied to the group counseling scenario. If the school attendance for the seven students in the "students of divorce group" improved by 27%, then the work of the school counselor is directly linked to academic success. If students aren't in school, students can't learn. The shift from "so what" data to impacting critical school-based data is most powerful when we can explain and prove that the divorce group was a necessary and successful intervention needed to improve a child's academic success. Reporting a positive change in attendance is the type of accountability data that has meaning and merit to school boards and certainly to a student's future! It is much more powerful than reporting that the school counselor conducted seven groups for 35 students this year. It also means that we have to view our world through a different lens. This lens is focused on the changing times and also on the changing needs of youth in dynamic educational systems that have become complex and accountable for student results.

Accountability Means

How would it look and how incredulous would it be if the accountability fire to which teachers', principals', and superintendents' feet were held involved only time-on-task numbers?

Dear Teacher:
It is time to submit your accountability report. To do this, answer these questions:

1. *How many students did you teach this year?*
2. *How many lessons did you deliver?*
3. *How many tests did you give?*
4. *How many students received your one-on-one instruction?*
5. *How many times did you stay after school to help students?*
6. *How many parent conferences did you hold?*

If your numbers are impressive, you pass the accountability test.

Sincerely,
Your Principal

Dear Principal:
It is time to submit your accountability report. To do this, answer these questions about your work this year:

1. *How many teachers did you serve as curriculum leader?*
2. *How many students did you serve as principal?*
3. *How many Parent Teacher Association meetings did you attend?*
4. *How many parent conferences did you hold?*
5. *How many student conferences did you conduct?*
6. *How many teachers did you conference with this year?*

If your numbers are impressive, you pass the accountability test and your principalship is safe for another year.

Sincerely,
Your Superintendent

Dear Superintendent:
It is time to submit your accountability report. To do this, answer these questions about your work this year:

1. *How many educators did you serve as superintendent?*
2. *How many students did you serve as superintendent?*
3. *How many parent conferences did you conduct?*
4. *How many school board meetings did you attend?*

If your numbers are impressive, you pass the accountability test and your contract will be renewed.

Sincerely,
Your School Board Members

Dear School Counselor:
It is time to submit your accountability report.
To do this, answer these questions:

1. *How many classroom guidance lessons did you deliver?*
2. *How many students received your individual counseling services?*
3. *How many small groups did you deliver?*
4. *How many parent conferences did you conduct?*

If your numbers are impressive, you pass the accountability test.

Sincerely,
Your Principal

Are these four scenarios realistic? Are teachers, principals, and superintendents allowed to count services delivered or time-on-task as a measure of accountability? Would such a shallow measurement be desirable? The answer is a resounding, "No." For these educators the question is not, "How much do you do?" but, "How are students better off academically because of what you do?" Nevertheless, we counselors still hold fast to counting services delivered or time-on-task as our primary measure of accountability. Time-on-task is useful, but without student impact data, time-on-task numbers are inadequate for all other educators and for school counselors also!

Needs Assessments, Surveys, and Pre- and Post-Tests

Dear Teacher:
It is time to submit your accountability report.
To do this, answer these questions:

1. *Did you give a needs assessment this year to see what your students were interested in learning? Did you implement the desires expressed by students in those needs assessments?*
2. *Did you give a pre-test and post-test following each lesson you delivered? Did your students pass your post-tests?*
3. *Did you give an opinion survey to your students and their parents about the effectiveness of your teaching? How many students self-reported that they learned a great deal from your lessons this year?*
4. *How many parents positively responded that their children learned a great deal in your class this year?*

If the results of these efforts are positive, you pass the accountability test.

Sincerely,
Your Principal

Dear School Counselor:
It is time to submit your accountability report.
To do this, answer these questions:

1. *Did you give a needs assessment this year to see what your students and parents needed from your school counseling program? Did you implement the desires expressed in those needs assessments?*
2. *Did you give a pre-test and post-test following each lesson you delivered? Did your students pass your post-tests?*
3. *Did you give an opinion survey to your students and their parents about the effectiveness of your school counseling program? How many students self-reported that they benefited from your school counseling program this year?*

If the results of these efforts are positive, you pass the accountability test.

Sincerely,
Your Principal

In this scenario we are moving closer to the expectations of the accountability climate, yet self-report, surveys, needs assessments, and interim post-tests still fall short. The hot fire of accountability would be less intense for teachers if their measures of accountability depended on students' self-report of what they learned or the results of post-tests following each lesson. Although post-tests, self-reporting, surveys, and needs assessments are moving us closer to accountability, these are still soft measures of accountability and not at the level of accountability expected by stakeholders.

To deem counting and results-based approaches as adequate without showing the impact of our work on school report card data places us at risk of being viewed as an ineffective utilization of financial resources in the climate of limited funding. Some policy makers, school boards, and school system leaders who are held accountable for increasing student achievement have viewed the counseling program as fiscally irresponsible and as an ineffective utilization of resources (Whiston, 2002). Public perception continues to beg frequent questions such as, "What do school counselors really do? Why do we need school counselors in our schools?" These are not newly raised concerns and school counselors have heard variations on this theme over and over again.

Accountability and School Counselors

Accountability, as expected by our 21st century stakeholders, has eluded the school counseling professional who has traditionally focused on a support role, addressing individual issues, and removed from the instructional arena of schools. Often the school counseling profession has responded that counseling is a personal relationship with too many variables, making it impossible to measure a counselor's effectiveness, or evaluate a series of services (Schmidt, 2000). This way of working appears as marginally related to teaching and learning. The cliché evolved that 10% of the students command 90% of school counselors' time. For more than 20 years the professional literature has called repeatedly for increasing counselor accountability (Nims, James, & Hughey, 1998).

Despite the calls for accountability, there continues to be some resistance on the part of the counseling profession. Perhaps this is because counselors believe that accountability as we have described it may not be possible. Understandably, it can be difficult for school counselors to see how they can use data to isolate the things they do that contribute to the academic success of students. Resistance also has emanated from years of frustration in not having access to students or becoming embroiled in administrative responsibilities. Frustration, perceived or real, lack of support, marginalization, and huge caseloads have also contributed to maintaining the status quo of presenting time-on-task, needs assessments, and counting contacts to demonstrate a measure of accountability.

> Take a moment to reflect on your personal feelings about accountability. In every counseling situation the need to explore motivation and emotions about an issue impact a student's ability to move in a positive direction. To contribute to the accountability agenda in our schools we need to apply the same principles to ourselves.

Accountability is not:

- The feedback you receive from your principal on your annual evaluation. This principal report is important, but accountability focuses on how student achievement has been impacted by the school counselor's work on the leadership team.
- Counting services delivered such as how many groups you ran, individuals you counseled, parent conferences you held.
- Showing how you spend your time such as a report that 75% of your time was in direct service with students.
- Survey results, needs assessments, pre- and post-tests.

Accountability is:

- A means of assessing the impact of the school counseling program on school improvement.
- Connecting our work to student outcome data.

Beliefs Inform Behaviors

Can we rise to meet this challenge? If we truly believe that all children can learn and achieve, then aligning the school counseling program with the academic mission of schools presents the school counselor as a champion and collaborator who encourages high aspirations and creates opportunities for students to realize their dreams. Accountability shows that school counselors act on their belief systems, not just talk about them.

School counselors demonstrate by words and actions that we accept the responsibility of removing barriers to learning and achievement. As a systemic change agent we can cultivate a belief that all children are capable of achieving (Johnson, 2000). School counselors who focus on improving student results will contribute to raising the achievement level for every student.

School counselors can:

- impact student achievement;
- improve student course-taking patterns that increase access to rigorous academic work;
- raise student aspiration and motivation;
- manage and access school and community-based resources;
- motivate students to assume responsibility for their educational and career planning;
- influence the school climate to ensure that high standards are the norm in a safe and respectful environment;
- work with our principals and faculties to create safe and drug-free communities; and
- use data to effectively identify institutional and environmental barriers that can impede student success.

The Achievement Gap

Working within an accountability framework shows that all educators, especially school counselors, intentionally and purposely act to close the achievement gap. Accepting the challenge of accountability propels school counselors into a higher-profile, more powerful role to challenge barriers to learning and achievement and to raise the level of expectations for those students from whom little is expected. School counselors can challenge the pervasive belief that socio-economic status and color determine a young person's ability to learn. Acting as agents of school and community change, school counselors can create a climate where access and support for quality and rigor is the norm. In doing so, underserved and under-represented students now have a chance to acquire the education skills necessary to participate fully in the 21st century economy.

School counselors can form partnerships with principals and key stakeholders to embrace accountability and to promote systemic change with the expressed purpose of furthering the academic success of every student (Stone & Clark, 2001). With an accountable school counseling program that can quantify success, school counselors are seen as partners and collaborators in school improvement and essential to fulfilling the mission of every school. Sharing accountability with stakeholders to improve our schools is a driving force for transforming the work of school counselors across the nation.

References

Gysbers, N. C. & Henderson, P. (2000). *Developing and managing your school guidance program* (3rd ed.). Alexandria, VA: American Counseling Association.

Johnson, C. D. & Johnson, S. K. (1991). The new guidance: A system approach to pupil personnel programs. *CACD Journal, 11,* 5-14.

Johnson, L. S. (2000). Promoting professional identity in an era of educational reform. *Professional School Counseling, 4,* 31-40.

Nims, D., James, S., & Hughey, A. (1998). The challenge of accountability: A survey of Kentucky school counselors. *Kentucky Counseling Association Journal, 17,* 31-37.

Rhode Island Department of Education (1997). *School accountability for learning and teaching (SALT).* Providence, RI: Author.

Schmidt, J. (2000). *Counseling in schools: Essential services and comprehensive programs.* Boston, MA: Allyn and Bacon

Stone, C., & Clark, M. (2001). School counselors and principals: Partners in support of academic achievement. *National Association of Secondary School Principals Bulletin, 85* (624), 46-53.

Whiston, S. C. (2002). Response to the past, present, and future of school counseling: Raising some issues. *Professional School Counseling, 5,* 148-155.

CHAPTER 2

Beyond Tradition

- Closing the Gap
- School Counselors: Leaving No Child Behind
- Respecting Tradition: A Retrospective
- Why Change? Well, It's a Different World
- Moving Forward

"School improvement is hard work. But if schools are not constantly improving and growing in their capacity to meet the needs of today's students, then they are losing ground and failing in their mission of service to young people."

-Fitzpatrick, 1997

School counselors can work with the same goals in mind as our colleagues to meet the needs of today's students. Acceptance as an equal player requires our willingness to be held to the same accountability standards as our fellow educators. School board members and parents do not focus on the number of students assigned to a secondary teacher during the course of an eight-period school day, nor do they concern themselves exclusively with the number of students in each fourth-grade teacher's class. The numbers are important, but administrators, parents, and taxpayers care most about the results of instruction in those classes. Did every elementary child gain, at the minimum, a full year of instructional growth? Did secondary students master the subject, pass the final exams, and accrue credit towards graduation? Our radar sensors told us that it was only a matter of time until school counselors would be expected to move beyond our tried and true ways of demonstrating accountability. But why now?

Since America 2000 (1990) and Goals 2000 (1994), educational requirements and expectations have demanded much more than accounting for time and tasks from all educators. Accountability is not a newly raised issue. Throughout the last decade, educators, policy makers, community groups, business leaders, and parents who work in boardrooms, in legislative arenas, in school districts, and at universities, and who sit at kitchen tables across the nation have diligently worked to reform and improve K-12 education. Today's accountability expectations emanate from *No Child Left Behind* (2001), which require every educator to use school-based data to demonstrate our engagement in the school mission and student achievement. This means school counselors too! Accountability represents our desire to effect school improvement through systemic change.

Closing the Gap

The heart of the national debate about education is simply about what is working and what is not in public schools. Policies and practices are concerned with every student having equitable access to educational opportunities and with creating settings in which all children are held to high expectations and are given a fair chance to achieve this goal. The influence of the differences in our classrooms, such as ethnicity, language, and economic means, is of major concern to educators and business persons alike (Sapon-Shevon, 2001). In the past some students went to "good" schools; others to the "poor" schools. Within our school buildings opportunities were too frequently stratified by race, ethnicity, and socio-economic status (SES). The quality of our public schools affects all of us, yet too many children in America are segregated by low expectations, low literacy, and self doubt (Bush, 2001). Let's look at the following table:

Achievement Level (in quartiles)	Low-Income	High-Income
Quartile 1 (Low)	36%	77%
Quartile 2	50%	85%
Quartile 3	63%	90%
Quartile 4 (High)	78%	97%

Source: USDOE, NCES, NCES Condition of Education 1997, p. 64

The data in the table above reveals poverty as the contributing factor. More than ever before we are reminded of the importance of the American education system's commitment to standards-based reform and the declaration to close the gap in student performance. This is the central goal of school-based accountability. Standards across academic areas are the basis to assess the quality of the program and the effectiveness of the curriculum. The use of demographic and performance data makes it possible to determine how policies and practices are affecting issues of equity and, in this case, the impact of wealth on achievement.

School counseling programs must respond to the implications of data such as this. Unknowingly and without malevolent intent, school counselors have played a central role in maintaining the status quo and supporting inequitable schools and have served as gatekeepers in the course selection and course placement process. It is time to show that within our sphere of influence we are willing to address some of the challenges in implementing a standards-based educational system. Specifically school counselors can impact:

- low expectations, specifically the pervasive belief that socioeconomic status and color determine young people's ability to learn; and
- the sorting and selecting process that acts as a filter, denying access to rigorous course content to students because of low expectations.

If school counselors are committed to high expectations for all students regardless of race, ethnicity, and SES, then every student requires the academic and life skills preparation that opens wide the door of opportunity to all options after high school, including college. To give all students extensive options, more stakeholders need to be involved and to demonstrate a commitment to equity. School counselors can systematically collect and analyze achievement data to inform and guide the development and construction of a school counseling program. This data can be used to address concerns regarding equity, access, and success that exist in both our affluent and poverty stricken school systems. In other words, school counseling programs can seek out those pockets of students left out of the academic success picture and contribute to creating opportunities for them. Indeed, when you read the MEASUREs from real counselors in real schools later on in this book, you will see how school counselors across this country are figuratively wrapping their arms around more students and providing them with many more opportunities.

School Counselors: Leaving No Child Behind

Everyone of us has been affected by the *No Child Left Behind* (2001) legislation. President George W. Bush has made education a domestic priority. *No Child Left Behind* (NCLB), the current reauthorization of the Elementary and Secondary Education Act, intends to close the achievement gap between disadvantaged students, students of color, and their peers. NCLB promotes stronger accountability for demonstrating results and expanded options for parents to seek a high-quality education experience for their children. Student progress and achievement is published annually. Mandated state reports include performance data disaggregated according to race, gender, and other criteria. This demonstrates not only how well students are achieving overall, but also depicts progress made to close the achievement gap between disadvantaged students and other groups of students.

No Child Left Behind (2001) embodies four basic principles:

a. Stronger accountability for results, which has created standards in each state determining what a child should know specifically in reading and math in grades 3-8. Student progress and achievement will be measured according to tests based upon those state standards and given to every child, every year.

b. Expanded flexibility and local control, which have allowed for local school districts to have more flexibility and a greater say in how federal funds are used in their schools to meet student needs.

c. Expanded options for parents of children from disadvantaged backgrounds whose children are trapped in failing schools. Providing funds to students in failing schools to use for supplemental educational services, including tutoring, after-school services, and summer school programs, and charter schools.

d. An emphasis on teaching methods that have been proven to work, strengthening teacher quality, and promoting English proficiency.

No Child Left Behind has five primary goals that are the foundation for this national educational agenda, which extends to the school year 2013–2014. The first three goals focus on the improvement of curriculum, learning, and achievement. Goals 4 and 5 address the other side of the report card, the aspect of student success that takes into consideration student personal-social development and motivation.

Let's look at how Goals 4 and 5 impact our work:

No Child Left Behind (2001) Elementary and Secondary Education Act
ESEA Goal 4 All students will be educated in learning environments that are safe, drug free, and conducive to learning.
ESEA Goal 5 All students will graduate from high school.

School counselors are ideally situated to impact Goals 4 and 5. We can share the pressures of school accountability by motivating students to achieve at their highest level of ability, demonstrate advocacy for every student to experience success in a safe and respectful environment, and work intentionally towards the goal of ensuring that every child graduates from high school, regardless of the level at which we work.

Who can better address these two goals than the school counselor who is committed to ensuring that students have equitable access to educational opportunities? NCLB urges school counselors to become involved in school-wide issues related to school improvement and to ensure that every student will be prepared fully to participate in the 21st century society and economy.

Raising student achievement in America's schools is the primary focus of school improvement. Legislators, school board members, teachers, school-site and district-level administrators, parents, employers, and other school and community members feel the pressures of raising academic standards and improving student academic success. Commitment to higher levels of student achievement and continuous improvement is a responsibility shared by all of the critical stakeholders, including school counselors. If we want to be key players in furthering the primary goals of our 21st century schools, then we too must become partners in systemic change with the express purpose of furthering the academic success of every student.

Respecting Tradition: A Retrospective

In the less complicated world of yesterday, counseling in schools was viewed primarily as an intervention for individual students. Were there fewer children who needed us? In the past, demands on children and educators were different. Not so long ago, a school counselor could spend the majority of her/his time working with students who were in crisis, in trouble, or applying to highly selective colleges. Despite large caseloads, our sphere of influence was small. One child at a time was the way we knew how to make a difference. Graduate training programs honed our skills in individual and group interventions. Our energies were expended on those who sought our assistance or with those students who were brought to our immediate attention for crisis intervention.

Despite these intensive efforts, we were concerned that our effectiveness was limited by time constraints and our own ability to intervene and impact more students. In some of our schools, counselors were (and are) tapped to become administrative and clerical support for overworked principals. Time and task assignments often spun out of control. The school counselor, not married to a classroom routine, often found her/himself enveloped in administrative duties. After all, we were considered ancillary services – supporting whatever needed to be accomplished.

It is also important to note that the tradition of school counseling preparation was firmly grounded in mental health theory, technique, and practice. Today's school counselor needs that solid foundation in counseling, but just as critically important is the need to understand the place called school, the expectations of the institution, and the dynamics of working with perhaps a hundred faculty members and several hundred students and parents, all of whom share the ultimate goal of ensuring that students succeed in school. Expectations for school counselors are changing; now too graduate preparation is changing (Stone & Hanson, 2002).

A profession does not evolve overnight despite the numbers or levels of courses required for degrees, or the sheer numbers of personnel in the field. Counseling in schools continues to move towards professional status. We have learned from our history that our roots are deeply embedded in the values that attracted each one of us to the helping professions in the first place.

School counseling is invested in tradition yet continues to evolve and change in focus and purpose. The first guidance program introduced into a Detroit high school by Jesse Davis in 1889 was intended to help students develop character, avoid problems, and relate vocational interests to course work (Brewer, 1932). Frank Parsons, often cited as the "father of guidance", is credited as the person who began this movement. Parson's attention to vocational guidance was coupled with his concern about society's failure to provide resources for human growth and development, especially for young people (Schmidt, 2000). Sound familiar? Perhaps, we have come full circle.

The impact of World War I and its aftermath, the Great Depression, resulted in a marked need for assisting students with vocational selection and placement. The term "vocational counselor", rarely heard before the Depression, entered the educational vocabulary (Wittmer, 2000). The use of new assessments led to the development of counseling approaches that related student traits with interests and abilities. Attempts to organize and expand guidance within the school setting in the 1930s led to the addition of educational and personal/social services

(Gysbers, 2000). The traditional way of describing guidance as a vocational service was no longer in vogue, thus contributing to broadening the goals of these programs and added the elements of counseling.

In the 1940s, the introduction of Carl Rogers' client-centered theory, the impact of World War II, and government's involvement in education strongly influenced the future direction of guidance and counseling (Gladding, 2000). The *George-Barden Act* of 1946 funded guidance and counseling in the schools and other settings. As these services expanded across the country, Mathewson promoted school guidance and counseling as a process that moves with the individual student and in a developmental sequence through the age of maturity (Wittmer, 2000).

Professional associations emerged as strong influences during this period, and the American School Counselor Association became a division of the American Personnel and Guidance Association in the mid-1950s. Additional funding channeled through the *National Defense Education Act* (NDEA) of 1956 tripled the number of secondary school counselors with the express intent of increasing the numbers of students going on to college. Once again the focus of the counselor shifted with a dual emphasis on delivering college admissions information and supporting the student in resolving personal problems that might be a barrier to academic success (Perry & Schwallie-Giddis, 1993). This emphasis on postsecondary opportunities and individual personal support created the perception that the work of school counselors was available only to the college bound or for those with personal problems.

Since the early 1980s, Gysbers and Henderson (2000) and Myrick (1997) have written extensively about redesigning school counseling programs into a comprehensive and developmental format. Social pressures and the emphasis on educational student support have reframed school counseling from individual student response and crisis intervention to a proactive series of strategies that engage every student. As a result many new models for program design and delivery systems were developed at the state and local level.

Despite these new models, the traditional viewpoint persisted and school counselors continued to deliver a constellation of responsive and reactive activities that serviced a small percentage of the student population. School counseling research studies examined the professional school counselor role, analyzed time and tasks, and explored the impact and significance of interventions and prevention initiatives. Commissioned reports of national significance such as Keeping the Options Open (1986, 1992) and High Hopes Long Odds (1994) praised school counselors for the work they do, condemned them for what they don't do, and accused school counselors of not appropriately contributing to the academic success of students. School counselors were accused of being gatekeepers, perpetuating the accepted rules and systematic barriers that cause inequities between achievers and non-achievers based on race and socio-economic status (Hart & Jacobi, 1992).

Throughout the 1980s and the 1990s school counseling was conspicuously absent in all the school reform efforts to promote higher levels of educational excellence.

The continued omission of school counseling from the educational reform agenda was the impetus for the American School Counselor Association's (ASCA) action to advocate for the establishment of school counseling programs as an integral component of the educational system. The development of the *National Standards for School Counseling Programs* (ASCA, 1997) was an important first step in engaging school counselors and stakeholders in a national conversation about the attitudes, knowledge, and skills, in academic, career, and personal-social development that every student should acquire as a result of participating in the school counseling program (Appendix B). The national standards, linked to the mission of the school, encouraged school counselors to evaluate and assess the impact of their program on student achievement and school success. Most importantly, the standards connected school counseling to the national school reform agenda of the 1990s (Campbell & Dahir, 1997). School counselors began to see themselves as key players in preparing students to meet the increasingly complex societal demands that require significant knowledge and skills to succeed in the 21st century. Taking a position on important educational issues, behaving as a systemic change agent, and advocating for change and continuous improvement was beginning to be the norm for school counselors (Clark & Stone, 2000).

The *National Model: A Framework for School Counseling Programs* (ASCA, 2003) (Appendix C) emphasized the importance of school counselors delivering accountable school counseling programs that carefully consider local demographic needs and the political climate of the community. The *National Model* (ASCA, 2003) speaks to the importance of having an accountability system and an organizational framework that documents how students are different as a result of the school counseling program. The four main components of the *National Model* are:

1) the foundation of the program, which requires the implementation of the belief and mission that every student will benefit from the school counseling program;

Accountability
Results Reports
School Counselor Performance Standards
The Program Audit

Management System
Agreements
Advisory Council
Use of Data
Action Plans
Use of Time
Calendars

Delivery System
School Guidance Curriculum
Individual Student Planning
Responsive Services
System Support

Foundation
Beliefs and Philosophy
Mission Statement
ASCA National Standards (Student Academic, Career and Social/Personal Development)

SYSTEMIC CHANGE · ADVOCACY · LEADERSHIP · COLLABORATION · SYSTEMIC CHANGE · ADVOCACY · LEADERSHIP · COLLABORATION · SYSTEMIC CHANGE · ADVOCACY · LEADERSHIP · COLLABORATION · SYSTEMIC CHANGE · ADVOCACY · LEADERSHIP · COLLABORATION

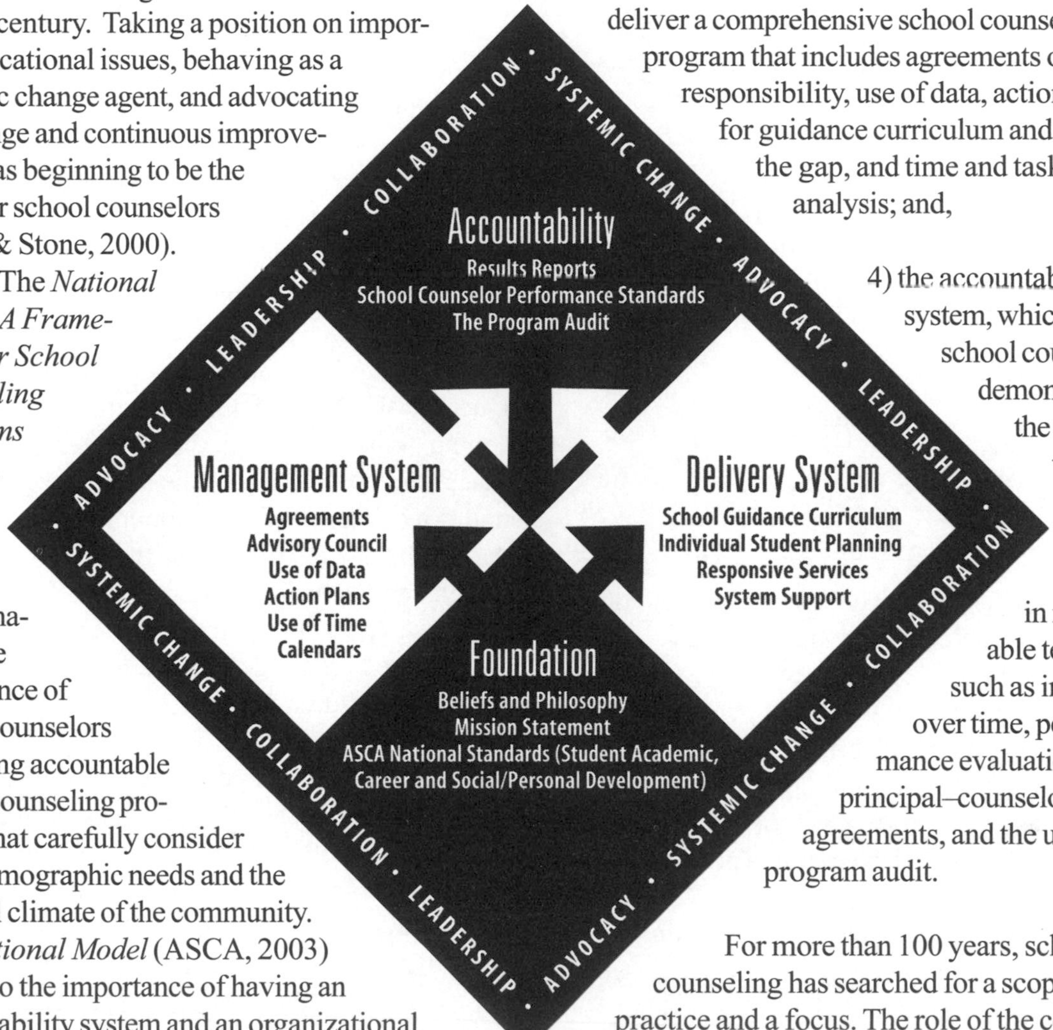

2) the delivery system, which defines the implementation process and the components of the comprehensive model, i.e., guidance curriculum, individual planning with students, responsive services, and system support;

3) the management system, which presents the organizational processes and tools needed to deliver a comprehensive school counseling program that includes agreements of responsibility, use of data, action plans for guidance curriculum and closing the gap, and time and task analysis; and,

4) the accountability system, which helps school counselors demonstrate the effectiveness of their work in measurable terms such as impact over time, performance evaluation, principal–counselor agreements, and the use of a program audit.

For more than 100 years, school counseling has searched for a scope of practice and a focus. The role of the counselor changed from vocational guidance advisor to psycho-matrician, to a responsive service provider. Today we want to be viewed as essential contributors to student success. With accountability driving the educational agenda, the 21st century school counselor must be seen as a highly visible and proactive professional directly involved in student achievement. Most importantly, we are willing to share accountability for school improvement.

Historical perspectives help us to understand our roots and the evolution of new trends and influences. Progression and professionalism in school counseling have been steady and focused. The school counseling program of the 21st century is different from the activities and service model of the 1980s. School counseling programs now have characteristics similar to other educational programs, including standards, a scope and sequence, student outcomes or competencies, activities and processes to assist students in achieving these outcomes, professionally credentialed personnel, materials, and resources, and methods to measure success. Most importantly, 21st century counselors avoid working in isolation, and are part of the team contributing to a school climate and the achievement of identified student goals and outcomes, and share accountability for student success.

Why Change? Well, It's a Different World

Change doesn't come easily in any educational arena, including school counseling. It has taken us 100 years to receive acknowledgement as an integral, but unmandated, component of the educational system in the majority of the 50 states. It has taken us an equal amount of time to transform ourselves to embrace school-based issues and student achievement concerns as a primary focus of our work.

If you have always been successful in your work with students you may be asking yourself, "What is the imperative to change?" Students present a myriad of needs that have evolved out of poverty, family dysfunction, prejudice, and learning abilities. In contemporary society, every child is at risk of some aberrant behavior. Societal influence is strong. Violence, gangs, suicide, child abuse, teen pregnancy, substance abuse, date rape, homelessness, hunger, and lack of access to postsecondary education lurk in every community and across all socio-economic boundaries. Digest the following statistics for a minute -

An American child:
- is reported abused or neglected every 11 seconds;
- is born into poverty every 43 seconds;
- is born to a teen mother every minute;
- is arrested for drug abuse every 4 minutes;
- is arrested for violent crimes every 8 minutes;
- is killed by a firearm every 3 hours;
- commits suicide every 5 hours;

(Children's Defense Fund, 2002, p. 14)

Millions of American children start school not ready to learn; a majority of fourth graders can't read or do math at a proficient level; and seven million children are home alone on a regular basis without adult supervision, often after school when they are at the greatest risk of getting into trouble (Children's Defense Fund, 2002).

Today's school counselor shows how much he/she cares by instilling the resiliency and coping skills in children that are necessary for a successful completion of the school year. The traditional way of working no longer produces the results needed to address the magnitude of societal and achievement challenges facing our students. All children and adolescents live more complicated emotional, social, and academic lives than children of even ten years ago. Working individually and not systemically risks leaving huge numbers of these students, all of whom need us, out of the success picture. Our imperative is to try to meet the needs of the greatest number of students in our charge. NCLB (2001) is also a constant reminder to us to carefully think and rethink about results and how we can influence our practice and programs

Moving Forward

The educational agenda of the 21st century has raised the bar for every student regardless of ability or disability. As educators, we now see ourselves as critical players in helping every student meet the rigorous curriculum of academic standards, pass the exit exams, and graduate high school with all options available to her/him for the next phase of the student's postsecondary plans. This shift in thinking and practice requires embracing a new vision with a strong emphasis on leadership, advocacy, and support for high levels of student achievement. (The Education Trust, 1997). It also requires us to rethink our current level of skill and where additional professional development may be helpful to us in this new way of working.

Expanding the Focus

Service driven model	Student competency driven model
• Counseling	• Counseling
• Coordination	• Coordination of services
• Consultation	• Consultation
	• Collaboration and teaming
	• Case management
	• Leadership
	• Advocacy
	• Management of resources
	• Assessment and use of data
	• Program design and evaluation

National associations such as the American School Counselor Association (Campbell & Dahir, 1997) and the Education Trust (1997) have suggested that school counselors need to be proficient in more than the traditional three C's: counseling, coordination of services, and consultation. Skills in collaboration and teaming, case management, leadership, advocacy, managing resources, assessment and use of data, and program design and evaluation are considered the essential elements of contemporary graduate preparation, professional development, and transformed school counselor practice (Education Trust, 1997). Let's explore what each of these mean:

Counseling
Counseling is the process of assisting a client in understanding, assessing, and making a change in behavior for the purpose of advancing self- awareness and understanding, increasing self -efficacy, and improving or enhancing relationships with others. Counseling also is a tool for enabling clients to make decisions to further improve their quality of life.

Coordination of Services
Counselors serve as liaisons between teachers, parents, support personnel, and community resources to facilitate successful student development. As student advocates, school counselors seek equitable access to programs and services for all students.

Consultation
The counselor as a consultant primarily helps parents and teachers to be more effective in working with others. Consultation helps parents and teachers think through problems and concerns, acquire more knowledge and skill, and become more objective and self-confident. This intervention can take place in individual or group conferences, through staff-development activities, or in parent education classes. The school counselor acting as a consultant provides information and skills to parents/guardians, teachers, and the community to assist them in helping students in academic, career, and personal/social development.

Collaboration and Teaming
School counselors, as education professionals who specialize in counseling and student growth and development, have joined with teachers, administrators, and stakeholders external to the school to improve student success and achievement.

Case Management
Counselors provide the necessary monitoring and coordinating of an individual student's progress towards achieving success in academic, career, and personal/social development, and secure the appropriate and necessary services and supports that are essential to the student's success.

Leadership
The school counselor serves as a leader as well as an effective team member, working with teachers, administrators, and other school personnel to make sure that each student succeeds. A comprehensive school counseling program now aligned with the school improvement agenda in your building is a proactive response to school improvement.

Advocacy
The school counselor advocates for the elimination of significant performance gaps among students from different economic classes, genders, races, or ethnic groups. Therefore, there is an alignment and consistency in expectations across all levels of education – elementary, middle, and high school.

Management of Resources
Counselors identify, access, and coordinate the resources within the school and community that are necessary to support school success for every child. The school counselor helps families, parents, guardians, and caretakers identify their children's needs and provides information and assistance by accessing resources internally and externally to the school.

Assessment and Use of Data
Data-driven results are the key to linking school counseling programs with higher levels of achievement. These results can be shared within the school community and with the school board, parents, business and industry, and higher education partners.

Program Design and Evaluation
Counselors continually assess the needs of their students, evaluate their programs, and make changes and revisions to the school counseling program to better meet the academic, career, and personal-social development of every student.

Take a moment to reflect on your feelings about expanding your repertoire of skills. What skills are strongest for you? What skills do you want to improve or refine?

____

____

The transformed school counselor articulates and communicates how her/his presence and work positively impact student achievement. The transformed school counselor uses a variety of strategies, activities, delivery methods, and resources to facilitate student growth and development. This foundation helps us in our role as student advocates, in our ability to provide direct and indirect services to every child, and also supports our belief that all children can learn and achieve.

On a daily basis, we are confronted with issues of equity and access to opportunity. The data and the students tell the tale. Students of color, students of poverty, and students of some ethnic groups are often denied access to educational opportunities that lead to quality postsecondary options after high school. Education and economic success are inextricably entwined. School counselors hold the key to student success and are ideally situated to identify policies and practices that stratify student opportunity (Stone & Clark, 2001). The accountable school counseling program, now aligned with the educational enterprise, is data driven, proactive and preventive in focus, and assists students in acquiring and applying life-long learning skills. School counseling in the 21st century is continually moving forward, seeking ways to better serve the needs of our students and our schools, while not losing sight of our rich history and our purpose to be counselors in schools, not counselors in agencies.

References

American School Counselor Association. (1997). *The national standards for school counseling, programs*. Alexandria, VA: Author.

American School Counselor Association. (2003). *American school counselor association national model: A framework for school counseling programs*. Alexandria, VA: Author.

Brewer, J. M. (1932). *Education as guidance: An examination of the possibilities of curriculum in terms of life activities in elementary and secondary schools and colleges.* New York: Macmillan.

Bush, G. W. (2001). *No child left behind.* Washington, DC: U. S. Department of Education.

Campbell, C., & Dahir, C. (1997). *Sharing the vision: The national standards for school counseling programs*. Alexandria, VA: American School Counselor Association.

Gysbers, N. C., & Henderson, P. (2000). *Developing and managing your school guidance program* (3rd ed.). Alexandria, VA: American Counseling Association.

Hart, P. J., & Jacobi, M. (1992). *From gatekeeper to advocate: Transforming the role of the school counselor.* NY: College Entrance Examination Board.

Lilly Endowment. (1994). *High hopes, long odds.* Chicago: Public Policy Research Consortium and The Indiana Youth Institute.

Myrick, R. D. (1997). *Developmental guidance and counseling: A practical approach.* Minneapolis, MN: Educational Media Corporation.

Perry, N., & Schwallie-Giddis, P. (1993). The counselor and reform in tomorrow's schools. *The Journal of Counseling and Human Development, 25,* 1-8.

Sapon-Shevin, M. (2001). Schools fit for all. *Educational Leadership, 58*, 34-39.

Schmidt, J. (2000). *Counseling in schools: Essential services and comprehensive programs.* Boston, MA: Allyn and Bacon.

Stone, C. B., & Clark, M. (2001). School counselors and principals: Partners in support of academic achievement. *National Association of Secondary School Principals Bulletin, 85* (624), 46-53.

Stone, C., & Hanson, C. (2002). Selection of school counselor candidates: Future direction at two universities. *Counselor Education and Supervision,* 41(3), 175-192.

U.S. Department of Education. (2001). *No child left behind* (ERIC Document No. ED 447 608). Washington, DC: Author.

U.S. Department of Education. (1994). *Goals 2000: The educate America act.* Washington, DC: Author.

U.S. Department of Education. (1990). *America 2000: An education strategy.* Washington, D.C.: U.S. Department of Education.

U.S. Department of Education. (1956). *National defense education act.* Washington, DC: Author.

Wittmer, J. (2000). *Managing your school guidance and counseling program: K-12 developmental strategies.* Minneapolis, MN: Educational Media Corp.

CHAPTER 3
Demystifying Data

"Using data to drive decisions....is critical. Teachers, principals, curriculum advisors, parents, and students all can work toward basing their decisions on objective data rather than opinion and hearsay. This will require each of us to do a little more checking, a little more questioning, and a little more listening, but the end result will be worth it."

Gina Burkhardt, NCREL, 2003

(This means school counselors too!)

Data First

What's driving the school improvement agenda? Accountability! What's driving accountability? Data-driven decision making! So what do school counselors need to do? Begin by using the data that is discussed in your school improvement plan to design and implement your comprehensive school counseling program. Just like the "chicken or the egg" debate, is it program development first or data? Consider this: data is knowledge. Knowledge is power. Thus let's begin with the critical data elements that are presented publicly about our schools. The data tells the story of our students' accomplishments and provides us with the knowledge to impact real needs, not the perception of need. Once we have the facts in hand, we can develop the strategies to support our comprehensive national standards-based program. These strategies also will support the necessary changes identified by the school improvement plan. Need we say more? The commitment of school counselors to sharing accountability will help to ensure that all students will progress through school and emerge more capable and more prepared than ever before to meet the challenging and changing demands of the new millennium. This cannot happen without the knowledge about who succeeds and who fails. School counselors who demonstrate accountability, document effectiveness, and promote school counseling's contributions to the educational agenda are in a unique position to exert a powerful influence (Clark & Stone, 2000).

Why Use Data?

Data paints a vivid picture of a school and its students. Our school report cards are graphic representations of the successes and failures in our buildings and systems. By using data, school counselors can accurately present the current situation of student challenges and accomplishments in all of the areas that are publicly displayed. These areas include attendance, promotion rates, number of suspensions, graduation rates, postsecondary attending, and standardized test results. Using data to tell the story identifies the needs of your students in your caseload and also reveals the school/system wide issues that impact success. Just as data can help us visualize the accomplishment picture, it also reveals achievement patterns. Data helps us to identify and eliminate school practices that may be impacting some students' ability to access higher-level academics, school and community resources, or educational opportunities after high school.

Disaggregated Data

School counselors understand the power of aggregated and disaggregated student information. Disaggregating data, that is, separating out the data by variables such as ethnicity, gender, socio-economic status, or teacher assignment, makes it possible to determine how policy and practices affect issues of equity, enabling all school counselors to work closely with building administrators and faculty to close the achievement gap. Disaggregating data reveals the dissonance between what people believe or assume is happening in schools and reality. Data brings attention to issues that are opportunities for school-wide attention through conversations and planning. Most importantly, data provides guidance for program development and implementation. School counselors who focus their school counseling program efforts on moving data in a positive direction demonstrate a strong commitment to sharing the responsibility and accountability for student outcomes.

The Power of Data

You can answer almost any question about the effectiveness of your school and the effectiveness of your school counseling program by gathering and analyzing different kinds of data. We have demographic data that describes the student body, the staff, and the community. Student achievement data talks to us about learning as an outcome of curriculum and instruction. Perception data is gathered through questionnaires, needs assessments, focus groups, and interviews. School process data tells us about classroom techniques, specific instructional strategies, and school-wide program adoption.

Data helps us to understand and apply the aggregation and disaggregation of student information to identify and eliminate school practices or individual practices that may be deterring access and success in higher-level academics. Data also demonstrates how the school counseling program is contributing to overall student progress and student achievement. Data tells us about our efforts and the efficacy of our program including the strategies or interventions that were developed and implemented.

Data: Friend or Pho-bia

Using data often conjures up the struggles and nightmares that some of us experienced with statistical analysis in our graduate programs. We looked at pages of printouts searching for meaningful interpretations. Statistical phobia can rear its head with the mention of the words "data analysis." This fear not only affects school counselors, but often can impact school administrators too!

Putting complex statistical analyses aside, the effective use of data in schools relies upon simplicity. Consider this a balm to cure data-phobia: ask yourself, "Which data do we need to examine to help us better understand our students' successes and failures?" The data can tell us how many students are passing and how many are failing. Within those two categories, those who are passing and those who are failing, we can now examine many of the factors that contribute to student success and failure.

This is a scenario to which you can probably relate. In Riverdale Middle School, 78% of the eighth graders passed the state Math exam. This exam is required for promotion to the high school, but the most recent results show that 22% of the student body must attend and pass summer school to move on to ninth grade. The students are upset, teachers are frustrated, and parents are complaining about their summer plans. How could this have happened? Placing blame will not resolve the frustration experienced by so many of the stakeholders, especially the students. Looking for ways to reduce retention in the future is the most significant contribution the school counselors can make to the school improvement agenda.

Research tells us that establishing specific school improvement goals and strategies is the most important action in the school improvement process (McGonagill, 1992; Schmoker, 1999, 2001). When the school improvement team convened immediately after the results arrived every grade level/department in the school building identified strategies to improve the eighth grade math scores for next year. The school improvement team determined that a school-wide effort was needed to reduce the number of failures from 22% to 10%.

Making Connections

How can the school counselors contribute to this goal of improving the eighth-grade math exam scores and moving the data in a positive direction? Let's start by disaggregating our thinking so we can figure out what we need to do.

*I already know*__________________________

____

*I need to know*__________________________

____

Who has or can help me locate the additional information that I need?

____

____

Large-scale data tells me only one part of the story. In what ways can I disaggregate the data to look for ways to improve the eighth-grade math scores?

____

____

Keep It Simple

We are not looking to do complex analyses and correlation studies (Schmoker, 2002). Complexity will only lead to overload and confusion. You begin to fill in the blanks:

I already know: that 22% of our students failed the state math exam.

I need to know: the impact of socio-economic status, absenteeism, and related academic achievement on math failure.

Who has, or can help me locate the additional information that I need? The assistant principal in charge of the student data management system; teachers from the math department; other members of the faculty who work with the eighth graders; students who passed and students who failed.

Large-scale data tells me only one part of the story. In what ways can I disaggregate the data to look for ways of improving the eighth-grade math scores? Let's start by disaggregating the data by gender, ethnicity, absenteeism, and SES status.

Now What?

After reviewing the disaggregated data you and the other school counselors know they can contribute by helping the teachers better understand not just the actual results and numbers, but which students and groups of students fell through the cracks and when problems began to surface. Many students exhibited warning signs way back in September. You and your colleagues also determine the need to address student perception about math, the teachers' disappointment in the results, and the parents' frustration about the failures. By intersecting several of these issues you now have a richer and more vivid picture of why certain students passed and others failed, and you can better help the faculty improve the passing rate for next year's eighth-grade math exam.

The Riverdale school counselors also discovered that there were no obvious differences in the performance of the boys and girls. "Female math phobia" was eliminated as a primary cause. However, it was discovered that the students who did the poorest were those who were mainstreamed from special education classes and the regular education students who were labeled "slow learners." When discussing this with the eighth-grade teachers, the counselors found out that none of these students ever stayed for extra help classes after school. The anonymity of failure had taken on shape, form, and personal characteristics. The data revealed that this pattern has been in place for several years, although it was not as problematic in the recent past. Looking at data longitudinally (looking at data patterns over time) also revealed that the majority of the students had extremely high absenteeism in the formative years of second and third grade. The majority of the students lagged behind their peers for years, which went unnoticed until this year's abysmal eighth-grade failure rate.

What a wealth of information came to light! Each piece of information prompted the school counselors to look further. The school counselors had slowly and methodically peeled away the layers that revealed annually recurring phenomena. As part of the school improvement team, the school counselors began to establish a student profile consisting of warning signs that could lead to failure. The math teachers could now target and intervene in September and not wait until the third marking period. Most importantly, the school improvement team also reached out to the Parent Teacher Association (PTA) to rally the eighth-grade parents to attend a series of workshops to help parents better understand math homework.

Following the *Understanding by Design* process (Wiggins & McTighe, 1998) the school counselors looked at the root causes of the present level of achievement and contributed to designing systemic actions to ultimately reduce eighth-grade math failure. Taking on the multiple roles of leader, advocate, manager of resources, and consultant, the counselors used the data to identify barriers and ultimately impact change where, when, and how needed. The counselors at Riverdale Middle School were never left out of a school improvement conversation again!

It is important in conquering data phobia to reemphasize that the school counselor does not need to know how to physically pull data from the school system's database or to manipulate the system to aggregate and disaggregate the data. Knowing the power of data to help all students be successful and knowing how to ask the right questions of the right people who can get us the data, are the needed skills.

From Perception to Reality

Building your school counseling program around critical data elements shows support for the issues and concerns that are important to all stakeholders including legislators, school board members, teachers, parents, and building and district level administrators. Using data is a powerful way to tell the story about how your school educates children. Data can take many forms but throughout these examples we are referring to the use of real numbers rather than relying on assumptions or perceptions. Concrete data such as enrollments in college prep courses, the graduation rate, retention rates, special education placements, attendance, grades, and standardized test scores are only a few examples that reveal a telling story of achievement patterns, equity issues, and the overall effectiveness of your school. A more complete list of critical and important data elements can be found in Appendix D. Data helps you write your story in a factual framework. No longer are we presenting perception; the descriptors in our school-based stories are rooted in fact. The analysis of data reveals every aspect of the conditions in our school and identifies those barriers that hinder student academic success.

> **Data Can:**
>
> a. Challenge attitudes and beliefs: data tells the story to staff, faculty, parents, and students in a visual and in a non-judgmental manner.
>
> b. Develop high expectations: the level of awareness and expectations differs among staff, parents, and students.
>
> c. Provide career and academic advising: information is readily available to provide students and parents with current figures on scholarship dollars and financial aid information and how to access the Internet for college and career advising.
>
> d. Change enrollment patterns to support success in rigorous academics: aggregated and disaggregated data graphically show the composition of our classrooms and course selection. Using data can influence course enrollment patterns.
>
> e. Impact the instructional program: school counselors can support the instructional program by assisting classroom teachers to use data to better understand the issues that impact achievement and behavior.

Challenge or Opportunity: Carpe Diem!

Many school counselors have access to databases that contain school demographic information, students' biographical information, as well as course information, student schedules, attendance, discipline, and test history. This information is useful in itself. These data elements can serve as the baseline for school improvement and school counseling program development.

Strategies and activities that are intended to move these data from the baseline position to the identified goals are monitored throughout the implementation process. Benchmark data is collected along the way to monitor progress toward the desired goal. When these indicators fall short, midstream course corrections can be put into place. School counselors can use data to demonstrate how intervention and prevention strategies contribute to improving student achievement and school improvement.

Monitor What Matters

School counselors naturally observe much of what is happening in schools. Often the primary focus has been on monitoring and properly documenting the Carnegie units that students must attain for graduation at the high school level or the basic skill attainment in reading and mathematics in K-8 assessments. These items still require careful scrutiny as schools and systems move toward a standards-based system of education. Beyond this monitoring, the following questions need to be asked:

- What? Did the school counseling program contribute to a positive difference in the data elements selected by the school improvement team?
- When? Within the timeline, did the benchmark assessments show a positive trend toward reaching the school improvement goals?

School counselors also contribute to the school improvement agenda by connecting their work to the *National Standards for School Counseling Programs* (ASCA, 1997). Each strategy can be aligned with one of the national standards, and competencies for students can be developed to show growth in attitudes, knowledge, or skills. See Appendix B for a summary of the national standards. Organized into personal-social, academic, and career domains, the competencies are also developmental. Measurable indicators are identified for each competency. Activities and strategies designed to improve student achievement are delivered in collaboration with teachers and others in the school setting. The comprehensive process (Gysbers & Henderson, 2000; ASCA National Model, 2003), using multiple delivery systems in classroom settings, group settings, or individually, is the method of delivery (see Appendix C).

Accountability shows that all educators, especially school counselors, intentionally act to close the gap. If administrators, faculty, and all stakeholders truly believe that all children can learn and achieve, then aligning the purpose of school counseling with the school improvement plan presents school counselors as champions and collaborators who encourage high aspirations and create opportunities for students to realize their dreams. Accepting the challenge of accountability propels school counselors to accept the responsibility of removing barriers to learning and achievement, and raise the level of expectations for those students of whom little is expected. We do this by using data to monitor progress and measure the results of our efforts as contributing members of our school's educational community.

Data should no longer be perceived as a mysterious or overwhelming set of numbers to be put aside or considered to be someone else's responsibility. We monitor what matters, that is, we pay close attention to the data that paints the picture of progress in our school. Even when the results are confusing or even disappointing, we can use data to shift our focus to the areas of school improvement that will make the greatest impact on student achievement and school success.

References

American School Counselor Association. (2003). *American school counselor association national model: A framework for school counseling programs*. Alexandria, VA: Author.

Campbell, C., & Dahir, C. (1997*). Sharing the vision: the national standards for school counseling programs.* Alexandria, VA: American School Counselor Association.

Gysbers, N. C., & Henderson, P. (2000). *Developing and managing your school guidance program* (3rd ed.). Alexandria, VA: American Counseling Association.

McGonagill, G. (1992). *Overcoming barriers to educational restructuring: A call for system literacy.* ERIC, ED 357-512.

Schmoker, M. (1999). *Results: The key to continuous school improvement (2nd edition*). Alexandria, VA: ASCD.

Schmoker, M. (2001) *The results fieldbook: Practical strategies from dramatically improved schools.* Alexandria, VA: ASCD.

Wiggins, G., & McTighe, J. (1998). *Understanding by design.* Alexandria, VA: ASCD.

CHAPTER 4

MEASURE: A Different Way of Focusing Our Work

"Using MEASURE has taken the guesswork out of what I do and provided me with a tool to see my efforts move from inception to fruition."
-Mary Ann Dyal, Alimacani Elementary School, 2003

"The era of shrinking budgets forces the bitter cry of reality. We must be accountable for our programs and show that what we are doing is working."
-Robert Becker, Lewis and Clark College, 2003.

"No longer will we say a 'Counselor Can Make a Difference.' Our new mantra will become 'A Counselor Is the Difference'."
-Linda Miller, District Supervisor of Guidance, Louisville, Kentucky, 2003.

- What do I need to do?
- **M**ission
- **E**lements
- **A**nalyze
- **S**takeholders-**U**nite
- **R**eanalyze
- **E**ducate
- Creating a SPARC

MEASURE is a six-step accountability process that helps school counselors demonstrate how their programs impact critical data, those components of a school report card that are the backbone of the accountability movement. Implementing a MEASURE is an easy way to connect to the school leadership team and demonstrate that you are helping to drive data in a positive direction. MEASURE will help organize your efforts and show your results. MEASURE is a way of using information to target critical data elements, such as retention rates, test scores, and postsecondary going rates, and to develop specific strategies to connect school counseling to the accountability agenda of today's schools. Let's learn how to use the six steps by using a very common goal for school districts, to improve the postsecondary going rates. MEASURE stands for: **M**ission, **E**lements, **A**nalyze, **S**takeholders-**U**nite, **R**eanalyze, **E**ducate.

Step One: **M**ission

What Do I Need to Do?

Connect the design, implementation, and management of the school counseling program to the mission of the school and to the objectives of the annual school improvement plan.

Student achievement and success in rigorous academics is at the heart of every school's mission statement. School counselors need to ask how every aspect of their program supports the mission of the school and contributes to student achievement. Preparing students to choose from a wide array of options after high school is part of every school district's mission of academic success for every student and is congruent with the wishes of your school board.

Mission *Connect your work to your school's mission.*
Your mission statement is: The mission of our school is to promote the conditions necessary so that each student experiences academic success. Each student will have the course work required to choose from a wide array of options after high school.

Step Two: Elements

What Do I Need to Do?

As a member of the school's leadership team, identify and examine the critical elements of the available data that are important to your school's mission. School counselors play a pivotal role in this process as they work collectively with all stakeholders to focus on areas of concern for student success. Critical data elements usually can be found on the school's district or building report card. School systems routinely collect and store academic and demographic data in a retrievable form. School counselors have ready access to data in areas that contribute to achievement such as course enrollment patterns and attendance. Disaggregating data into separate elements in a variety of ways ensures that the system addresses access and equity issues. This approach to looking at data guarantees that no group of students is ignored.

Let us assume that the number of students in your school district going on to postsecondary educational institutions is not what it should be. The critical data element to address might be the postsecondary going rates for your school district, which have been holding steady around 50% for the last five years.

Current Critical Data Element *What indicator of school success are you trying to positively impact? Grades? Test scores? Attendance? Promotion Rates? Postsecondary going rate?*
The school counselor as part of the leadership team identified these critical data elements to try to impact: 50% of our students access postsecondary education (college and other educational opportunities after graduation).

Step Three: Analyze

What Do I Need to Do?

Analyze the critical data elements to determine which areas pose problems. Analysis will determine the institutional or environmental barriers that may be impeding student achievement and adversely influencing the data elements. School counselors can initially determine which elements to tackle first and which elements the school counseling program can move in a positive direction to specific targets. A quick look at data alone does not tell the whole story. It is important to disaggregate the critical data elements on which you are focusing, and to look at them in terms of gender, race/ethnicity, socio-economic status, and perhaps by teacher to shed light on areas of success or on areas in need of attention. You will also be able to see which data elements impact your school improvement plan.

Analyze the data to see what it reveals, to identify the problem areas, to establish your baseline, and to set your goal. It may be necessary to disaggregate the data, e.g., race, ethnicity, gender, SES, teacher assignment.	
Baseline: Where is this data element currently? 50% of our students access postsecondary education.	***Goal: Where do you want the data element to be in a year?*** A 5% increase in the postsecondary going rate

What other information do you need to know? Which student groups are represented in the 50% accessing postsecondary education? Which students comprise the 50% not accessing this option? Disaggregate the data to answer these and other questions. You can disaggregate data in a number of ways: gender, ethnicity, SES, home location, teacher or counselor assignments, course taking patterns, feeder schools, and so on. This information can be gathered through the student information management system, school report card, and from other sources.

What does the data tell us?

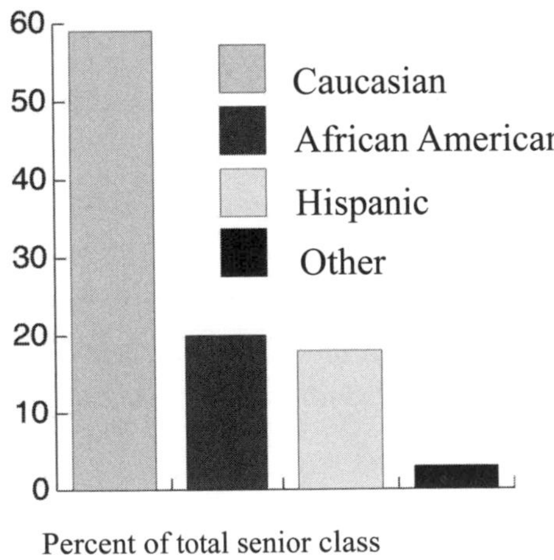

Percent of total senior class

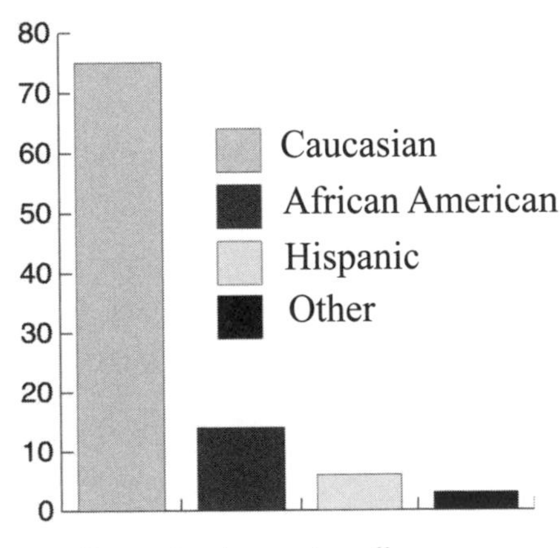

Percent going on to college

Assume that these tables represent last year's graduating class. What do these tables tell you? When the data is disaggregated by ethnicity it paints a picture of inequitable opportunity. As part of the leadership team trying to positively impact this data, what else do you need to know about this data? What are the key issues? How do you want this data to look next year and in the subsequent years? How will the school counseling program contribute toward positively improving these critical data elements and connecting the work of school counselors to better results for students?

And the Data Said...

The data revealed (among other important things) that of the 50% of your students seeking postsecondary education, the majority or 34% came from one particular feeder middle school where all students were assigned to algebra classes in eigth grade and were supported with mentors and tutors to be successful. The feeder middle school placed every student in algebra, a positive practice that could be replicated by the other feeder schools.

Step Four: Stakeholders-Unite

Identify Stakeholders to Help and Unite to Develop an Action Plan.

What Do I Need to Do?

Identify stakeholders who need to become involved and part of a team who can address the movement of critical data elements. All concerned members of the internal and external school community should be included. Determine how to secure their commitment and who will bring them together. If possible, use an existing school action committee. Accountability for school counselors is about collaborating with other stakeholders and avoiding tackling issues in isolation. Examples of stakeholders are:

Internal Community
- Principal
- Teacher
- School Board Member

External Community
- Parent
- Business Representative
- Faith Represenative

What Do I Need to Do?

Unite with stakeholders and develop and implement strategies to move critical data elements in a positive direction. With your stakeholders, begin to develop and implement an action plan that contains strategies, a timeline, and responsibilities in order to move the postsecondary going rates to 55%. The table on the next page gives a high school example of stakeholders and strategies that could be used to increase postsecondary going rates. Similar tables can be created for middle and elementary schools based on the target results from Step Three.

Develop an Action Plan *School counselors, as managers of resources, join existing groups of stakeholders, such as the school improvement team, or bring other stakeholders and resources into the task of creating and implementing an action plan. Strategies are developed that will change systems as well as impact individual students and targeted groups of students.* *Impacting systems means (1) replicating successful programs and interventions; (2) identifying barriers that adversely stratify students' opportunities to be successful learners; and (3) developing strategies to:* *• change policies, practices, and procedures* *• strengthen curriculum offerings* *• maximize the instructional program* *• enhance the school and classroom culture and climate* *• provide student academic support systems (safety nets)* *• influence course enrollment patterns to widen access to rigorous academics* *• involve parents and other critical stakeholders (internal and external to the school)* *• raise aspirations in students, parents, teachers, the community* *• change attitudes and beliefs about students and their abilities to learn*	
Stakeholders	***Strategies*** *Connect your strategies to the American School Counselor Association (ASCA) National Standards and the ASCA National Model.*
	Beginning date: September 2002 ***Ending date:*** June 2003
School Counselors	• Implement a career awareness program for every student in the school to help each see the interrelatedness between postsecondary education and his or her future economic opportunities. • Advocate for a systemic change in course enrollment patterns to support more students to access higher level academics. • Use data and anecdotal information about student success in higher level academics to try to change attitudes and beliefs about widening opportunities for higher level academics.
Teachers	• Have students research their career goals and project how their career paths fit with economic trends and the business climate. • Have students write essays for scholarships. • Integrate financial aid calculations into lessons.

Administrators	• Provide professional development for the faculty on raising aspirations. • Orchestrate collaboration with feeder schools to see how to replicate the practices that are proving successful in raising aspirations.
School Psychologists	• Provide additional group and individual counseling to high-risk students on motivation and problem solving.
School Social Workers	• Work with parents and caretakers on teaching students the importance of attendance for school success.
Clerical Staff	• Monitor student progress in submitting applications for postsecondary admissions. • Organize group meetings between the counselors and the students who are not submitting information in a timely manner to postsecondary institutions.
School Clubs	• Invite community leaders to talk about career opportunities and the education and skills needed to be successful in the work environment. • Help close the information gap by sponsoring awareness activities regarding postsecondary opportunities.
Parents	• Assist in establishing a tutoring program. • Create a phone chain to call parents to remind them of important school events.
Volunteers	• Work with individual students on the power of financial aid to impact their future.
Business Partners	• Assist in establishing a mentoring program. • Provide site visits to their businesses. • Help organize and participate in career fairs.
Community Agencies	• Assist in establishing a mentoring program. • Run evening and Saturday programs with school personnel for parents and students on raising aspirations, homework help, technology awareness, etc.
Colleges and Universities	• Host "College for a Day" programs for elementary and middle school students. • Offer diagnostic academic placement testing to tenth and eleventh graders. • Provide targeted interventions for underrepresented populations.

Step Five: **R**eanalyze, Reflect, and Revise

What Do I Need to Do?

Even if the targeted results were met there is still reflection and refining to do. Did the results of everyone's efforts show that the interventions and strategies successfully moved the critical data elements in a positive direction? If so, reassess your efforts to develop your next steps toward continuous school improvement, including any changes in the school counseling program.

If the targeted results were not met, the next step would be to reanalyze and refocus the efforts to determine why the interventions were unsuccessful in moving the data in a positive direction. Identify the components of the effort that worked. Reanalyzing means replicating what is working and developing new or different strategies for what did not work. Based on your analysis determine what changes need to be made to the school counseling program to keep the focus on student success. We can't hold fast to programs and strategies that do not help our students become more successful learners. There is too much work and too little time to accomplish all that needs to happen for our students. A school counselor recently was lamenting, "What if I find that my conflict resolution program did not really impact the discipline rate?" (It did with a 54% decrease). If the program had not made a difference we would have to rethink investing so much time and energy. In other words, if the horse is dead, get off!

It is always necessary to reanalyze and refocus to determine whether you met your targeted results. If the targeted results were met, set new targets, add new strategies, and replicate what was successful. If the postsecondary rates increased by only 2% and thus fell short of the targeted results, it will be necessary to refocus efforts to determine which strategies were successful and which need to be replaced or revised. Stakeholders will examine what efforts worked well, and which strategies need to be modified, adjusted, or perhaps changed altogether. The next steps will be to revise the action plan for the following year and to continue to move the critical data elements in a positive direction.

Reanalyze *Restate the baseline data. Where is the data after the action plan? Did the strategies have a positive impact on the data?* *Restate the baseline data:* -50% postsecondary going rate *Data after action plan:* -56% postsecondary going rate *Impact:* -Yes, the goal was not only reached but exceeded! Postsecondary rates grew by 6%.	***Reflect and Revise*** *Reflect on why the stakeholders were successful or unsuccessful. Revise the action plan so that progress can be made and you can continue to get better results.* *Which of the strategies worked?* -All of them contributed *Which strategies should be replaced? Added?* -None noted at this time *Based on what you have learned, how will you revise the action plan?* -Next year we are going to focus on the discrepancies in postsecondary going rates among Caucasians, African Americans, and Hispanics.

Look at that high school profile now! Now 56% of our students are accessing postsecondary opportunities, slightly better than the goal of 55%. What did we learn from this process?

- critical data element analyses helped us focus our efforts;
- district-wide systemic change issues must begin in elementary school;
- stakeholders across all levels were willing to share responsibility for moving critical data elements;
- changes in data clearly demonstrated the intentional focus of the school counseling program on improving the postsecondary going rate;
- collaborative effort made the change happen;
- the school counselors' commitment as key players in school improvement was well established and acknowledged;
- strategies delivered K through 12 positively moved this data forward; and,
- measurable results showed how the school counseling program worked to increase the postsecondary going rate through a system-wide focused effort.

Step Six: **E**ducate

What Do I Need to Do?

Disseminate to internal and external stakeholders the changes in the targeted data elements that show the positive impact the school counseling program is having on student success. Publicizing the results of an effective school counseling program is a vital step in the accountability process and key to garnering support for your program. This can be a time to celebrate success and recognize and applaud your partnerships. Through this education, stakeholders will have a deeper understanding about the contributions of the school counseling program focused on student achievement. School counselors will be seen as partners in school improvement and will have demonstrated a willingness to be accountable for changing critical data elements. Because of these efforts, school counselors are viewed as essential to the mission of our school.

Systemic Changes and Other Interim Data

Whenever you implement a MEASURE you will contribute to systemic change. Each MEASURE will in some way change a school, home, or community system to enhance student learning. Capture these systemic changes here and record them on your School (counseling) Program Accountability Report Card (SPARC).

When you tackle delivering a data-driven school counseling program, you become a systemic change agent impacting policies and procedures that will widen opportunities and empower more students to be successful learners. If the system is working optimally then a MEASURE would not be necessary; we can't drive data without changing systems. So, when you are gathering stakeholders and developing strategies, make certain you implement a MEASURE that intentionally tackles systemic barriers. Give yourself credit for impacting systems.

Impacting systems means:

1) replicating successful programs and interventions,
2) identifying barriers that adversely stratify students' opportunities to be successful learners, and
3) developing strategies to:
   - -change policies, practices, and procedures
   - -strengthen curriculum offerings

-maximize the instructional program
-enhance the school and classroom culture and climate
-provide student academic support systems (safety nets)
-influence course enrollment patterns to widen access to rigorous academics
-involve parents and other critical stakeholders (internal and external to the school)
-raise aspirations in students, parents, teachers, and the community
-change attitudes and beliefs about students and their abilities to learn

The Starfish Story

A man was walking along the beach. Hundreds of starfish had washed up on the shore. As he walked along he would pick up one and toss it back into the ocean. A passerby observed him and commented, "There are thousands, you can't possibly save them all!" The man smiled as he looked up and responded, "Yes, but I can save this one!"
(source unknown)

The systemic change agent will not allow hundreds of starfish to swelter and die to save one. Rather, the systemic change agent will build a net to keep the starfish from beaching, study the situation to see what is causing the starfish to beach, or call in resources to help.

For an example of how to educate others, look at the report card called a SPARC that follows. SPARC is a continuous improvement document sponsored by the California Department of Education and the Los Angeles County Office of Education. SPARC has been adapted with permission as a complement to MEASURE. Additional MEASURE and SPARC examples are presented in the next chapter.

Our MEASURE of Success

SPARC - School Counseling Program Accountability Report Card

School: Presidential High School
Enrollment: 2112
Principal: Elsie Davis
Counselors: Timothy Bishop, Gray Howell, Katie Handel, Amanda Riemer

Principal's Comments

Preparing students to choose from a wide array of options after high school is part of our district's mission of academic success for every student. Our counselors worked very hard this year to impact the school board's desire to improve the postsecondary going rate for every student. They looked at the important data elements that contribute to improving our students' futures and used their leadership, advocacy, teaming, and collaboration skills to make a positive difference.

School Improvement Issues

Postsecondary rates are stagnant. Underrepresented students do not transition to a wide variety of options after high school.

Critical Data Elements:

Postsecondary going rate is 50%.

Stakeholders

Parents: Assisted in establishing a tutoring program; created a phone chain to call parents to remind them of important school events.
Community: Assisted in establishing a mentoring program; ran evening and Saturday programs with school personnel for parents and students on raising aspirations, and provided homework help, technology awareness.
Volunteers: Participated in training delivered by financial aid officers on the Free Application for Federal Student Aid (FAFSA); worked with individual students on the power of financial aid to impact their future.
Business Partners: Assisted in establishing a mentoring program. Provided site visits to their businesses. Helped organize and participate in career fairs.

Results

Comparative Changes In Postsecondary Rates

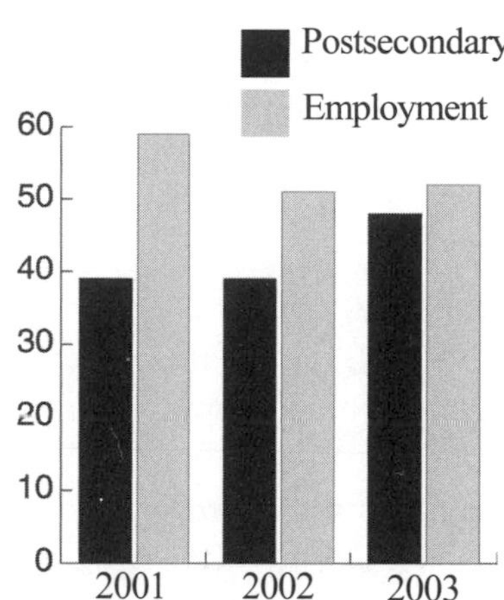

Percentages Of Students By Ethnicity Accepted To Postsecondary Institutions

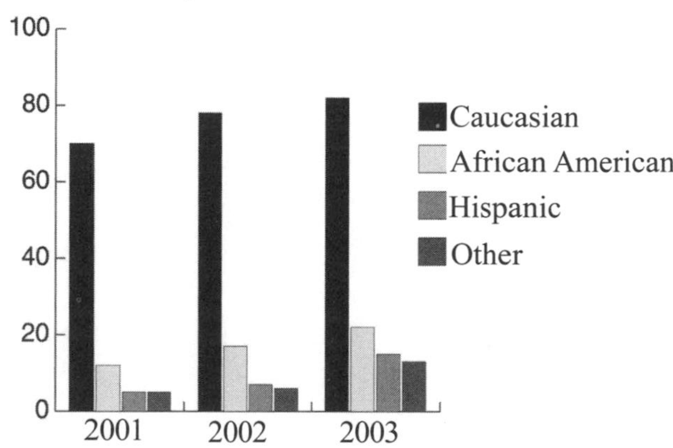

Systemic Changes

For the first time ever, our school and community came together to talk about improving our seniors' options after high school. The action planned focused on this graduating class, but we now know that this effort needs to start in the ninth grade.

Faces Behind the Data

A parent approached her child's school counselor at the end of the graduation ceremony: "I didn't think my child's dream of going to college was going to happen this year. I am recently divorced and did not realize that financial aid would be available. Thank you for keeping after both of us to fill out the FAFSA so that it wasn't too late to get some help."

Practice What You Have Learned

It is your turn to complete a MEASURE. Take one of the three scenarios below and fill in the blank MEASURE. For additional assistance, you can refer to the MEASURE examples in Chapter 5.

High School Counselors:

Imagine that as part of the leadership team at your school you are trying to help improve the number of students who complete the college preparation curriculum, i.e., three years of rigorous mathematics (algebra, geometry, trigonometry, etc.), three years of science including chemistry, two years of a second language, and the high school graduation requirements for social studies and English.

Middle School Counselors

Imagine that as part of the leadership team at your school you are trying to help impact the number of students who are promoted from eighth grade to ninth grade.

Elementary School Counselors

Imagine that as part of the leadership team at your school you are trying to help impact the number of students promoted from third grade to fourth grade.

1 2 3 4 5 6 7 8 9 10 11 12

MEASURE

Mission, **E**lements, **A**nalyze, **S**takeholders-**U**nite, **R**eanalyze, **E**ducate,
a Six-step Accountability Process for School Counselors

Name and Address of School:
Name of Counselor Leading the Initiative:
Principal:
Enrollment:

School Demographics:
Caucasian/Non-Hispanic
African American
Hispanic
Asian
Other

Free/Reduced lunch
ESL

Step One: **M**ission

Mission *Connect your work to your school's mission.*
Your mission statement is:

Step Two: **E**lements

Current Critical Data Element *What indicator of school success are you trying to positively impact? Grades? Test scores? Attendance? Promotion Rates? Postsecondary going rate?*
The school counselor as part of the leadership team identified these critical data elements to try to impact:

Step Three: **A**nalyze

Analyze the data to see what it reveals, to identify the problem areas, to establish your baseline, and to set your goal. It may be necessary to disaggregate the data, e.g., race, ethnicity, gender, SES, teacher assignment.	
Baseline: Where is this data element currently?	***Goal: Where do you want the data element to be in a year?***

Step Four: **S**takeholders-**U**nite

Develop an Action Plan
School counselors, as managers of resources, join existing groups of stakeholders, such as the school improvement team, or bring other stakeholders and resources into the task of creating and implementing an action plan. Strategies are developed that will change systems as well as impact individual students and targeted groups of students.

Impacting systems means (1) replicating successful programs and interventions; (2) identifying barriers that adversely stratify students' opportunities to be successful learners; and (3) developing strategies to:
- *change policies, practices, and procedures*
- *strengthen curriculum offerings*
- *maximize the instructional program*
- *enhance the school and classroom culture and climate*
- *provide student academic support systems (safety nets)*
- *influence course enrollment patterns to widen access to rigorous academics*
- *involve parents and other critical stakeholders (internal and external to the school)*
- *raise aspirations in students, parents, teachers, and the community*
- *change attitudes and beliefs about students and their abilities to learn*

Stakeholders	***Strategies*** *Connect your strategies to the American School Counselor Association (ASCA) National Standards and the ASCA National Model.*
	Beginning date: ***Ending date:***

School Counselors	
Teachers	
Administrators	
Students	
Technology	
Community Agency Members	
Local Colleges	
Grants	
Parents	
Teacher Assistants	
School Improvement Team (may also include a number of stakeholders)	

Step Five: **R**eanalyze, Reflect, and Revise

Reanalyze *Restate the baseline data. Where is the data after the action plan? Did the strategies have a positive impact on the data?* *Restate the baseline data:* *Data after action plan:* *Impact:*	***Reflect and Revise*** *Reflect on why the stakeholders were successful or unsuccessful. Revise the action plan so that progress can be made and you can continue to get better results.* *Which of the strategies worked?* *Which strategies should be replaced? Added?* *Based on what you have learned, how will you revise the action plan?*

Systemic Changes Made

Whenever you implement a MEASURE you will contribute to systemic change. Each MEASURE will in some way change a school, home, or community system to enhance student learning. Capture these systemic changes here and record them on your SPARC.

Step Six: **E**ducate

Promote and publicize the results of your work. Develop a report card for your own program to let the internal and external school members know your work is connected to the mission of the school and to student success. The School Counseling Program Accountability Report Card (SPARC) is a way to do this.

Our MEASURE of Success

SPARC - School Counseling Program Accountability Report Card

School:
Enrollment:
Principal:
Counselor:

Results

Principal's Comments

School Improvement Issues

Systemic Changes

Stakeholders

Faces Behind the Data

SPARC is a continuous improvement document sponsored by the California Department of Education and the Los Angeles County Office of Education. SPARC has been adapted with permission as a complement to MEASURE.

References

Becker, R. (2003). *Personal conversation.* Lewis and Clark College. Portland, OR.

Dyal, M. (2003). *Personal conversation.* Alimacani Elementary School. Jacksonville, FL.

Miller, L. (2003). *Personal conversation.* Jefferson County Public Schools. Louisville, KY.

CHAPTER 5
School Counselors Demonstrating Accountability

- Alimacani Elementary School
- Bryceville Elementary School
- S.A. Hull Elementary School
- Piscataway Township Elementary & Middle Schools
- Chelsea Career & Technical Education High School
- Darnell-Cookman Middle School
- Pike High School
- Stanton College Preparatory High School
- Jefferson County Public Schools

School counselors are challenged to demonstrate the effectiveness of their program in measurable terms. School counselors must collect and use data that support and link the school counseling program to students' academic success.

-The ASCA National Model, p. 59

Forty-nine hard-working, forward-thinking school counselors agreed to implement data-driven school counseling programs this year. Their admirable efforts resulted in nine MEASUREs that represent elementary, middle, high schools and an entire district. In Step 5 of each counselor's MEASURE you will see the change in data. These school counselors contributed to the academic success picture of their schools and, furthermore, they showed their contribution with hard data—not perceptions, not time-on-task, but real numbers that represent thousands of students who are better off as a result of their work! As part of their schools' leadership teams, just look at what these counselors have accomplished: increasing ninth-grade promotion rates; dramatically reducing discipline referrals; increasing state test scores; increasing the postsecondary going rates; reducing the gap in the completion of the college core; increasing Algebra I completion rates; increasing the number of National Merit qualifiers; and decreasing suspension rates. The proof is here in the student outcomes.

These counselors will tell you that working in a focused way and connecting their efforts to the mission of the school have positioned them in a more powerful, important light with the stakeholders of their schools. In the words of these school counselors:

"MEASURE has helped me to break down the problems of my school by unbundling the data so that I can get to the specifics of who needs help" (Turba, 2003).

"This work has received a favorable response from my principal because the MEASURE shows that my program is working" (Parikh, 2003).

"We sometimes don't take the time to collaborate even though we know the benefits. Doing a MEASURE has reminded me of the power of collaboration and shows the positive results when you team" (Vanderhoek, 2003).

As you read these MEASUREs think about all the important changes these counselors were able to make on a macro systemic level. Systemic change is a powerful, heady role for a school counselor because when you make a systemic change the number of students impacted increases exponentially.

Think about the many uses that can be made of the SPARCs (the school counselors' report cards). Bob Tyra of the Los Angeles County Office of Education, the creative force behind the design of the SPARC, explains that they widely distribute them to realtors, businesses, the chamber of commerce, and the Parent Teacher Association. In other words, the school counselors use their SPARCs as important public relations tools for their programs and use them to educate their internal and external community as to the contributions school counselors are making to improving student success. The SPARC template has been adapted with permission for these purposes as a complement to MEASURE.

1 2 3 4 5 6 7 8 9 10 11 12

MEASURE

Mission, **E**lements, **A**nalyze, **S**takeholders-**U**nite, **R**eanalyze, **E**ducate,
a Six-step Accountability Process for School Counselors

Name and Address of School:
Alimacani Elementary School
2051 San Pablo Road
Jacksonville, FL 32224
(904) 221-7103

Name of Counselor Leading the Initiative:
Mary Ann Dyal

Principal:
Pamela Rogers

Enrollment:
1,110 - suburban setting

School Demographics:
Caucasian/Non-Hispanic: 70%
African American: 15%
Hispanic: 4%
Asian: 4%
Other: 7%
Free/Reduced lunch: 23%

Step One: **M**ission

Mission *Connect your work to your school's mission.*
Your mission statement is: Alimacani Elementary School will implement the standards-based curriculum required by the Duval County Public School System by providing an environment for all students where education is a treasure and children are inspired to reach for their dreams by fostering academic growth for all learners to meet or exceed local and state performance standards.

Step Two: **E**lements

<table>
<tr><td>Current Critical Data Element
What indicator of school success are you trying to positively impact? Grades? Test scores? Attendance? Promotion rates? Postsecondary going rate?</td></tr>
<tr><td>The Alimacani school counselor as part of the leadership team identified this critical data element to try to impact:
• School-wide discipline referrals</td></tr>
</table>

Step Three: **A**nalyze

<table>
<tr><td colspan="2">Analyze the data to see what it reveals, to identify the problem areas, to establish your baseline, and to set your goal. It may be necessary to disaggregate the data, e.g., race, ethnicity, gender, SES, teacher assignment.</td></tr>
<tr><td>Baseline: Where is this data element currently?

• 2000–2001 Discipline Referrals - 183</td><td>Goal: Where do you want the data element to be in a year?

• Decrease discipline referrals by 10% for the school year 2001–2002</td></tr>
</table>

Step Four: **S**takeholders-**U**nite

<table>
<tr><td>Develop an Action Plan
School counselors, as managers of resources, join existing groups of stakeholders, such as the school improvement team, or bring other stakeholders and resources into the task of creating and implementing an action plan. Strategies are developed that will change systems as well as impact individual students and targeted groups of students.

Impacting systems means (1) replicating successful programs and interventions, (2) identifying barriers that adversely stratify students' opportunities to be successful learners, and (3) developing strategies to:
• change policies, practices, and procedures
• strengthen curriculum offerings
• maximize the instructional program
• enhance the school and classroom culture and climate</td></tr>
</table>

• provide student academic support systems (safety nets) *• influence course enrollment patterns to widen access to rigorous academics* *• involve parents and other critical stakeholders (internal and external to the school)* *• raise aspirations in students, parents, teachers, and the community* *• change attitudes and beliefs about students and their abilities to learn*	
Stakeholders	***Strategies*** *Connect your strategies to the American School Counselor Association (ASCA) National Standards and the ASCA National Model.*
	Beginning date: 2000–2001 school year ***Ending date:*** 2001–2002 school year
School Counselors	• Established a bullyproofing program that involved the entire internal and external school community • Developed an alliance with the Parent Teacher Association (PTA) to partner on delivering the bullyproofing program and other strategies • Delivered faculty and staff training for bullyproofing • Set up action plans for teachers in response to bullying behaviors • Delivered classroom guidance lessons on bullyproofing • Conducted parent education through monthly newsletter articles and a workshop • Implemented and managed quarterly student contests that involved poetry, posters, and essays about bullying • Provided materials to teachers for follow-up classroom guidance lessons • Established a mentoring program with aircraft carrier pilots • Helped establish a tutoring program • Worked diligently with local businesses and volunteers to provide incentives for classes to reduce their bullying behavior • Implemented a parent fair that attracted over 100 parents who chose from a variety of topics designed to reduce bullying and increase their children's social and school success skills
Teachers	• Supported the bullyproofing program by following through with lessons provided by the counselor • Participated in training strategies to educate about bullying • Implemented conflict resolution strategies such as teaching students to identify bullying behavior and charting it as a class • Held weekly class meetings to discuss any bullying problems and gave students ownership of the program
Administrators	•Provided leadership and support for all facets of the program •Continually emphasized to faculty the importance of the bullyproofing program, mentoring program, and other strategies designed to reduce

	bullying • Took a decisive role in the discipline process when a bullying incident did occur
Students	• Worked together to stand up to bullies • Learned to watch for and identify bullying; learned a common language to combat bullying; learned to feel empowered to stop bullying • Participated in weekly class meetings to discuss bullying as a group • Actively and enthusiastically participated in classroom guidance lessons that focused on social skills and tolerance for individual differences
Technology	• Provided daily films with a bullyproofing theme on closed circuit television • Used closed circuit television for daily skits and dramatization about bullying
Media Specialist	• Developed daily closed circuit television clips to be shown at the beginning of each day that addressed bullying and its effects • Delivered lessons and activities aimed at eliminating bullying
Music Teacher	• Established lessons that were integral to the schoolwide effort to eliminate bullying
Art Teacher	• Established lessons and activities designed to eliminate bullying
Business Partners	• Provided incentives for classes to reduce their bullying behavior • Provided meals for Parent Night training session (Bonos Restaurant) • Purchased a character education program for the school (Chic-fil-A Restaurant) • Donated food for the mentoring program (Publix Groceries) • Helped with parent fair training sessions (two agencies)
Community Agency Members	• Provided speakers for a parent fair on areas that impact discipline such as "How to Know If Your Child is a Victim of Bullying" and "How to Prevent Your Child from Becoming a Bully" (10 agencies were involved in the Parent Fair)
Military	• Provided mentors for students with a history of problems in the area of conflict resolution (Navy helicopter pilots) • Provided volunteer tutors to work with students needing extra academic assistance (U.S.S. Kennedy)
Local Colleges	• Provided two interns in school counseling who implemented strategies to enhance the climate of the school

Literacy Coach	• Selected books with a bullying theme and the entire school would read and discuss these books
Grant Writers	• Wrote grants to obtain materials for the bullyproofing program (university interns)
Parents	• Acted as co-program leaders for bullyproofing program • Found volunteers and set up programs (PTA) • Funded entire bullyproofing program (PTA)
Teacher Assistants	• Participated in training and responded to bullying in areas such as the cafeteria, bus loading zone, playground
School Improvement Team	• Made bullyproofing part of the School Improvement Plan

Step Five: **R**eanalyze, Reflect, and Revise

Reanalyze
Restate the baseline data. Where is the data after the action plan? Did the strategies have a positive impact on the data?

2001 Discipline Referrals Baseline Date	2002 Discipline Referrals Data after the Action Plan
183	98 (a 54% reduction)

The strategies made a tremendous impact on our discipline problems.

Reflect and Revise
Reflect on why the stakeholders were successful or unsuccessful. Revise the action plan so that progress can be made and you can continue to get better results.

Which of the strategies worked?
-We used collaboration among all the internal and external school community members.

Which strategies should be replaced? Added?
-None noted at this time.

Based on what you have learned, how will you rewrite the action plan?
-Next year we will also focus on attendance data.

Systemic Changes Made
Whenever you implement a MEASURE you will contribute to systemic change. Each MEASURE will in some way change a school, home, or community system to enhance student learning. Capture these systemic changes here and record them on your SPARC.

1. A school-wide approach to impacting bullying was institutionalized.
2.Tutoring and mentoring became part of the regular program.
3. Students became active participants in changing the school climate and teachers changed their attitudes and beliefs about the powerful role students can play in impacting the school climate.

Step Six: **E**ducate

Promote and publicize the results of your work. Develop a report card for your own program to let the internal and external school members know your work is connected to the mission of the school and to student success. The School Counseling Program Accountability Report Card (SPARC) is a way to do this.

Our MEASURE of Success

SPARC - School Counseling Program Accountability Report Card

School: Alimacani Elementary
Enrollment: 1110
Principal: Pamela Rogers
Counselor: Mary Ann Dyal

Principal's Comments

Mary Ann has taken a leadership role in trying to help all students be successful learners. She has impacted hundreds of students and her bullyproofing program is just one more example of how she sees her role as helping students have a healthy academic life. What a joy to have a counselor who cares about student achievement and who makes a difference in areas such as the school's learning climate.

School Improvement Issues

Discipline referrals can impact school climate; decrease the number of discipline referrals.

Critical Data Element(s):

School-wide discipline referrals

Stakeholders

Counselor: Established and infused a bullyproofing program that involved the entire school body and community
Administrators: Provided leadership and support for all facets of the program
Teachers: Supported every effort of the bullyproofing program from weekly class meetings to charting bullying behaviors
Parents: Acted as co-program leaders for bullyproofing program and provided all the necessary funding and volunteers
Students: Worked together to stand up to bullies
Higher Education: Provided two school counseling interns who implemented strategies that enhanced the program
Business Partners: Provided incentives, meals for a parent fair, a character education program, food for the mentoring program, mentors for students and tutors

Results

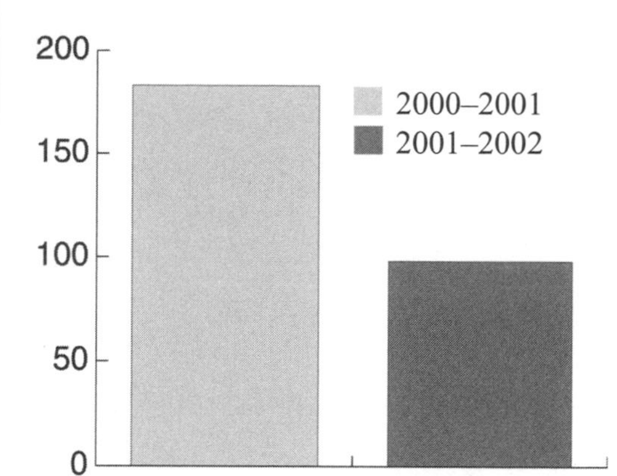

2001 Discipline Referrals	2002 Discipline Referrals
183	98 (a 54% reduction)

Systemic Changes

1. The school and classroom approaches to bullying were improved.
2. Approaches to handling discipline were positively changed.
3. Tutoring and mentoring programs were institutionalized.
4. Students became part of prevention and changing the school climate.
5. The external community such as businesses and parents found a medium in which to become active participants of the school.

Faces Behind the Data

A new second grader entered Alimacani distressed over having to leave her former school. She could not stop crying and clinging to the teacher. Another student observing this student's distress came up and said, "It's okay, no one will bother you here because we are bullyproofed!"

The assistant principal overheard a student admonishing a boy in the throes of bullying another student, "Leave him alone. We don't bully here at Alimacani."

MEASURE

Mission, **E**lements, **A**nalyze, **S**takeholders-**U**nite, **R**eanalyze, **E**ducate,
a Six-step Accountability Process for School Counselors

Name and Address of School:
Bryceville Elementary
6504 Church Avenue
Bryceville, FL 32009
(904) 266-9241

Name of Counselor Leading the Initiative:
Laura Lee Kinard

Principal:
Eric Larsen

Enrollment:
229 students - rural setting

School Demographics:
Caucasian/Non-Hispanic: 97%
African American: 1%
Hispanic: 1%
Other: 1%
Free/Reduced lunch: 31%

Step One: **M**ission

Mission
Connect your work to your school's mission.

Your mission statement is:
It is the mission of Bryceville Elementary School to foster positive attitudes and high expectations throughout the school and community. Bryceville Elementary School will provide a wide and varied curriculum built upon the basic skills using interactive methods to guide the students to achieve adequate progress throughout their academic career and beyond.

Step Two: **E**lements

Current Critical Data Element
What indicator of school success are you trying to positively impact? Grades? Test scores? Attendance? Promotion rates? Postsecondary going rate?

The Bryceville school counselor as part of the leadership team identified this critical data element to try to impact:
• FCAT Scores in third and fourth grades

Step Three: **A**nalyze

Analyze the data to see what it reveals, to identify the problem areas, to establish your baseline, and to set your goal. It may be necessary to disaggregate the data, e.g., race, ethnicity, gender, SES, teacher assignment.

Baseline: Where is this data element currently?

2001–2002	
3rd Math	81%
3rd Reading	66%
4th Math	57%
4th Reading	63%
4th Writing	84%

Goal: Where do you want the data element to be in a year?

Increase the number of students scoring at or above level 3 by 4%

Step Four: **S**takeholders-**U**nite

Develop an Action Plan
School counselors, as managers of resources, join existing groups of stakeholders, such as the school improvement team, or bring other stakeholders and resources into the task of creating and implementing an action plan. Strategies are developed that will change systems as well as impact individual students and targeted groups of students.

Impacting systems means (1) replicating successful programs and interventions, (2) identifying barriers that adversely stratify students' opportunities to be successful learners, and (3) developing strategies to:
• *change policies, practices, and procedures*
• *strengthen curriculum offerings*

• *maximize the instructional program* • *enhance the school and classroom culture and climate* • *provide student academic support systems (safety nets)* • *influence course enrollment patterns to widen access to rigorous academics* • *involve parents and other critical stakeholders (internal and external to the school)* • *raise aspirations in students, parents, teachers, and the community* • *change attitudes and beliefs about students and their abilities to learn*	
Stakeholders	***Strategies*** *Connect your strategies to the American School Counselor Association (ASCA) National Standards and the ASCA National Model.*
	Beginning date: 2001–2002 school year ***Ending date:*** 2002–2003 school year
School Counselor	• Conducted classroom guidance lessons on communication skills, higher order thinking skills, and character education topics • Participated in the School Advisory Council • Incorporated character education into classroom guidance lessons and delivered these lessons with the FCAT skills in mind focusing on higher-order thinking skills and incorporating writing assignments • Provided a writing workshop for teachers • Supported an after-school tutoring program • Advocated for a change in the ESE schedule for the school so that students would benefit more from this support program • Organized a teacher tutoring program • Implemented "Bobcat Buddies," a reward program that focuses on completing work • Organized the implementation of a summer reading program called the Learning Academy • Conducted "Go For It" groups; small group counseling for study skills • Conducted faculty and parent workshops on study skills, FCAT reading strategies, and parent conferencing
Teachers	• Delivered after-school tutoring and collaborated with the new Elementary Director of Nassau County (third grade teachers) • Implemented cross-grade-level program development • Helped research reading strategies and train peers
Administrators	• Provided a method for the ESE teacher to be able to collaborated with the regular education teacher (ESE Director, Nassau County) • Coordinated time between grade levels and scheduled substitutes for second-grade teachers to articulate with third-grade teachers (principal) • Continually advocated for the three reading support programs, i.e., Saxon phonics, Title 1, and Reading Rescue

	• Supported the efforts of all stakeholders to impact the FCAT scores
Students	• Worked as peer tutors to other students
Volunteers	• Assisted teachers so they can work one-on-one with targeted students • Helped run the Bobcat of the Month Program (PTA)
Grant Writers	• Wrote a grant for Principle Woods character education program, which includes reading and higher order thinking skills
Funding Agents	• Supported tutoring and summer reading programs (Title 5 funds from the Elementary Director)
Parents	• Supported and implemented Principle Woods Reading Program • Participated in Parent Workshops

Step Five: **R**eanalyze, Reflect, and Revise

Reanalyze
Restate the baseline data. Where is the data after the action plan? Did the strategies have a positive impact on the data?

	2001–2002	2002–2003
3rd Math	81%	91%
3rd Reading	66%	83%
4th Math	57%	67%
4th Reading	63%	77%
4th Writing	84%	86%

The strategies moved the data in a positive direction.

Reflect and Revise
Reflect on why the stakeholders were successful or unsuccessful. Revise the action plan so that progress can be made and you can continue to get better results.

Which of the strategies worked?
-All strategies contributed to impacting the FCAT scores.

Which strategies should be replaced? Added?
-Study skills for all students will be added.

Based on what you have learned, how will you rewrite the action plan?
-The plan will include all grade levels next year.

Systemic Changes Made
Whenever you implement a MEASURE you will contribute to systemic change. Each MEASURE will in some way change a school, home, or community system to enhance student learning. Capture these systemic changes here and record them on your SPARC.

1. Permanent changes were made to the district ESE schedule to optimize this support.
2. The school's approach to reading success was changed.

Step Six: **E**ducate

Promote and publicize the results of your work. Develop a report card for your own program to let the internal and external school members know your work is connected to the mission of the school and to student success. The School Counseling Program Accountability Report Card (SPARC) is a way to do this.

Our MEASURE of Success

SPARC - School Counseling Program Accountability Report Card

School: Bryceville Elementary
Enrollment: 229
Principal: Eric Larsen
Counselor: Laura Lee Kinard

Principal's Comments

During the past several years, Mrs. Kinard's efforts helped the students scoring in the lower quartile and I am convinced that she is one of the primary reasons that over 80 percent of these students experienced learning gains on the FCAT Reading Test. These results, in addition to my personal observations, offer strong evidence that Mrs. Kinard's strategies are successful.

School Improvement Issues

The number of students scoring at or above a level 3 on the FCAT should be increased.
Critical Data Element(s):
FCAT scores at or above level 3 in third grade math and reading, and fourth grade math, reading, and writing

Stakeholders

Counselor: Looked at disaggregated data and developed strategies with stakeholders to impact the FCAT scores
Administrators: Devised a better schedule for the Exceptional Student Education students; gave priority to planning time among grade levels
Teachers: Delivered tutoring after school; attended workshops
Parents: Implemented Principle Woods Reading Program; participated in parent workshops
Students: Behaved as peer tutors to other students
Volunteers: Assisted teachers so they can work one-on-one with targeted students; ran student awards programs

Systemic Changes

1. Permanent changes made to optimize the schedule for ESE students
2. Changed the approach to teaching reading
3. Established cross-grade-level planning as standard operating procedure

Results

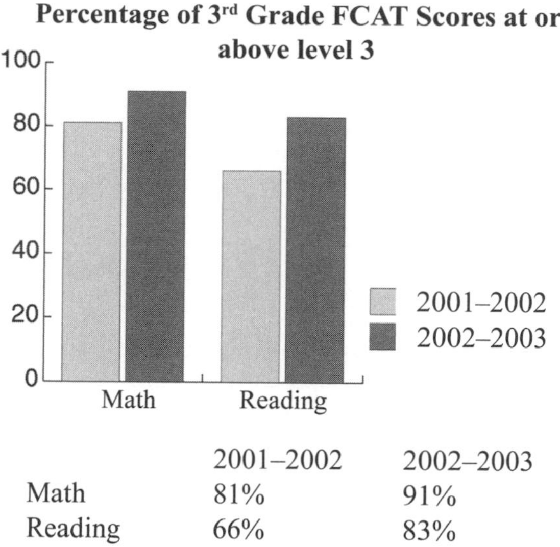

	2001–2002	2002–2003
Math	81%	91%
Reading	66%	83%

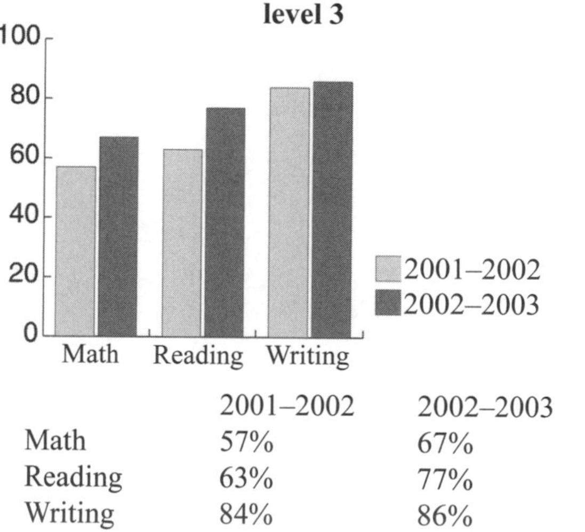

	2001–2002	2002–2003
Math	57%	67%
Reading	63%	77%
Writing	84%	86%

Faces Behind the Data

A student with a severe learning disability worked very hard to complete his assignments in order to be awarded a "trinket" from my box. One day this student said to me, "Mrs. Kinard, I don't need trinkets anymore. I want to be a Bobcat of the Month now." I said, "You do?" And he looked at me with a puzzled look and said, "Yeah, I want to stand on the stage." He did. He also scored a level 3 in Reading on the FCAT!

MEASURE

Mission, **E**lements, **A**nalyze, **S**takeholders-**U**nite, **R**eanalyze, **E**ducate,
a Six-step Accountability Process for School Counselors

Name and Address of School:
S. A. Hull Elementary School
7528 Hull Street
Jacksonville, FL 32219
(904) 924-3136

Name of Counselor Leading the Initiative:
Sejal Parikh

Principal:
Carrie Price

Enrollment:
335 students - urban setting

School Demographics:
Caucasian/Non-Hispanic: 4%
African American: 93%
Hispanic: 1%
Asian: 0%
Other: 2%
Free/Reduced lunch: 88%
ESOL: 0%

Step One: **M**ission

Mission *Connect your work to your school's mission.*
Your mission statement is: It is the mission of S. A. Hull Elementary School to provide quality instruction so students progress satisfactorily and above through the school years and are prepared for the succeeding years.

Step Two: **E**lements

Current Critical Data Element *What indicator of school success are you trying to positively impact? Grades? Test scores? Attendance? Promotion rates? Postsecondary going rate?*
The S.A. Hull school counselor as part of the leadership team identified this critical data element to try to impact: • Discipline referrals in fourth and fifth grades

Step Three: **A**nalyze

Analyze the data to see what it reveals, to identify the problem areas, to establish your baseline, and to set your goal. It may be necessary to disaggregate the data, e.g., race, ethnicity, gender, SES, teacher assignment.

Baseline: Where is this data element currently?

4th and 5th Grade Discipline Referrals
February
23

Goal: Where do you want the data element to be in a year?

• Decrease discipline referrals by 1 percent each month for the remainder of the school year

Step Four: **S**takeholders-**U**nite

Develop an Action Plan

School counselors, as managers of resources, join existing groups of stakeholders, such as the school improvement team, or bring other stakeholders and resources into the task of creating and implementing an action plan. Strategies are developed that will change systems as well as impact individual students and targeted groups of students.

Impacting systems means (1) replicating successful programs and interventions, (2) identifying barriers that adversely stratify students' opportunities to be successful learners, and (3) developing strategies to:

- *change policies, practices, and procedures*
- *strengthen curriculum offerings*
- *maximize the instructional program*
- *enhance the school and classroom culture and climate*

• *provide student academic support systems (safety nets)* • *influence course enrollment patterns to widen access to rigorous academics* • *involve parents and other critical stakeholders (internal and external to the school)* • *raise aspirations in students, parents, teachers, and the community* • *change attitudes and beliefs about students and their abilities to learn*	
Stakeholders	***Strategies*** *Connect your strategies to the American School Counselor Association (ASCA) National Standards and the ASCA National Model.*
	Beginning date: February, 2003 ***Ending date:*** June, 2003
School Counselors	• Disaggregated data to identify problem areas; found that fourth and fifth grades had the largest number of discipline referrals • Assisted in the formation of a new discipline committee to rewrite the discipline plan • Collaborated with the entire internal and external school to decrease referrals, giving everyone ownership and a defined role • Implemented written policies for all school wide areas, i.e., what behavior is expected in playground, cafeteria, classrooms • Assisted in the formation of intervention teams on every grade level for discussion of chronic referrals • Delivered conflict resolution guidance lessons • Recommended books to the librarian to use in lessons • Provided teachers with materials for lessons on conflict resolution
Teachers	• Supported the bullyproofing program by actively implementing the components in their classrooms • Consulted with the school counselor and infused lessons into their daily curriculum • Referred students to the school counselor for interventions instead of first seeking discipline • Collaborated with the school counselor to decrease the number of child study team screenings and staffing • Supported and participated in training for optimum implementation of the discipline program • Wrote intervention plans for students receiving two or more referrals in a two-week period
Administrators	• Supported a collaborative team between school counselor and the fourth and fifth-grade teachers • Recommended classroom management training • Participated in the intervention teams • Supported writing of new policies for expectations of student behavior • Provided teachers with opportunities to visit effective classrooms

Students	• Led classroom discussions on bullying behavior • Utilized assertive skills learned from lessons • Learned to prevent and counter bullying
Technology	• Allowed for retrieval of disaggregated data
Local Colleges	• Provided interns who assisted with lessons on bullyproofing
Art teacher	• Used art to support bullyproofing
Music teacher	• Infused the bullyproofing into the music program
Librarian	• Provided lessons in bullyproofing • Used books suggested by school counselors
Parents	• Provided money for incentives • Supported behavior management program in the cafeteria

Step Five: **R**eanalyze, Reflect, and Revise

Reanalyze

Restate the baseline data. Where is the data after the action plan? Did the strategies have a positive impact on the data?

4th and 5th Grade Discipline Referrals	
February Baseline Data	April Data After the Action Plan
23	8

The strategies significantly reduced our discipline referrals.

Reflect and Revise

Reflect on why the stakeholders were successful or unsuccessful. Revise the action plan so that progress can be made and you can continue to get better results.

Which of the strategies worked?
-The conflict resolution lessons were effective.

Which strategies should be replaced? Added?
-None noted at this time.

Based on what you learned, how will you rewrite the action plan?
-Work will be done around impacting discipline referrals for all grade levels.
-Efforts will be made to reduce the number of child study team referrals.

Systemic Changes Made

Whenever you implement a MEASURE you will contribute to systemic change. Each MEASURE will in some way change a school, home, or community system to enhance student learning. Capture these systemic changes here and record them on your SPARC.

1. A completely new discipline plan was initiated.
2. Intervention teams on each grade level are the norm.
3. Everyone now takes responsibility for a climate that fosters optimum learning conditions.

Step Six: Educate

Promote and publicize the results of your work. Develop a report card for your own program to let the internal and external school members know your work is connected to the mission of the school and to student success. The School Counseling Program Accountability Report Card (SPARC) is a way to do this.

Our MEASURE of Success

SPARC - School Counseling Program Accountability Report Card

School: S. A. Hull Elementary
Enrollment: 335
Principal: Carrie Price
Counselor: Sejal Parikh

Principal's Comments

Sejal takes a leadership role and collaborates so that our students can succeed in the classroom. I continually encourage teachers to use the resources provided by Sejal such as classroom management. I am pleased that Sejal is so involved in reducing the number of discipline referrals. Every student should be lucky enough to have a counselor who collects and analyzes data and implements programs to help them succeed academically.

School Improvement Issues

Discipline referrals for the 2002–2003 school year were at unacceptable levels (382 for all grades).

Critical Data Element(s):
Reduce discipline referrals in fourth and fifth grades

Stakeholders

Counselor: Disaggregated the data and identified the discipline problem areas; assisted in the formation of a discipline committee to rewrite a discipline plan; led classroom and school-wide effort on bullyproofing
Administrators: Supported the collaboration between Sejal and the fourth and fifth grade teachers; recommended classroom management training
Teachers: Actively implemented a bully proofing program; referred discipline problems first to the counselor for interventions
Parents: Provided money for incentives; supported school-wide behavior management programs
Students: Led classroom discussions on bullying behavior; prevented bullying; enthusiastically embraced the school-wide effort
Higher Education: Provided interns who assisted with lessons on bullying

Results

4th and 5th Grade Discipline Referrals for February and April 2003

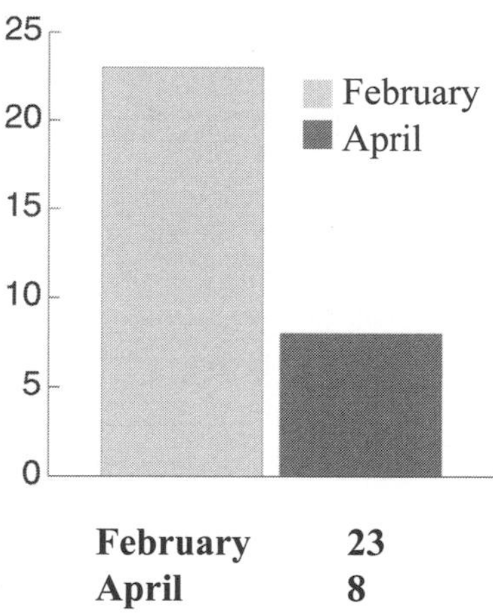

February	**23**
April	**8**

Systemic Changes

1. A completely new discipline plan was initiated.
2. Intervention teams on each grade level will be the norm in the future.
3. A climate that supports learning is a focused effort on everyone's part.

Faces Behind the Data

In disaggregating data on discipline referrals, I found that one student was responsible for a disproportionately large number of the referrals. For two weeks I interviewed his teachers and observed him in various settings. I came to the conclusion that he was bored and that he should be tested for the gifted program. He qualified, is happy in the gifted program, and is no longer a discipline problem; and, not one referral since he was placed in the gifted program!

MEASURE

Mission, **E**lements, **A**nalyze, **S**takeholders-**U**nite, **R**eanalyze, **E**ducate,
a Six-step Accountability Process for School Counselors

School District and Schools Participating:
Piscataway Township Elementary and Middle Schools
Piscataway, New Jersey

Arbor Elementary School
Eisenhower Elementary School
Grandview Elementary School
Randolphville Elementary School
King Elementary School
Knollwood Elementary School

Conackamack Middle School
Quibbletown Middle School
Schor Middle School

Leading the Initiative:
Dr. Dorothy J. Youngs, Assistant Director for Counseling K-12

Elementary School Counselors:
Jill Brown, Gillian Roth, Susan Manley, J. Courtney Boyd-Moscowitz, Irene Guarino, Carmen Campoverde, Sherri Griffith, Jaime Schnirman, Rebecca Walker, Ildiko Henni-Jones, Robyn Rosenthal, Deirdre McClafferty

Middle School Counselors:
MaryAnn Lombardi, Margo Shapiro, Marge Delaney, C. Alex Gray, Dan Rothberg, Wendy Johansen

Principals:
Susan Chalfin, Arbor Elementary School
Wayne Rose, Grandview Elementary School
Barry Glickman, Knollwood Elementary School
Dr. Willa Pryor, Eisenhower Elementary School
Alice Rothberg, King Elementary School
Shirley Eyler, Randolphville Elementary School

Dr. Suzanne Westberg, Conackamack Middle School
Mario Tursi, Quibbletown Middle School
Richard Gardner, Schor Middle School

Enrollment and Setting (urban, suburban, or rural):
4688 students   K-8 – suburban setting

K-8 School Demographics 2002–2003:
Caucasian/Non-Hispanic: 31%
African American: 32.5%
Hispanic: 12%
Asian: 24%
Other: 0.5%
Free/Reduced Lunch: 21%
ESL: 5%
Special Education: 14.6%

Step One: **M**ission

Mission *Connect your work to your school's mission.*
Your mission statement is: The mission of the Piscataway Public Schools is the continual development of each child's intellectual, aesthetic, social, and physical abilities in a positive environment that fosters self-esteem. Students in the Piscataway Public Schools will be confident, productive members of a changing society.

Step Two: **E**lements

Current Critical Data Element *What indicator of school success are you trying to positively impact? Grades? Test scores? Attendance? Promotion rates? Postsecondary going rate?*
The Piscataway Public Schools District elementary and middle school counselors as part of the leadership team identified this critical data element to try to impact: •Suspension rate for the elementary and sixth grade students

Step Three: Analyze

Analyze the data to see what it reveals, to identify the problem areas, to establish your baseline, and to set your goal. It may be necessary to disaggregate the data, e.g., race, ethnicity, gender, SES, teacher assignment.	
Baseline: Where is this data element currently?	***Goal: Where do you want the data element to be in a year?***
2001–2002 suspensions 176	• Decrease suspensions by 1%

Step Four: Stakeholders-Unite

Develop an Action Plan
School counselors, as managers of resources, join existing groups of stakeholders, such as the school improvement team, or bring other stakeholders and resources into the task of creating and implementing an action plan. Strategies are developed that will change systems as well as impact individual students and targeted groups of students.

Impacting systems means (1) replicating successful programs and interventions, (2) identifying barriers that adversely stratify students' opportunities to be successful learners, and (3) developing strategies to:
- *change policies, practices, and procedures*
- *strengthen curriculum offerings*
- *maximize the instructional program*
- *enhance the school and classroom culture and climate*
- *provide student academic support systems (safety nets)*
- *influence course enrollment patterns to widen access to rigorous academics*
- *involve parents and other critical stakeholders (internal and external to the school)*
- *raise aspirations in students, parents, teachers, and the community*
- *change attitudes and beliefs about students and their abilities to learn*

Shareholders	***Strategies*** *Connect your strategies to the American School Counselor Association (ASCA) National Standards and the ASCA National Model.*
	Beginning date: September, 2002 ***Ending date:*** June, 2003
School Counselors	• Implemented a Peace Pledge program

	• Developed anti-bullying classroom guidance lessons • Trained peer mediators • Raised awareness through a school-wide education campaign • Worked closely across schools (elementary with middle school counselors) to continue and extend the skills taught in K-5 • Reviewed and reinforced conflict resolution skills • Taught students how to manage anger and frustration • Taught students "I" messages • Conducted problem-solving groups • Monitored attendance patterns, provided interventions • Conducted lunch groups with students • Disaggregated and studied attendance, suspension, discipline referral data (time in district, gender, grade, ethnicity, situation)
Teachers	• Reinforced classroom guidance lessons as a follow-up • Used writing as a medium to help students describe anger management situations • Learned to identify and remediate stress and anxiety in children • Created bullyfree class environments • Used conflict resolution strategies in their classrooms • Referred students for mediation as an alternative to discipline • Collaborated with counselors on creating safe classrooms • Addressed all bullying incidents
Administrators	• Encouraged mediation first • Enforced consequences • Used conflict resolution strategies with students • Worked with staff to improve classroom school climate • Created a teacher/student united hotline with staff feedback • Continued conflict resolution training for staff and students • Compared end-of-year data (2002) to end-of-year data (2003)
Students	• Participated in the Peace Pledge Program at a rate of 85% (elementary students) • Created anti-bullying posters • Collected kindness coupons • Served as peer mediators • Learned when to seek help from an adult • Learned to recognize signs of tension or stress and utilize skills that have been taught
Student Services Personnel	• Collaborated with the child study team to look at alternative ways of discipline for identified students • Worked with students on rules and consequences • Collaborated with outside agencies

	• Provided internal testing and home visits as needed • Identified students with history of conflict • Provided consultation with teachers and parents
Technology	• Used technology to disaggregate, access, compile, and display data
Media Specialist	• Delivered story time using books and stories for class presentations that addressed resolving conflict peacefully • Developed a thought for the day – appropriate AM readings • Developed a parent library
Music Teacher	• Taught songs that supported friendships and resolving problems
Art Teacher	• Worked with students on designing posters and displaying bullyfree posters
Community Agency and Business Community Members	• Conducted an assembly on positive decision making (police department) • Spoke with students about collaborating and working together • Met with each student who was suspended twice (student resource officer) • Hosted students for job shadowing • Served as mentors and tutors
Local Colleges	• Offered a mentoring program (Kean University) • Facilitated a tutoring program (Rutgers University)
Parents	• Participated in workshops and reading material that focused on resolving conflict peaceably • Attended meetings to discuss their child's behavior • Reinforced the code of conduct at home
Teacher Assistants	• Participated in conflict resolution training • Trained custodians to be more observant of student behavior in the cafeteria and to openly discuss bus incidents • Monitored behavior and consistently enforced the rules • Participated in respect reminders program
School Improvement Team	• Aligned the district strategic action plan • Brainstormed activities, programs, assemblies that targeted a safe school environment • Developed a management plan to improve climate for difficult areas (cafeteria, bus loading zones)

Step Five: **R**eanalyze, Reflect, and Revise

Reanalyze

Restate the baseline data. Where is the data after the action plan? Did the strategies have a positive impact on the data?

2001–2002 suspensions Baseline Data	2002–2003 suspensions Data after Action Plan
176	124

Impact: Suspension incidents were reduced at both the elementary and middle schools. This is especially powerful because it was the first sixth-grade class impacted by a targeted collaboration.

Reflect and Revise

Reflect on why the stakeholders were successful or unsuccessful. Revise the action plan so that progress can be made and you can continue to get better results.

Which of the strategies worked?
-Especially effective were the collaboration efforts and the Peace Program.

Which strategies should be replaced? Added?
-None noted at this time.

Based on what you learned, how will you rewrite the action plan?
-Next year we will include all discipline incidents, not just suspensions, and work on promotion rates.

Systemic Changes Made

Whenever you implement a MEASURE you will contribute to systemic change. Each MEASURE will in some way change a school, home, or community system to enhance student learning. Capture these systemic changes here and record them on your SPARC.

1. The work of the counselors became part of the school improvement team's strategic plan.
2. A safe and respectful school became a school-wide effort involving all internal and external stakeholders, resulting in a change in the school climate.
3. A stronger collaboration between elementary and middle school counselors became our new way of operating to deliver the K-8 comprehensive school counseling program.

Step Six: **E**ducate

Promote and publicize the results of your work. Develop a report card for your own program to let the internal and external school members know your work is connected to the mission of the school and to student success. The School Counseling Program Accountability Report Card (SPARC) is a way to do this.

Our MEASURE of Success

SPARC - School Counseling Program Accountability Report Card

District: Piscataway Elementary and Middle Schools
Enrollment: K-8 4688
Principals: Susan Chalfin, Wayne Rose, Barry Glickman, Dr. Willa Pryor, Alice Rothberg, Shirley Eyler, Dr. Suzanne Westberg, Mr. Mario Tursi, Mr. Richard Gardner
Assistant Director for Counseling: Dr. Dorothy J. Youngs
Counselors: Jill Brown, Gillian Roth, Susan Manley, J. Courtney Boyd-Moscowitz, Irene Guarino, Carmen Campoverde, Sherri Griffith, Jaime Schnirman, Rebecca Walker, Ildiko Henni-Jones, Robyn Rosenthal, Deirdre McClafferty, MaryAnn Lombardi, Margo Shapiro, Marge Delaney, C. Alex Gray, Dan Rothberg, Wendy Johansen

Director of Counselors' Comments

Collaboration was key to our success this year with elementary and middle school counselors working together to build on skills and knowledge that students acquired in the elementary schools. The sixth-grade suspension rate was strongly impacted as a result of this effort. Training was provided for staff in conflict resolution skills to manage student behavior. We pulled together toward the common goal of creating a climate of caring and respect in our schools.

School Improvement Issues

Suspension rates were at unacceptable levels.

Critical Data Element(s):
Reduce the number of K-6 suspensions

Stakeholders

Counselors: Involved students in the Peace Pledge program; developed anti-bullying classroom guidance lessons; trained peer mediators; implemented a school-wide program; collaborated with counselors across schools to continue the skills taught in K-5; taught conflict resolution skills; used disaggregated data to identify problem areas
Administrator: Encouraged mediation first; enforced consequences; used conflict resolution strategies with students
Teachers: Reinforced conflict mediation skills; created bullyfree class environments; referred students for mediation as an alternative to discipline
Parents: Participated in workshops that focused on resolving conflict peacefully; reinforced the code of conduct at home
Students: Created an anti-bullying school; served as peer mediators; took the "peace pledge," learned when to seek help from an adult and how to confront bullying
Higher Education: Provided mentors and tutors for children who displayed at-risk behavior
Business Partners: Spoke to students about the importance of working together

Results

Number of Student K-8 Suspensions

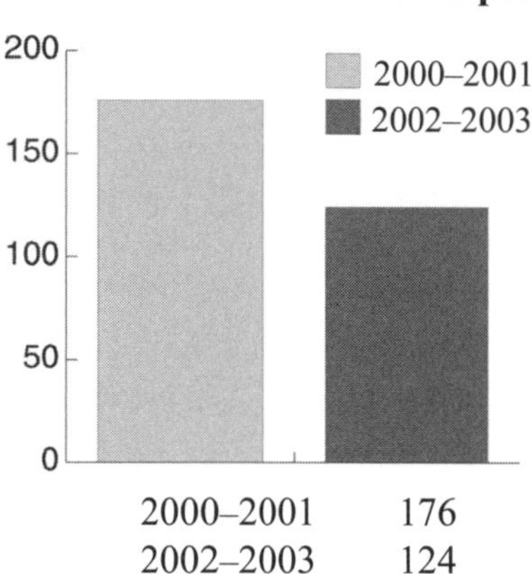

2000–2001 176
2002–2003 124

Systemic Changes

1. The elementary and middle school counselors began the process of annually establishing goals and collaborating to achieve them.
2. A safe and respectful school climate became a focus of each school with multiple stakeholders seeking attainment.
3. Choosing a goal and having the entire faculty focus on that goal became the district practice, with a safe and respectful school climate becoming the first such goal.

Faces Behind the Data

Shortly after Irene Guarino taught her second graders anti-bullying strategies, a second grader ran up to her, "Mrs. Guarino," she excitedly said, "here's the story. So far I told them to stop. I stood up to the whole group. I told them how I felt. I gave them an "I" message. And now I'm telling a grown-up."

Counselor Marge Delaney always goes out of her way to compliment her students when she "catches" them doing something good! One student looked quizzically at her and responded, " But I just listen to you."

MEASURE

Mission, **E**lements, **A**nalyze, **S**takeholders-**U**nite, **R**eanalyze, **E**ducate,
a Six-step Accountability Process for School Counselors

Name and Address of School:
Chelsea Career and Technical Education High School
131 Avenue of the Americas
New York, NY 10013
(212) 925-2871

Name of Counselor Leading the Initiative:
Joan Apellaniz

Principal:
Timothy Timberlake

Enrollment:
950 students - urban setting

School Demographics:
Caucasian/Non-Hispanic: 4.3%
African American: 38.5%
Hispanic: 55.1%
Other: 2.2%
ESL: 6%
Free/Reduced lunch

Step One: **M**ission

Mission *Connect your work to your school's mission.*
Your mission statement is: The mission of Chelsea High School is to provide an environment that nurtures and values each individual, and that expands the intellectual, social, and physical capabilities of all students. By providing academic intervention services, career-informed courses, and work-based learning experiences, we believe that each student, upon graduation, will have marketable skills as well as the qualifications to attend college if he/she desires.

Step Two: **E**lements

Current Critical Data Element *What indicator of school success are you trying to positively impact? Grades? Test scores? Attendance? Promotion rates? Postsecondary going rate?*
The school counselor as part of the leadership team identified these critical data elements to try to impact: 1. Improve the ninth grade promotion rate 2. Reduce suspensions

Step Three: **A**nalyze

Analyze the data to see what it reveals, to identify the problem areas, to establish your baseline, and to set your goal. It may be necessary to disaggregate the data, e.g., race, ethnicity, gender, SES, teacher assignment.

Baseline: Where is this data element currently?	***Goal: Where do you want the data element to be in a year?***
Baseline Data: • Fall 2002 = 21 suspensions • Spring 2003 3rd Marking Period = 55.2% promotion rate	1. Decrease suspensions for ninth graders by 5% 2. Increase promotion rates for ninth graders by 5%

Step Four: **S**takeholders-**U**nite

Develop an Action Plan

School counselors, as managers of resources, join existing groups of stakeholders, such as the school improvement team, or bring other stakeholders and resources into the task of creating and implementing an action plan. Strategies are developed that will change systems as well as impact individual students and targeted groups of students.

Impacting systems means (1) replicating successful programs and interventions, (2) identifying barriers that adversely stratify students' opportunities to be successful learners, and (3) developing strategies to:

- *change policies, practices, and procedures*
- *strengthen curriculum offerings*
- *maximize the instructional program*

• *enhance the school and classroom culture and climate* • *provide student academic support systems (safety nets)* • *influence course enrollment patterns to widen access to rigorous academics* • *involve parents and other critical stakeholders (internal and external to the school)* • *raise aspirations in students, parents, teachers, and the community* • *change attitudes and beliefs about students and their abilities to learn*	
Stakeholders	***Strategies*** *Connect your strategies to the American School Counselor Association (ASCA) National Standards and the ASCA National Model.*
	Beginning date: November, 2002 ***Ending date:*** June, 2003
School Counselors	• Mentored students in an after-school program • Worked with students individually who were in conflict during the school day • Delivered career and academic classroom information sessions about the interrelatedness between academic performance and future economic opportunities, financial aid, and other critical, timely information • Implemented a rewards ceremony and distributed certificates to students based on grades and courses passed • Developed a program where honor roll students mentored at-risk students • Advocated for a change in policy to give students in conflict a time-out or "cooling off" period instead of suspension
Administrators	• Continued to deliver strategies already implemented such as the fall ninth-grade information sessions • Continued to support the counselors (they expressed appreciation for the collaboration from the administration) • Began the planning process for after-school discussion groups for at-risk students
Social Worker	• Held ninth-grade discussion groups (rap sessions) for students who were in danger of dropping out
Student Support Personnel	• Established a Freshman Parent Night with enhanced strategies to bring in more parents • Established a group for students who have been suspended for fighting
Manhattan High School District Staff	• Provided Department of Education consultants to help support the school's efforts • Provided periodic meetings for the Chelsea faculty and staff to come together and exchange ideas with counselors from other high schools on how to increase retention and promotion rates

District Office Consultants	• Provided technical support in gathering data and reporting successes to district administrators • Provided a celebration of successes
Teachers	• Delivered an initial technical support meeting for the school counseling staff • Visited the school and helped develop this action plan • Offered technical support by phone • Delivered a central workshop for all counselors and facilitated a counselor exchange of strategies to use at their school
Students	• Widened the reach of support to students by developing more peer helper programs to include peer tutoring and peer mediation
Technology	• Served as mentors to freshman (honor roll students) • Gave testimonials to students who were struggling (former at-risk students)
Attendance Officer	• Generated automated attendance and cut reports
School Clubs	• Monitored attendance of targeted students and reported to counselors • Expanded clubs to reach out to students not yet connected to the school, e.g., book club, video club
Alumni	• Gave testimonials to inspire students
Business Partners	• Supported the Freshman Parent Night Dinner

Step Five: **R**eanalyze, Reflect, and Revise

Reanalyze

Restate the baseline data. Where is the data after the action plan? Did the strategies have a positive impact on the data?

Baseline Data:	Data after Action Plan:
• Fall 2002 = 21 suspensions	• Spring 2003 = 14 suspensions
• Spring 2003 3rd Marking Period = 55.2% promotion	• Spring 2003 6th Marking Period = 59.2% promotion

Reflect and Revise

Reflect on why the stakeholders were successful or unsuccessful. Revise the action plan so that progress can be made and you can continue to get better results.

Which of the strategies worked?

-The rewards ceremony and certificates based on grades and courses passed were effective.

Which strategies should be replaced? Added?

-None noted at this time.

Impact: The strategies moved the data in a positive direction.	*Based on what you have learned, how will you revise the action plan?* -We will continue to work with the tenth graders and add the incoming ninth graders to our plan.

Systemic Changes Made

Whenever you implement a MEASURE you will contribute to systemic change. Each MEASURE will in some way change a school, home, or community system to enhance student learning. Capture these systemic changes here and record them on your SPARC.

1. The school climate was positively impacted by moving to a reward system for courses passed.
2. Data-driven decision-making was implemented across the ninth-grade staff.

Step Six: Educate

Promote and publicize the results of your work. Develop a report card for your own program to let the internal and external school members know your work is connected to the mission of the school and to student success. The School Counseling Program Accountability Report Card (SPARC) is a way to do this.

Our MEASURE of Success

SPARC - School Counseling Program Accountability Report Card

School: Chelsea Career and Technical Education High School
Enrollment: 950
Principal: Timothy Timberlake
Counseling Department Member(s): Joan Apellaniz, Risa Marlne, Diance Lucas, Ayoka Cox

Principal's Comments

Our counselors worked very hard this year to impact the District Office's desire to improve promotion and discipline rates. They did this by looking at the important data elements that contribute to improving our students' futures. They used their leadership, advocacy, teaming, and collaboration skills to make a positive difference.

School Improvement Issues

Promotion rate of ninth graders needs to be increased. Suspension rates are at unacceptable levels.

Critical Data Element(s):
Passing rate of ninth graders
Number of suspensions

Stakeholders

Counselors: Studied data and implemented strategies to reduce suspensions and failures.
Administrators: Supported the counselors and continued to implement strategies to reduce failure rates
Teachers: Developed peer tutoring and mediation programs
Students: Served as mentors to peers; gave testimonials to students who were struggling
Business Partners: Supported the Freshman Parent Night Dinner

Results

2003 Passing Rates for 9th Graders

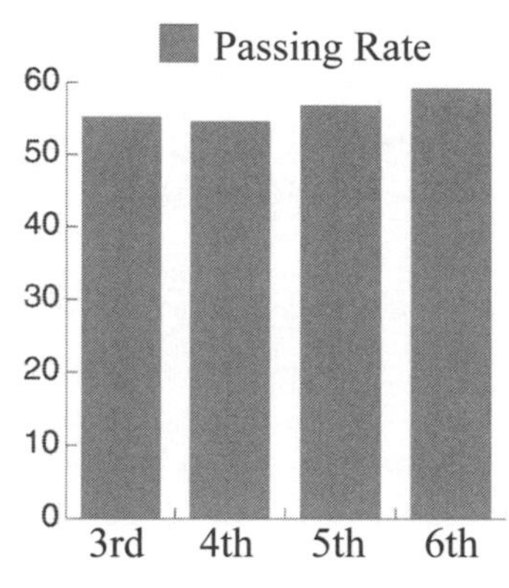

3rd Marking Period (MP)	55.2%
4th MP	54.6%
5th MP	56.8%
6th MP	59.2%

2002–2003 Number of Students Suspended

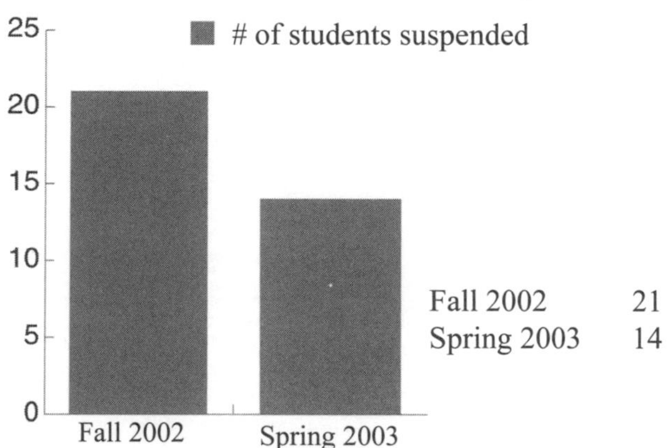

Fall 2002	21
Spring 2003	14

Systemic Changes

1. The collaboration changed school climate by moving to a reward system for courses passed.
2. The counselors initiated data-driven decision making.

Faces Behind the Data

Certificates were given out at the first awards assembly to our ninth graders passing their subjects and we fully expected to find the hall littered with discarded certificates. Not one! We inquired of the custodians who confirmed that the certificates all made it out of the building, testament to their value to our students.

MEASURE

Mission, **E**lements, **A**nalyze, **S**takeholders-**U**nite, **R**eanalyze, **E**ducate,
a Six-step Accountability Process for School Counselors

Name and Address of School:
Darnell-Cookman Middle School
1701 Davis Street
Jacksonville, FL 32209
(904) 630-6805

Name of Counselor Leading the Initiative:
Edith Vanderhoek

Principal:
Cheryl Hough

Enrollment:
1255 students - urban setting

School Demographics:
Caucasian/Non-Hispanic: 56%
African American: 33%
Hispanic: 3%
Asian: 5%
Other: 2%
Free/Reduced lunch: 16.1 %
ESL: 0.3%

Step One: **M**ission

Mission *Connect your work to your school's mission.*
Your mission statement is: The mission of Darnell-Cookman is to prepare students for success in high school by offering a rigorous, standards-based curriculum, which allows students opportunities to think and work creatively and critically, and to learn to work together in an ever-changing society.

Step Two: **Elements**

Current Critical Data Element *What indicator of school success are you trying to positively impact? Grades? Test scores? Attendance? Promotion rates? Postsecondary going rate?*
Darnell-Cookman school counselors as part of the leadership team identified these critical data elements to try to impact: • FCAT scores in sixth, seventh, and eighth grades

Step Three: **Analyze**

Analyze the data to see what it reveals, to identify the problem areas, to establish your baseline, and to set your goal. It may be necessary to disaggregate the data e.g. race, ethnicity, gender, SES, teacher assignment.

Baseline: Where is this data element currently?

2002 FCAT scores at or above level 3*

6th Math	75%
6th Reading	84%
7th Math	83%
7th Reading	85%
8th Math	94%
8th Reading	83%

*The Florida Comprehensive Assessment Test (FCAT) scores are reported in terms of five achievement levels (1-low to 5-high).

Goal: Where do you want the data element to be in a year?

• Increase FCAT scores so that the number of students scoring at or above a level 3 increases in each area by 4%

Step Four: **Stakeholders-Unite**

Develop an Action Plan

School counselors, as managers of resources, join existing groups of stakeholders, such as the school improvement team, or bring other stakeholders and resources into the task of creating and implementing an action plan. Strategies are developed that will change systems as well as impact individual students and targeted groups of students.

Impacting systems means (1) replicating successful programs and interventions, (2) identifying

barriers that adversely stratify students' opportunities to be successful learners, and (3) developing strategies to: *• change policies, practices, and procedures* *• strengthen curriculum offerings* *• maximize the instructional program* *• enhance the school and classroom culture and climate* *• provide student academic support systems (safety nets)* *• influence course enrollment patterns to widen access to rigorous academics* *• involve parents and other critical stakeholders (internal and external to the school)* *• raise aspirations in students, parents, teachers, and the community* *• change attitudes and beliefs about students and their abilities to learn*	
Stakeholders	***Strategies*** *Connect your strategies to the American School Counselor Association (ASCA) National Standards and the ASCA National Model.*
	Beginning date: 2001–2002 school year ***Ending date:*** 2002–2003 school year
School Counselors	• Studied data and developed strategies with the stakeholders • Communicated with parents through mailings to let parents know that their student is having difficulty and to offer strategies • Requested a parent conference with each struggling student • Created contracts for student and parent signature listing activities that will improve grades • Contributed to the newsletter study skills and other strategies to support learning • Helped establish Saturday classes for academic support
Teachers	• Administered FCAT practice tests • Implemented TEAM UP, an after-school program for homework help • Suggested after-school help for struggling students • Offered individual after-school tutoring • Wrote a study skills program for the school • Established a separate reading class for sixth grade • Began research classes for students scoring low on the FCAT in lieu of an elective class • Implemented peer tutoring • Contributed to newsletters on test-taking strategies and study tips • Adjusted their elective schedule to give students additional help
Administrators	• Implemented Saturday school for math and language arts • Expanded the Saturday school to include science and history

Student	• Participated in after-school and Saturday school tutoring programs • Acted as peer tutors
Technology	• Provided on-line FCAT practice tests for students
Business Partners	• Provided after-school mathematics tutors from Bank of America
Local Colleges	• Provided tutoring, study skills, and mentors
Teacher Assistants	• Provided FCAT test-taking strategies; acted as FCAT coaches
Technology Specialist	• Developed the parent newsletter

Step Five: **R**eanalyze, Reflect, and Revise

Reanalyze

Restate the baseline data. Where is the data after the action plan? Did the strategies have a positive impact on the data?

	2002 Baseline data	2003 Data after Action Plan
6th Math	75%	70%
6th Reading	84%	85%
7th Math	83%	86%
7th Reading	85%	87%
8th Math	94%	96%
8th Reading	83%	88%

The strategies impacted the test scores in all but one area.

Reflect and Revise

Reflect on why the stakeholders were successful or unsuccessful. Revise the action plan so that progress can be made and you can continue to get better results.

Which of the strategies worked?
-Communication efforts with parents and the Saturday school

Which strategies should be replaced? Added?
-None noted at this time.

Based on what you have learned, how will you rewrite the action plan?
-Next year we will add attendance as a critical data element.

Systemic Changes Made

Whenever you implement a MEASURE you will contribute to systemic change. Each MEASURE will in some way change a school, home, or community system to enhance student learning. Capture these systemic changes here and record them on your SPARC.

1. A tight network of collaboration between teachers, parents, administrators, and school counselors replaced a loosely established student assistance program.

2. After-school homework help was institutionalized.

Step Six: Educate

Promote and publicize the results of your work. Develop a report card for your own program to let the internal and external school members know your work is connected to the mission of the school and to student success. The School Counseling Program Accountability Report Card (SPARC) is a way to do this.

Our MEASURE of Success

SPARC - School Counseling Program Accountability Report Card

School: Darnell-Cookman Middle
Enrollment: 1255
Principal: Cheryl Hough
Counselors: Edith Vanderhoek, Erika Gilbert

Principal's Comments

At Darnell-Cookman, our school counselors are truly role models for student advocacy through collaboration, inspiring and supporting all stakeholders, students, parents, teachers, administrators, and staff members. Our counselors work collaboratively to carry out and initiate programs and strategies for the success of all students.

School Improvement Issues

The Florida Comprehensive Assessment Test (FCAT) is a standards-based test used in promotion. The FCAT has 5 achievement levels, with level 1 being the lowest and level 5 the highest. Too many students are scoring below level 3.
Critical Data Element(s):
Percentage of students scoring at or above a level 3 on the FCAT

Stakeholders

Counselor: Used data to develop strategies to impact success on the FCAT
Administrator: Supported the stakeholders' efforts; implemented Saturday school for math, language arts, science, and history
Teachers: Implemented peer tutoring, test-taking strategies; championed the counselor's efforts
Students: Participated in after-school and Saturday school tutoring programs; acted as peer tutors
Higher Education: Provided tutoring, study skills, and mentors
Business Partners: Provided mathematics tutors twice each week

Results

6th Grade FCAT Scores at or above level 3

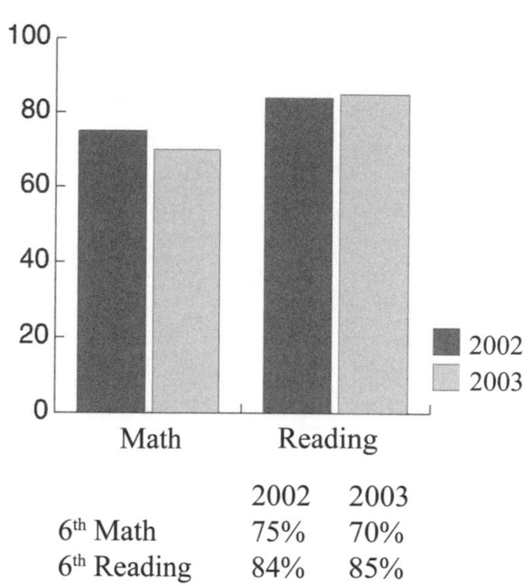

	2002	2003
6th Math	75%	70%
6th Reading	84%	85%

7th Grade FCAT Scores at or above level 3

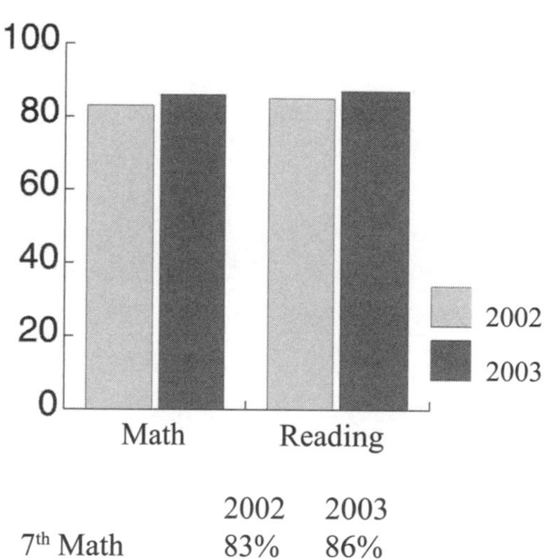

	2002	2003
7th Math	83%	86%
7th Reading	85%	87%

8th Grade FCAT scores at or above level 3

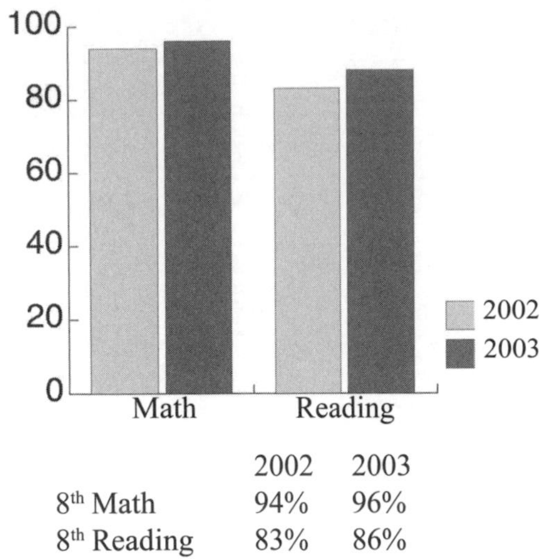

	2002	2003
8th Math	94%	96%
8th Reading	83%	86%

Systemic Changes

1. Institutionalized a tight network of collaboration between teachers, parents, administrators, and school counselors
2. Created permanent after-school homework help

Faces Behind the Data

Our school offers only advanced classes. One sixth grader who was learning-disabled had the fight of his life this year. Through intense collaborative interventions (face-to-face parent conferences, brief counseling, enrollment in both math and reading research classes, teacher tutoring, Saturday school) this shy, quiet young man passed the advanced program with a 2.17 GPA and raised his FCAT scores from level 3 to 4 in reading and from level 2 to 3 in math!

MEASURE

Mission, **E**lements, **A**nalyze, **S**takeholders-**U**nite, **R**eanalyze, **E**ducate,
a Six-step Accountability Process for School Counselors

Name and Address of School:
Pike High School
5401 W 71st Street
Indianapolis, IN 46268
Phone- (317) 387-2600
Fax- (317) 328-7239

Name of Counselor Leading the Initiative:
Jim MacGregor

Principal:
Stan Hall

Enrollment:
2492 - urban setting

School Demographics:

1989:	66% Caucasian/Non-Hispanic	2000:	39% Caucasian/Non-Hispanic*
	30% African American		51% African American
	4% Other		10% Other

Free and reduced lunch ranged for the time period between 16–22%.

* A major shift in demographics occurred from 1993 from a predominately Caucasian school to a predominately African American school.

Step One: **M**ission

Mission *Connect your work to your school's mission.*
Your mission statement is: Pike High School, a culturally diverse public educational institution, engages students through exceptional learning opportunities in a safe, secure, and stimulating environment. The staff, parents, and community work as partners to enhance the academic, social, physical, and ethical development of all students. Lifelong learning is encouraged through an emphasis on a challenging academic curriculum and career choices.

Step Two: Elements

Current Critical Data Element

What indicator of school success are you trying to positively impact? Grades? Test scores? Attendance? Promotion rates? Postsecondary going rate?

Pike school counselors as part of the leadership team identified these critical data elements to try to impact:

1. Higher level mathematics course enrollment
2. Percentage of students graduating with a college core
3. Postsecondary and college going rates

Step Three: Analyze

Analyze the data to see what it reveals, to identify the problem areas, to establish your baseline, and to set your goal. It may be necessary to disaggregate the data, e.g., race, ethnicity, gender, SES, teacher assignment.

Baseline: Where is this data element currently?

1. Completion of the following mathematics courses 1991–1992:

(Course completion meant passing with at least a "D")

	1991–1992
ALG 1 & 2	71%
GEO	66.1%
ALG 3 & 4	55.4%
Pre-CAL	31.5%
CAL 1 & 2	11%

2. Postsecondary and college going rate:

1989	60%

3. Students graduating with college core:

	1994
Caucasian	62.5%
African American	26.7%

Goal: Where do you want the data element to be in a year?

1. Increase higher level mathematics enrollment by 1% each year

2. Increase the postsecondary and college going rate by 1% each year

3. Decrease the gap between Caucasian and African American (AA) students graduating with a college core by 5% each year

Step Four: **S**takeholders-**U**nite

Develop an Action Plan
School counselors, as managers of resources, join existing groups of stakeholders, such as the school improvement team, or bring other stakeholders and resources into the task of creating and implementing an action plan. Strategies are developed that will change systems as well as impact individual students and targeted groups of students.

Impacting systems means (1) replicating successful programs and interventions, (2) identifying barriers that adversely stratify students' opportunities to be successful learners, and (3) developing strategies to:

- *change policies, practices, and procedures*
- *strengthen curriculum offerings*
- *maximize the instructional program*
- *enhance the school and classroom culture and climate*
- *provide student academic support systems (safety nets)*
- *influence course enrollment patterns to widen access to rigorous academics*
- *involve parents and other critical stakeholders (internal and external to the school)*
- *raise aspirations in students, parents, teachers, and the community*
- *change attitudes and beliefs about students and their abilities to learn*

Stakeholders	***Strategies*** *Connect your strategies to the American School Counselor Association (ASCA) National Standards and the ASCA National Model.*
	Beginning date: 1991–1992 school year ***Ending date:*** 2000–2001 school year
School Counselors	• Implemented a career awareness program for every student to help them see the relationship between postsecondary education and their future economic opportunities • Advocated for a systemic change in course enrollment patterns to support more students to access higher level academics • Used data and anecdotal information about student success in higher level academics • Changed attitudes and beliefs about widening opportunities for higher level mathematics • Impacted the instructional program by helping teachers understand students' strengths and weaknesses through disaggregated test results • Led large and small group sessions to raise aspirations • Tracked through technology every student's course selections and the match with their career goals (led to increased enrollment in rigorous mathematics) • Established a mentoring program • Brought in role models who represented careers that required higher level mathematics

	• Assisted in establishing a tutoring program • Disaggregated course enrollment patterns by counselor and discovered that some counselors were allowing students to opt out of rigorous academics at much higher rates • Garnered support to add additional counselors • Created an alliance with district administrators to widen access to higher level mathematics • Managed resources and brought more people in to help with the school counseling program • Collaborated with teachers to increase algebra completion • Recruited parents to develop and run a career center • Eliminated the requirement for teacher approval for all upper level classes • Created a Career course to teach study skills and to provide school tours, job shadowing, and career searches • Provided classroom guidance lessons on career development • Provided a career center orientation for all ninth- and eleventh-grade students • Implemented a highly successful cafeteria-style parent conference event (spread to every school in the district) • Worked with the math department chairperson to receive approval for every ninth grader to enroll in algebra
Teachers	• Opened access to all students to enroll in higher level math • Discontinued the practice of asking counselors to remove struggling students from their math courses • Integrated into the curriculum writing assignments related to scholarship and college applications, financial aid calculations, and career searches (math, English, and social studies teachers) • Tried new ideas and influenced reluctant peers to make changes • Traveled to 20 locations for professional development in block scheduling and math teaching strategies • Tutored 30 minutes before and after school for minimum pay • Advocated for the peer tutoring program
Administrators	• Supported the efforts of the school counselors with time, money, and endorsements • Made instructional changes such as block scheduling • Made curriculum changes such as eliminating dead-end math courses • Added and supported safety nets such as double math periods • Opened access to upper level classes • Supported personnel to develop and implement new initiatives • Approved a career course for all students

21st Century Team	• Brought leadership and clout to the establishment of Pike as a state model for a career academy and supported efforts at school improvement (Stan Hall, Chair)
Students	• Delivered peer tutoring • Convinced their fellow students to participate in the tutoring program • Made their four-year plans a meaningful document and actively sought the school counselor's help to revise them as needed
Technology	• Allowed tracking of four-year plans • Eliminated course scheduling by counselors • Allowed college advisors to interact electronically with students about their course taking, grades, career plans, college admissions • Provided tenth-graders computer placement testing to show their progress towards math for college success
Community Agency Members	• Advocated to school board members in favor of requiring algebra and other rigorous course work (influential community leaders) • Worked to change attitudes that contributed toward wider opportunities for students • Continued advocating until curriculum changes were institutionalized and fully implemented • Published a convincing newsletter to all parents supporting higher level academics
Local Colleges	• Implemented computer placement testing for tenth graders to help them with early awareness as to their academic progress towards college success • Implemented technology so that college advisors could interact electronically with students • Researched and hailed the school's transition efforts, which resulted in support for the counselors' efforts
Grants	• Funded counselors to work in the summer to improve student course taking (Lily Endowment Grant). When funding ended the school district picked up the obligation
Parents	• Manned and financially supported the career center • Advocated to keep the career center open two nights a week • Worked to make certain that their children were taking advantage of tutoring, their four-year plans, and the career center
Teacher Assistants	• Helped run the career center

School Improvement Team	• Publicized the school's success in higher level academics to the school board and larger community. Acted as the point person for controversial issues such as block scheduling

Step Five: **R**eanalyze, Reflect, and Revise

Reanalyze

Restate the baseline data. Where is the data after the action plan? Did the strategies have a positive impact on the data?

1. Completion of higher level mathmatics courses:

	1991 Baseline Data	1995–1996 Interim Data	2000–2001 Data after Action Plan
ALG 1 & 2	71%	94%	99%
GEO	66.1%	83%	96%
ALG 3 & 4	55.4%	63%	65%-
Pre-CAL	31.5%	39%	46%
CAL 1 & 2	11%	20%	20%

2. Postsecondary and college going rate:

1989	2000
60%	70%

3. Students graduating with college Core:

	1994	2000
Caucasian	62.5%	78%
African American	26.7%	66%

Reflect and Revise

Reflect on why the stakeholders were successful or unsuccessful. Revise the action plan so that progress can be made and you can continue to get better results.

Which of the strategies worked?

-Peer and teacher tutoring were very successful (when active failure rates dropped to 9%).

Which strategies should be replaced? Added?

-Technology must be enhanced for placement testing and college advising.

Based on what you have learned, how will you rewrite the action plan?

-We will add stakeholders and seek an International Baccalaureate Program.

Systemic Changes Made
Whenever you implement a MEASURE you will contribute to systemic change. Each MEASURE will in some way change a school, home, or community system to enhance student learning. Capture these systemic changes here and record them on your SPARC.

Systemic Changes:
1. Transitioning between middle and high school (named by Butler University as a model) became seamless.
2. The school district added counselors and funded counselors to work in the summer because of their success rate in increasing higher level mathematics enrollment.
3. Double mathematics periods were implemented.
4. A change in attitudes and beliefs on the part of teachers, other educators, and community members opened higher level academics to all students.
5. Algebra became a required course.

Step Six: **E**ducate

Promote and publicize the results of your work. Develop a report card for your own program to let the internal and external school members know your work is connected to the mission of the school and to student success. The School Counseling Program Accountability Report Card (SPARC) is a way to do this.

Our MEASURE of Success

SPARC - School Counseling Program Accountability Report Card

School: Pike High School
Enrollment: 2492
Principal: Jim Rollins
Assistant Principal: Stan Hall
Counselor: Jim MacGregor

Principal's Comments

Pike High School has seen many positive changes as a result of the data-driven decisions that were made during Jim MacGregor's tenure as Guidance Director. The work Jim spearheaded resulted in systemic changes such as our six small learning communities, our open access to AP enrollments, and our application for an International Baccalaureate program.

School Improvement Issues

Students were not enrolling in higher level math courses, postsecondary and college going rates were stagnant, and a gap existed among college core completers.

Critical Data Element(s):
Increase the number of students completing higher level mathematics and the college core, and entering college upon graduation

Stakeholders

Counselors: Advocated for systemic change to support more students to access higher level academics; impacted the instructional program by using disaggregated test results so that teachers understood student weaknesses
Administrators: Supported block scheduling to add safety nets for students, allowing for double math
Teachers: Supported block scheduling; served as tutors before and after school
Parents: Advocated for a career center to demonstrate the connection between math and careers
Students: Participated in peer tutoring
Higher Education: Helped students understand about non-credit courses in college if their skills are weak; studied and informed the transition process from eighth to ninth grade
Community: Spoke in favor of curriculum reform; developed a newsletter for parents

Results

Percent of Graduates Completing Higher Level Math Courses

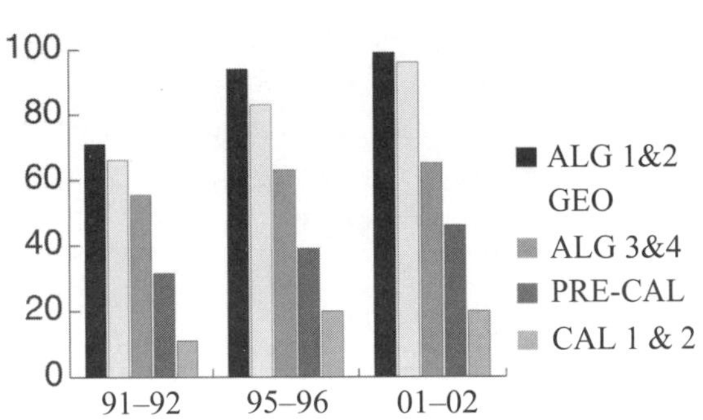

	91–92	95–96	01–02
ALG 1 & 2	71%	94%	99%
GEO	66.1%	83%	96%
ALG 3 & 4	55.4%	63%	65%
Pre-CAL	31.5%	39%	46%
CAL 1 & 2	11%	20%	20%

Postsecondary and College Going Rates

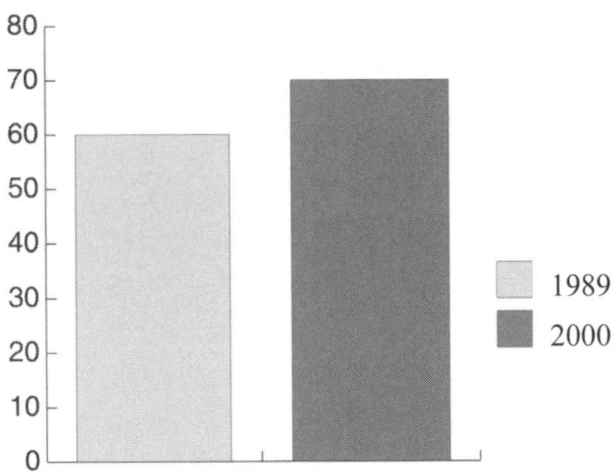

1989	2000
60%	70%

Students Graduating with the "College Core"

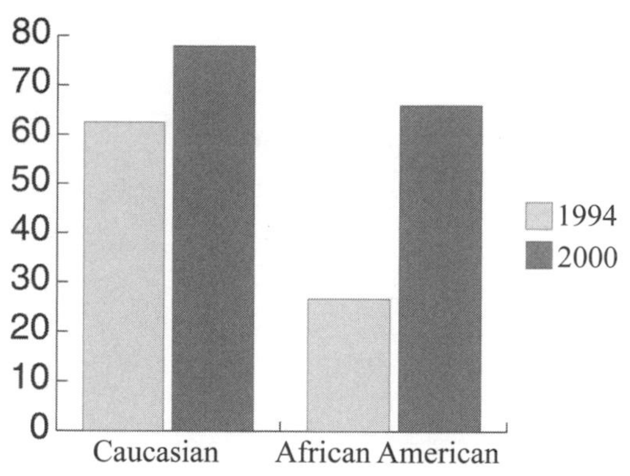

	1994	2000
Caucasian	62.5%	78%
African American	26.7%	66%

Systemic Changes

1. A collaborative, smooth approach to transitioning middle schoolers to high school became the norm (named by Butler University as a model).
2. The school district added counselors and funded counselors to work in the summer based on their success rate in increasing higher-level mathematics enrollment.
3. Double mathematics periods were implemented.
4. Attitudes and beliefs changed on the part of teachers, other educators, and community members about opening higher-level academics to all students.
5. Algebra became a required course.

Faces Behind the Data

A mother of a ninth grader lamented the fact that her son had not passed any of his math tests during his three years of middle school. With peer tutoring and other interventions he not only started passing his tests, he continued to take the math courses necessary for admission to Indiana University (two years of algebra and a year of geometry) and he was admitted!

When we implemented "real" algebra for every ninth grader we added a "help" class for those who needed more support than double math periods. Twin sisters, one of whom had learning disabilities, had D's and F's in mathematics throughout middle school. With the extra support, both sisters shot up to B averages and went on to be successful in higher level mathematics.

1	2	3	4	5	6	7	8	9	10	11	12

MEASURE

Mission, **E**lements, **A**nalyze, **S**takeholders-**U**nite, **R**eanalyze, **E**ducate,
a Six-step Accountability Process for School Counselors

Name and Address of School:
Stanton College Preparatory High School
1149 West 13th Street
Jacksonville, FL 32209
(904) 630-6760

Name of Counselor Leading the Initiative:
Robert Turba

Principal:
Jim Jaxon

Enrollment:
1,520 students - urban setting

School Demographics:
Caucasian/Non-Hispanic: 57.4%
African American: 29.4%
Hispanic: 1.1%
Asian: 11.4%
Other: 0.7%

Step One: **M**ission

Mission *Connect your work to your school's mission.*
Your mission statement is: The mission of Stanton College Preparatory School is to foster an environment of academic excellence through balanced and comprehensive curricula, rigorous academic standards, and challenging assessments. Faculty members guide students to master intellectual, physical, and creative skills; to acquire knowledge; and to think critically, creatively, and independently. Stanton endeavors to develop the individual talents of young people to teach them to relate the experiences of the classroom to the realities of our changing world. Stanton emphasizes teaching cultural understanding and responsible citizenship to its diverse student body in order that those students may become compassionate, informed participants in local and world affairs.

Step Two: Elements

<table>
<tr><td>Current Critical Data Element
What indicator of school success are you trying to positively impact? Grades? Test scores? Attendance? Promotion rates? Postsecondary going rate?</td></tr>
<tr><td>Stanton school counselors as part of the leadership team identified this critical data element to try to impact:
Increase scores on the Preliminary Scholastic Aptitude Test (PSAT), which determines:
1. National Merit Finalists
2. Merit Commended
3. National Achievement
4. Achievement Commended</td></tr>
</table>

Step Three: Analyze

Analyze the data to see what it reveals, to identify the problem areas, to establish your baseline, and to set your goal. It may be necessary to disaggregate the data, e.g., race, ethnicity, gender, SES, teacher assignment.

Baseline: Where is this data element currently?

From the 11th Grade PSAT Scores 2001:

	2001 Baseline Data
National Merit	6
Merit Commended	33
National Achievement	5
Achievement Commended	9

Goal: Where do you want the data element to be in a year?

• Increase the total number of finalists in all areas by 1% each year

Step Four: **Stakeholders-Unite**

<table>
<tr><td colspan="2">

Develop an Action Plan
School counselors, as managers of resources, join existing groups of stakeholders, such as the school improvement team, or bring other stakeholders and resources into the task of creating and implementing an action plan. Strategies are developed that will change systems as well as impact individual students and targeted groups of students.

Impacting systems means (1) replicating successful programs and interventions, (2) identifying barriers that adversely stratify students' opportunities to be successful learners, and (3) developing strategies to:
• change policies, practices, and procedures
• strengthen curriculum offerings
• maximize the instructional program
• enhance the school and classroom culture and climate
• provide student academic support systems (safety nets)
• influence course enrollment patterns to widen access to rigorous academics
• involve parents and other critical stakeholders (internal and external to the school)
• raise aspirations in students, parents, teachers, and the community
• change attitudes and beliefs about students and their abilities to learn

</td></tr>
<tr><td>Stakeholders</td><td>Strategies
Connect your strategies to the American School Counselor Association (ASCA) National Standards and the ASCA National Model.</td></tr>
<tr><td></td><td>Beginning date: 2000–2001 school year
Ending date: 2002–2003 school year</td></tr>
<tr><td>School Counselors</td><td>• Purchased PSAT data on disk so that scores could be disaggregated by a current teacher
• Established database for student information from the PSAT
• Provided data to teachers just prior to the PSAT so that information gained from going over the past year's test would increase students' knowledge about their current performance on the PSAT
• Provided teachers with class sets of PSAT preparation booklets
• Ensured that all tenth & eleventh graders took the PSAT to increase opportunities to qualify for National Merit Scholar status (leads to complete college funding for any FL state school)
• Met with tenth-grade students to discuss the importance of the eleventh- grade PSAT; offered scholarship information and anecdotal stories to illustrate how beneficial a high score on the PSAT could be for a student's future; used database to illustrate to students how many others have benefited from doing well on the PSAT; "shocked" students out of their comfort zone to ensure that they took advantage of all opportunities</td></tr>
</table>

11th Grade Teachers	• Applied student's PSAT results to instruction and taught gaps in skills • Supported and emphasized the PSAT Week through focused instruction
Administrators	• Supported teachers by allowing for PSAT Week
Students	• Participated in PSAT Week to "cheer" each other on for high performance
Technology	• Allowed for a database to track student scores from the PSATs
Funding Agents	• Funded all tenth graders to take the PSAT (State of Florida)

Step Five: **R**eanalyze, Reflect, and Revise

Reanalyze
Restate the baseline data. Where is the data after the action plan? Did the strategies have a positive impact on the data?

	2001 Baseline Data	2003 Data after Action Plan
National Merit	6	25
Merit Commended	33	34
National Achievement	5	6
Achievement Commended	9	5

Impact: Our results tell the story and more students qualified for National Merit status.

Reflect and Revise
Reflect on why the stakeholders were successful or unsuccessful. Revise the action plan so that progress can be made and you can continue to get better results.

Which of the strategies worked?
-Teaching with PSAT scores as a tool increased PSAT scores and prepared students for SAT.

Which strategies should be replaced? Added?
-None noted at this time.

Based on what you have learned, how will you rewrite the action plan?
-Next year we will look at the impact we can have on raising the national achievement and commended results.

Systemic Changes Made
Whenever you implement a MEASURE you will contribute to systemic change. Each MEASURE will in some way change a school, home, or community system to enhance student learning. Capture these systemic changes here and record them on your SPARC.

1. The instructional program was impacted and teachers were helped to address gaps in skills that are needed on the PSAT and other critical tests.

2. The climate of the school was influenced by infusing excitement about the PSAT.
3. The aspirations of students were raised, which impacted the students' and families' understanding of the future scholarship opportunities that come with the PSAT and SAT.
4. We influenced a change in policy to support all students in taking the PSAT.

Step Six: **E**ducate

Promote and publicize the results of your work. Develop a report card for your own program to let the internal and external school members know your work is connected to the mission of the school and to student success. The School Counseling Program Accountability Report Card (SPARC) is a way to do this.

Our MEASURE of Success

SPARC - School Counseling Program Accountability Report Card

School: Stanton College Preparatory School
Enrollment: 1,520
Principal: Jim Jaxon
Counselor: Robert Turba

Principal's Comments

Bob has successfully used data to impact our students' achievement on standardized tests. Through his advocacy, Bob has been instrumental in helping more students acquire the PSAT scores necessary to bring more scholarship opportunities.

School Improvement Issues

PSAT scores impact National Merit qualifiers and scholarship dollars.

Critical Data Element(s):
Increase PSAT scores to increase the number of students who are identified as National Merit Finalists, Merit Commended, National Achievement, and Achievement Commended

Stakeholders

Counselor: Collected and disseminated data on PSAT scores and disaggregated it for teachers so that gaps in learning could be closed; supported a PSAT week
Administrator: Supported a PSAT week during which teachers went over skills needed
Teachers: Used student score analysis to determine needs and taught gaps in skills
Students: Participated in PSAT Week to "cheer" students' performance
Technology: Designed a database to track student PSAT scores
Funding Agents: State paid for all tenth graders to take the PSAT

Results

Students Who Achieved High Scores on the PSAT 2001 and 2003

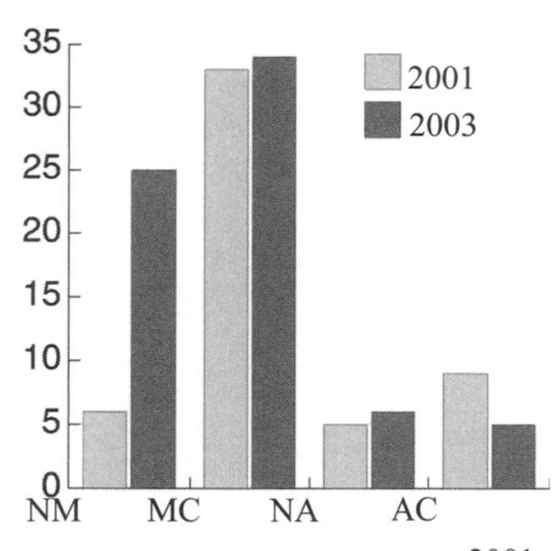

	2001	2003
National Merit (NM)	6	25
Merit Commended (MC)	33	34
National Achievement (NA)	5	6
Achievement Commended (AC)	9	5

Systemic Changes

1. The instructional program was impacted.
2. Aspirations of students and teachers were raised.
3. The PSAT and SAT became a school-wide focus for more scholarship opportunities.
4. A change in policy was implemented to support all students to take the PSAT.

Faces Behind the Data

The PSAT database described in this MEASURE allows me to compare the students' scores from year to year. Querying the database, I have found that students' scores go up an average of 17 points from tenth to eleventh grade. Tenth graders are not aware of the National Merit Program and the scholarship money it brings, so I educate students as to how many more points they would need to reach qualifier status. For example, this year I explained to Rhoda that an additional 3 points in her score could potentially qualify her as a National Merit finalist with huge scholarship dollars. She said, "Do you mean 3 more points is all it will take? I didn't even really try last year!" Motivated by the information, Rhoda made the cutoff score in eleventh grade and gained scholarship money that made the difference for her.

MEASURE

Mission, **E**lements, **A**nalyze, **S**takeholders-**U**nite, **R**eanalyze, **E**ducate,
a Six-step Accountability Process for School Counselors

Name and Address of School:
Jefferson County Public Schools
Louisville, KY 40232-4020
(502) 339-9808

Superintendent:
Dr. Stephen Daeschner

Leading the Initiative:
Linda Miller, Director, School Program and Services

School Counselors:
Rebecca Ansari
Diana Apel
Donna Block
Julianne Davis
Faryl Edelen
Mary Grace Feltham
Trish Foy
Carmen Harris
Linda Ilnick
Cassandra Jackson
Cyndi Lampton
Lynne Macpherson
Joe Prather
Jane Prince
James Ray
Tracy Reed
Pam Robertson
Terri Sgro
Linda Stallings
Diane Stogner
Inman Talaat
Brad Weston
Debra Wilson

Principals and High Schools:
John Hudson, Atherton HS
Sandy Allen, Ballard HS
Ron Freeman, Brown HS
Kenneth Frick, Butler HS
Daniel Withers, Central HS
Glenn Beale, Doss HS
Beverly Keepers, duPont Manual
James Sexton, Eastern HS
Linda Brown, Fairdale HS
Tito Castillo, Fern Creek HS
Brian Schumate, Iroquois HS
Marsha Donn, Jeffersontown HS
David Wilson, Lou Male Traditional HS
Ward Weber, Moors Traditional HS
Charles Miler, Pleasure Ridge Park HS
John Locke, Seneca HS
Buton Martin, Shawnee HS
Jerry Keepers, Southern HS
Dan Hampton, Valley Traditional HS
James Jury, Valley Traditional HS
Geneva Price, Western HS

Enrollment and Setting (urban, suburban, or rural):
96,500 urban, suburban, and rural settings

School Demographics:
Caucasian/Non-Hispanic: 58%
African-American: 36%
Other: 6%

Step One: Mission

Mission *Connect your work to your school's mission.*
Your mission statement is: The Jefferson County Public School District is committed to the education and well-being of students. This commitment is evidenced by our focus upon student success, family/community collaboration, employee efficacy, and by the infusion of each into every aspect of the District's programs and activities.

Step Two: Elements

Current Critical Data Element *What indicator of school success are you trying to positively impact? Grades? Test scores? Attendance? Promotion rates? Postsecondary going rate?*
Jefferson County high achool counselors as part of the leadership team identified this critical data element to try to impact: • Retention rates

Step Three: Analyze

Analyze the data to see what it reveals, to identify the problem areas, to establish your baseline, and to set your goal. It may be necessary to disaggregate the data, e.g., race, ethnicity, gender, SES, teacher assignment.
Goal: Where do you want the data element to be in a year? • Decrease retention rates for each school by 5%
Baseline: Where is this data element currently? 2000–2001 9th grade retention rates: Atherton High 29.75% Ballard High 13.47%

2000–2001 9th grade retention rates: (cont'd)

School	Rate	School	Rate
Breckenridge Metropolitan	61.02%	Liberty High	67.30%
Brown High	1.92%	Male Traditional High	4.96%
Buechel Metropolitan	60.00%	Manual High/Ypas	0.82%
Butler Traditional	8.25%	Moore Traditional HS	36.97%
Central High	32.26%	Pleasure Ridge Park	26.04%
Doss High	21.85%	Seneca High	20.20%
Eastern High	18.16%	Shawnee High	34.68%
Fairdale High	24.54%	South Park Tapp	67.74%
Fern Creek Traditional	26.61%	Southern High	22.66%
Iroquois High	49.28%	Valley Traditional HS	40.35%
Jeffersontown High	36.09%	Waggener Traditional	36.20%
		Western High	43.10%
		Westport Tapp	55.36%

Step Four: **S**takeholders-**U**nite

Develop an Action Plan

School counselors, as managers of resources, join existing groups of stakeholders, such as the school improvement team, or bring other stakeholders and resources into the task of creating and implementing an action plan. Strategies are developed that will change systems as well as impact individual students and targeted groups of students.

Impacting systems means (1) replicating successful programs and interventions, (2) identifying barriers that adversely stratify students' opportunities to be successful learners, and (3) developing strategies to:

- *change policies, practices, and procedures*
- *strengthen curriculum offerings*
- *maximize the instructional program*
- *enhance the school and classroom culture and climate*
- *provide student academic support systems (safety nets)*
- *influence course enrollment patterns to widen access to rigorous academics*
- *involve parents and other critical stakeholders (internal and external to the school)*
- *raise aspirations in students, parents, teachers, and the community*
- *change attitudes and beliefs about students and their abilities to learn*

Stakeholders	***Strategies*** *Connect your strategies to the American School Counselor Association (ASCA) National Standards and the ASCA National Model.*
	Beginning date: 1991–1992 school year ***Ending date:*** 2000–2001 school year

School Counselors	• Collected data from freshman retention rates • Submitted action plans to the district supervisor of guidance on how they were going to help reduce ninth grade retention • Conducted classroom guidance lessons on "freshman survival skills" to teach them about high school expectations and college admissions • Sent informative letters to parents on current issues and ways to help their child pass • Developed contracts for parents and students to sign to ensure student academic advancement • Called parents to keep them involved • Developed a brochure on college preparation and advanced placement credits for students and parents • Helped to align curriculum and set standards to improve retention rates • Conducted assessments every three weeks • Developed the materials and curriculum for the advisor/advisee program • Developed a PowerPoint presentation for use with all ninth graders across the district • Held small group counseling sessions for students • Developed ninth-grade teams • Developed a transition class for at-risk incoming ninth graders which met all year for one period and awarded one credit • Met with each freshman for individual counseling for a minimum of two times to discuss graduation plans, college plans, etc. • Helped to develop double time blocks for at-risk ninth graders in reading and math
Teachers	• Worked with newly aligned curriculum and provided consistency in the classroom • Identified students experiencing difficulties and provided them with extra assistance • Conducted and assisted in the development of an advisor/advisee program
Administrators	• Took data to ninth-grade counselors and challenged them to make a difference (District Supervisor of Guidance) • Developed double time blocks for at-risk ninth graders in reading and math • Raised district-wide requirements for graduation to include Algebra I, Algebra II, Geometry; eliminated lower level math • Involved principals in every school when the assistant superintendent brought the focus to retention rates • Reduced the amount of paperwork required for ESE students so that the counselor had more time to focus on shifting data • Hired more clerical help to assist counselors
Students	• Participated in classroom guidance lessons

Students	• Signed contracts with parents and school counselors to reinforce efforts toward advancement
Technology	• Helped to reduce the amount of paperwork required of school counselors
Volunteers	• Assisted in school counseling offices to help reduce the amount of paperwork
Parents	• Signed contracts and became more involved with the school about their children

Step Five: **R**eanalyze, Reflect, and Revise

Reanalyze

Restate the baseline data. Where is the data after the action plan? Did the strategies have a positive impact on the data?

	2000–2001	2002–2003
Atherton High	29.75%	21.40%
Ballard High	13.47%	7.28%
Breckenridge Metropolitan	61.02%	39.13%
Brown High	1.92%	4.35%
Buechel Metropolitan	60.00%	56.82%
Butler Traditional	8.25%	8.26%
Central High	32.26%	6.05%
Doss High	21.85%	14.98%
Eastern High	18.16%	19.70%
Fairdale High	24.54%	18.55%
Fern Creek Traditional	26.61%	25.22%
Iroquois High	49.28%	43.62%
Jeffersontown High	36.09%	28.92%
Liberty High	67.30%	48.45%
Male Traditional High	4.96%	8.53%
Manual High/Ypas	0.82%	0.87%
Moore Traditional HS	36.97%	25.14%
Pleasure Ridge Park	26.04%	20.82%
Seneca High	20.20%	15.82%
Shawnee High	34.68%	22.83%
South Park Tapp	67.74%	52.17%
Southern High	22.66%	18.21%
Valley Traditional HS	40.35%	32.80%
Waggener Traditional	36.20%	30.00%
Western High	43.10%	31.22%
Westport Tapp	55.36%	38.10%

Reflect and Revise

Reflect on why the stakeholders were successful or unsuccessful. Revise the action plan so that progress can be made and you can continue to get better results.

Which of the strategies worked?
-We used data analysis to help us see which students were lagging behind and needed help.

Which strategies should be replaced? Added?
-None noted at this time.

Based on what you have learned, how will you rewrite the action plan?
-We will try to expand the one-credit classes and continue to add stakeholders.

Systemic Changes Made
Whenever you implement a MEASURE you will contribute to systemic change. Each MEASURE will in some way change a school, home, or community system to enhance student learning. Capture these systemic changes here and record them on your SPARC.

1. Collaboration among schools was institutionalized to improve the promotion rate for the ninth grade.
2. The practice was changed so that every counselor and administrator will disaggregate data on a regular basis to see which students need more attention.

Step Six: Educate

Promote and publicize the results of your work. Develop a report card for your own program to let the internal and external school members know your work is connected to the mission of the school and to student success. The School Counseling Program Accountability Report Card (SPARC) is a way to do this.

Our MEASURE of Success

SPARC - School Counseling Program Accountability Report Card

School: Jefferson County Public Schools
Enrollment: 96,500
Superintendent: Dr. Stephen Daeschner
Supervisor of Guidance: Linda Miller
Counselors: Diane Stogner, Terri Sgro, Faryl Edelen, James Ray, Julianne Davis, Carmen Harris, Cyndi Lampton, Jane Prince, Brad Weston, Diana Apel, Trish Foy, Lynne Macpherson, Inman Talaat, Joe Prather, Linda Ilnick, Mary Grace Feltham, Debra Wilson, Linda Stallings, Tracy Reed, Rebecca Ansari, Donna Block, Pam Robertson, Cassandra Jackson

Supervisor of Guidance Comments

This initiative has shown what counselors can do when they function as leaders focusing on student achievement. These counselors partnered with administrators, teachers, and parents and as a result, they are seen sharing the mission of raising student achievement. No longer will we say, "A counselor can make the difference." Our new mantra will become "A counselor IS the difference."

School Improvement Issues

Our schools need to focus on retention, especially at the ninth-grade level.
Critical Data Element(s):
Rate of retention

Stakeholders

Counselors: Submitted action plans to the district supervisor of guidance on strategies to reduce retention
Administrators: Introduced analyzing data; raised graduation requirements to include Algebra I & II and Geometry; focused on retention rates; reduced paperwork; hired more clerical help, increased availability of technology
Teachers: Worked with newly aligned curriculum; identified students experiencing difficulties; provided extra assistance and participated in an advisor/advisee program
Parents: Signed contracts and worked with teachers
Students: Signed contracts with parents and counselors to reinforce efforts toward advancement
Volunteers: Assisted in the counseling office to free school counselors from paperwork to help ninth graders

Results

	2000–2001	2002–2003
Atherton High	29.75%	21.40%
Ballard High	13.47%	7.28%
Breckenridge Metropolitan	61.02%	39.13%
Brown High	1.92%	4.35%
Buechel Metropolitan	60.00%	56.82%
Butler Traditional	8.25%	8.26%
Central High	32.26%	6.05%
Doss High	21.85%	14.98%
Eastern High	18.16%	19.70%
Fairdale High	24.54%	18.55%
Fern Creek Traditional	26.61%	25.22%
Iroquois High	49.28%	43.62%
Jeffersontown High	36.09%	28.92%
Liberty High	67.30%	48.45%
Male Traditional High	4.96%	8.53%
Manual High/Ypas	0.82%	0.87%
Moore Traditional HS	36.97%	25.14%
Pleasure Ridge Park	26.04%	20.82%
Seneca High	20.20%	15.82%
Shawnee High	34.68%	22.83%
South Park Tapp	67.74%	52.17%
Southern High	22.66%	18.21%
Valley Traditional HS	40.35%	32.80%
Waggener Traditional	36.20%	30.00%
Western High	43.10%	31.22%
Westport Tapp	55.36%	38.10%

Systemic Changes

1. Institutionalized collaboration among schools to improve ninth grade promotion
2. Changed practice so that every counselor and administrator will look at disaggregated data on a regular basis

Faces Behind the Data

Hundreds of students in these 26 schools were helped to navigate ninth grade. There are dozens of success stories behind the data. One such story is Jeremy who was in danger of failing ninth grade for the second time. The disaggregated data brought him to our attention, and through focused interventions he made progress by leaps and bounds.

References

Parikh, S. (2003). *Personal conversation.* S. A. Hull Elementary School.

Turba, B. (2003). *Personal conversation.* Stanton College Preparatory High School.

Vanderhoek, E. (2003). *Personal conversation*. Darnell-Cookman Middle School.

CHAPTER 6

Transforming Our Future: Impacting the System

"Congratulations!
Today is your day.
You're off to great places!
You're off and away!
Your mountain is waiting
So.....get on your way!"

-Dr. Seuss, 1990

- Systemic Change Agent
- Looking to the Future

In just a few short hours we hope that your relationship with data has moved from nonexistent, or perhaps neutral at best, to a relationship that can become positive and proactive. Let's examine some of the lessons learned from the MEASUREs presented in Chapter 5. These MEASUREs graphically show us the power of data to vividly paint the picture of student achievement in your school. Look at the reduction in ninth grade retention rate that the Louisville, Kentucky counselors were able to accomplish! This data dramatically demonstrates what a focused effort can accomplish. Behind the Kentucky data stand hundreds of students whose lives were positively impacted. This MEASURE, as well as the others, depicted how school counselors can rectify issues that impact every student's ability to achieve at expected levels. All of the counselors who participated with MEASUREs used advocacy and leadership skills and changed attitudes with evidence. Students benefited from the effort and the system changed. The use of school-wide data demonstrated school counselor support for the school mission, student success, and a desire to affect school improvement by positively impacting the system.

Some of the counselors introduced to you in the MEASUREs of Chapter 5 started small by focusing on one important data element such as Mary Ann Dyal's concentration on discipline referrals and Edith Vanderhoek's sincerity at trying to impact state tests. You don't have to start with multiple data elements and a complicated approach. Look what Jim MacGregor accomplished with his Algebra 1 success rate. He developed his strategies pushing and prodding over time. Jim did not move this mountain in a year.

As data unveils the story about our students, it informs and challenges our thinking to determine what needs to be changed in the system while also confirming progress and revealing shortcomings about student performance. In this climate of school improvement, school counselors can play a proactive role in identifying and responding to the issues, policies, and practices that stratify and impede student opportunity. Systemic change is a critical area in the academic success picture.

Systemic Change Agent

In developing MEASUREs with counselors across the nation in urban, suburban, and rural settings, we learned that whenever you move data in a positive direction you contribute to systemic change. Systemic change is just a natural byproduct of impacting data! Without exception, each MEASURE you were introduced to in Chapter 5 contributed in some way to changing a school, home, or community system that was adversely stratifying student opportunities. These MEASUREs also changed or implemented new systems such as policies, procedures, instruction that positively impacted student success. So by implementing a MEASURE you are being a systemic change agent. Call yourself a mover and a shaker. Your MEASURE will naturally alter a system that stratifies, or enhance a system that bolsters student learning.

Closing the gap in student performance is at the heart of systemic change. The use of demographic and performance data makes it possible to determine how policies and practices are affecting issues of equity, that is, disaggregated data can reveal that certain groups of students are accessing higher level academics at lower rates. Systemic issues, or broken systems, are contributing to the gap, more so than student performance. MEASUREs can help you find and repair or change these broken systems and move us away from always looking at low performance as a broken child or broken family problem. Through collaboration with their principals and faculties, school counselors can identify broad system-wide practices that contribute to inequitable situations, or enhance practices that reduce inequitable situations for individual students and groups of students. For example, Jim MacGregor along with the leadership team implemented double mathematics periods; a systemic change that helped to considerably reduce the gap between Caucasian students completing a college core and African American students completing a college core. Good systems can make the difference between a contributing member of society and a marginal participant. Develop a MEASURE and watch the system change.

The waterfall story is an example of systemic change. We first heard the story told by Patricia Martin (Education Trust, 1997), the architect of the *Transforming School Counseling Initiative*.

The Waterfall Story

A school counselor was standing at the bottom of a waterfall catching students as they came crashing over the waterfall. This dedicated counselor was able to save only a few and others perished as they fell on the rocks. This counselor was not willing to meet the needs of the few to the exclusion of all students so she went to the top of the waterfall to see who was pushing these students over the edge. She built a safety net to keep others from crashing down and studied the problem to see how the students got into the water in the first place.

-(author unknown)

This is the work of a systemic change agent, figuring out how to change the system to help all students. Test your understanding of systemic change. Go back and reread the MEASUREs and SPARCs of the school counselors in Chapter 5. We listed only a few of the systemic changes these counselors made. Identify other systemic changes that were intentional byproducts, and sometimes unintentional or natural byproducts, of the strategies implemented by the stakeholders of these MEASUREs.

Looking at the Future

Imagine a world in which every student receives an optimum education, all students are given the support they need, and the achievement gap no longer exists. School counselors and other educators who envision this world as possible represent our best hope for making it a reality. Developing MEASUREs can help you begin to create that vision. Start now. Examine the issues of your school as revealed by data and establish some baseline data that you want to impact. If you cannot start full force with a half-dozen stakeholders at the table, start with two stakeholders. Just get started! You will grow your stakeholders and your strategies. Work for, but don't wait for all the pieces to be firmly in place before you make your pledge to position yourself in the middle of accountability with your own MEASURE.

Now, move the calendar forward to a year from now. With MEASUREs in hand, you have student outcome data. You are able to show with hard data how your school counseling program contributed to student academic success. You have anecdotal stories that put a human face on the data as you talk about how students' lives were touched, you have changed the system, and you are speaking the accountability language that is understood by all your school system's stakeholders. You collaborated and sent the message that you are a team player with a high-profile role aimed at supporting all students in the learning success equation. You are considered a vital force in the accountability picture and you have garnered support for your program from all levels. You are acting with focused purpose.

There are so many unalterable factors in children's lives. As school counselors, we cannot change children's families, give them a secure home, or establish for them conditions to make their time away from school happy, but we can influence their ability to be successful learners and give them a chance through education to change their circumstances and to be productive citizens. Optimum learning conditions are a gift we can give students; it's the best gift we can give students in the forty hours a week in our schools.

References

Dr. Seuss. (1990). *Oh the places you will go*. New York: Random House.

Appendix A

Participants in the 2001 Education Trust Accountability Meetings

Anderson, Laurel
Past Supervisor of Guidance Services
Duval County Public Schools
Jacksonville, FL

Anderson, Ron
Senior Director of Guidance and Social Work
Wake County Public Schools
Raleigh, NC

Colbert, Robert
Associate Professor
University of Massachusetts
Amherst, MA

Dahir, Carol
Assistant Professor
New York Institute of Technology
Old Westbury, NY

Gysbers, Norm
Professor
University of Missouri
Columbia, MO

House, Reese
Principal Investigator
The Education Trust
Washington, DC

Jackson, Greg
Assistant Professor
California State University, Northridge
Northridge, CA

Johnson, Curly
Professional Update
San Juan Capistrano, CA

Kaye, Dawn
State Department of Education
Salt Lake City, UT

Lockhart, Trish
Director of Guidance
Palmdale High School
Palmdale, CA

MacGregor, Jim
Guidance Director
Pike High School
Indianapolis, IN

Martin, Patricia
School Counselor Liaison
The College Board
Washington, DC

Meyers, Paul
Consultant
California Department of Education
Sacramento, CA

Myrick, Robert
Professor
University of Florida
Gainesville, FL

Paisley, Pam
Associate Professor
The University of Georgia
Athens, GA

Reynolds, Sue
Guidance and Counseling Specialist
Indiana Department of Education
Indianapolis, IN

Rich, Dave
Director, Student Support Services
Antelope Valley Union High School District
Lancaster, CA

Stone, Carolyn
Associate Professor
University of North Florida
Jacksonville, FL

Turba, Robert
Chairperson of Guidance Services
Stanton College Preparatory School
Jacksonville, FL

Whitfield, Edwin
Associate Director
Ohio Department of Education
Columbus, OH

Appendix B

The National Standards for School Counseling Programs: What Students Should Know and Be Able To Do

The national standards identify the attitudes, knowledge, and skills that students should acquire in a proactive and preventive manner through a broad range of experiences. The adoption and implementation of the national standards also have changed the way school counseling programs are designed and delivered across our country. The emphasis is on academic success for all students, not just those students who are motivated, supported, and ready to learn. The school counseling program based upon the national standards supports every student to achieve success in school and to develop into a contributing member of our society.

The nine national standards are based on the three widely accepted and interrelated areas of student development as described in the counseling literature and research: academic, career, and personal/social development.

Academic Development

The three standards for academic development guide school counselors as they implement school counseling program strategies and activities to support and maximize student learning. Academic development includes students acquiring attitudes, knowledge, and skills that contribute to effective learning in school and across the lifespan; employing strategies to achieve success in school; and understanding the relationship of academics to the world of work, and to life at home and in the community. The academic development standards are:

Standard A. Students will acquire the attitudes, knowledge, and skills that contribute to effective learning in school and across the life span.

Standard B. Students will complete school with the academic preparation essential to choose from a wide variety of substantial postsecondary options, including college.

Standard C. Students will understand the relationship of academics to the world of work, and to life at home and in the community.

Career Development

The standards for career development guide school counselors as they implement school counseling program strategies and activities to assist students acquire attitudes, knowledge, and skills to successfully transition from grade to grade, from school to postsecondary education, and ultimately to the world of work. Career development activities include the employment of strategies to achieve future career success and job satisfaction, as well as fostering understanding of the relationship between personal qualities, education and training, and future career goals. The three career development standards are:

Standard A. Students will acquire the skills to investigate the world of work in relation to knowledge of self and to make informed career decisions.

Standard B. Students will employ strategies to achieve future career success and satisfaction.

Standard C. Students will understand the relationship between personal qualities, education and training, and the world of work.

Personal-Social Development

The standards for personal-social development guide school counselors as they implement school counseling program strategies and activities to provide personal and social growth experiences to facilitate students' progress through school and help them make the transition to adulthood. Personal-social development contributes to academic and career success, and includes the acquisition of attitudes, knowledge, and skills to help students understand and respect self and others, acquire effective interpersonal skills, understand safety and survival skills, and develop into contributing members of society. The three personal-social development standards are:

Standard A. Students will acquire the attitudes, knowledge, and interpersonal skills to help them understand and respect self and others.

Standard B. Students will make decisions, set goals, and take appropriate action to achieve goals.

Standard C. Students will understand safety and survival skills.

Appendix C

American School Counselor Association National Model: A Framework For School Counseling Programs

The recently released ASCA National Model (ASCA, 2003) reinforces the importance of delivering a comprehensive, developmental, and results-based program that carefully considers local demographic needs and the political climate of the community. The four main components of the model are: 1) the foundation of the program requires the implementation of the belief and mission that every student will benefit from the school counseling program; 2) the delivery system defines the implementation process and the components of the comprehensive model, i.e., guidance curriculum, individual planning with students, responsive services, and system support; 3) the management system presents the organizational processes and tools needed to deliver a comprehensive school counseling program. These processes and tools include: agreements of responsibility, use of data, action plans for guidance curriculum and closing the gap, and time and task analysis; and, 4) the accountability system helps school counselors demonstrate the effectiveness of their work in measurable terms such as impact over time, performance evaluation, and a program audit.

The National Model speaks to the importance of having an organizational framework that documents and demonstrates "how are students different as a result of the school counseling program?" A commitment to accountability shifts public perception from questions such as "What do school counselors really do?" to showing how school counselors are key players in the academic success story for students and are partners in student achievement.

Appendix D

Critical Data Examples

Measures of Achievement:

• Test results
• State exams such as the Florida Comprehensive Achievement Test (FCAT); New York State Regents Examinations
• Preliminary Scholastic Achievement Test (PSAT) and Scholastic Achievement Test (SAT)
• ACT
• Armed Services Vocational Aptitude Battery (ASVAB)
• Standardized achievement tests such as the Iowa Tests, Stanford Achievement Tests, National Assessment of Educational Progress (NAEP), etc.
• Number of credits taken per year
• Retention rates
• Drop-out rates
• Postsecondary enrollment (four-year-college, community college, apprenticeship, career and technical, military training)
• Grade point averages
• Rank in class

Impacts on Achievement

• Course enrollment patterns that demonstrate commitment to high achievement
• Numbers of National Merit/Achievement semi-finalists
• Enrollment in honors, advanced placement (AP), international baccalaureate (IB), or college level courses
• Enrollment in general, remedial courses.
• Exceptional student/ special education screening & placement
• Gifted screening & enrollment
• Alternative school enrollment

Demographics of the Internal and External School Community

• Entry and withdrawal information
• Ethnicity
• Gender
• Number and type of discipline referrals to include suspension rate
• Attendance rate
• Single family situations
• School geographic areas
• Free/Reduced lunch students and other available socio-economic measures
• History and patterns of changes in community
• Community crime rate

Remember: A quick look at data alone does not tell the whole story. It is important to disaggregate all critical data elements and look at them in terms of gender, race/ethnicity, socio-economic status, and perhaps by teacher to shed light on areas of success or areas in need of attention.

Other Important data elements include:

• Course taking patterns in rigorous academic program
• Course pass/fail rates
• Number of credits taken per year
• Discipline/suspension rates
• Gifted and talented program enrollment
• Graduation rates
• Definitive exit plans for twelfth graders
• Honor roll
• Promotion/retention rates

Appendix E

Sample MEASURE and SPARC

MEASURE

Mission, **E**lements, **A**nalyze, **S**takeholders-**U**nite, **R**eanalyze, **E**ducate,
a Six-step Accountability Process for School Counselors

Name and Address of School:
Name of Counselor Leading the Initiative:
Principal:
Enrollment:

School Demographics:
Caucasian/Non-Hispanic
African American
Hispanic
Asian
Other

Free/Reduced lunch
ESL

Step One: **M**ission

Mission *Connect your work to your school's mission.*
Your mission statement is:

Step Two: **E**lements

Current Critical Data Element *What indicator of school success are you trying to positively impact? Grades? Test scores? Attendance? Promotion rates? Postsecondary going rate?*
The school counselor as part of the leadership team identified these critical data elements to try to impact:

Step Three: **A**nalyze

Analyze the data to see what it reveals, to identify the problem areas, to establish your baseline, and to set your goal. It may be necessary to disaggregate the data, e.g., race, ethnicity, gender, SES, teacher assignment.	
Baseline: Where is this data element currently?	***Goal: Where do you want the data element to be in a year?***

Step Four: **S**takeholders-**U**nite

Develop an Action Plan

School counselors, as managers of resources, join existing groups of stakeholders, such as the school improvement team, or bring other stakeholders and resources into the task of creating and implementing an action plan. Strategies are developed that will change systems as well as impact individual students and targeted groups of students.

Impacting systems means (1) replicating successful programs and interventions; (2) identifying barriers that adversely stratify students' opportunities to be successful learners; and (3) developing strategies to:

- *change policies, practices, and procedures*
- *strengthen curriculum offerings*
- *maximize the instructional program*
- *enhance the school and classroom culture and climate*
- *provide student academic support systems (safety nets)*
- *influence course enrollment patterns to widen access to rigorous academics*
- *involve parents and other critical stakeholders (internal and external to the school)*
- *raise aspirations in students, parents, teachers, and the community*
- *change attitudes and beliefs about students and their abilities to learn*

Stakeholders	***Strategies*** *Connect your strategies to the American School Counselor Association (ASCA) National Standards and the ASCA National Model.*
	Beginning date: ***Ending date:***
School Counselors	
Teachers	
Administrators	
Students	
Technology	
Community Agency Members	
Local Colleges	
Grants	
Parents	

Teacher Assistants	
School Improvement Team (may also include a number of stakeholders)	

Step Five: **R**eanalyze, Reflect, and Revise

Reanalyze *Restate the baseline data. Where is the data after the action plan? Did the strategies have a positive impact on the data?* *Restate the baseline data:* *Data after action plan:* *Impact:*	***Reflect and Revise*** *Reflect on why the stakeholders were successful or unsuccessful. Revise the action plan so that progress can be made and you can continue to get better results.* *Which of the strategies worked?* *Which strategies should be replaced? Added?* *Based on what you have learned, how will you revise the action plan?*

Systemic Changes Made

Whenever you implement a MEASURE you will contribute to systemic change. Each MEASURE will in some way change a school, home, or community system to enhance student learning. Capture these systemic changes here and record them on your SPARC.

Step Six: **E**ducate

Promote and publicize the results of your work. Develop a report card for your own program to let the internal and external school members know your work is connected to the mission of the school and to student success. The School Counseling Program Accountability Report Card (SPARC) is a way to do this.

Our MEASURE of Success

SPARC - School Counseling Program Accountability Report Card

School:
Enrollment:
Principal:
Counselor:

Principal's Comments

School Improvement Issues

Stakeholders

Results

Systemic Changes

Faces Behind the Data

SPARC is a continuous improvement document sponsored by the California Department of Education and the Los Angeles County Office of Education. SPARC has been adapted with permission as a complement to MEASURE.

11613019R00064

Made in the USA
San Bernardino, CA
06 December 2018

GoPro®

HOW TO USE

THE GoPro® HERO 6 BLACK

PUBLISHED BY **Kaisanti Press**

GOPRO: HOW TO USE THE GOPRO HERO 6 BLACK.

FIRST EDITION: November 2017

Copyright

Trademarks

This book is in no way affiliated, authorized, sponsored, or endorsed by GoPro, Inc. or any other companies mentioned in this book. All references to GoPro and other trademarked properties are used in accordance with the Nominative Fair Use Doctrine and are not meant to imply that this book is a GoPro, Inc. product for advertising or other commercial purposes.

All terms mentioned in this book that are known to be trademarks or service marks have been appropriately capitalized. The author cannot attest to the accuracy of this information. Use of a term in the book should not be regarded as affecting the validity of any trademark or service mark.

GoPro®, HERO®, SuperView® & 3-Way® are trademarks or registered trademarks of GoPro, Inc. in the United States and other countries. Any other trademarks remain property of the trademark holder.

Warning and Disclaimer

This book nor its author does not endorse any of the dangerous sports/activities shown in this book. If you choose to participate in these activities, do so at your own risk. This book does not guarantee that by following the advice in this book, your camera will not be damaged. Always refer to your camera's user manual. Always check with your camera manufacturer and follow recommendations before getting your camera wet. The author accepts no liability for any harm done to your camera or selves.

INTRODUCTION

That little GoPro camera that you hold in your hand is the result of years of testing, revising, and perfecting. What started as a simple desire to carry a camera for surfing pics of some friends grew, grew, and grew some more.

The same convenience that GoPro founder Nick Woodman was searching for when he strapped a camera onto his wrist is what has attracted millions of people to these powerful storytelling devices. Everyone has moments in his or her life to be remembered, and there is no easier way to record them than with a GoPro camera. These cameras are waterproof, shockproof, tough little cameras that are fully capable of recording life's moments in such crisp, clear high quality that we can replay them over and over to feel like we are there again.

When the first GoPro was released, I had already been using big, bulky water housings to take photos of surfers, bodyboarders and windsurfers around the world for years. The resulting images were worth the hard work, but when I got my first GoPro camera, the struggle of the big camera was gone and just the fun remained. That's when it all clicked. Everyone was going to want one of these, and people were going to need help. So I set out on a mission to figure out the clearest, most logical way for people to learn how to use their GoPro cameras from start to finish.

Seven years, ten books, and millions of readers/viewers later, you are reading the evolution of my intent to help you, written specifically for the GoPro HERO6 Black.

This how-to-use guide will teach you how to use your HERO6 Black camera with confidence from the initial setup all the way through to sharing your edited photos and videos. Let me teach you everything you need to know. I'm so happy to have you on board!

Jordan Hetrick

Bestselling Author on GoPro Cameras

CONTENTS

CONTENTS

ABOUT THE HERO6 BLACK

This book covers the GoPro HERO 6 Black- the newest addition to GoPro's lineup of filmmaking and photo-capturing tools! The HERO6 Black is the ultimate tool for capturing your magic moments at the highest quality ever from a GoPro camera.

From the outside, the HERO6 Black looks identical to the HERO5 Black, but the true innovation lies inside the HERO6's waterproof camera body. For the first time ever, the Hero6 Black uses GoPro's own GP1 chip. The biggest deal about the new processing chip is that GoPro is no longer limited to using chips from other manufacturers. They can now push the limits on their own hardware. What that means for you is that your camera's chip is designed specifically for your camera, resulting in smoother operation, amazing video quality and most likely, more improvements through firmware updates in the future.

Straight out of the gates, the HERO6 Black's GP1 chip offers you 2x faster video frame rates for 4k and 1080p video, as well as vastly improved image quality and color. Plus, GoPro's best stabilization yet is now available for 4k video, giving you smoother high resolution videos than ever before. The settings on this camera give you the freedom to record all of life's exciting moments in full 4k resolution. On top of the GP1 chip, the HERO6 Black features 5 GHz Wi-Fi for more convenient mobile editing and Touch Zoom for easier composition.

As filmmaking technology continues to evolve at lightning speed, the GoPro HERO6 Black leads the evolution, putting GoPro's most powerful storytelling tool yet in a tiny package that fits in your pocket. Grab your HERO6 Black and let's get to know the ins and outs of your new GoPro camera!

HOW TO USE THIS GUIDE

Now that you've decided to really learn how to use your GoPro® HERO6 Black camera, the information in this guide will teach you everything you need to know to get the shots you've always wanted.

This guide is organized into 7 Steps, which were written to logically guide you through the learning process. By the end of this book, you will have a clear and thorough knowledge of your GoPro camera and everything about the GoPro world.

In Step One- Get To Know Your HERO6 Black, you will learn how to unlock the full potential of your new camera. This section includes essential information to familiarize you with your camera and to get you started, as well as get you connected to the GoPro App. You can also download the HERO6 Black User Manual from GoPro's Support page on their website to be used in conjunction with the information in this guide. Your camera's User Manual tells you all of the little details about every setting option, while this guide provides you with the vital knowledge to understand what you really need to know to use your HERO6 Black.

The Go Deeper sections provide more advanced tips for using your HERO6 Black camera. You may want to come back and reread these sections after learning the basics.

If you just bought your camera, before you buy the wrong mounts for your lifestyle, check out the Mounting Section in Step 3 to see which mounts are right for you and your passions!

Take your time, go step by step and by the time you finish this book, you will finally know how to use your HERO6 Black camera to record, edit and share your unique point of view!

STEP ONE

GET TO KNOW YOUR HERO6 BLACK

Learn To Navigate Your New Camera

Welcome to the HERO6 Black! This first section gives you hands on practice to easily navigate your new camera and access its features so you can focus on filming. Once you know your way around, you will be able to unlock the full potential of the HERO6 Black to capture your exciting moments in the best way possible.

So let's get to know your new camera!

SETTING UP YOUR CAMERA FOR THE FIRST TIME (It's Easy!)

1

2-4

5

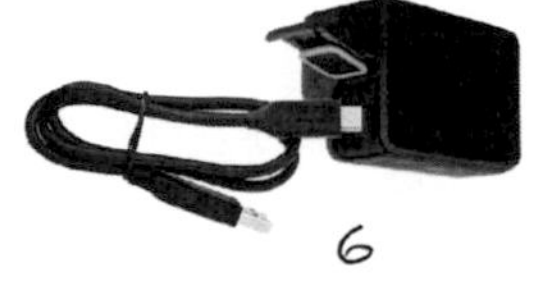

6

7

1. **Remove your camera from the frame** by lifting the latch on the Frame from the front of the camera.

2. On the **bottom of your camera**, press the Latch Release Button and slide the door to **open the bottom door** that covers the battery and microSD card slot.

3. **Insert the battery** with the GoPro logo facing the front of the camera

4. **Insert the microSD Card** with the text facing the battery. A 32GB microSD card is included in some HERO6 kits as a bonus. The Black requires a Class 10 or UHS-1 microSD card up to 256GB. Lexar or SanDisk are the most well-known brands.

5. **Close the bottom door**, making sure the door closes completely and the latch release button returns to its original position.

6. **Charge your camera**. Open the **side door on the right side** of your camera by pressing the Latch Release Button and sliding down. Plug one end of the USB cable into the port on your camera and the other end to a computer or USB power supply. Your camera battery comes partially charged and using it with a partial charge will not affect the battery life. Charging typically takes about 2 hours.

7. After your camera has charged, remove the USB cable and **close the side door**.

Your camera is ready to use. It's that easy! Now let's go through elements of your camera.

NOTE: Make sure you are running the most current firmware (v01.51 or higher) to take advantage of the modes and settings as shown in this book. To see which version is installed on your camera, turn on your camera and swipe down from the top of the screen to expose the top tray. The firmware version is located under Preferences>About This GoPro. **If your camera's firmware needs to be updated, the easiest way to update is to connect to the GoPro App, which you will learn how to do here in Step One.**

TIP: Hold onto the plate your camera was mounted on in the packaging. A lot of people throw this away, but it's like a free bonus mount that can come in handy. You can **drill holes through it**, **glue it to a surface**, or **cut it down to size** for a custom mount.

WHAT ARE THESE BUTTONS AND PORTS FOR?

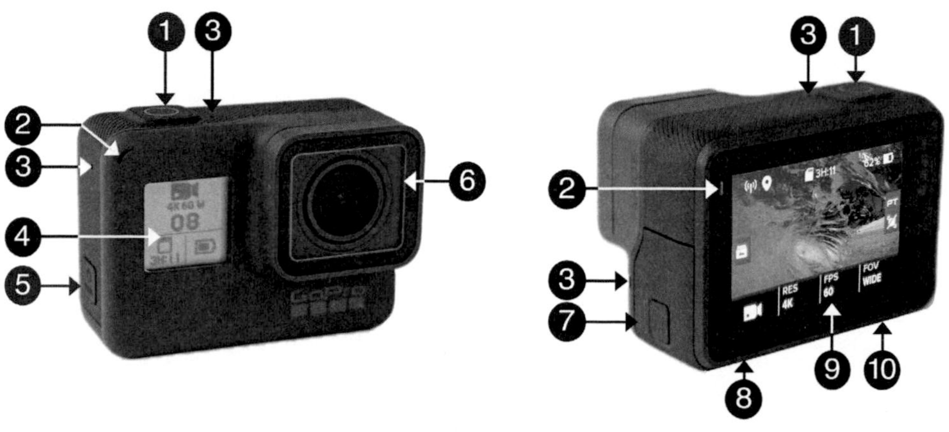

1. SHUTTER Button
Press this button to start and stop recording or to take photos.

2. Camera Status Lights
These red lights turn on when the camera is recording video and when taking photos. You can turn off the front light or all three of the lights (one is also on the bottom) in the Preferences Menu.

3. Microphones
Three microphones record stereo sound.

4. Camera Status Screen
This screen tells you about your camera's settings. See the detailed Camera Status Screen diagram for an explanation of what this screen displays.

5. POWER/MODE Button
Press this button to turn your camera ON.

Once your camera is powered on, press this button to scroll through shooting modes. Press this button to escape out of Settings or Media screens for a quick return to shooting modes.

Hold down this button down for 2 seconds to turn your camera OFF.

6. Lens Port
This replaceable glass protects your camera's lens. See how to fix it if it gets scratched in Step 7.

7. Latch Release Tab/Side Door
The USB and micro HDMI ports are inside this door. The USB port is for charging and transferring files. Step-by-step instructions for transferring your files are provided in Step 5- Creation.

The micro HDMI port is to connect your camera to a TV/HDTV.

Always close this door completely before you begin filming. The rubber gasket inside keeps water out of your camera.

8. Speaker (underneath)
This speaker puts out audio when you watch videos on your Touch Display.

9. Touch Display Screen
The Touch Display is a built-in LCD Screen that can be used as a viewfinder for composing shots, to change settings and to play back your footage. The Touch Display section gives you an explanation of everything you can do using this screen.

10. Battery and Micro SD Card Door (underneath)
Open this door to install or replace the rechargeable battery and to insert or remove your micro SD card. The rubber gasket on the door keeps water out of your camera, so make sure it is always closed securely.

CAMERA STATUS SCREEN

The Camera Status Screen tells you the following information about your camera settings, modes and status:

1. Camera Mode
This icon indicates which recording mode you are currently using (Video, Photo, Time Lapse, etc.)

2. Settings
This displays the current recording settings for the selected mode, which include:
Resolution (4k, 2.7k, 1080, etc. for Video or 12MP for Photo Modes),
Frame Rate (30, 60, 120, etc. for Video only) or Interval (for Burst and Time Lapse Modes), and
Field of View (Wide, Linear or Superview)

3. Counter
In Video Mode, this tells you how many videos you have recorded. When recording, this displays a time counter showing the length of your recorded video.

In the Photo Modes, the number indicates the TOTAL number of photos you have taken.

4. Time/Storage/Files
In Video Mode, this displays the remaining number of minutes you can record on your memory card at the current video resolution. (This time will change when you change settings because different file sizes require different amounts of memory)

In Photo Modes, this tells you how many photos you have remaining at the current setting.

5. Battery Life
This shows the remaining battery life. The Touch Display on the back displays an exact percentage.

NAVIGATING YOUR HERO6 BLACK

Let's turn your camera on and learn to navigate your new camera so you can tap into all of the fun features of this powerful little camera.

GoPro has given you a few options for getting around the HERO6 Black, but the simplest way is to use the camera's integrated Touch Display. All of the modes, settings and setup options are available through the Touch Display.

There are lots of setting options on the HERO6 Black (which we will get into in the next step), but after a little practice, you will be able to get around your camera with ease. If you want to take a moment to practice getting around, **follow the steps to take a short tour**.

1. **Press the Power/Mode Button on the left side of your camera to turn your camera on.** It may take a few seconds for your camera to power on.

2. Once your camera is on, **tap the Video mode icon at the bottom left of the Touch Display screen**.

3. **Along the top of the next screen, you will see the three main modes.** The three modes are: Video, Photo, and Time Lapse.

4. Within each mode, **there are several Capture Modes you can choose from**. A Capture Mode defines how your camera will function within that mode, which will make more sense as we get into the next step. When you **tap each icon along the top**, you will see the available Capture Modes for that Mode. In Video Mode, for example, there are two Capture Modes: 1) Video and 2) Looping. The next chapter will help you understand the various modes.

5. Under the Video icon, **tap the Video option** to stay in Video Capture Mode and return to the previous screen. (You can also Swipe Down or press the Mode Button to exit that screen.)

6. **Each Capture Mode has its own settings**. You can use the Touch Display screen to change the settings for that Capture Mode. To try this out, **Tap on the Res option** and a screen with the Res options will open.

7. On the Res Options screen, **Swipe Left or Right to scroll through the resolution options**. Or you can Tap on any of the

options around the edges. You will learn which settings to use in the next chapter. For now, you can select 1080 to exit out of that screen.

8. To begin recording after selecting your settings, you would press the top Shutter Button.

TIP: Using the Buttons to Change Modes and Settings. When the Touch Display is inaccessible, you can easily change modes by pressing the Mode Button on the left side of your camera to scroll through Video, Photo, Burst and Time Lapse modes, in that order. The most recently selected Capture Mode within each of the modes is available.

Secret Menu. When you want to change capture modes and settings and are filming in a situation where the Touch Display won't work, for example underwater or while wearing snow gloves, use the buttons to access the button menu. Here is how it's done using the buttons:

1. It's best to **lock the screen first** when you know you are not going to be able to change settings using the Touch Display.
2. Once you have scrolled to the desired mode, **hold down the Mode Button and press the Shutter Button quickly** after to bring up the settings options. (If you wait too long to press the Shutter Button, you may accidentally turn off the camera.)
3. **Press the top Shutter Button** to select capture modes and settings until your desired setting is shown.
4. **Press the Mode Button** to move to the next item.
5. When you are finished, **Hold Down the Shutter Button** for 2 seconds or scroll to Done to exit the menu.

Go Deeper

The settings you choose in one mode will not change the settings in another mode. For example, changing the field of view in Photo Mode will not change the field of view in Night Photo Mode. You can leave the settings adjusted to your favorite settings for each mode.

ONE BUTTON CONTROL

When you want to get straight into recording, you can utilize One Button Control, which gives you quick access to video recording and time lapse photos with the push of a button. **To begin recording video, Press the top Shutter Button and your camera will power on and begin recording. Or Hold down the top Shutter Button for at least 3 seconds and your camera will begin taking time lapse photos.**

Once you **press the Shutter Button again, your camera will stop recording and turn off**. This feature, called QuikCapture, can by turned on or off in the Preferences menu.

One Button Control is a great tool for specific filming situations once you know your HERO6 Black and your favorite settings. One Button Control also conserves battery life that would be used during standby time.

VOICE CONTROL

At first, Voice Control may seem a bit like a gimmick, but as you start to use it, you will realize that it's actually very useful, especially when using a GoPro. When your camera is out of reach, or your hands are busy, Voice Control gives you easy hands-free access to control your HERO6 Black. With a simple command, you can start recording or taking photos in a variety of modes. It's also much easier to change modes using Voice Control. Instead of scrolling through the modes, you can go straight to the mode you want to record with.

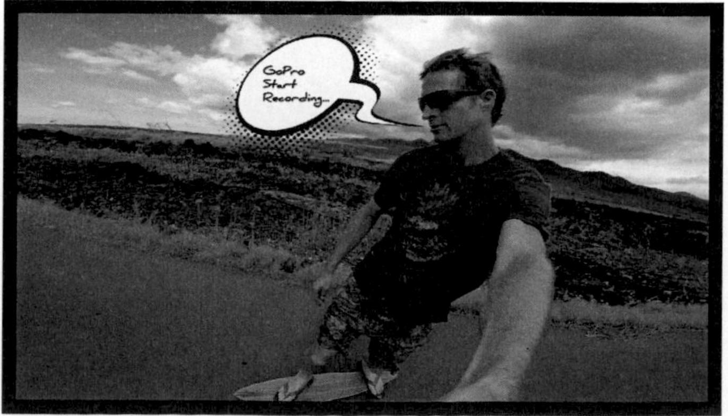

To activate Voice Control, Pull Down the top tray on the Touch Display Screen. Tap the Voice Control Icon at the top right to remove the "x". The preferred Voice Control language can be changed using the Voice Control options in the Preferences Menu.

You can't do everything with Voice Control, but there is a lot you can control. **Here is a list of the commands you can use with your HERO6 Black:**

TO CHANGE MODES AND POWER OFF

"GoPro Video Mode"
"GoPro Photo Mode"
"GoPro Time Lapse Mode"
"GoPro Burst Mode"
"GoPro Turn Off"

TO START AND STOP RECORDING OR TAKING PHOTOS

"GoPro Start Recording" (for video or time lapse, depending on current mode)
"GoPro Stop Recording" (for video or time lapse, depending on current mode)
"GoPro HiLight", "Oh Sh*t", "That was Sick" (all set a HiLight Tag)
"GoPro Take a Photo" (if your camera is not recording a video)
"GoPro Shoot Burst"
"GoPro Start Time Lapse"
"GoPro Stop Time Lapse"

TO OPERATE WITH THE POWER OFF

(Turn on "Wake On Voice" in Preferences>Voice Control. Commands can be used for 8 hours after powering off your camera.)

"GoPro Turn On"
"GoPro Start Recording"
"GoPro Stop Recording"

Of course, as with anything, there are good times to use voice control and not such good times. For best results, use Voice Control when there is **not too much ambient noise** around you. If you are recording video or a time lapse, you need to stop recording before issuing a new command.

Also, keep your GoPro **within a few feet** to make sure it can hear you, especially if there is ambient noise, such as the ocean or wind. Speak clearly and say the exact command. Voice Control doesn't work too well with kids' voices.

Also, Voice Control will not work when your camera is underwater, or even sometimes after you have been in the water (if there is sand or water covering the speaker). Make sure to blow the water out of the speaker opening after going in the water.

THE TOUCH DISPLAY SCREEN

The Touch Display is a very convenient feature of the HERO6 Black and one that was missing from the first few generations of GoPro cameras. The Touch Display gives you the ability to preview and compose your shots, as well as see a Live View of how changes to your settings will affect your videos and photos. If you like to get muddy or sandy, consider using GoPro's Screen Protectors to keep your Touch Display scratch free.

TIP: There are several mounting positions and/or backdoors that prevent you from using the Touch Display to change settings. Also, the Touch Display doesn't work when your hands are wet, like when you are surfing, or you are wearing gloves in the snow. For these situations, use the buttons to change settings as shown in the section on Navigating Your Camera.

USING THE TOUCH DISPLAY

You've already learned how to navigate the Touch Display to change modes and basic settings, but the following section provides more information about other useful ways to tap into the convenience of the Touch Display. The Touch Display serves three primary functions: as a **viewfinder**, to **change settings**, and to **view your recorded photos and videos**:

1. AS A VIEWFINDER

The Touch Display provides an easy way to **set up and compose your shots**. Using the Touch Display, you can preview how your shots will look with the selected settings.

When composing your shots through the Touch Display as you film, keep the Touch Display on so you can continue to watch the action. If the Touch Display goes to sleep while you are filming, tap the screen or press the side Power/Mode Button to wake it back up.

When using the Touch Display **to set up mounted shots**, preview the composition on the Touch Display. Once the shot is set up and your mounting position is secured, **let the Touch Display go to sleep** to conserve battery life. You can set the Touch Display turn off after 1, 2, or 3 minutes (you can select the time in the Preferences Menu). Allowing the Touch Display to turn off when you are not actively using it will extend battery life.

2. TO SELECT AND CHANGE SETTINGS

As you learned previously, all of the modes and settings can be changed using the Touch Display.

- Setting options for the current mode are at the bottom of the screen.
- The advanced setting menu is hidden on the right.
- To show settings info (including current mode, the counter, capture settings and battery status) on the preview screen, Tap the Screen. To hide this info, Tap the Screen again.
- To close a Setting Option Menu, select a Setting, Swipe Down from the top edge, or press the Power/Mode Button.

3. TO VIEW AND TRIM YOUR RECORDED PHOTOS AND VIDEOS

After a session, use the Touch Display to view your videos and photos. One of the great things about your HERO6 Black is the instant gratification of seeing your photos and videos right away on the Touch Display. The built-in screen lets you view your footage immediately.

The Touch Display has some intelligent features, like recognizing if you recorded burst photos or a time lapse sequence of photos. Instead of scrolling through hundreds of photos of a time lapse sequence, your camera batches them into one file for playback. The sequences will be available as separate photo files on your computer.

- **Swipe Right** from the left side of the screen to open your media.
- Use the top bar with the date to **filter your media by media type**, for example clips, photos or videos.
- **Scroll up** to view any photos or videos that you have already recorded. The most recent files are shown first.
- **Tap on the photo or video** you would like to watch.
- **Push play** to watch the video, view a single shot photo or view a sequence of photos.
- Use the scissors icon to **create a trimmed 5, 15, or 30 second clip**. This will create a new trimmed clip and will not affect the original clip.
- **Press the Image icon** to grab a still image from a video.
- Use the **Trash Can icon** to delete one file or multiple files.
- **Swipe Up** from the bottom for the Volume option. You can raise or lower the playback volume on your camera.

WIFI / BLUETOOTH

The HERO6 Black uses a combination of 5GHz WiFi and Bluetooth to connect to external devices, such as a remote or a phone/ tablet. Your camera emits its own signal, so you don't need to be within range of any WiFi signals to use your camera's WiFi features. Unlike older GoPro models, there is no indicator light to tell you if your WiFi signal is on. When your camera's WiFi is enabled and your camera is turned on, you will see a WiFi icon on the top left of the Touch Display Screen. There is no way of checking your WiFi status when the camera is off.

The HERO6 Black automatically manages your camera's WiFi, switching from WiFi to Bluetooth to reduce battery drain. The WiFi signal should turn off automatically after about 8 hours, but if you will not be using your camera for an extended period, you may want to make sure the WiFi Signal is off. The drain on your battery is minimal, about 3% over 12 hours, but over time it could drain your battery if it hasn't turned off automatically.

To access the Connections dialog, pull the top tray down on the Touch Display screen. Tap Connections to access the WiFi settings. To manually turn on or off the WiFi, press the Power button icon under Wireless Connections.

USING THE GOPRO APP

The GoPro App works on your tablet or smartphone and is available for free from the App Store (iOS) or Google Play (Android).

In addition to giving you remote access to your camera's Shutter Button, modes and settings, the GoPro App allows you to view the action as you record videos and photos when you can't see your camera's Touch Display. This is extremely useful for composing your mounted shots. You will see the benefit of this technology when you learn to set up your shots in Step 3- Mounting.

You can also **update your camera's firmware wirelessly through the App**. Updating your camera will ensure that your camera is equipped with the most up-to-date features and settings. The App will notify you when an update is available.

> **TIP:** Live View (viewing what you are filming while your camera is recording) compatibility depends on your device, but if you see a "Preview Not Available" message once you start recording, you are filming in a resolution that is not compatible with your device. Your camera is still able to record video, but you are not able to preview it using the App. Start with 1080-60 if higher resolutions are not working with your device and increase resolution from there to see where your device maxes out.

QuikSTORIES The GoPro App can also automatically transfer the most recent files from your camera to your device to create an auto edit for you. This feature, called QuikStories, uses the GoPro App and Quik to make it easier than ever to share your most recent adventures. Learn more about using Quik and QuikStories in Step 5- Editing.

TO CONNECT YOUR HERO6 BLACK TO THE GOPRO APP:

Download the GoPro App from your app store. The GoPro App is free so make sure you don't accidentally download an app that looks similar but charges a fee. There are no additional upgrade options for the GoPro App.

After you install and open the App, the App will walk you through the setup. When reconnecting to the App, make sure your camera's WiFi is turned on.

UNDERSTANDING THE APP

Once your camera is connected wirelessly to the App, the following buttons give you remote access to the full range of settings and modes on your HERO6 Black:

1. GOPRO MEDIA

Tap this icon to view the videos and photos that are currently on your camera's memory card. You can view, trim, download, delete and share these files.

2. SHUTTER BUTTON

Press this button to begin recording video or taking photos.

3. MODE

This icon displays the current recording mode. Tap this icon to change modes.

4. SETTINGS

This icon takes you to the Settings dialog, where you can change video and photo settings as well as access the Set Up Menu. In Step 2- Settings, you will learn which settings to use.

5. HILIGHT TAG (displayed only when recording video)

Press this button while recording video to add a HiLight Tag.

After filming, you can view, browse, delete, download and even trim the content from your camera's memory card. When you record video, your camera automatically records a LRV (Low Resolution Video) file along with the full resolution file. You can share the LRV file through the App, since it is a smaller file for uploading and viewing on small devices. If you plan on using GoPro's mobile editing apps, you will need to save the photos and videos you want to use to your phone.

When you finish using the App, turn off your camera by pressing the power icon on the top right corner of the App screen. You can also turn your camera back on using the App if the camera's WiFi is still enabled.

If you want to manually turn off the WiFi, pull the top tray down on the Touch Display screen. Tap Connections and turn off Wireless Connections.

Now that you've got your camera up and running, let's go to Step 2 to learn about the modes and settings.

STEP TWO

THE SETTINGS

Choose Your Settings to Get the Shot

When it comes to capturing unforgettable moments with your GoPro® HERO6 Black, the options are endless. Your HERO6 Black is a powerful little camera, capable of recording broadcast-quality video and eye-grabbing photos. Because it is such a powerful recording tool, there are lots of setting options to choose from! The single biggest factor to recording those moments is setting up your shots correctly. To a new GoPro user, the options may be a bit hard to filter through. In this step, we will break it down and give you the simplified guide to your GoPro's settings and modes so you can learn which modes and settings to use and when.

Choosing the right settings with your finished product (video or photos) in mind is almost as important as the action you are recording. Unfortunately, explaining the settings is the most technical step, so once you get through this first step, the rest will be a breeze. Just try to get a basic understanding of what the settings mean and the rest will fall into place.

This step is separated into four sections to give you a rundown of which settings to choose whether you are shooting videos, photos, or time lapses. The fourth section highlights some of the useful camera settings available in the Preferences menu to customize your filming experience. So, let's get into the business of having fun.

NOTE: Make sure your camera is running firmware version 01.51 or higher so that the following information matches your camera's settings.

RECORDING VIDEOS

This section will help you understand when and how to use the different modes and settings when using your HERO6 Black to record videos. After learning about the different video capture mode options, you will learn how to select the correct settings for the videos you are filming.

There are two things you need to do to set up your camera to record videos:

1) Choose your Video Capture Mode

2) Choose your Settings

#1- Choose your VIDEO CAPTURE MODE

VIDEO MODE

The HERO 6 Black offers two capture options in Video Mode. You will probably use the first capture mode (Video) most of the time, but it is helpful to understand how to use the other option.

 VIDEO

When you are in Video Capture Mode, your camera will **just record video**. Press the Shutter Button once to start recording video. Press the Shutter Button again to stop recording the clip.This is the standard video mode which you will use 99% of the time for recording video.

Video recorded on the HERO6 Black at 4k 4:3 @ 30 FPS Wide handheld with the GoPole Triad Mount and Dome (a 50/50 dome port- see Step 7).

 LOOPING

In Looping Mode, the **video keeps recording over itself until you stop recording**. You can select the looping interval in the settings menu. The available looping intervals are MAX, 5, 20, 60 and 120 minutes as long as you have enough available space on your camera's memory card.

After your camera has recorded the selected amount of time, it will begin to overwrite (delete) the previous video. MAX will begin to overwrite the video once the card is full. This mode works well for long stints of video where nothing is really happening, but you want to record continuously in case something does happen. For extended recording times, connect your camera to an external USB power source.

This mode is also useful if you are using your camera as a dashboard camera in your vehicle or as a security camera. Push the Shutter Button to stop recording when something happens and you will have the most recent video available to review.

#2- Choose your VIDEO SETTINGS

Selecting the best video settings for your moment will help you achieve the shot you want and give you the freedom to edit your video how your mind envisions. Whether your camera is mounted near or far, you are filming fast action or scenery, full sun or low light, the settings you choose will give you the high quality footage you need when you begin editing your videos.

There are three things you should understand when choosing your video settings and we will walk you through each one:

A) Understand what File Size means

B) Choose the Aspect Ratio

C) Select a setting based on the type of action you are filming

A) UNDERSTAND WHAT FILE SIZE MEANS

When deciding which settings to choose, you will see the file size displayed like this: 4k-30, which is also sometimes written like this: 4k @ 30FPS.

What does this mean? This refers to two things:

1) RESOLUTION

Resolution refers to **the size of your video image**. The first number before the dash ("4k" in 4k-30) tells you the size of the video image. So, why does resolution matter?

In simple terms, a video "image" is made up of a bunch of small dots, called pixels. A video comprised of many pixels creates a larger, more detailed image.

The resolution name (4k, 1080p, etc.) defines how many lines of pixels exist within the video frame. The higher the number, the better the quality. As you can see in the chart below, a 4k video is much larger than a 1080p video and produces more detailed video.

In 4k and 2.7k, the names refer to the width of the image in pixels. For example, a 4k video is about 4000 pixels wide.

In other resolutions, such as 1080p, the number 1080 refers to the vertical height of the image being recorded. In other words, the image is 1,080 pixels high. (The "p" after the number stands for "progressive scan", which, without getting too technical, creates smoother, more detailed video).

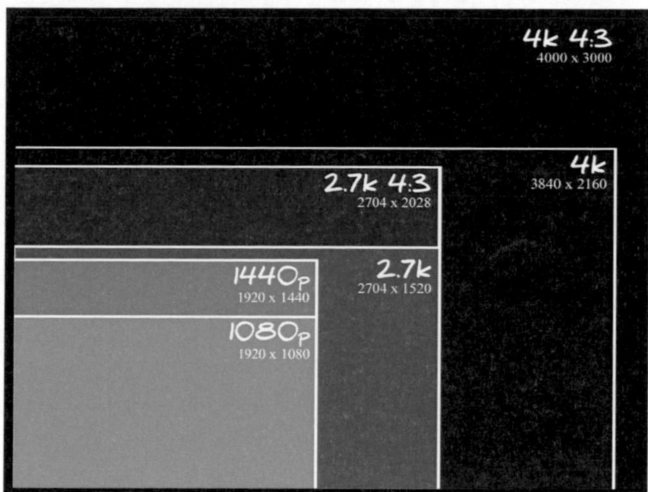

This chart shows the relative pixel dimensions (width x height) of the most useful file sizes available on the HERO6 Black. (720p is intentionally left out for clarity)

FPS 2) FRAMES PER SECOND (FPS)

The number after the dash (30 in this example) tells you how many frames are being recorded each second. **Frames Per Second (FPS) refers to the number of individual frames (similar to photos) the camera records each second.**

A video typically needs to play a minimum of 24 frames per second for the video to flow smoothly. Anything less than 24 frames per second and the eye can begin to distinguish individual frames (almost like a quick slideshow). When you record video at 24 frames per second and play it back at normal speed, this looks great. But when you record at a higher frame rate, say 60 frames per second, you can slow that video clip down to play 24 frames per second, which effectively makes that clip take 2.5x longer to play, giving it a slow motion effect.

Capturing footage at a higher frame rate (higher number FPS, such as 60, 120, or 240FPS) is better if you are planning to play back your footage in slow-mo, which a lot of action clips need to look good. All of the video frame rates play back at regular speed by default, but with a higher frame rate, you have the option to edit it to play back in slow motion.

The important thing to remember is that a higher frame rate equals slower slow motion, but as the frame rates increase, the

available resolution decreases. **Finding the right balance of resolution and frame rate for your scene is the secret to getting the footage you want.**

NOTE: Many film and video makers display their footage at 24FPS because the on-screen "look" most closely matches film. Other professional video producers use 30FPS as a standard frame rate, arguing that 24FPS is only useful if you are transferring digital footage to film, which never really happens. 30 frames per second is better suited for viewing on televisions and computers. However, because it is a debatable topic and you can get "slower" slow motion at 24 frames per second, this book uses 24 frames per second as a standard.

B) CHOOSE YOUR ASPECT RATIO - 16:9 WIDESCREEN OR 4:3 STANDARD

WHAT IS AN ASPECT RATIO?

The Aspect Ratio (16:9 or 4:3) refers to the ratio (width: height) of the image you will capture. There are **two ratios to choose from:**

16:9 WIDESCREEN ASPECT RATIO

• 16:9 Widescreen is a widescreen format for HDTV's, plasma widescreen TV's, and cinema screens. This is how you see most videos and movies. YouTube, Vimeo and Hulu support this ratio. Using this ratio gives your footage the cool **widescreen cinematic look**. The Widescreen ratio also offers **faster frame rates** to create smoother slow motion. Widescreen is the **best choice for most shots when you have enough distance to capture what you want in the frame**. 4k, 2.7k, 1080p, and 720p are all 16:9 Widescreen resolutions.
*SuperView resolutions play in 16:9 Widescreen.

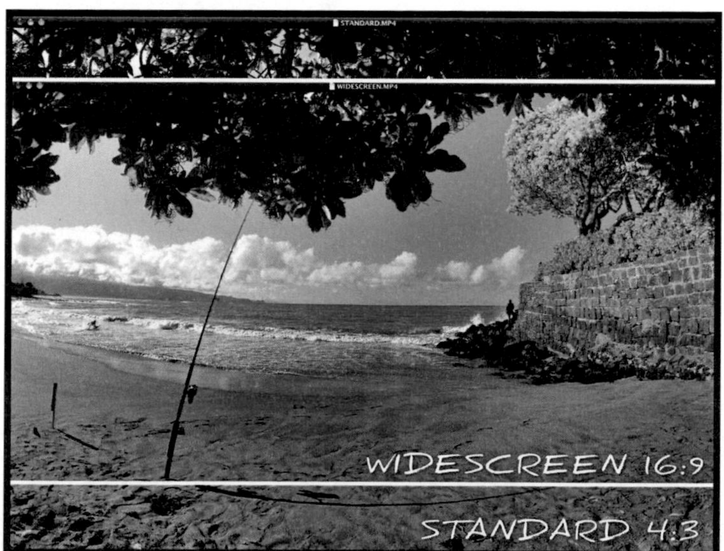

*The image above shows how the **Widescreen 16:9** shot in the middle crops out the top and bottom of what's captured in a **Standard 4:3** frame.*

4:3 STANDARD ASPECT RATIO

• 4:3 Standard was the "default" ratio all videos used to be before widescreen came around. YouTube, Vimeo and Hulu also support this ratio, but you will see black bars on the sides so that the video fits in the widescreen player. The benefit of using a 4:3 ratio is that you capture the full frame, giving you **more top-to-bottom viewing area**. This makes it **easier to get your entire body in the shot**, especially when you are shooting at a close angle or when your camera is mounted on your body or equipment. 4:3 resolutions **can be used for point of view (POV) shots** when your camera is mounted close to you. 4k 4:3, 2.7k 4:3, and 1440p are 4:3 Standard resolutions.
*SuperView captures the full frame of a 4:3 Standard Aspect Ratio.

TIP: Since you will most likely want to display your footage in a 16:9 Widescreen Aspect Ratio, any footage filmed in a 4:3 Aspect Ratio will need to be edited to fit a widescreen frame. If you need to film in a 4:3 Aspect Ratio for a particular scene, you can crop or scale it when editing to make it match. (We will get to that in Step 5-Creation.) 4k 4:3 crops to 4k, 2.7k 4:3 crops to 2.7k, and 1440p crops to 1080p without losing quality.

C) SELECT A SETTING BASED ON THE TYPE OF ACTION YOU ARE FILMING

You can select the right settings for your shot (slow motion, regular speed, etc.) by changing Resolution and FPS. The following list of recommended settings makes it a lot easier to remember which settings to use.

When choosing settings for a specific activity, consider the following tips:

TIP #1: If you know what frame rate you are going for, select your frame rate first on the Touch Display. Then tap to see which resolutions are available for that frame rate. Use the highest resolution that suits your needs. It's always better to reduce a file size rather than increase it.

TIP #2: Changing the frame rate for slow motion during editing will also affect the audio speed. Just because you record at a faster frame rate, doesn't mean you must use the clip for slow motion. You can play a clip recorded at any frame rate in regular motion video. If you record a video clip at 30FPS and you want to play it at regular speed, when you export it to 24FPS, the extra 6 frames will be removed without affecting the audio.

PAL vs. NTSC: Most countries outside of North America use a format called PAL instead of NTSC. If you are in a country that uses PAL and your camera is set to shoot at PAL, the available frames per second rate will be different while using certain settings. The PAL frame rates that differ from the NTSC frame rates are noted below.

NTSC (in frames per second)	PAL (in frames per second)
30	25
60	50
120	100
240	200

HERO6 BLACK HIGH-PERFORMANCE RESOLUTIONS

As you are selecting video settings on the Touch Display, some settings display HEVC under the Res/Frame Rate setting. These are the HERO6 Black's high-performance video settings that set this camera above and beyond the rest. If you can, utilize these settings for the highest quality videos possible with this camera.

This relatively new HEVC (High Efficiency Video Coding or H.265) compression is 30-40% more efficient than other GoPro resolutions (which use H.264), and the difference is obvious in image quality. GoPro had to use the latest technology available to offer users the best video settings at high quality, even though not everyone's computers are up to speed.

Since HEVC is still being implemented into our computers and phones, there will be a lot of GoPro users who will have trouble viewing these settings. The same thing happened when GoPro first introduced 4k video on the HERO4 Black, but slowly technology will catch up.

Old model computers will most likely not be able to view these files. If you are using a newer model computer (some 2015-2017 Apple or 2017 Windows computers), make sure you are running the latest operating system. Depending on your computer model, on a Mac, High Sierra OS can view these files, and on a PC, Windows 10 is compatible. Newer iPhones (7 and newer) and some Android 5.0+ devices (such as the Galaxy S7 and newer) are compatible with these new settings.

If you are not able to view the HEVC files on your computer yet, you have two options: The first option is to import the videos to your computer and then convert the videos to H.264 using Handbrake, which is a free open-source app for your computer. You will still benefit from the improved quality of these settings. The other option is to use the second-best setting options, which are also provided in this book and have quite a few advantages over the high-performance settings.

If you choose to use Handbrake to convert your HEVC files, use the Normal Preset and make sure to output your videos to H.264. Now, let's check out the best settings to use.

THE HERO6 BLACK EDITION RECOMMENDED HIGH-PERFORMANCE (HEVC) VIDEO SETTINGS

Use this simplified list of the most useful settings to choose based on what you are filming. These high-performance settings are recommended for desktop editing to take advantage of the full resolution available on the HERO6 Black. These HEVC settings produce the highest quality videos, but some advanced features such as Stabilization and Linear/ SuperView are not available with these settings.

16:9 (WIDESCREEN) VIDEO RESOLUTIONS

If you choose a 16:9 widescreen aspect ratio, here are the 3 settings you will need and what they are useful for:

*A) FOR **REGULAR SPEED OR SLOW MOTION** 4k or 1080p PLAYBACK, CHOOSE **4k @ 60FPS (4k-60)***

• *60 frames per second means you can play back the footage at regular speed or* **slow down the footage 2.5x to 24 frames per second for really smooth slow motion in full 4k resolution.**

• If you are filming for a 4k video clip, this is **the most useful all-around setting for general lifestyle and action in daylight** because you can achieve high quality slow motion at the highest resolution available. In low light- lower the frame rate to 4k @ 30 frames per second for better low light performance.

• If you are downsizing your footage to 1080p hd, you can zoom in 200% and still maintain full 1080p resolution. The 4k resolution gives you the ability to crop, reframe or stabilize your footage during editing and still maintain high-quality 1080p footage.

*B) FOR **SUPER SLOW MOTION** 4k or 1080p PLAYBACK, CHOOSE **2.7k @ 120FPS (2.7k-120)***

• *120 frames per second means you can dramatically* **slow down the footage 5x to 24 frames per second for really smooth super slow motion.**

• If you are editing a 4k video, even though 2.7k is lower resolution, 2.7k still produces usable footage when upscaled to 4k.

• For 1080p videos, 2.7k resolution gives you enough extra space to zoom in 141% and still maintain full 1080p resolution. The extra resolution gives you the ability to crop, reframe or stabilize your footage during editing and still maintain high-quality 1080p clips.

• This setting is **ideal for fast action sports in bright daylight** where you want to play back your footage in the highest quality slow motion possible.

*C) FOR **SUPER, SUPER SLOW MOTION** 1080p PLAYBACK, CHOOSE **1080 @ 240FPS (1080-240)***

• *240 Frames per second means you can* **dramatically slow down the footage 10x to 24 frames per second for ultra smooth super slow motion.**

• 1080p resolution is good for 1080p playback and web content, or exporting to Instagram. It is **ideal if you need SUPER SLOW MOTION and can sacrifice some quality.**

• Because of the high frame rate and lower resolution, the quality of each frame is not as high as 4k or 2.7k footage. For best results, choose Low Sharpness in ProTune and sharpen when you edit (if needed). However, for most viewing purposes, the slow motion achieved is worth the slightly diminished quality.

THE HERO6 BLACK EDITION RECOMMENDED HIGH-PERFORMANCE (HEVC) VIDEO SETTINGS

4:3 (STANDARD) VIDEO RESOLUTIONS

As mentioned before, the 4:3 Aspect Ratio is especially useful for body-mounted shots where your camera is mounted close to you and you need the full top-to-bottom height of the image. If you choose a 4:3 standard aspect ratio, here are the 2 settings you will need:

*A) FOR **REGULAR SPEED** 4k or 1080p PLAYBACK, CHOOSE 4k 4:3 @ 30FPS (4k 4:3-30)*

- 30 frames per second means you can play your footage at regular speed. You can also slightly slow down the footage to 24 frames per second and still have smooth video.
- The 4k 4:3 resolution is a lot taller (840 pixels) and a little wider than widescreen 4k. The extra resolution gives you the ability to crop or reframe your footage for 4k output. When creating 1080p clips, the extra resolution gives you even more freedom for creativity.
- This setting is ideal **when you need the full top-to-bottom view, but it is not ideal for high action sports because of the low frame rate. This setting is also a great alternative to Single Photo and Burst Photo modes because you can extract high quality full resolution still frames from the video.**

*B) FOR **SLOW MOTION** 4k or 1080p PLAYBACK, CHOOSE 2.7k 4:3 @ 60FPS (2.7 4:3-60)*

- *60 frames per second means you can* **slow down the footage 2.5x to 24 frames per second for really smooth slow motion.**
- *The extra resolution gives you the ability to crop, reframe or stabilize your footage during editing and still maintain high-quality 1080p clips.*
- *You can also crop and upscale to 4k resolution if you are editing a video in 4k.*
- *This setting is ideal for* **action sports when you need to use a 4:3 Aspect Ratio to get the shot you want and want to freedom to play back the footage in slow motion.**

THE HERO6 BLACK EDITION B-LIST SETTINGS

If you can't yet utilize the high-performance HEVC video settings on your computer, use this list of the most useful "second best" settings, which don't use HEVC compression. They are a step down in frame rates from the new HEVC settings, but most computers can play these files. These settings are recommended if you cannot yet take advantage of the latest HEVC video technology or don't want to take the extra step of converting the files to H.264.

A benefit of using these settings is that you can use Electronic Image Stabilization (which you will learn about soon) and select Field of View options. Also, depending on your device, you are more likely able to see a Live View while you film using the GoPro App on your device.

THE HERO6 BLACK EDITION
B-LIST SETTINGS

16:9 (WIDESCREEN) VIDEO RESOLUTIONS

If you choose a 16:9 widescreen aspect ratio, here are the 3 settings you will need and what they are useful for:

*A) FOR **REGULAR SPEED** 4k or 1080p PLAYBACK, CHOOSE **4k @ 30FPS (4k-30)***

• 30 frames per second means you can play back the footage at regular speed in full 4k resolution.

*B) FOR **SLOW MOTION** 4k or 1080p PLAYBACK, CHOOSE **2.7k @ 60FPS (2.7k-60)***

• *60 frames per second means you can slow down the footage 2.5x to 24 frames per second for really smooth slow motion.*

*C) FOR **SUPER SLOW MOTION** 1080p PLAYBACK, CHOOSE **1080 @ 120FPS (1080-120)***

• *120 Frames per second means you can dramatically slow down the footage 5x to 24 frames per second for ultra smooth super slow motion.*

4:3 (STANDARD) VIDEO RESOLUTIONS

If you choose a 4:3 standard aspect ratio, here are the 2 settings you will need:

*A) FOR **REGULAR SPEED** 4k or 1080p PLAYBACK, CHOOSE 2.7k 4:3 @ 30FPS (2.7k 4:3-30)*

• 30 frames per second means you can play your footage at regular speed. You can also slightly slow down the footage to 24 frames per second and still have smooth video.

*B) FOR **SLOW MOTION** 1080p PLAYBACK, CHOOSE 1440p @ 60FPS (1440-60)*

• *60 frames per second means you can DRAMATICALLY slow down the footage 5x to 24 frames per second and have really smooth slow motion.*

MOBILE FRIENDLY SETTINGS

The settings above are recommended for 4k or 1080 output that is being edited on a desktop computer. Mobile editing is also popular and serves a different purpose, such as instant sharing on Social Media. The best advice for choosing resolution is to always shoot in the maximum resolution possible so that you have the high-resolution video available. Newer smart phones, such as the iPhone 7 and newer, and some Android 5.0+ devices are compatible with all of the HERO6 Black files including HEVC.

If you are filming video with the sole intention of mobile editing, you can use 1080p in a variety of frame rates, depending on your action. Use 1080-60 as a minimum and step up to 1080-120 or 1080-240 as needed for fast action.

OTHER USEFUL VIDEO SETTING OPTIONS

The following additional video settings give you even more control over the look and quality of your videos.

FOV FIELD OF VIEW (FOV)

Changing the field of view is like changing lenses. When you tap FOV on the Touch Display, you can scroll through the field of view options for a live view of how the different fields of view affect your shots. Once you understand the field of view options, you can select a field of view that will best create the perspective you want.

On the HERO6 Black, there are three field of view options to choose from- Wide, Linear, and SuperView. Not all fields of view are available in every resolution.

First, let's look at a quick comparison of the three FOV options. (These examples are all fully zoomed out. We will learn about Touch Zoom next.)

As you can see, changing field of view creates a different look, even when filmed from the exact same location. Linear creates the tightest shot with straighter lines than Wide, while SuperView is the most pulled back with extra curvature around the edges of the frame.

Wide FOV

Point of view shots, equipment-mounted shots, expansive skies

The Wide FOV offers the traditional GoPro perspective of the built-in wide angle lens. When you select Wide, you see the actual optics viewed through the 3mm lens (equivalent to a 15mm lens on a full frame 35mm camera).

Wide FOV allows for some amazing perspectives, even when objects are extremely close to the camera. Wide FOV creates some curvature around the edges of the frame, which you will learn to work with in Step 4.

Wide FOV is available in all resolutions and is the only option for the high-performance widescreen resolutions.

Use Wide FOV as your standard FOV to start with and change field of view to Linear or SuperView when needed to capture the perspective you want.

Linear FOV

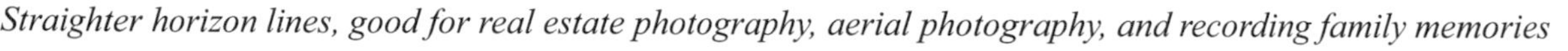

Straighter horizon lines, good for real estate photography, aerial photography, and recording family memories

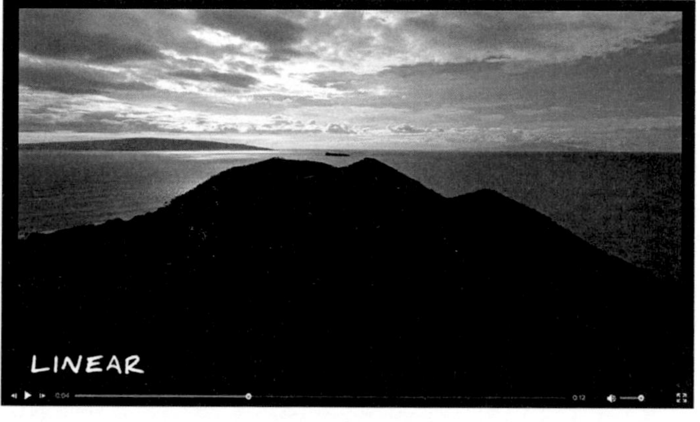

In the videos above, you can see how the Linear FOV straightens the horizon (especially when the horizon is not centered in the frame) but also zooms in slightly. Linear FOV is a common choice for drone footage because the curvature of the horizon is so obvious. Videos shot using the GoPro Karma drone at 2.7k @ 60 FPS.

The Linear FOV was developed to reduce the curvature caused by the GoPro's wide angle fisheye lens. Linear FOV uses framing adjustments within the camera to flatten the "bubble" in the middle of the wide angle shots. This results in straighter horizon lines through the middle and less curvature around the edges of the frame. Since your camera is still filming through a wide angle lens, you may notice some strange stretching effects at the edge of the frame.

Linear FOV does not capture as wide of an angle as Wide FOV and can be used to film more traditional-looking video shots. Linear FOV is especially useful for real estate videos, where viewers want a more realistic preview of a building. Linear FOV also works well for aerial drone footage where panning can accentuate the curvature caused by the wide angle lens.

The drawbacks of Linear FOV are that you lose a bit of that GoPro-style immersion we are used to seeing.

Also, Linear FOV is not available in 4k or the high-performance widescreen resolution settings, so if you want to use Linear FOV, you need to step down the resolution to 2.7k-60 or lower. The **best settings for filming in Linear FOV are 2.7k-60 or 1080-120.**

SuperView

For close up body-mounted shots, in tight spaces

GoPro calls SuperView "the world's most immersive wide angle perspective" because it captures the top to bottom field of view of a Standard 4:3 Aspect Ratio but displays it as a Widescreen shot. This is great for up close or body-mounted shots where you cannot get the entire subject in the frame. Be aware that there is distortion around the edges of the frame when shooting in SuperView because the camera is using framing adjustments to transform a video captured in Standard 4:3 Aspect Ratio into a Widescreen 16:9 shot. SuperView is best for shots with the subject centered in the frame, like surfing or biking.

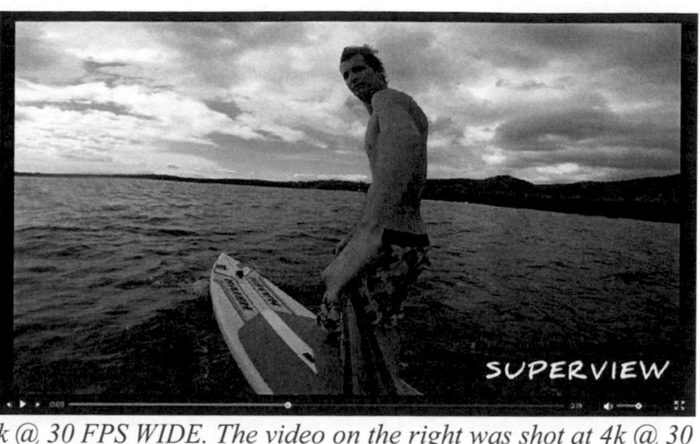

The video on the left was shot on the HERO6 Black Edition at 4k @ 30 FPS WIDE. The video on the right was shot at 4k @ 30 FPS SuperView. The camera was mounted on the paddle using the Handlebar Seatpost Mount. Notice how much more of the scene is visible above and below the subject.

SuperView can be shot in Widescreen resolutions in 4k (at 30 or 24FPS), 2.7k (at 60FPS), or 1080p (at 120FPS and lower). An "S" next to the video resolution indicates a SuperView setting.

If you record a video clip in a 4:3 aspect ratio (4k 4:3, 2.7k 4:3, or 1440p) and decide you want to convert the clip to Widescreen 16:9 during editing, you can get a similar effect to SuperView by using one of the GoPro Studio Presets when you edit. You will learn how to do that in Step 5- Editing Your Video.

The following are the most useful SuperView resolutions:

• 4k-30 S: SuperView in full 4k resolution. Because of the low frame rate, this resolution is perfect for shots where your camera is mounted in a stable position to eliminate shake or turn on Stabilization (which we will cover next) to smooth out the shots. This setting is great for scenic shots and panoramas that won't be affected by the distortion around the sides of the frame. Use this 4k setting for body-mounted shots in bright light that do not require slow motion playback.

• 2.7k-60 S: Perfect for body-mounted shots and full action shots because the high frame rate allows for super high quality slow motion upscaled to 4k or downscaled to 1080p.

• 1080-120 S: Use this setting when you want the extra frames for slow motion and plan to play back your footage in 1080p.

Touch Zoom

The HERO6 Black is GoPro's first camera to feature Touch Zoom. Predecessors offered a Medium or Narrow FOV, but Touch Zoom gives you more control over your composition. Touch Zoom gives you the freedom to fine-tune zoom to compose your shots exactly how you want them to look.

To use Touch Zoom, enter the Field of View setting on the Touch Display. Simply move the slider up to zoom in on your subject. Touch Zoom can also be adjusted through the GoPro App directly on the Live Preview in compatible resolutions.

The white box represents the maximum zoom in Wide or Linear FOV. When the zoom slider is all the way up, the image will only include the area in the white box.

Touch Zoom is available in Linear and Wide FOV's in 2.7k and lower. Touch Zoom uses the extra size of the sensor when filming in 2.7k and lower to zoom in and maintain the selected resolution. Touch Zoom is not available in SuperView because SuperView is used for extremely wide angle shots.

In 2.7k, the picture becomes noisy when you zoom all the way in, especially in Linear FOV. Stick to about halfway up the zoom slider and the image will still maintain its high quality. In 1080p, feel free to zoom all the way in without losing image quality.

ADVANCED VIDEO SETTINGS

These advanced settings are only available when using Video Capture Mode, not with Looping Video. To bring up the Advanced Settings options, Swipe Left from the right side of the Touch Display screen. Even though Protune is the first option in the Advanced Settings, we will go over it last since there are lots of useful Protune options to cover.

VIDEO STABILIZATION (EIS)

The HERO6 Black features GoPro's most effective stabilization yet! Video stabilization helps keep your footage steady, even when you are rocking and rolling. When the Electronic Image Stabilization (EIS) is enabled, your camera continually adjusts to keep a steady horizon. The camera uses the area around the edges of the frame to shift and rotate the video to keep it stable. Because of this, you will lose about 5% of the frame when stabilization is enabled in SuperView or Wide FOV. You won't lose any of the frame in Linear FOV, and the stabilization is more effective in shots that are zoomed in. However, you will most often need stabilization when your camera is mounted to you, so the narrower perspectives are not quite as useful for body mounted shots.

Stabilization is most effective for shots where a steady horizon would be natural, such as a mountain bike shot or driving offroad. An easy way to see the results of EIS is to hold your camera in a fixed direction and then move it side to side slightly. The video movement will be much less noticeable than your actual movement.

Stabilization is not available in HEVC resolutions. For regular speed 4k shots, use 4k-30 Wide or SuperView. 2.7k-60 is your best bet for most stabilized shots since you have a few FOV's available and a higher frame rate for slow motion. For super slow motion, go with 1080-120. Also, use Stabilization with a low ISO (which you will learn about in ProTune) because the camera has a difficult time compensating for movement when the video is full of noise.

AUTO LOW LIGHT

When Auto Low Light is turned on, your camera will automatically shift to a lower frame rate in low light situations. For example, if you are recording at 60 FPS, Auto Low Light will force your camera to record at 30 FPS in low light situations to allow your camera to take in more light. Auto Low Light is only available for slow motion frame rates (60 FPS – 120 FPS).

Typically, it's better to manually change your frame rate. Choose a lower frame rate (24 or 30 FPS) in the settings menu when you will be shooting in a low light situation. Choose a slow motion frame rate (60-240 FPS) during bright daylight. This gives you better control of your footage.

MANUAL AUDIO CONTROL

This setting is used to override your HERO6 Black's audio intelligence, which automatically switches between trying to reduce wind noise (Wind Only) and Stereo recording. If you are going to be in a setting where wind is not a factor and you want to make sure your camera constantly records audio in Stereo mode, select Stereo Only. If you are out moving around quickly where wind might be an issue, you can usually leave this option turned off and let the camera do its best to create a quality audio track. If it's going to be constantly windy, filming kitesurfing for example, select Wind Only.

PT PROTUNE (Video Settings available in Video Capture Mode ONLY)

• Protune is an advanced group of settings that gives you fine-tuned control over your video quality. It is mostly aimed towards experienced image-makers (which you will be soon) who want to affect the look and quality of their videos by adjusting manual settings.

• Turn on Protune to automatically boost your videos' quality (in terms of bitrate), even if you don't change any settings.

• Protune settings in photo and video modes are slightly different. Protune can be turned on in one mode and off in another simultaneously. Changing Protune settings in Video mode will not affect Protune settings in Photo modes.

Go Deeper

Advanced Protune Settings

After you turn on Protune in the Advanced Settings tray on the right side of the Touch Display, you can select and change the following Protune setting options. These recommendations are for video. As you gain experience, you can customize these settings to your particular tastes.

If you decide to enable Protune, start with the following recommended settings:

Shutter: Auto

The Shutter setting defines how long the camera's shutter stays open for each video frame. Auto is typically your go-to for Shutter settings. But, if you want to lock exposure to keep the Shutter open for a specific amount of time per frame, you can select a Shutter setting. A manual Shutter setting creates constant exposure throughout a video that will not adjust as lighting changes. In bright light, you will need to use a faster shutter with a low ISO to avoid overexposure. A slower shutter (1/30 or 1/60) can be used to create motion blur but needs a stable mounting position to keep some objects in focus. A faster shutter (1/240, 1/480) gives you sharper images with less blur. You can see a live view of how the Shutter speed affects exposure by previewing the Live View on the Touch Display.

Both videos were shot on the HERO6 Black at 4k @ 30 FPS WIDE with the same amount of movement. The top image was shot with a Shutter Speed of 1/30 sec. creating the motion blur. This motion blur effect disappears with a fast shutter speed.

Available shutter speeds are 1/30 sec, 1/60 sec, 1/120 sec, 1/240 sec up to 1/3840 sec for higher frame rates. If you record at 60 FPS, the minimum shutter time available will be 1/60 sec. At 30 FPS, 1/30 will be available. These are the slowest shutter times possible to capture the desired frame rate. Not all Shutter speeds are available for every frame rate.

Because the available shutter speeds are typically slower than the Auto shutter speed, your shots may be overexposed in bright daylight. The best way to counteract this is to use a neutral density (ND) filter. Learn more about using an ND filter in Step 7.

Exposure Value Compensation: 0

EV Comp tells your camera to make the footage brighter or darker than the exposure reading from the camera. You only need to adjust this manually if you are going for an overexposed or underexposed look, or if your camera is taking an inaccurate reading of a scene and you want to manually override the exposure reading. For example, if you are filming a scene with bright and dark

areas, you can adjust the EV to +1 to brighten the scene one stop. Exposure Control is an easier way to do this, but it's useful to be aware of how to use EV Comp.

ISO ISO MIN + MAX: 100 MIN / 400 MAX for sunlight or cloudy conditions

To set a specific ISO (100 for example), set the MIN and MAX to the same number.

The ISO determines the sensor's sensitivity to light. If you want to record the cleanest, noise-free video possible, tap into the lowest ISO available on your camera, which is 100 ISO. Because a low ISO is less sensitive to light, it absorbs light more slowly resulting in high quality video without any noise. Always keep your MIN ISO at 100 and if you need a higher ISO for cloudy conditions, set the MAX to 400 or 800. Try to stay below 1600 ISO max, even for low light conditions. A high ISO (3200-6400) absorbs light more quickly and will allow you to record twilight or night video, but the video will be full of noise and appear to be low quality. Noise is all those little specks that make your footage look grainy like you may have noticed in videos you've recorded at night. Noise can be corrected to a certain extent when you edit, but it's best to start off with high quality, noise-free video.

White Balance : Auto

White balance refers to the color temperature- a lower number creates a colder (bluish) look and a higher number creates a warmer (more yellowish) tone. Unless you have experience setting white balance, or have a very specific need, Auto White Balance is your best option.

Sharpness: Medium

Sharpness refers to the amount of digital sharpness that is added to your footage in the camera after it is shot. A medium amount of sharpness will make your footage look crisp, but not overly sharpened. Choose Low if you would prefer to sharpen the video in post-production. Also, if you are recording at 1080-240, choose Low and sharpen when you edit for the best results.

Color : GoPro Color

GoPro Color adjusts colors to add vibrance and give your footage pop, just like when Protune is turned off. GoPro really fine-tuned the color profiles in the HERO6 Black, making the raw videos ready to share without much color correction. To take advantage of these adjustments, choose GoPro Color. Flat produces videos with a more even tone if you prefer to adjust colors from scratch when you edit in post-production or if certain shots look over-saturated.

Both videos were shot on the HERO6 Black at 2.7k @ 60 FPS Linear. Notice how the colors are much more vibrant when GoPro Color is used.

RAW Audio: Off

When you turn on RAW Audio, your camera records a separate audio file recorded as a .wav, in addition to the audio on your video file. The audio track is saved with the same name as the video so you can locate the file on your microSD card and sync it to your video when you edit. Select Low if you want to make your own adjustments to the audio or High for a track that is already pre-processed.

That covers video settings on the HERO6 Black. Before we move onto photo modes, here is a Summary of the MOST USEFUL VIDEO SETTINGS for the HERO6 Black:

MOST USEFUL VIDEO SETTINGS FOR THE HERO6 BLACK EDITION

Here is a little cheat sheet of the most useful video settings we covered.

HIGH-PERFORMANCE (HEVC) SETTINGS (no EIS)

16:9 Aspect Ratio- 4k-60, 2.7k-120, and 1080p-120

4:3 Aspect Ratio- 4k 4:3-30, 2.7k 4:3-60

B-LIST (H.264) SETTINGS

16:9 Aspect Ratio- 4k-30, 2.7k-60, and 1080p-120

4:3 Aspect Ratio- 2.7k 4:3-30, 1440-60

FOV

Wide- All of the settings above

Linear- 2.7k-60 or 1080-120

SuperView- 4k-30 S or 2.7k-60 S, 1080-120 S

VIDEO STABILIZATION (EIS)

4k-30 (Wide, SuperView), 2.7k-60 or 1080S-120

TAKING PHOTOS

The HERO6 Black Edition offers a wide variety of photo modes to help you achieve amazing photos. Because of the versatility of GoPro cameras, there are à variety of ways you can set up your camera to take photos, from taking a single photo to taking a speedy burst of 30 photos in one second. The photo-taking capability of this camera is top-notch, and that is great motivation to understand the various shooting modes. This section includes Photo and Time Lapse Modes.

This section will help you understand when and how to use the different modes when using your HERO6 Black to take photos. After learning about the different photo modes, you will learn how to select the correct settings for the photos you are taking.

There are two things you need to do to set up your camera to take photos:

1) Choose your Shooting Mode

2) Choose your Field of View

#1- Choose your SHOOTING MODE

Two of your HERO6 Black's main modes are designated to taking photos- Photo Mode and Time Lapse Mode. Within both modes, there are also several Capture Modes to choose from. We will look at the Photo Mode options first.

PHOTO MODE

The Capture Modes within Photo Mode are designed for you to operate your HERO6 Black like a standard point and shoot camera, where pushing the Shutter Button tells your camera to take a photo.

The following three Capture Modes are available within Photo Mode:

A) PHOTO- The Highest Quality Scenic Photos or Portraits

Photo taken with the HERO6 Black camera at WIDE FOV in Single Photo Mode. The camera was mounted on the Joby Gorillapod.

Photo is your standard photo mode in which your camera takes one photo per push of the Shutter Button (or when you say, "GoPro Take A Photo"). Because your camera is only taking one photo, photos taken in photo mode are noticeably higher quality than photos taken in other photo modes. Photo mode is **best for shots that don't involve high action**, like a scenic photo or portrait.

As an added feature, if you hold down the Shutter button, your camera will continuously take a sequence of 30 photos max. This feature is useful when you want to **capture spur of the moment bursts of action**. When you don't have time to switch your camera over into Burst or Time Lapse modes, holding down the Shutter button gives you the freedom to snap a sequence anytime. You cannot use Voice Control to continuously take photos in this mode. Continuous photos will not work if HDR or RAW is enabled in the advanced settings, which you will learn about next.

When taking photos in Single Photo Mode, hold your camera steady and keep your subject around the middle of the frame for the least distortion. You can also rotate your camera 90 degrees to take vertical photos.

Your camera will take the photo immediately after you press the Shutter Button.

B) NIGHT PHOTO- Long Exposure Photos for Dark Scenes

Night Photo mode allows you to set your camera's shutter to stay open for 2-30 seconds. The long exposure, as it is called, allows light to slowly "write" an image in low light situations. Long exposure photos can be taken at dawn or dusk (up until about 30 minutes before sunrise or after sunset) or nighttime with your camera mounted in a stationary position.

Use Night Photo mode to create stunning waterfall or ocean photos with a mysterious soft water appearance. Or capture a scene that is too dark to photograph using Single Photo mode.

Photo taken with the HERO6 Black camera at WIDE FOV in Night Photo Mode with a Shutter Time of 5 seconds with RAW photo enabled. The camera was mounted on the GoPro Shorty as a tripod. This photo was taken about 30 minutes after sunset. Because there was still ambient light in the sky, the 5 second shutter time which was necessary to create the blurred ocean also made the photo overexposed. The RAW file was then edited to reduce the exposure and bring back the scene's vivid color.

Go Deeper

Night Photo Mode opens up a new realm of possibilities for night shots, especially when combined with Night Lapse Mode, which enables you to take a series of long exposure photos in sequence. Long exposure photos can look stunning, but taking them is an art in itself. **The following tips will help you capture the night photo you envision.**

• Because of the long Shutter times in Night Photo mode, the Touch Display doesn't preview how the Shutter setting will affect exposure. **Always take some test shots** to determine which Shutter/ISO setting is right for a scene.

• If the scene has a lot of ambient light, use Protune to lower the ISO to 100 so your camera absorbs light more slowly.

• When photographing a night photo, remember that any incoming light that lands on your camera's sensor will leave its imprint. If the shutter is open for 30 seconds and you are photographing **stars with no ambient light**, 30 seconds will be just enough time to be able to see the stars. On a pitch-black night, set the ISO to 800 to absorb as much light as possible.

• If you are riding your bike around the city at night, 30 seconds of city lights will leave too much of an imprint and create a blown-out background. A **short shutter time with a low ISO works better for night shots with ambient or city lights**.

• The following settings give you a starting point for choosing the Shutter time depending on your scene (with the ISO set to 800 ISO):

Auto (up to 2 seconds)- Best for times when there is still ambient light in the sky, for example around sunset or just before sunrise.

2 sec- Up until about 30 minutes before sunrise or 30 minutes after sunset. Night driving in a semi-urban setting at this setting will produce great streaks of light as you pass by lights and other vehicles.

5 sec- When there is a decent amount of ambient light, like from a busy city scene or at an amusement park. Driving in a rural setting with occasional passing cars.

10 sec or 15 sec- A small urban scene where there is not too much light from building and street lights.

20 sec- Dark night sky with some ambient light reflecting off trees or clouds.

30 sec- Completely dark night sky like if you were out camping or away from any city lights.

• The LED lights on your camera will not flash until AFTER the photo is taken, so the **red LED light does not need to be turned off**.

• **Keep your camera still while the shutter is open.** In Night Photo mode, there is a **2 second delay** between when you push the shutter button and when your camera's shutter opens to take the photo. This delay prevents camera shake from pushing the button. However, your camera needs to be still while "writing" the photo. **Mount your camera on a tripod or in a stable**

position with another mount. Moving the camera while the shutter is open will result in blurred photos.

• You can **mount your camera to a moving object** (like a bike, car, motorcycle, etc.) as long as your camera is securely mounted and you can see the object in the foreground. This will give your photo a focal point, while the surrounding objects will create blurred streaks of light.

• **Light painting** is a cool effect you can create using a long exposure photograph. Find a dark place to shoot your photo. Mount your camera so it will not move while the shutter is open. Depending on how much ambient light is around you, set your camera shutter to 10, 20, or 30 seconds. In Protune, set your ISO to 100 for the longest exposure possible to give you more time to write with light. After you press the shutter button, use a candle, lighter, flashlight, or sparkler to write something in the sky. If you get really into light painting, there are all sorts of fun light painting tools such as the Pixel Stick to get really creative. Lume Cubes are another useful light painting tool. (You will learn more about portable lights in Step 7.)

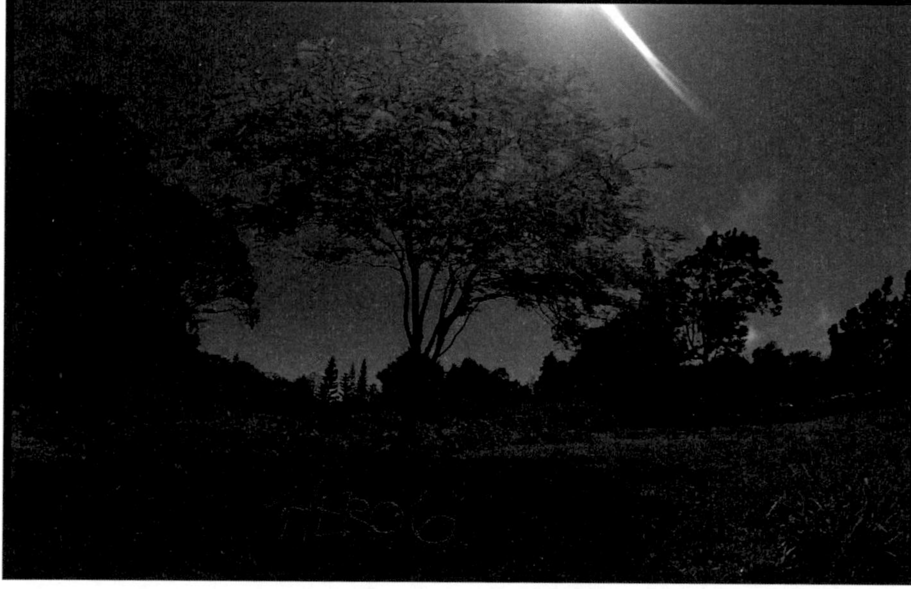

Photo taken with the HERO6 Black camera in Night Photo Mode at WIDE FOV with a Shutter time of 30 seconds at 100 ISO (which was set using Protune controls) on a bright moon night. The exposure was tested to make sure the stars were visible in the sky. The camera was set up on a tripod. The words Hero 6 were written with a laser light and the tree was "painted" with light using a Lume Cube while the shutter was open.

When writing words, you have to write backwards (so the words read correctly in the photo) and imagine where you are writing. Anywhere you move the bright light will leave its imprint in the photo- kind of like painting with light!

If you find it too hard to write backwards, you can flip the photo during editing, but make sure there are no other words on your clothing or in the background because they will read backwards.

> **TIP:** Using Auto White Balance for night shots will sometimes result in inconsistent color tones. To get a realistic looking bluish hue **in a dark night scene, turn on Protune and set the White Balance to 3000k. A higher number white balance (6500k) will give your photos a reddish hue.**

C) BURST- High Action Sports, Handheld Shots, Action Sequences

Burst Mode is **great for high action** where timing is everything. Use this mode when shooting high action sports and choose the winning shot later. You won't miss a moment. This mode is best used when holding your camera, or if you are using the Smart WiFi remote, you can push the shutter button on the remote and get photos of yourself at just the right moment. If you are close enough to your camera, say "GoPro Shoot Burst" to start shooting.

Burst Mode photos can also be used to make an action sequence, where there are multiple photos of one subject edited into a single frame. Combining the multiple images is not done automatically in the camera, but you can do this with photo-editing software (See Step 5- Editing an Action Sequence).

Photo taken with the HERO6 Black camera at WIDE FOV in Burst Mode at 30 photos over 2 seconds at 200 ISO. The fast burst provided lots of photos to choose from to find that magic moment. The camera was mounted on the GoPro Shorty as a tripod.

Because your camera is taking a quick burst of photos in a short amount of time, when shooting Burst photos in low light, many will come out blurry. Usually you can pick out the best ones and come up with some usable photos. It is best, however, to **shoot Burst Mode photos in bright daylight** to give your camera enough light to produce in-focus photos. Use an ISO of 400 MAX for quicker shutter speeds to freeze the action. If you are filming in cloudy or shady conditions, 4k 4:3 @ 30 FPS video is a better option for low light conditions.

The HERO6 Black Edition shoots up to 30 photos in one second in this mode. You can also space out the 30 photo burst over 2, 3 or 6 seconds, which is more useful for most action sports.

> **TIP:** The new 4k 4:3 HEVC video setting produces high quality still frames which compare to the quality of the photos taken in photo modes with your HERO6 Black camera. Because of the high quality still frames, this video setting makes **a great alternative to Single Photo and Burst Modes**. You can record 30 frames per second for long periods and pull still photos from the video. Keep that in mind the next time you want photos and videos simultaneously.

#2- Choose your FIELD OF VIEW

FOV FIELD OF VIEW (not available with RAW photos)

Photo modes offer two fields of view to choose from- **Wide or Linear**, both with the option of using Touch Zoom. Photos taken in photo modes are always captured at a 4:3 ratio and photos taken in any field of view/zoom result in a 12 MP photo. Wide and Linear fields of view are similar to the field of view options in video, however, since we showed a comparison of Widescreen video frames in the video section, 4:3 comparisons (taken vertically) are shown here so you can easily compare.

When selecting a field of view or zooming, you can see a live preview of your composition on the Touch Display as you select your field of view. This can be helpful for many shots where you are framing your composition.

• When you change field of view in video, you can truly keep the same resolution because you are just using portion of the sensor. However, with photos, quality diminishes slightly as you zoom in, even though the result is a 4000px by 3000px photo in any field of view at any zoom level.

• You can also get a similar look to a zoomed in photo by cropping a Wide field of view photo and upsizing it if you need to. (We will get to that in Step 5-Creation).

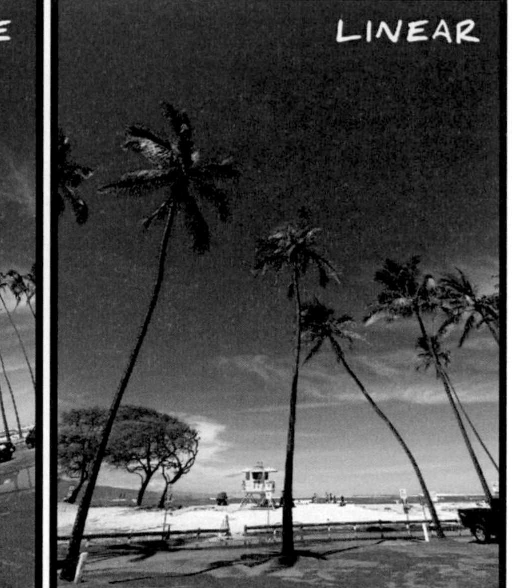

The example above shows a comparison of the Wide and Linear fields of view. Notice how the Linear FOV is much more zoomed in than Wide FOV.

• Linear FOV is great for everyday photos, such as portraits or aerial photos. There is minimal distortion around the center of the frame when compared to the Wide FOV, as you can see in the example above. If you captured a moment in Wide field of view and want to remove the fisheye effect after the fact, you can also easily replicate a Linear FOV when you edit. We will show you that also in Step 5-Creation- Removing Fisheye (for photos).

ADVANCED PHOTO SETTINGS

These advanced photo settings will give your photos some extra punch when the lighting gets tricky. To bring up the Advanced Photo Settings options, Swipe Left from the right side of the Touch Display screen.

RAW RAW (only available when using WIDE FOV)

A RAW file gives you the ability to **process your image with all of the original data** so you can get more detail out of the bright and dark areas when you edit. RAW is useful **for backlit or contrasty scenes** where the camera might have a hard time capturing detail in shadowy areas. These RAW files can handle more adjustments than a compressed jpeg.

When taking photos with RAW enabled, your camera will save a JPEG, as well as an unprocessed image file, also known as a RAW file with a .gpr extension. This RAW file will not be visible when you download your files in Quik (which you will learn about in Step 5-Creation), but it will be saved in the folder with the JPEG that shares the same name. The jpeg will have a similar color range to an HDR photo.

When you want to find the RAW file, right click (Cntrl+Click on a MAC) and select "Show in Finder". The .gpr file should be there next to the JPEG. The RAW file can then be opened in Adobe Lightroom or Camera Raw for editing.

Shooting in RAW takes about twice as much storage as just taking a JPEG or HDR photo because your camera creates two photo files. The camera also takes a little longer to process and save the file after pressing the Shutter button. You should have plenty of storage on your microSD card since photos take very little space compared to video, but it is something to be aware of when you get short on storage space.

RAW is available in Photo and Night Photo Modes, as well as Time Lapse Photo and Night Lapse Photo Modes with an interval of 5 seconds or longer. RAW is only available in these modes when WIDE FOV is selected. Once you select RAW, the Touch Zoom features becomes unavailable.

HDR (only available in Photo Capture Mode)

When you enable HDR (High Dynamic Range), your camera compiles three photos taken at different exposures (called bracketing) to **improve the level of detail in an image's dark and bright areas**. HDR is useful for **backlit scenes or scenes with a lot of contrast** (dark and bright areas). HDR produces a JPEG file with an improved range of tones even in a scene with tricky lighting. Use HDR when you want good-looking photos straight out of the camera in high contrast scenes. The HDR setting won't produce a RAW file for editing, so you won't have as much freedom when you edit. HDR is not available when taking RAW photos, so you have to choose one or the other.

Photos taken with HDR enabled take longer to process after pressing the Shutter button. Also, make sure you hold the camera relatively still when pressing the Shutter button to give the camera time to capture the bracketed photos. If you are too active while photographing HDR photos, you may see that the multiple exposures don't line up correctly in the photo.

HDR is a great option for scenes that need the multiple exposures, but don't keep it on for everyday shooting.

In this comparison, the backlit tree was much darker than the bright sky which made it difficult to photograph. Both images were brightened equally, but no other color adjustments were made. As you can see, HDR brought out deeper colors and more details in the shadowed areas and the sky.

PROTUNE PHOTO SETTINGS (available in all Photo modes)

Some of the Protune settings for photos are the same as video settings, but there are a few differences.

- When you change Protune settings in Single Photo Mode, Protune settings in a different Capture mode won't be affected.
- After you turn on Protune in the Advanced Settings on the Touch Display, the following setting options can be adjusted. If you decide to turn on Protune, **start with the following recommended settings**:

Shutter: Auto (available in Photo Mode only)

In Photo Mode, the Auto Shutter setting lets the camera select the right setting for your scene. However, by selecting a set ISO and Shutter speed, you can manually set your exposure. This is very useful for certain situations where you want a fixed exposure throughout a range of shots.

The most obvious application for this would be when photographing a series of panoramic photos that will be edited together. A fixed exposure will save you the extra work of trying to match exposures before merging the photos.

The Touch Display shows a live view of how the manual Shutter setting will affect the photos, but it's still a good idea to take a few test shots to determine the correct exposure for your scene. A faster shutter setting (1/1000 sec. or 1/2000 sec.) lets in less light and will be most common for bright scenes.

For this panorama, the Shutter was set to 1/1000 sec. @ 100 ISO to take a series of 5 photos, which were then merged into a panorama using Photoshop. The manual shutter setting maintained a consistent exposure throughout the sequence for easier editing.

The available Shutter settings are AUTO, 1/125, 1/250, 1/500, 1/1000, or 1/2000.

Exposure Value Compensation: 0

If you notice that your images are consistently turning out over or underexposed, use this to fine tune the exposure to your tastes. Most photographers typically like to avoid overexposing photos too much because the details in the highlights are easily lost. When taking RAW photos, the raw data from the highlights is still there so overexposure is not as much of an issue.

ISO Minimum: 100

You can always keep the minimum ISO at 100 to get the highest quality images when there is enough light.

ISO Maximum: 100 in daylight/400 in cloudy conditions

As mentioned in the section on video ISO, when there is enough light to keep the ISO down, you will get less noise in your photos, resulting in cleaner, clearer images. When you really want the highest quality photos and are photographing in bright light, set the max ISO to 100. Setting a max ISO of 400 gives your camera a range so that photos in low light situations will also come out sharp. In Night Photo Mode or Burst Mode, you may need to use 800 ISO.

White Balance: Auto

Auto White Balance is your best option. The exception is when you are taking a Night Photo in a dark night sky: you can set the White Balance to 3000K to achieve a realistic-looking night sky.

Sharpness: Medium

Sharpness refers to the amount of digital sharpness that is added to your photos in the camera after it is shot. A medium amount of sharpness will make your photos look crisp, but not overly sharpened. You can easily sharpen your photos when you edit them if they need further sharpening.

Color: GoPro Color

GoPro Color adjusts colors to add vibrance and give your photos pop, just like when Protune is turned off. Flat will produce photos without as much color, but it does pick up more details in the shadows and highlights. If you use Flat, you will need to adjust the colors in post-production.

TIME LAPSE MODES

Time lapse modes give you the option to set an interval between photos, spacing out your sequence over a longer period of time. The main purpose of these modes is to create a gap between moments, which when played as a video, makes time speed up. The HERO6 Black is an excellent tool for creating time lapses, and there are several modes available to achieve the shot you want. And, as you will see, there is more than one way you can use time lapse modes to get the shot!

Time lapses make an artsy addition to a video. Learning the art of creating a visually-appealing time lapse takes some experimentation to get right, so don't be discouraged if you don't get a great one on your first try. The following tips will help you with some of the more technical aspects of recording a memorable time lapse.

• The interval setting defines the amount of time between each photograph (or frame in Time Lapse Video Mode).

• Choose a *short interval (.5, 1, 2, or 5 seconds) for a scene with continuously moving action like waves lapping on the beach or traffic in a city for example. A short interval is also useful for an event that happens over a relatively short period of time, like a sunrise or preparing your gear to go ride.*

• Choose a *long interval (10, 30 or 60 seconds) for a scene where there is not a lot of movement, like slow-moving clouds, or for longer duration events, like road trips, construction or long art projects.*

• For a still time lapse, use a tripod or set your camera in a stationary position so the scene creates the movement instead of your camera. Any movement of your camera will be intensified.

• You can also film a hyperlapse, where your camera changes position throughout the clip. This involves patiently and slowly moving your camera from spot to spot. See more tips in the time lapse section in Step 4- Capture Your Action.

The HERO6 Black offers **three time lapse modes to choose from** depending on what you are filming and how you want to capture it:

TIME LAPSE VIDEO- Automatic Time Lapse Videos

In Time Lapse Video Mode, your camera records one frame (similar to one photo) at the selected interval (.5 sec, 1 sec, etc.). The individual frames are then automatically stitched together in the camera and played back as a video at 30 frames per second. Because the frames are spaced apart and then played back quickly, there are gaps in between moments and time appears to speed up, creating the time lapse effect.

Shot on the HERO6 Black in Time Lapse Video Mode at 4k with a .5 second interval. The camera was mounted to the roof racks using the Handlebar Seatpost Mount.

Although this mode lacks some of the advanced controls available in Time Lapse Photo Mode, the instant gratification of viewing your time lapses as a video on your camera will probably make this one of your favorite time lapse modes.

Go Deeper

This section will help you with some of the more technical aspects of Time Lapse Video Mode.

• Unlike other video modes, the time counter will **display the playback duration of the video**, not the recording time. To **capture one second of video, you need to record 30 frames**. The time counter will remain at 00:01 (1 second) until you have recorded 30 frames.

INTERVAL (in seconds)	RECORDING TIME REQUIRED FOR A 1 SEC. CLIP
.5	15 seconds
1	30 seconds
2	1 minute
5	2.5 minutes
10	5 minutes
30	15 minutes
60	30 minutes

This chart tells you how long you need to record in Time Lapse Video Mode at each interval for 1 second of video.

• Advanced video settings such as Protune, Video Stabilization and Auto Low Light are not available when using Time Lapse Video Mode.

• There are three resolutions available in Time Lapse Video Mode: 4k is for 16:9 Widescreen shots in Wide FOV. Use 2.7k 4:3 for Standard Aspect Ratio shots in Wide FOV with the ability to zoom in. For more field of view options, choose 1080p.

• Battery runtime in Time Lapse Video Mode is similar to recording normal video in the same resolution even though you are capturing far fewer frames.

TIME LAPSE PHOTO- Artsy Video Clips, Action Photos while Mounted, Self-Timer Portrait Photos

In time lapse photo mode, you can set the time interval between photos and the camera will **continue shooting automatically until you push the shutter button again (or your memory card fills up).** The camera takes a sequence of photos at whatever time interval you set it to. Your end result will be a batch of individual photos, which can be edited individually or easily combined for a time lapse video.

Protune Settings are available in Time Lapse Photo Mode.

There are three things Time Lapse Photo Mode is really useful for:

1) Use Time Lapse Mode to create a time lapse video. A batch of photos taken sequentially in Time Lapse Mode can be easily edited together to create a time lapse video. (You will learn how to edit a time lapse video clip from photos in Step 5-Creation.)

Photo taken with the HERO6 Black camera in Time Lapse Photo Mode at WIDE FOV with one photo every .5 seconds. The camera was mounted on a tripod using the Tripod Mount.

There are several benefits of using Time Lapse Photo Mode instead of the automated Time Lapse Video Mode. One benefit is that Time Lapse Photo Mode creates an individual photo file for each frame. These photos can be batch processed using photo-editing software, or you can easily extract single photos from the batch. Also, the photo mode uses the full sensor so you can capture 4k files at a Standard Aspect Ratio, giving you more flexibility to zoom in or stretch to a Widescreen Aspect Ratio, creating a SuperView effect.

Also, once you become familiar with the advanced settings of your camera, you can access the full range of Protune photo settings in Time Lapse Photo Mode for extra control over the appearance of your images.

INTERVAL (in seconds)	RECORDING TIME REQUIRED FOR A 30 SEC. CLIP @ 24 FPS
.5	6 minutes
1	12 minutes
2	24 minutes
5	1 hour
10	2 hours
30	6 hours
60	12 hours

Refer to this chart when planning your Time Lapses for video. Since the battery will run out after a couple hours max, you will need extra batteries or an external power supply for longer interval time lapses. You can connect to external power without moving your angle when your camera is mounted in the Frame with the side door removed. (Your camera is not waterproof with the door removed.)

2) Use Time Lapse Photo Mode to **shoot photos of yourself in action by setting the interval and pushing the Shutter button before you want to start taking pictures. This technique results in a lot of photos, but you can select the best of the bunch and delete the extras.**

Photo taken with the HERO6 Black camera at WIDE FOV in Time Lapse Photo Mode with one photo every .5 second. The camera was mounted on the Shorty on the ground as a tripod.

• For *sports where the action happens in short bursts, you will want to shoot at the shortest interval possible (.5 or 1 second) so you don't miss the best moments.*

• *For sports where the action doesn't come in such short spurts, like snowkiting/kitesurfing, windsurfing, biking or canoeing, you might want to use a slightly longer interval (5 or 10 seconds).*

3) Since the HERO6 Black camera doesn't have a self-timer mode built-in, you can use Time Lapse Photo Mode to capture self-portrait photos of you or a group. Set your camera up for the shot you want, push the shutter, step into the frame and keep the best photos out of the bunch.

NIGHT LAPSE- Time Lapse Videos of a Night Scene, such as a city buzzing by or clouds moving through a starry sky.

A night lapse is simply a series of night photos taken in sequence, which can then be combined during editing into a video clip. The most common uses for Night Lapse Mode are to record a city night scene, night driving, or the stars moving across the sky.

Since you will be taking a series of Night Photos, refer to the tips in Night Photo Mode to determine the right Shutter time for your shot. If possible, test your shutter setting with one photo and preview it on the Touch Display before you record an entire night of time lapse photos. And don't forget that you can also utilize Protune settings in Night Lapse Mode to fine tune your shots.

Photo Taken with the HERO6 Black camera at WIDE FOV in Night Lapse Mode with a 10 second Shutter at Auto intervals. Other settings: 100 ISO, RAW Enabled. The camera was set down on the grass facing towards the sky to capture the wind on the palm trees with clouds passing by.

The Interval setting defines the amount of time between when one photo finishes and the next photo begins. The interval options for night lapse photos range from Auto up to 60 minutes between photos. If you choose Auto Interval, your camera will automatically take the next photo as soon as the prior photo is taken. For most circumstances, choose a shorter interval, such as Auto up to 2 minutes, so you capture enough photos to put together a night lapse video. There are very limited uses for the longer intervals (30 min or 60 min) since you will only end up with a few photos over a long period of time.

Many night lapses require more time and power because each photo takes longer to capture than daytime photos. For maximum shooting time, connect your camera to an external USB power source like a portable phone charger.

For more time lapse tips and ideas, see the time lapse section in Step 4- Capture Your Action!

ADVANCED VIDEO & PHOTO SETTING OPTIONS

After you familiarize yourself with your new camera and become comfortable with the basic operations, you may want to utilize the following setting options for specific shooting needs. The following setting options can be utilized when recording videos or photos.

EXPOSURE CONTROL

Exposure Control allows you to specify a particular area of the frame to determine exposure. This is especially useful for high contrast scenes, for example if part of the scene is in complete shade and the other area is in bright sunlight. Your camera would naturally try to set an exposure that balances the two extremes. With Exposure Control, you can tell it to expose for the shady area, or just the bright area.

There are two options for Exposure Control- one, called Auto Exposure, is to continually set exposure based on a particular area of the image. When you move your camera, the exposure will change as the lighting changes in that region. The second option, called Locked Exposure, allows you to set the exposure based on a certain area of the image, then lock that exposure until you deactivate it, or switch modes.

It's important to note that if you lock an exposure using Exposure Control, it will override manual Shutter and ISO settings that were selected using Protune.

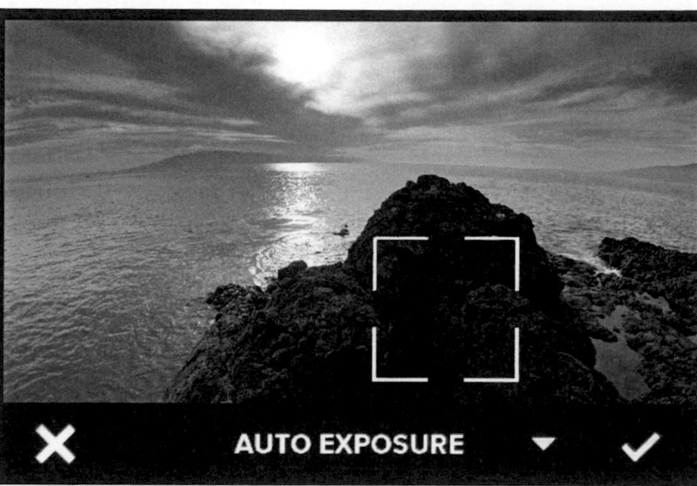

To activate Auto Exposure or Locked Exposure:

1. Press the Touch Display until a box appears and then shrinks to the area where you are pressing.
2. Drag the box to the area where you would like to determine exposure. Or tap another area of the frame.
3. If you are using Locked Exposure, tap Auto Exposure to change it to Locked Exposure.
4. Click the check box to enable Exposure Control.

Exposure Control can be disabled by changing modes, turning off your camera, or pressing the screen and tapping the "x".

PREFERENCES

The Preferences Menu allows you to change various settings on your camera.

After powering on your camera, Swipe Down on the Touch Display to bring up the Connect and Preferences Options. The following options are found in the Preferences Menu. Some of these options, such as Voice Control and checking your camera's firmware version were discussed in Step 1.

You can come back to revisit most of these settings once you are comfortable using your camera.

Two of the settings, Date and PAL/NTSC, should be checked now, but the rest can wait until you begin using your camera. If you have not done so yet, start by setting the date so you can keep your files organized. Also, if you are outside of North America, check to see if your camera is set to PAL or NTSC.

SCREEN LOCK

With the Preference Menu open, at the top left corner of the Touch Display screen, you will see the Screen Lock option. When Screen Lock is enabled, the Touch Display Screen will automatically lock to prevent settings from accidentally being changed, or Exposure Control to be set. This is especially useful when you are going in the water or when you are carrying your camera in your pocket. To unlock Screen Lock, tap on the screen, Swipe Down and then tap on the lock. This will allow you to make changes before the screen automatically locks again.

CAMERA INFORMATION

 **Date /Time**

Set the date on your camera. If you have any hope of staying organized with the huge number of files produced by a GoPro camera, you need to be able to search through your files by date. So, before you record any more footage, go into the Preferences Menu and make sure the date is correct. When you connect your camera to the GoPro App or Quik for Desktop, the date will set automatically.

GENERAL SETTINGS

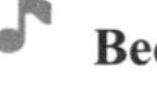 **Beep Volume**

This allows you to adjust the volume of the beeps to High, Medium, Low or completely silent. The beeps are helpful to let you know if your camera stops recording when your camera is mounted out of sight, on your helmet for example.

If you are recording nature or music, the beeps tend to be loud and distracting so you may want to lower the volume or turn them off completely.

LED Lights

You can control the amount of LED lights that light up on your camera. The options are All On, All Off, or Front Off Only. The LED lights flash while videoing or taking photos. The lights are pretty small, but sometimes if you are filming close to your subject, the red glow from the LED lights can show up on your subject. Also, if you are recording video at night, turn off the LED lights if they are affecting your scene.

QuikCapture

One Button recording was covered in Step One. This is where you can enable or disable QuikCapture.

DFLT Mode

This defines which capture mode you want to be available when you turn your camera on. The default is Video Mode/Video, but if you find that you are using a different mode most the time, set your preference here.

Auto OFF

If you find that you keep forgetting to turn off your camera and the battery dies before you get a chance to use your camera, you can set your camera to shut off automatically after 5, 15 or 30 minutes of inactivity, or Never. 30 minutes is a good option to prevent an accidental dead battery.

TOUCH DISPLAY SETTINGS

Screensaver and Brightness

This option allows you to change the settings for the Touch Display screen on the back of your camera.

Under the Screensaver option, you can set the Touch Display to sleep after 1, 2, or 3 minutes or never. Setting the display to sleep after a short period will help to maximize the battery life but may cause the screen to sleep while you are filming longer clips.

You can also adjust the Brightness to Low, Medium or High or turn off the Touch Display completely even when the camera is powered on.

Auto Rotation

With this setting, you can tell the camera which way is up or down so that it records in the correct orientation. This can be useful when mounting your camera upside down using some of the mounts shown in Step 3, such as mounted on the side or front of a helmet.

If you choose Auto, your camera will attempt to automatically adjust to the correct orientation. After rotating your camera, make sure the camera has changed to correct orientation by looking at the Camera Status or Touch Display Screen icons to make sure they are in the correct orientation. In Auto, the orientation is based on the beginning of your video clip and once you start recording, the orientation is locked.

REGIONAL MENU

GPS

When GPS is enabled, your camera will record key GPS stats, which can be used to show gauges (Speed, Path, G-Force, etc.) in Quik for Desktop, show speed in Quik, or for geotagging your photos.

Video Format

If you are in North America, film in NTSC. If you are outside of North America, most televisions outside of North America use PAL, so set your camera to PAL. Setting your camera to PAL will affect the frame rates as shown in the video settings section.

I/O RESET/FORMAT

Format SD Card

After you transfer footage to your computer, select All/Format to erase all of the files. You can also erase just the most recent file.

Congratulations, you've made it through the technical settings step. You are now ready to move on to Step 3 where you will learn how to mount your camera!

STEP THREE

MOUNTING

Set Up Your Camera To Work The Angles

The quality that really makes GoPro cameras stand out is their ability to be mounted in unique locations to capture angles that used to be unwieldy or nearly impossible. When it comes to mounting your HERO6 Black, think outside the box. Look for angles you've never seen before. Or use others as inspiration to record your life in a way you never thought to do before. **Getting creative with mounts is what will make your footage truly unique.**

There are hundreds of ways to mount your HERO6 Black and the possibilities keep expanding as creative users come up with new mounts and new mounting techniques. If there is an angle you can imagine, there is a way to capture it with your HERO6 Black. And the best part is that this camera is so small and lightweight that it's hardly even noticeable as you carry it along with you on your big and small adventures.

So study up and learn how these mounts work so you can decide which ones will best capture your point of view.

This chapter begins with **the basic elements- the camera, the frame and buckles**- and then gets deeper into the wide variety of mounts you can use with your HERO6 Black to get the angles you want to capture.

Other companies besides GoPro make versions of many of these mounts, however this book only points out other available options when they offer something unique from the original GoPro mounts.

GETTING STARTED

Your HERO6 Black is **part of a unique mounting system** that is what made GoPro cameras stand apart from other cameras in the first place. Your **camera** is inserted into the **frame** which can be attached to a variety of **mounts** using a **thumbscrew**. This basic combination is what made GoPro cameras stand out from the rest and is the starting point for a whole world of fun, creative mounting techniques.

Let's get started with one of the most exciting and creative aspects of using your HERO6 Black- mounting!

ACTIVITY LEGEND

As you learn about each mount, you will see the following icons which are shown to recommend which activities each mount is most useful for.

MOUNTING YOUR CAMERA

THE HERO6 BLACK CAMERA

Yes, The Camera is Waterproof!

The HERO6 Black camera is **waterproof to 33' (10m) without an additional case**. For years, the earlier generations of GoPro cameras had to be inserted into a waterproof case to create a waterproof camera set up.

With the HERO6 Black, your camera is always ready to get wet! The Black cannot go as deep as the previous GoPro cameras which required a separate waterproof housing, but 33' (10m) is deep enough for most activities besides scuba diving. If you want to go deeper, GoPro makes **the SuperSuit**, which encases the HERO6 Black and can withstand up to 196ft (60m) of depth.

As long as the side door is securely closed, the HERO6 Black camera itself is always ready for the water. You don't need to worry about it. This means there are no cases to worry about and no prep to get your camera ready to film in the water.

Whenever you finish accessing the side door or the bottom door and are ready to start using your camera again, **make sure the door is closed completely**. You'll notice a small rubber gasket around the opening. That gasket keeps water out of your camera. Having this door closed securely is essential to keeping your camera waterproof.

When your camera is new, the door should smoothly and securely latch when you close the door. But after time, some dust or dirt may accumulate and make closing it a little rougher. Make sure to keep any sand or dirt off the gasket by cleaning it periodically.

CARING FOR YOUR CAMERA

There are a few simple steps you can take to keep your camera working like new for years:

• **Rinse off your camera and mounts with fresh water** after using them in the ocean or getting them dirty. Gently dry your camera with a soft cloth and **blow off the residual water** around the doors before opening either one.

• The glass piece directly over the lens of your camera is called a "lens port". Don't touch the lens port with your fingers. You don't want grease or sunblock on the lens port. **Make sure your lens port is always clean!** This is your camera's window to the world. The flat lens port that comes on the HERO6 Black **works great for clear, in-focus shots underwater and on land**, as long as it is clean. Fortunately, GoPro sells a replacement lens cover so you can easily replace the lens cover if it gets scratched or damaged.

• If you are going above and below the surface, water drops on your lens port will quickly ruin your shot. **To prevent water drops in front of your lens when your housing gets wet, lick your lens port** and let it dry before you get in the water. When you get in the water, dip the housing to give it a quick rinse. This is an old surf photographer trick and it works really well to prevent water from beading up into visible drops on the lens port. You may need to repeat it a few times during your session. Although GoPro recommends it, don't use Rain-X on the outside because this makes water bead up and get in the way of your shot.

FOGGING ISSUES

• Since the HERO6 Black doesn't require a separate waterproof housing, fogging (moisture on the inside of the lens) is not a major problem, but **some fogging can occur under the lens port in humid environments**. If you notice excessive fogging on the inside of the glass that protects the lens, stop recording when it is convenient to let the camera cool down. As the camera cools off, you will notice that the moisture inside of the glass will start to dry out. The fogging is caused by the difference in

temperature inside of the glass and outside, just like a car window fogs up. You can minimize this by letting your camera adjust to the climate. For example, if you come out of an air-conditioned room into 100-degree heat, wait a bit for the air inside the camera to adjust.

• If you are experiencing fogging problems during a filming session, try to record only when you need to. This will allow your camera to cool off in between shots. **After the session**, rinse off your camera, dry it well and **leave your camera to dry out with the side door open** to let any moisture escape.

THE FRAME

The HERO6 Black comes mounted in a "frame". The Frame holds your camera securely allowing you to mount it to a variety of mounts using a thumbscrew. When your camera is mounted in the Frame, the microphones and lens are open for clear video and audio, especially in low-speed situations.

Tips for Using the Frame

• To insert your camera into the frame, **lift the tab on top** of the frame to release the backdoor. Lower the backdoor and **slide your camera into the frame from the back**. Close the backdoor, **hooking the latch onto the backdoor before closing it.** Always **make sure the latch on the Frame is completely closed all the way across** when getting ready for any extreme activities. It is a common mistake for the latch to grab the lip of the housing on one side, but not be fully latched all the way across.

• The Frame **can be used with any of the buckles** or attached directly to some mounts. Use the **long Thumbscrew to connect the Frame to a mount**. A short Thumbscrew only needs to be used when connecting any additional mounting pieces together.

• **Keep the Shutter Button at the top or bottom of your desired frame** so you record horizontally-framed videos. If you forget to orientate your camera correctly, you will record a vertical video, which is common with phone videos and great for photos, but not very useful for viewing your GoPro videos.

• If you remove the side door, you can **access the side ports** to charge the battery, transfer files or connect to external USB power while your camera is still in the frame. However, **your camera is NOT waterproof with the door removed**.

• The HERO6 Black comes in the Frame. If you are going deeper than 33' underwater or just want the extra protection, **the SuperSuit has a depth rating of 196' and can be purchased separately. The lens cover must be removed to insert your camera into the SuperSuit.**

• **The HERO6 Black, like all** GoPro cameras, **does NOT float. Whenever you are going in the water, make sure you use a Floaty or a floating handle** that will float your camera. A floating handle is the best option if you are holding your camera so you can still view the Touch Display. Otherwise, use a Floaty when your camera is mounted to your equipment. The Floaty attaches to the backdoor of the Frame (the Floaty comes with a solid backdoor) to **float your HERO6 Black** in case your setup accidentally comes out of a mount in the water. You don't want to watch your camera sink out of your hands and into the depths!

THUMBSCREW BASICS

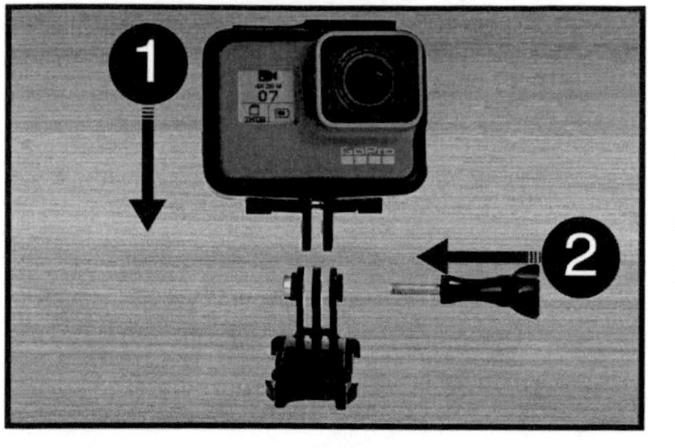

Your HERO6 Black attaches to mounts using a thumbscrew. Although this is a simple step, there are a couple basics you should know about connecting your camera using a thumbscrew.

- **Secure your angle!** Once you have figured out exactly how you want the camera pointing, **use a Philips screwdriver to tighten any thumbscrews** that hold the camera in place. If you don't tighten the screws properly, especially when you are in water, the camera will probably move around and you won't know if you are still capturing the right angle. Even small bumps and shakes can move your camera around very easily, so use a screwdriver to tighten the thumbscrews as tight as you can. Alternatively, GoPro makes the Tool, which is used to tighten thumbscrews and fits into your pocket better than a screwdriver.
- You can use **an extension arm** with many of the mounts to capture unique perspectives. An extension arm can be used to lift your camera up from a low position or to move your camera out and away from a helmet or board. Using an extension on a helmet tends to feel awkward because of the weight, but it can produce some unique perspectives. The Smatree Aluminum Arm or the GoPole Arm are two of the best premade extensions. In dry conditions, the Karma Grip can also be mounted and used as an extension arm for stabilized footage.

BUCKLES

Many of the mounts in the following two sections require that you use a "Buckle" to slide your HERO6 Black into the mount. As you just saw, your camera is attached to a buckle using a long thumbscrew. The **buckle then slides into the mount**, locking your camera in place.

There are **three buckle options to choose from** when mounting your camera on a mount base and each has its benefits. The Mounting Buckle comes with your HERO6 Black. The other two buckles are included with other mounts as you expand your mounting options.

Tips for Using the Buckles

- The buckles can be inserted into the mount bases **facing either direction**.
- Except for the Swivel Buckle, your camera can't rotate in the buckle. You can **add more extensions to the buckle** if you need to change the orientation of your camera. A 3-Way Pivot Arm can be used to rotate the camera 90 degrees, so if you are just looking for more height but want your camera to point the same direction, you will need to use two extension pieces. Make sure to **tighten each joint** so there is no weak point that will move under pressure.
- After inserting the buckle into a mount, push down the **attached black locking plug** to secure your mount in place. This prevents the buckle from accidentally releasing from the mount. The locking plug also helps to reduce vibrations.

MOUNTING BUCKLE

The Mounting Buckle is **for low-profile mounting positions** where you don't need a lot of front to back rotation to get the angle you are looking for. Because of its limited range of motion, this buckle works best for horizontal surfaces. With its low-profile, this buckle provides a securely mounted position that **can handle a lot of impact** for extreme moments.

VERTICAL MOUNTING BUCKLE

The Vertical Mounting Buckle allows for a **greater range of motion than the Mounting Buckle**. When using this buckle, you can flip your camera around 180 degrees from front to back. The name "Vertical Mounting Buckle" is somewhat confusing because this buckle is not only used for vertical mounting positions.

The Vertical Mounting Buckle is usually the best option for vertical mounting positions. Because the Frame mounts from the bottom, this buckle provides an easy way to mount your camera vertically, either right side up or upside down. You can also use this buckle on a horizontal surface to get a little extra distance from the mounting surface.

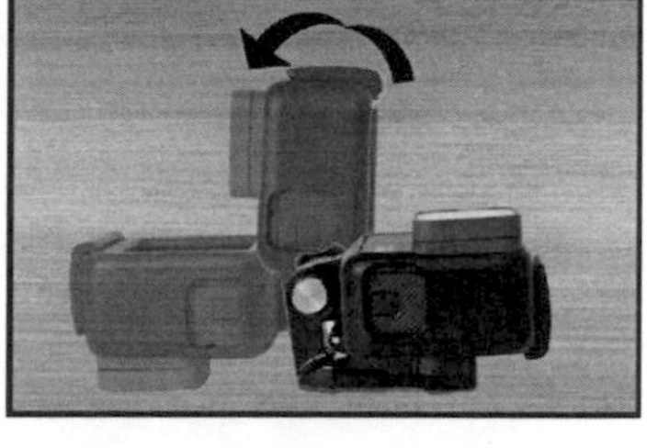

Range of Motion using the Vertical Buckle

SWIVEL BUCKLE

The Swivel Buckle/Mount **can be tilted 30 degrees in any direction**, which allows you to fine tune your angles when your camera is already mounted. The Swivel Buckle also allows you to turn your camera around completely, which makes it easy to capture different angles from one mounting position. The Swivel Buckle is a bit tricky to adjust because the joint is tight, which is needed to prevent accidental slipping.

• Use this buckle **if you need to make minor adjustments to straighten the camera's angle** after the camera is mounted.

• When the Swivel Buckle is used **for helmet mounting positions**, this compact camera setup can be adjusted easily for a straight horizon.

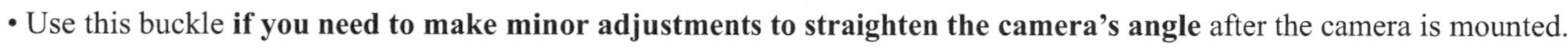

ADHESIVE MOUNTS

When properly applied, Adhesive Mounts are **the most secure base for mounting your camera to most surfaces**. The Adhesive Mounts stick to smooth surfaces using a super strong adhesive tape. They are single use and removable, but they are **typically left on for more permanent use**. It is especially important to follow the mounting instructions if you are using the mount in cold weather. The following tips will help you use the Adhesive Mounts to their full potential.

Tips For Using Adhesive Mounts

• **Do not apply the mounts to a flexible surface**, like the nose of a snowboard. The mount can come off when the surface flexes.

• To **remove a mount** from a tough surface, you can usually pry it off with a butter knife. If you are worried about damaging the surface, use a hairdryer to soften the adhesive and slowly peel it off.

• When setting up a new angle, the best option is to **always use a new mount**. If you must reuse a mount, make sure to use a new piece of a super strong adhesive. **3M VHB 4991** is a super strong adhesive bonding tape that comes on GoPro® mounts. You can pick up a roll online and it's always good to have on hand if you plan to reuse any mounts. To reuse a mount, peel off

the old adhesive and stick on the new mounting tape. If the mounting tape is in strips that are narrower than the mount, use multiple strips as close together as possible. Then trim the excess using scissors.

• When possible, use a camera tether for backup.

• Adhesive mounts can withstand temperatures up to 250ºF (121ºC).

• When mounting your camera, **make sure the buckle "clicks" into place** so it is locked into the mount.

• **ADHESIVE MOUNT MOUNTING INSTRUCTIONS:** Follow these steps to securely mount your camera using an adhesive mount:

1. First check to **make sure you are using the right adhesive mount** for the surface you are mounting to. If you are mounting to a flat surface, use the Flat Adhesive Mount or Surfboard Mount. When mounting to a curved surface, use the Curved Adhesive Mount. Before removing the backing from the adhesive, test the mounting position to make sure the edges of the mount sit flush on the surface.

2. Use isopropyl alcohol to **clean the surface** where you are going to place the mount. Make sure there is no wax or sand on the surface. Let the alcohol dry or wipe clean before moving to the next step.

3. Decide which direction you want the camera to face when mounted and **make sure the groove for the camera to slide into faces that direction**. You can insert the camera forwards or backwards, but you can't easily rotate the camera once it is mounted.

4. The mount works best if **applied at room temperature**. Peel the paper backing from the mount and stick the mount to the surface. NOTE: The adhesive does not feel extremely sticky to the touch and needs to be pressed hard onto the mounting surface. For tricky surfaces, use a hair dryer to heat up the red plastic liner that covers the adhesive before removing it. This will make the adhesive tackier and improve the adhesion. Some people use a lighter to soften the adhesive, but be careful not to burn it.

5. For the strongest bond, **wait 24 hours before placing your camera into the mount** to let the adhesive form a strong bond. After 72 hours, the mount will be fully set to the surface.

CURVED ADHESIVE MOUNT

The Curved Adhesive Mount has a slightly curved base **for mounting to rounded objects**, most commonly a helmet or a curved surface of a vehicle. The Curved Adhesive Mount can be easily distinguished from the Flat Adhesive Mount by its square corners.

Mounting Tips:

• Follow the Adhesive Mount Mounting Instructions in the beginning of the Adhesive Mount Section to set up a secure mount.

• When using this mount on a helmet, **find the best position and curve to match the base of the mount**. Inspect all the edges of the mount to make sure you have a good fit. If the edges of the mount lift slightly because the curve of the mount doesn't match the curve of your helmet, you can secure it using a small amount of epoxy or sun-curing surfboard resin (like Solarez). Make sure to just apply the resin around the base of the mount, not on the part of the mount where the camera slides in.

• This is the best mounting base to use for mounting your GoPro on a helmet. See the Helmet Mounting Tips in the Helmet and Wearable Mounts section for more ideas on where to use this mount for Helmet Cam angles.

Mounting Example:

MOUNTED ON TOP OF A HELMET

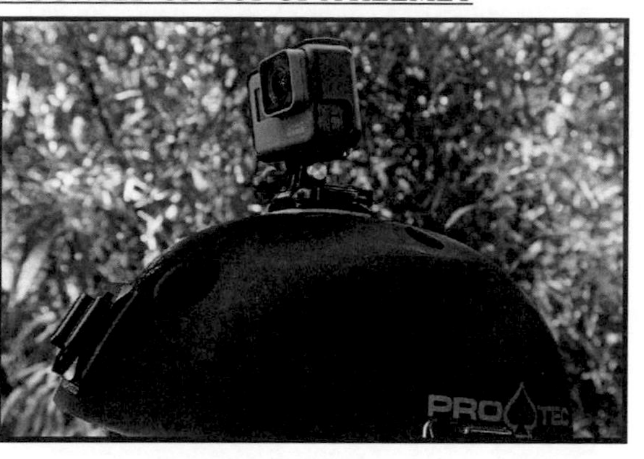

• When riding a bike or other vehicle, this angle captures a forward view of your action, but is difficult to include your body in the frame. The Helmet Front Mount is a better option if you want to capture more of your handlebars in the shot.

• You can easily flip the camera around 180 degrees for a rear-facing view.

FLAT ADHESIVE MOUNT

The Flat Adhesive Mount is a simple, low-profile mount that you can **stick to flat, non-flexible surfaces**. The Flat Mount has a flat base and rounded corners. When mounted properly to a flat surface, this mount provides a secure, semi-permanent base to hold your camera. The best application for the Flat Adhesive Mount is to a location where you can use the mount repeatedly- e.g. your own car, plane, boat, or sporting equipment.

Mounting Tips:

• Follow the Adhesive Mount Mounting Instructions in the beginning of the Adhesive Mount Section to set up a secure mount. The mount is very unlikely to fall off if mounted as instructed on a non-flexible surface.

• If you are mounting it to a board at deck level, **angle the camera back** so you get more of you and less of the board in the frame.

• **Drilled Mount.** For a secure mount in applications where a typical adhesive mount might come off, you can **modify the mount so that it can be drilled into a surface**. To do this: 1) Drill a hole in the middle of the mount, 2) Countersink a hole for the head of the screw (so it doesn't interfere with your camera sliding on) and 3) Screw or bolt your mount onto your board, surface, etc.

• The **Surfboard Mount** is a flat adhesive mount with **more surface area** than the standard Flat Adhesive Mount. It comes with a separate tether mount that fits together snugly with the cutout on the Surfboard Mount. The extra surface area creates a stronger bond, and along with the included tether mount, this mount is a safe bet for holding onto your camera, even in big surf. To put your camera into the Surfboard Mount, **with the tether attached to your camera, insert the tether through the tether mount** first. Then, **loop the tether over your camera** to form a loop at the tether mount. Your camera will fit through even with a Floaty. Finally, **slide your camera** into the Surfboard Mount.

• Do not use an Adhesive Mount on a **SoftTop surfboard or bodyboard**. If you are riding a SoftTop surfboard or a bodyboard, **use the GoPro Bodyboard Mount** instead.

• **Removable Instrument Mounts can be used repeatedly for a more temporary mounting option. The adhesive as not as secure and can be removed easily.**

Mounting Example:

SURFBOARD MOUNT ON THE NOSE OF A STANDUP PADDLEBOARD

• SETTING USED FOR THE ACTION SHOT: Video Mode at 4k @ 30 FPS without Stabilization. The resolution was chosen for full 4k video without the additional camera strain of the higher performance 4k @ 60 FPS setting since the camera would be recording for an hour-long paddle. Wide field of view was selected to capture a wide view of the action without the extra curvature of SuperView.

• When your camera is mounted at foot level and close to you, angle the camera back in the mount to capture more of the subject and less surfboard in the foreground.

• The Floaty was used on the Frame to float the camera in the rare event that the mount was pulled off the board. The Touch Display was locked to prevent water from accidentally changing settings.

Other Available Versions:

• K-Edge's Go Big GoPro Adapter Mount comes with two counter sunk holes so you can screw your mount onto any surface you drill holes into.

• BRLS Removable Suction Cup Surfboard Mount- Three suction cups attach the mount securely to any surfboard or clean, flat surfaces and can be easily removed. This is a non-adhesive alternative to the Surfboard Mount which is a great option when you are using someone else's surfboard.

CAMERA TETHER MOUNT

A Camera Tether Mount is a separate adhesive mount with a lanyard/ leash that attaches to the camera to **provide backup in case the primary mount fails**. You can use camera tethers anywhere that you can apply an adhesive mount. The adhesive mounts are unlikely to come off if applied correctly, but it's reassuring to know your camera will still be attached (albeit flapping around) if the primary mount fails.

If the primary mount does fail and the camera tether is holding your camera, you will want to stop whatever you are doing as soon as possible to prevent damage to your camera or the surface it is attached to.

Mounting Tips:

• Find a flat spot on whatever surface you are mounting the tether to. If you are mounting to a helmet, there should be a flat enough spot to adhere the small tether mount. Make sure it does not block the view of the shot when your camera is mounted.

• Follow these **steps to attach the tether to your camera**:

1. Insert the end of the tether string around the bar on the bottom of the backdoor. It should slide right in between the two clasps.
2. Insert the end of the tether string through itself to form a loop.
3. Before attaching your camera to the mount, insert the end of the tether string through the opening on the tether mount.
4. Pull the string through and loop it over the camera.
5. Pull the string tight just under the camera so you have formed a loop that holds tight onto your camera.

Other Available Versions:

• You can also make a chain of clear zip ties to connect your camera to a stable object. Attach one end of the chain to a stable object and the other end to your camera. Make sure the diameter of the zip tie connected to your mount is small enough that the camera or mount can't slip through it.

HELMET & WEARABLE MOUNTS

Helmet and wearable mounts provide **the ultimate point of view perspective**. These types of mounts put the camera right next to you for an intimate first person view. There are several ways to mount your HERO6 Black in a wearable position and each has its time and place. How and where you mount your camera while wearing it has a huge impact on whether you capture footage you want to watch or something that will just make you dizzy.

Tips For Helmet & Wearable Mounts

Follow these tips when setting up your camera with a helmet or a wearable mount:

• When your camera is mounted in a location where you can't see your camera's Touch Display, use the **GoPro App for a live viewfinder** to see what your angle looks like while you are setting up your camera. This will help you to make minor adjustments to get the angle you want. The Touch Display on your camera is not very helpful when setting up Helmet and Wearable Mounts because you often can't see the back of the camera to adjust the angle.

• For the most interesting footage, **set up your angle with something in the foreground** (your arms, board, vehicle, etc.) to give you a perspective of what is going on.

• **Use the GoPro App or Smart WiFi Remote while filming** so that you know if and when your camera is recording and to see

what mode you are in. It's really hard to tell whether you are recording by listening to the beeps and it is inconvenient to pull your camera off to look at the Camera Status Screen. You can also use Voice Control and try to use the beeps to determine if your camera is recording. **One beep sounds when recording starts or stops. 3 beeps sound after a file is saved.**

• While filming with your GoPro mounted to your body, the steadier you can stay, the better your footage will be. Using a video resolution that is compatible with stabilization (EIS) produces smooth footage for wearable mounts. If your footage still comes out shaky, **play your footage back in slow motion to help steady the shots**. The best option, although it's a pricey one, is to use a wearable gimbal for super silky smooth video. (See the Gimbal/Stabilizer section in Step 7).

• Check the angle of your camera to **make sure the horizon is level**. It's a lot easier to make minor adjustments before filming than to correct them during editing.

• **Best Settings for Wearable Mounts.** Because wearable mounts usually require Wide Angle shots and your camera is so close to you, a **Standard 4:3 Aspect Ratio or SuperView resolution will capture more of the action in the frame**. If you choose a Standard 4:3 Aspect Ratio and you want to show your footage in a Widescreen 16:9 Aspect Ratio, you can choose which part of the frame you would like to crop out or you can use the GoPro Studio presets to fit the Widescreen 16:9 Aspect Ratio.

Also, because you are usually moving a lot, **record at a high frame rate >60 FPS** so you can slow down your footage to reduce shakiness. 2.7k @ 120 FPS Wide or 2.7k @ 60 FPS SuperView are two of the best choices for body mounted shots.

• **Make sure your helmet fits correctly**. If your helmet is loose, the extra weight of the camera will make your helmet move around on your head.

• **Helmet Mounting Positions.** The three best locations for mounting your camera to a helmet are:

1. Directly **on top of your helmet** using a Curved Adhesive Mount or a Vented Helmet Strap for vented helmets.
2. For helmets without a lip on the front, you can adhere a mount **on the front of your helmet** and use the Helmet Front Mount for some unique angles.
3. On the **side of your helmet,** use the Helmet Side Mount as shown in the Helmet Front and Side Mount section.

HELMET FRONT AND SIDE MOUNT

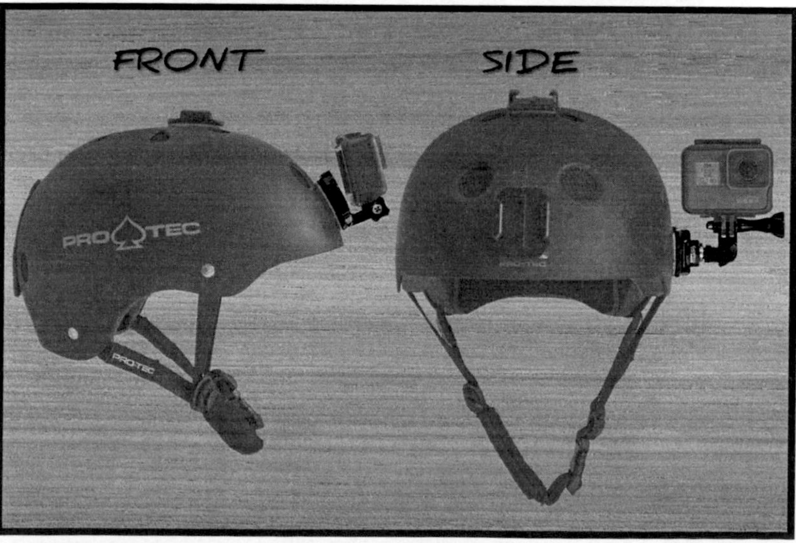

The **Helmet Front Mount** holds your camera onto the front of your helmet and can either point straight forward or point downward for self-portrait shots. The Helmet Front Mount is a great choice for **extreme sports where you want first person point of view footage**. This mount allows for a lower profile angle (as opposed to having the camera on top of your helmet), which means you don't have to compensate for the extra height of the camera above your head. This is especially helpful when going through trees on a bike or snowboarding.

The **Side Mount** is designed for mounting your camera to the side of a helmet for an **eye-level point of view**. With the Side Mount, you can get a portion of your helmet in the foreground for perspective. The Side Mount can also be used to mount your camera to the side of vehicles or any vertical surface.

Using these mounts gives you the best possible helmet cam angles.

Mounting Tips:

• **Both mounts are** used with a Curved Adhesive Mount adhered to your helmet.

• A helmet that has a visor or lip on the front will prevent you from being able to mount this on the very front of your helmet, where it works best. For a helmet with a visor, attach an adhesive mount directly under the visor for a similar perspective.

• **For the Front Mount**: Extending your camera out from the front of your helmet pointing down for a self-portrait perspective creates a unique, but very distorted view that makes your head look large and body small. Using an extension to add more distance can help to improve the angle.

• **For the Side Mount**: One way to use the Side Mount is to mount your camera upright as pictured. You can also flip your camera upside down so the camera angle is closer to your eye level. Your camera will automatically flip the orientation if Auto Orientation is selected.

• If you are using **a vented helmet that doesn't have enough room for a Curved Adhesive Mount, use the Vented Helmet Strap mount. The** Vented Helmet Strap Mount features two straps that are designed to be fed through the vents on your **vented helmet** and tightened for a secure temporary mounting position. This is a popular choice for bikers.

• Make sure your helmet fits securely so that the extra weight of the camera doesn't move your helmet. The weight of the camera on your helmet is minimal but noticeable, especially when using the Side Mount with a loose helmet.

• Depending on what type of action you are filming, when the camera is mounted on front of your helmet, **point the camera slightly down** so that you don't just record footage of the sky.

• For **low-impact activities** or **sports where you aren't always wearing a helmet**, check out the **Head Strap** and QuickClip. With the Head Strap, you can film a similar angle to the Front Mount even when you aren't wearing a helmet. Just throw it on for casual filming or mellow activities. Wear it over a hat or beanie for a more low-pro look. The center strap can be removed when wearing the Head Strap on your head or left on if you are wearing it over a helmet. The Head Strap is not recommended for watersports because if it comes off, it's gone.

Mounting Example:

MOUNTED UPSIDE DOWN ON THE SIDE OF HELMET

• SETTING USED FOR THE ACTION SHOT: Video Mode at 4k @ 60 FPS WIDE. This resolution was chosen for the highest possible resolution at 60 frames per second so the footage could be played back in slow motion. Slow motion helped to smooth out the footage since Stabilization is not available at this resolution and the helmet-mounted angle tends to be shaky. Another setting option for this shot would have been 4k @ 30 FPS SuperView with Stabilization enabled, but there would be no possibility of slow motion for the clip.

• The camera was mounted to the front of the helmet using the Helmet Front Mount as shown. This creates a point of view angle that creates a better angle than mounting the camera directly on top of your helmet.

CHEST HARNESS (AKA CHESTY)

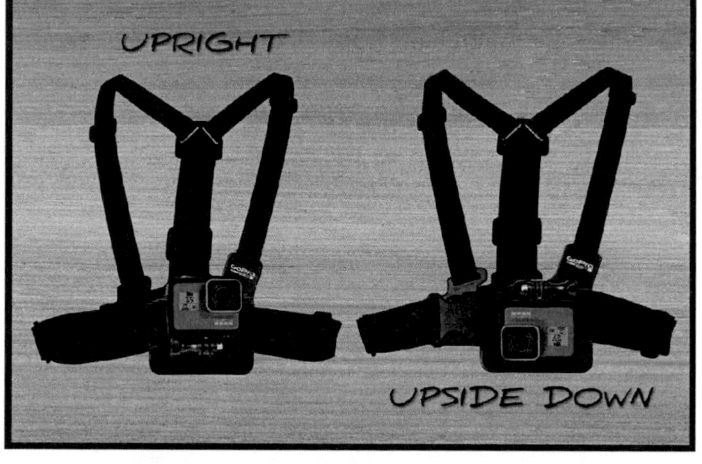

The Chesty (which also comes in a Junior Chesty size for kids 3 years and older) straps over your shoulders and around your body to put your camera right at the middle of your chest. This mount gets your **arms in the shot for a great point of view perspective** for a variety of activities like biking, snowboarding, skiing, motocross, and standup paddling. Since your torso doesn't generally move around as much as your head, the Chest Harness often produces more stable shots than a helmet/head mounted position.

Mounting Tips:

- Mount your camera **upside down for biking or other activities where you are leaning forward** so that you can rotate the camera up, pointing it away from the ground.
- Mount your camera **right side up for shots where you are upright** so that you can slightly angle your camera down to get some of your body in the frame.
- You can easily adjust the angle of your camera while it is still mounted on your body to see where your camera is pointing.
- The Chest Harness typically can't be used during activities where you lie on your stomach, like while paddling a surfboard.

Mounting Examples:

<u>MOUNTED ON CHEST WITH CAMERA UPSIDE DOWN</u>

- SETTING USED FOR THE ACTION SHOT: Video Mode at 4k @ 30 FPS SuperView with Stabilization turned on. SuperView was used to capture the widest view of the scene since the action was so close to the camera. 30 FPS was selected to take advantage of Stabilization since the clip would be played at regular speed to sync with the drum music.
- The Frame was mounted to the Vertical Mounting Buckle to allow for more rotation to capture the forward-facing angle.
- The camera was mounted upside down so it could be tilted up to capture more of the drums and background.

MOUNTED ON CHEST WITH CAMERA RIGHT SIDE UP

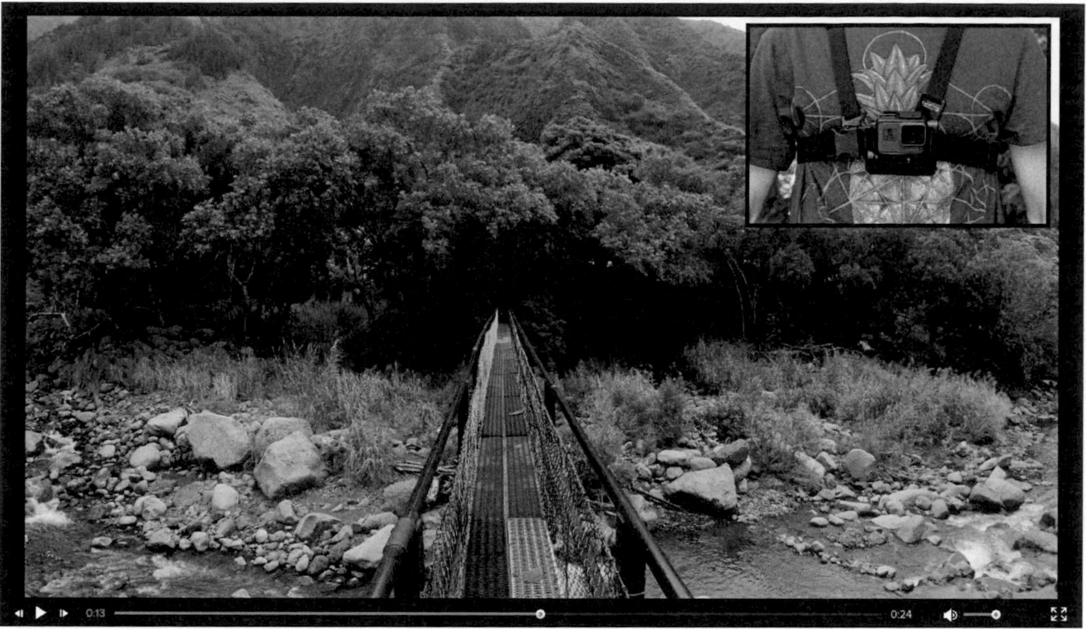

• SETTING USED FOR THE ACTION SHOT: Video Mode at 4k @ 30 FPS WIDE. 30 FPS was chosen to enable Stabilization which made this clip easy to watch without any post production stabilization.

• The Frame was mounted to the Vertical Mounting Buckle to allow for more rotation and to capture the forward-facing angle.

• The camera was mounted right side up so it could be tilted down slightly to capture more of the trail on this river crossing.

HAND + WRIST STRAP

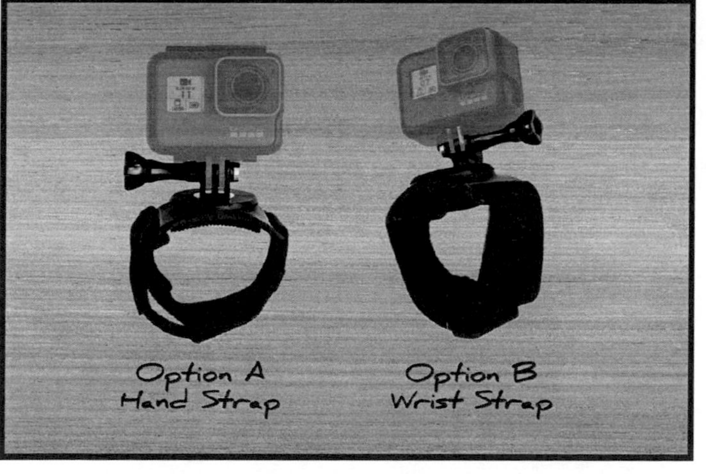

The Hand + Wrist Strap is a **very versatile wearable mount** because it comes with two straps **to fit different diameter objects**. The Strap can be worn around your hand, wrist, ankle, or other round objects (such as a tree branch or pole) for unique angles that are difficult to capture with other mounts. The mounting piece rotates 360 degrees allowing you to adjust your camera and change your angle while your camera is mounted.

Mounting Tips:

• **Choose a high frame rate** when using this mount for videos with a lot of movement so you can slow down the footage to stabilize it. Because your camera is mounted on your limbs, which tend to move a lot, slow motion helps to smooth the shaky shots.

• **Reattaching the straps** can be confusing if you forget how they were attached. When changing straps, each end is inserted into the mounting piece and folded back onto itself so the GoPro logo is showing.

• When wearing a backpack, you can tighten the hand strap **around one of the backpack straps** for a forward-facing view.

Mounting Example:

MOUNTED ON HAND

• SETTING USED FOR THE ACTION SHOT: 4k @ 60 FPS WIDE. Wide FOV worked well for this mounted position because SuperView created some distortion around the edges of the frame near the subject's arm. A higher frame rate allowed for the possibility of slow motion to smooth out shaky shots.

• During the hike, the HERO6 Black was rotated on the Hand Strap mount to create a variety of angles depending on the terrain.

VERSATILE MOUNTS

The mounts in this section **can be used in a variety of ways to capture unique angles**. These mounts are grouped together because they can be mounted temporarily to a variety of objects. Each of these mounts is quite unique and specific usage tips are given at each mount.

HANDLE OR POLECAM/MONOPOD

Attach your HERO6 Black to a handle (typically about 6"-8") or a pole (18"+) for an easy way to hold your camera and **capture multiple angles with one mount**. A handle or pole (also known as a selfie stick) enables you to capture some of the best angles possible for any activity where you have a free hand. The pole creates more distance between you and your camera so you can capture more of the scene in handheld self-portraits. You can **film yourself, follow behind your friends, or hold the pole vertically** to get more height on your shots.

There are tons of options available for a well-designed handle or pole, or you can easily make your own (see the Handlebar/ Seatpost Mounting tips for simple instructions).

If you are looking to purchase a premade handle, check out the Handler (by GoPro), or the Bobber (by GoPole). Both options are waterproof and will float your camera.

For a well-designed pole, the 3-Way by GoPro (pictured above) is very versatile and can capture multiple angles when used with the extension arm. GoPro also makes El Grande, which is an extension pole that can reach from 15" up to 38" for a heavier duty selfie stick. GoScope also makes a telescoping pole and GoPole makes the Evo, which is clear, floats and is extendable from 14"-24". The PowerPole (by PolarPro) is not waterproof, but it features a built-in battery that allows you to film for 10 hours on a single charge. A cheap lightweight option is the Bower Xtreme Action Monopod.

For the smoothest footage, the Karma Grip, with its built-in stabilization, is the ultimate handheld filming tool.

Mounting Tips:

• **Hold the pole steady** while filming for smooth shots.

• See the examples for the **three primary ways to hold your camera** when using a handle or polecam.

Mounting Examples:

THE FOLLOW-ALONG ANGLE

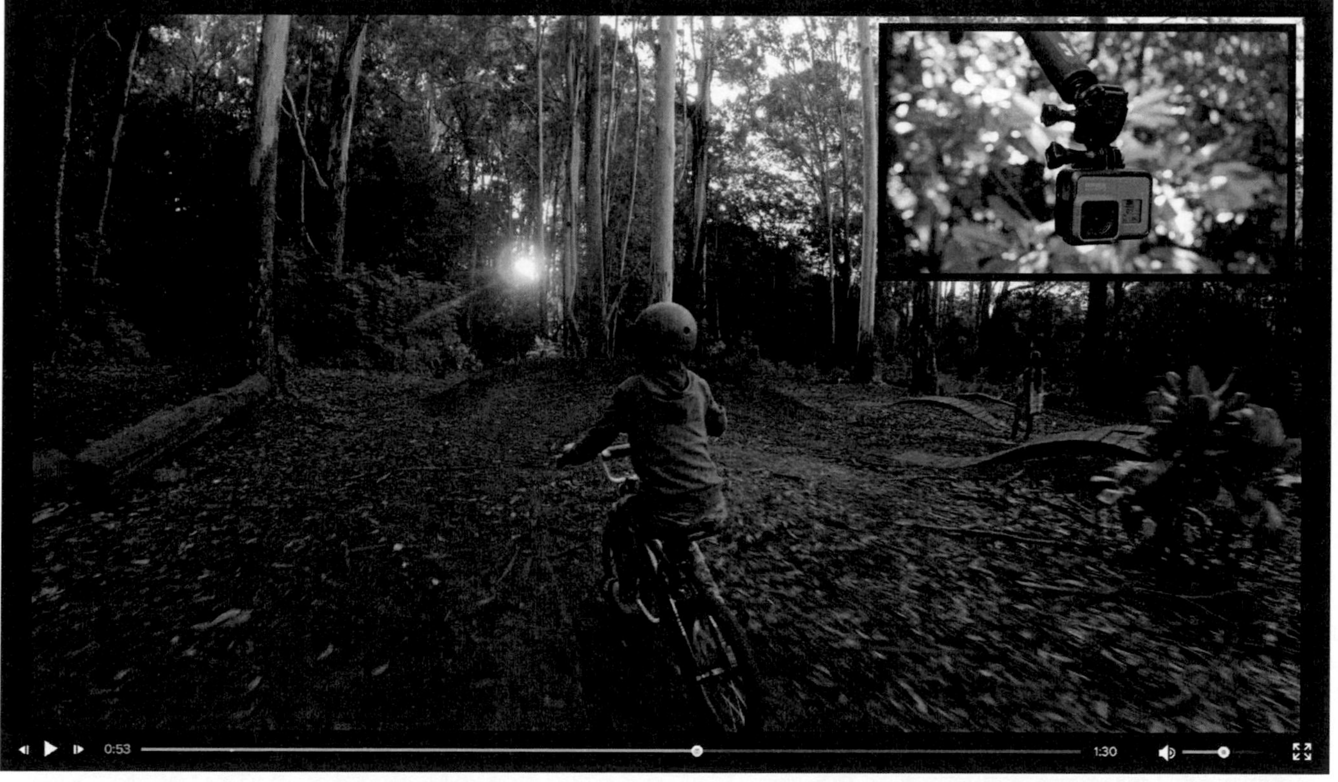

• Because the camera is upside down and facing out, this angle provides **optimal stability for following behind your friends**. The weight of the camera naturally helps to stabilize your shots.

• SETTING USED FOR THE ACTION SHOT: 4k @ 60 FPS WIDE using GoPro's El Grande pole. 60 FPS was chosen so that the clip could be played back in slow motion in 4k. The ISO was set to 400 max. since there was only filtered light through the trees. The exposure originally came out a little dark and was brightened in postproduction, but the low ISO produced super high quality, low noise footage. This mounting position worked well for following along with the subject and capturing a steady shot.

• The Frame was mounted on the Vertical Buckle to El Grande.

• When your camera is set up like this, set your orientation to Auto to automatically flip your camera's filming orientation so you can preview your footage right side up.

UPRIGHT POLECAM

• The upright mounting position gives you **extra height to take photos or videos**, usually of other people. When using a long pole, mounting the Smart WiFi Remote to the base of the pole is extremely useful for this mounting position, especially when shooting Burst action photos. If you can't easily reach your camera, in some situations you can also use Voice Control to start recording or to take a Burst of photos.

• SETTING USED FOR THE ACTION SHOT: Burst Mode at 30 photos over 2 seconds on the GoPro Handler. The upright position created the easiest way to get the right angle of this wave. The Shutter Button on the camera had to be pressed at just the right time- about .5 second before the action. Because the waves were so small, the quick burst of photos increased the odds of capturing just the right moment of this fast-moving action.

• By mounting the camera upright on the end of the handle or pole, you can get more vertical height for a better angle.

SELFIE SHOT

• When you have a free hand to hold the handle or pole, this mounting position **allows you to film yourself** and get extra distance between you and the camera for a better shot. Rotate the camera back slightly as shown so you capture less of the pole and more of you in the shot.

• SETTING USED FOR THE ACTION SHOT: 4k 4:3 @ 30 FPS Wide. This resolution was selected to capture full-frame 4k video for either cropping to Widescreen or pulling out high-quality still frames. El Grande pole was used fully extended to create the most distance between the camera and subject.

• The Frame was mounted to El Grande using the Vertical Buckle for maximum rotation.

HANDLEBAR / SEATPOST POLE MOUNT (PICTURED) & LARGE TUBE MOUNT

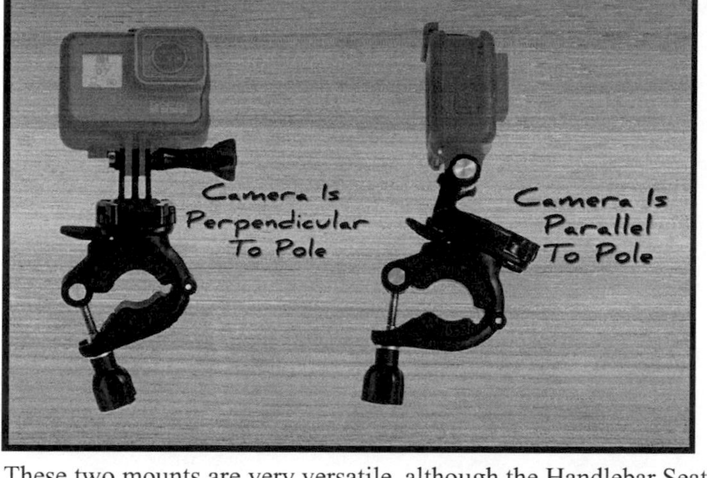

The Large Tube Mount and the Handlebar/Seatpost Pole Mount are very similar. Both mounts consist of a round piece that **clamps together around a pole** and tightens using a single bolt. The Pro Handlebar/Seatpost Pole Mount is made of aluminum for extra strength, specifically for biking. The mounting buckle on top can be rotated 360 degrees with 16 locking positions to adjust your camera for the perfect angle.

The Handlebar Seatpost Mount fits poles and tubes that are .75" to 1.40" (1.90cm - 3.50cm) in diameter. The Large Tube Mount fits onto larger pipes and poles with a diameter from 1.40" to 2.50" (3.50cm-6.35cm).

These two mounts are very versatile, although the Handlebar Seatpost Mount fits on a wider variety of objects.

Some of the things you can do **with the Handlebar/Seatpost Mount** are:

- Mount it on a piece of PVC pipe for an **easy homemade polecam.**
- Mount it **to a paddle** while riding waves standup paddling.
- Put it **on ski poles** or on the ski rack in a sled.
- Attach your camera on **bike handlebars, a seatpost or a bike frame**.

Use the **Roll Bar Mount to**:

- Mount your camera to **the strut of an airplane.**
- Attach it **to a bike frame** (for larger diameter frames).

Mounting Tips:

- **When mounting the Handlebar Seatpost Mount to your bike, if your bike seatpost is long enough, mount the Handlebar Seatpost Mount low on the seatpost with the camera mounted upright so that your legs don't rub on it while riding.**
- Tighten the thumbscrew that connects your camera with the GoPro Tool or a screwdriver so your camera doesn't change position on bumpy roads or when hit by a wave.
- **Make your own polecam/handle** by attaching the Handlebar/Seatpost Mount to the end of a 3/4" diameter piece of PVC pipe. Spray paint the PVC pipe with a matte black paint so it looks more stealth in your shots. If you are using the pole in the water, seal both ends with waterproof epoxy (Waterweld Epoxy works well) so it floats. Slide a rubber bike handlebar grip on the end if you want the extra grip. See the previous mounting section (Handle and Polecam) for more tips on how to use a polecam.
- When mounting to painted metal or other slippery surfaces, put the included protective liner around the pole to **prevent the mount from slipping**. The rubber also reduces vibration during filming.
- The Vertical Mounting Buckle gives you a wider range of motion to adjust your camera's angle, while the Mounting Buckle creates a more low-profile setup.

Mounting Example:

MOUNTED TO PADDLE (CAMERA PERPENDICULAR TO POLE)

- The Handlebar Seatpost Mount is mounted near the base of a paddle. The mount can be rotated to capture the angle you want, like the one captured in the Wide vs. SuperView Video example.
- When mounted to a stick or pole like shown, tilt your camera back to capture less of the pole in the foreground and more of the scene.

SUCTION CUP MOUNT

A suction cup mount uses an industrial strength suction cup at the base of the mount to **temporarily mount your GoPro camera** to a variety of surfaces including cars, trucks, boats and some sporting equipment. It comes with adjustable arms so you can customize the camera orientation for the shot you want.

The Suction Cup Mount is **the perfect travel mount** because you can temporarily mount your GoPro camera without using an adhesive mount. This mount also gives you the freedom to **quickly move your camera** to capture several angles.

Mounting Tips:

• Make sure you **attach the Suction Cup Mount to a flat, clean and smooth surface**, such as glass or smooth metal. Check to see that the suction cup is clear of debris. The suction cup will not stick well to a porous, curved or flexible surface.

• The Suction Cup Mount is **NOT recommended for high-impact sports** like snowboarding, motocross, or surfing.

• Do NOT apply the Suction Cup Mount in an environment where the temperature is drastically different than where you will be using the Suction Cup Mount. If you are in the snow for example, don't attach the Suction Cup Mount in your heated car and then jump outside into the cold. This may affect the suction.

• **Wet the edge of the ring** with a little bit of saliva or water before pushing the suction cup onto the surface to get better suction.

• After pushing down the button and flipping over the lever to secure the mount, **pull firmly on the mount to test its suction**. When mounted correctly, the mount should not move at all.

• If you are using this mount in a situation where you will lose your camera if the mount comes off, **use a leash tether or lanyard attached to a separate Tether Mount** as backup in case the suction cup does fail. You can also use a chain of zip ties attached to a part of your vehicle if you don't want to apply an adhesive tether. Attach the other end of the zip tie chain to the arm of the Suction Cup Mount. You don't want to lose your camera!

• Use the Suction Cup Mount in the water cautiously. If you are using a Suction Cup Mount in water, be sure to use a Floaty to provide flotation for your camera. And use a tether mount when possible just in case the Suction Cup fails.

Mounting Example:

FOR WINDSHIELD/WINDOW MOUNTING

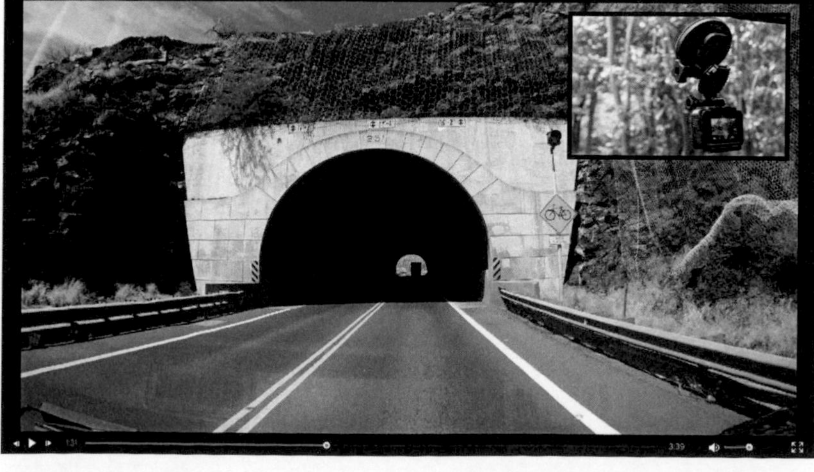

• When mounting your camera to a car windshield or airplane window, mount your camera upside down to get as close to the glass as possible, which will reduce reflections.

• SETTING USED FOR THE ACTION SHOT: Shot in Video Mode at 4k @ 60 FPS WIDE. The highest resolution and frame rate was used for this video to allow for the most creativity when editing. Even though the wiper blades can be seen in the frame, a slight zoom in editing can easily crop them out.

• The Frame was mounted to the Vertical Mounting Buckle for more clearance past the edge of the Suction Cup Mount.

Other Available Versions:

• **The** RAM Suction Cup Mount for GoPro has ball joints on the end for easy adjusting.

• VectorMount features three suction cups and a naturally rotating head, made specifically for vehicles, but based on the price, you may be better off with a mountable gimbal.

TRIPOD MOUNT

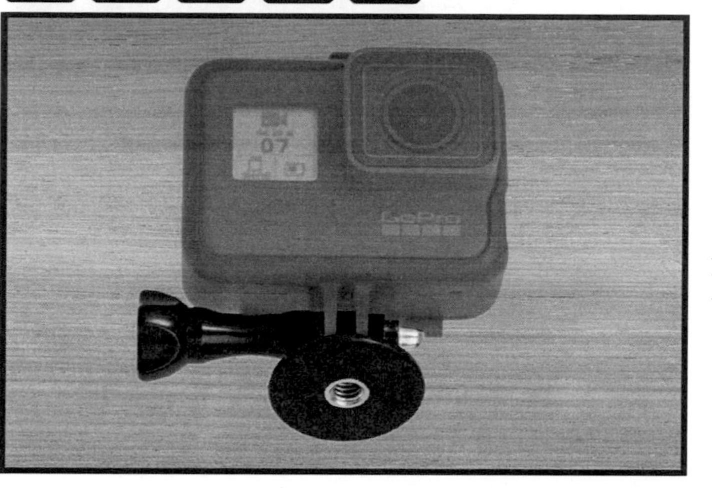

The Tripod Mount is a small mount that has a standard 1/4"-20 threads per inch screw so you can **mount your camera to any tripod**. This mount, as small and simple as it is, really opens up a lot of possibilities for different shots to mix in with your other action shots, such as scenic shots and self-portraits where you set up the shot and then pass by the camera.

Mounting Tips:

• A tripod is the best partner to utilize this mount. The mount comes with a basic tripod. A small, flexible tripod like the inexpensive Dynex Flexible Tripod or the Joby GorillaPod opens up a myriad of options for unique angles.

• The Tripod Mount also comes with a Quick Release Tripod Mount allowing you to easily slide your camera on and off of a tripod.

• Because this mount enables you to attach your camera to any 1/4"-20 screw, there are tons of custom mounting options, including on top of a DSLR or mirrorless camera to record video in addition to the photos you take with your DSLR. (See ON TOP OF A DSLR Example for mounting instructions.)

Mounting Examples:

ON A TRIPOD

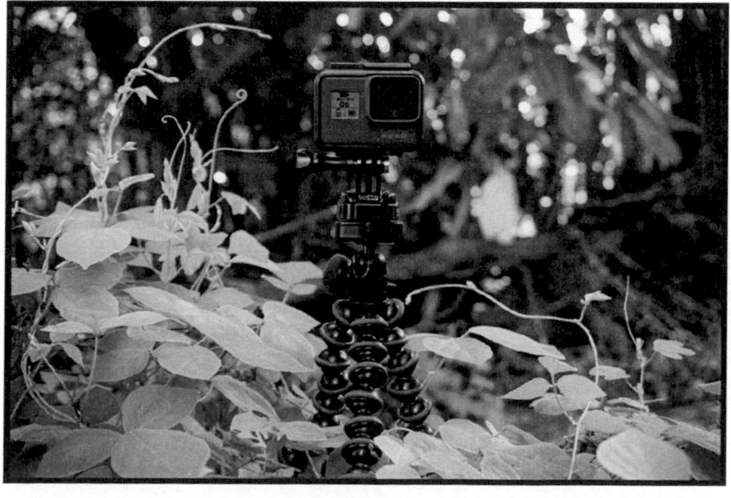

• Use the Tripod Mount or the Quick Release Tripod Mount (shown on the Joby GorillaPod) to mount your HERO6 Black on any mini or full-size tripod. For a full-size tripod, a fluid-head is the best option for smooth video movements.

ON TOP OF A DSLR

• Use a Hot Shoe to 1/4"-20 Tripod Screw Adapter (available online, but not from GoPro) along with the Tripod Mount to mount your HERO6 Black to the top of your DSLR so you can record video or time lapse photos with your GoPro while taking photos with your DSLR.

• If you are shooting with a standard lens on your DSLR, the lens will most likely be out of the GoPro video frame. However, check the shot on the Touch Display If the lens is in your shot, rotate your HERO6 Black up to get the lens out of the frame or zoom in to get a tighter shot.

JAWS: FLEX CLAMP

The Jaws: Flex Clamp has a **very strong grip** and comes with a flexible arm that can be used for a variety of mounting options. The clamp can be quickly and easily mounted and removed for **easy shots on the go**.

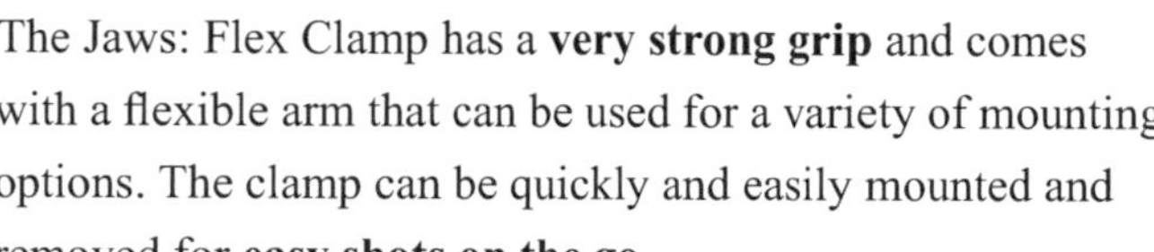

Mounting Tips:

• Use a **Vertical Mounting Buckle in conjunction with the clamp** so that you can rotate your camera all the way back as shown in the mounting photo above.

• The Gooseneck Extension gives you **flexibility to reposition your camera** into multiple angles from one clamping location.

• The **rubber tab on the clamp can be pulled to tighten the grip when you are clamped onto a round object.**

• **Jaws can also be used as a handle. Hold the clamp in your hands with the camera upside down facing out for maximum stability.**

• The Jam (Adjustable Music Mount) by GoPro is another clamp-style mount designed for mounting to musical instruments. The clamp is more lightweight if you are looking for a lighter option.

Mounting Examples:

WITH THE GOOSENECK ON A TREE

• The Frame was mounted to the Vertical Mounting Buckle on the Gooseneck for the widest range of motion to capture a good angle.

Other Available Versions:

(Both of the following options require the Tripod Mount to mount your GoPro to their products)

• ActionPod offers the Action Clamp, which is a clamp with a bendy arm.

• Pedco also makes a wide variety of camera clamps.

CHEAP & EASY DO-IT-YOURSELF GOPRO MOUNTS

GoPro'ers are a creative bunch who have taken underground no-frills filmmaking to the next level. Custom mounts are one of the easiest ways to get unique shots. The key is to keep them cheap or else you might as well go buy a professionally made version. These cheap and easy custom mount ideas will give you a head start on your image-making.

ROLLING DOLLY

You can easily attach wheels to the base of a flexible tripod for a quick and easy rolling dolly. This custom mount can be used for smooth dolly shots at ground level.

Just drill holes through the last link of the tripod legs, bolt on some old inline skate or skateboarding wheels and attach them with a ¼" bolt and thumbscrew. You can take the wheels on and off as you like. If you are filming on a rough surface, grab a wood plank and you can roll your dolly across it for a smooth shot.

CABLE SLIDER

A cable slider allows you to slide your camera along a cable for a smooth movement through the air. If you are using a drone, you wouldn't really need to make one of these because this shot resembles a drone shot. But, for those of you who don't have a drone, there are some relatively easy DIY versions online for making your own cable slider.

To use a cable slider, you will need the right filming location with two high objects for connecting the cable. These shots look great with your camera traveling through the trees along a path.

BACKPACK POLECAM (THIRD PERSON MOUNT)

The Backpack Pole Mount creates one of the coolest angles around. Also called the Third Person Mount, this custom mount **captures a perspective of your camera following you** from behind. This mount is NOT MADE for HIGH-IMPACT activities and is not waterproof, but for leisurely activities, this mount is perfect to get a full angle of the action with you in center stage. The mount is framed into your backpack so it creates a steady shot of you as the scenery moves around you.

To make this mount, use three pieces of PVC pipe and four 90º PVC Elbows to build a frame that fits around the bottom and sides of your backpack. Then join the top of the PVC pipe together using two short pieces of PVC pipe with a PVC Tee in the middle. Add another PVC pole into the tee with the Handlebar Seatpost mount on the end to mount your camera and you are ready to go film.

EGG TIMER TIME LAPSE

The Ikea Ordning Egg Timer costs about $6 and works great for a rotating camera mount to shoot time lapse photos for video clips. You can stick a mount directly on top of the timer, set the time lapse settings and the egg timer will slowly move counterclockwise. You can't adjust the rotating speed of the timer (360 degrees in one hour), which is far too slow for regular speed video, but for $6 US, this is a great way to add some movement to your time lapse clips.

FOLLOW YOUR PASSION

The following diagrams illustrate some of the best mounts and mounting locations for some of the most popular adventure sports. Of course, there are more sports and activities for your adventurous lifestyle, but **these are a starting point to inspire you to get out there and start filming with your HERO6 Black**. As you figure out which angles and locations work well for you, your ideas and knowledge will expand and even more ideas for creative mounting locations will come to mind.

The following setting recommendations are for Wide FOV, unless noted otherwise. The recommended settings are to provide you with an initial setting to use for each mounting position if you are just getting started. As you gain experience using your camera, **you will undoubtedly develop your personal favorite settings to film your action**.

NOTE: If you are editing a 4k video, use the 4k or 2.7k setting options in the examples. For a 1080p video, any of the example settings can be used. If you prefer to use H.264 (not the high-performance settings), step the resolution down one notch (4k down to 2.7k, for example) and use the recommended frame rate.

WATER SPORTS

Use a Floaty Backdoor (when the mounts allow it) or a floating handle for all watersports. Also, since the touch functions won't work properly with wet hands, lock the Touch Display screen and use the alternative button method to change settings.

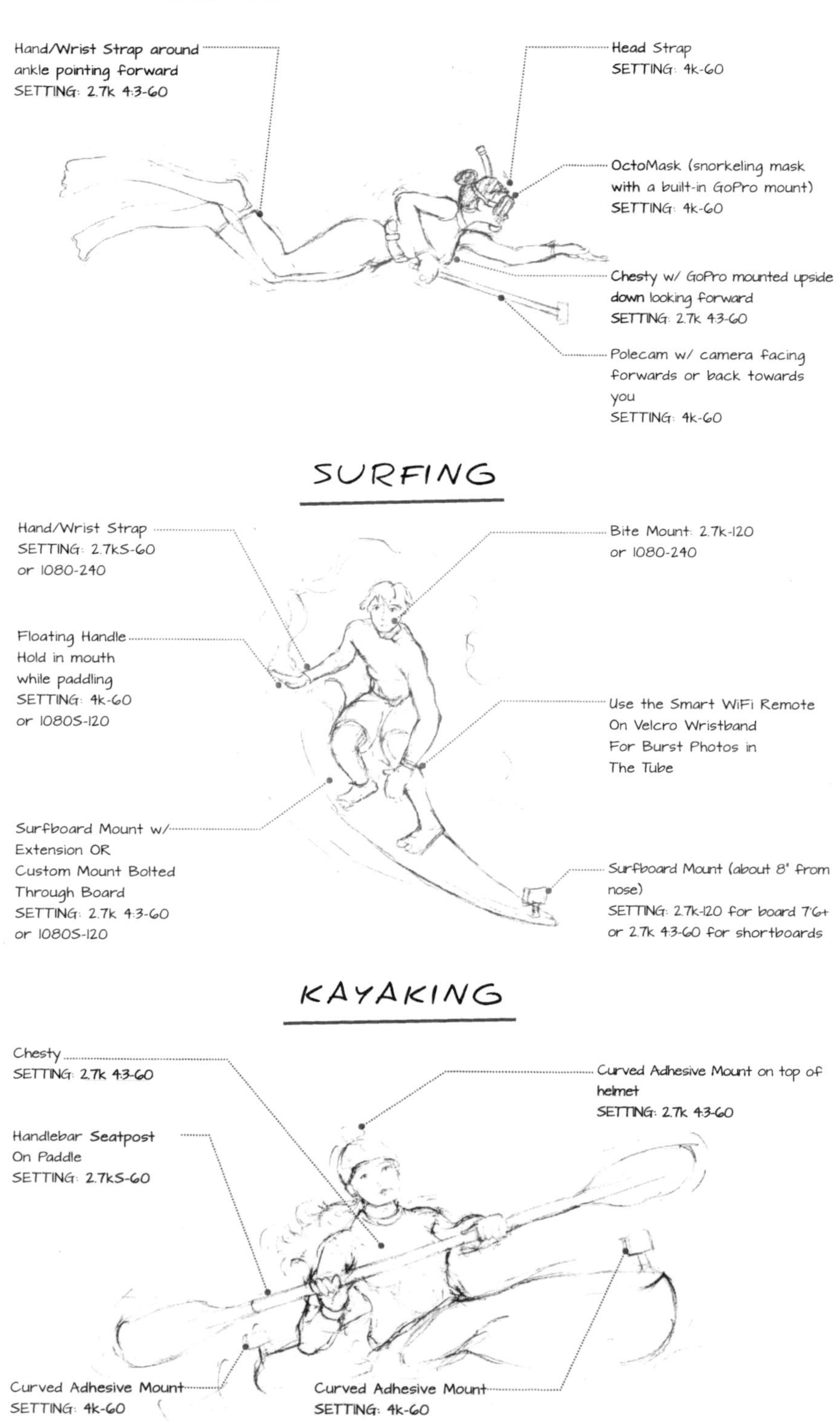

STAND UP PADDLING
Head Strap
(Flat Water Only)
SETTING: 4k-60
FLAT WATER
Suction Cup
SETTING: 4k-60
WAVERIDING
Surfboard Mount
SETTING: 2.7k-120
Chesty
SETTING: 2.7k 4:3-60
Handlebar Seatpost (for
waveriding)
SETTING: 2.7kS-60 OR
1080S-120
FLAT WATER
Suction Cup
SETTING: 4k 4:3-30
WAVERIDING
Surfboard Mount w/
extension
SETTING: 2.7k 4:3-60

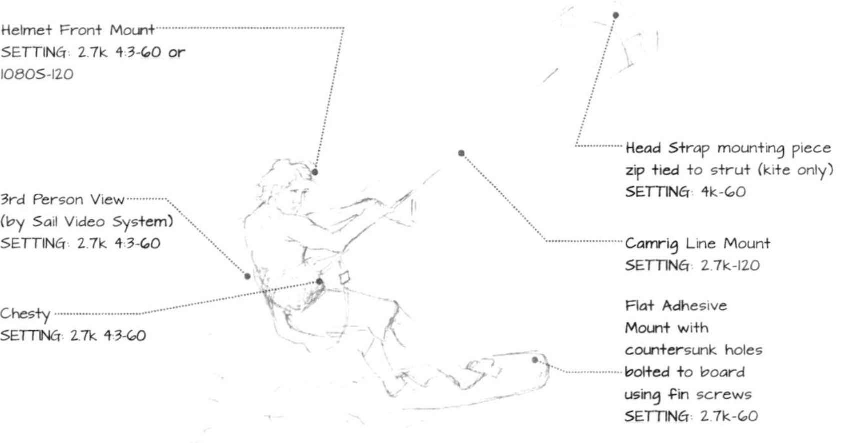
KITE/WAKEBOARDING
Helmet Front Mount
SETTING: 2.7k 4:3-60 or
1080S-120
3rd Person View
(by Sail Video System)
SETTING: 2.7k 4:3-60
Chesty
SETTING: 2.7k 4:3-60
Head Strap mounting piece
zip tied to strut (kite only)
SETTING: 4k-60
Camrig Line Mount
SETTING: 2.7k-120
Flat Adhesive
Mount with
countersunk holes
bolted to board
using fin screws
SETTING: 2.7k-60

LAND SPORTS

HIKING
Seeker Backpack
W/ 3-Way Pole
SETTING: 4k 4:3-30
Head Strap or The Strap
SETTING: 4k-30 (stabilization)
The Strap on backpack strap
or The Seeker Backpack
SETTING: 4k-30 (stabilization)
Chesty
SETTING: 4k-30 (stabilization)
Handle or Polecam (if you
have a free hand)
SETTING: 4k-60

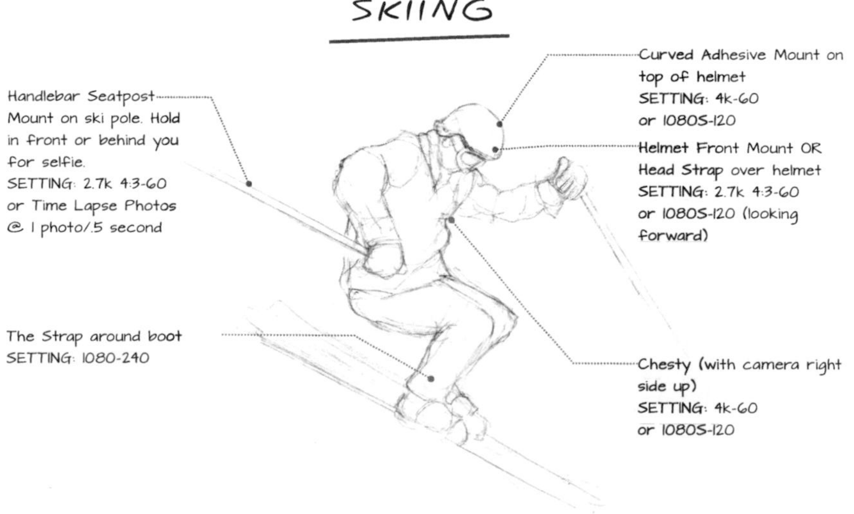
BIKING & MOTORCYCLE
Mountain, BMX & Road
Helmet Side Mount
SETTING: 2.7k 4:3-60 (with GoPro right side up or upside down)
Vented Helmet Strap or Curved Adhesive Mount on top of helmet
SETTING: 2.7k 4:3-60
Handlebar Seatpost Mount
SETTING: 2.7k 4:3-60
Chesty w/ GoPro upside down tilted up
SETTING: 2.7k 4:3-60
Roll Bar Mount
SETTING: 2.7k-120
Handlebar Seatpost Mount
SETTING: 4k-60

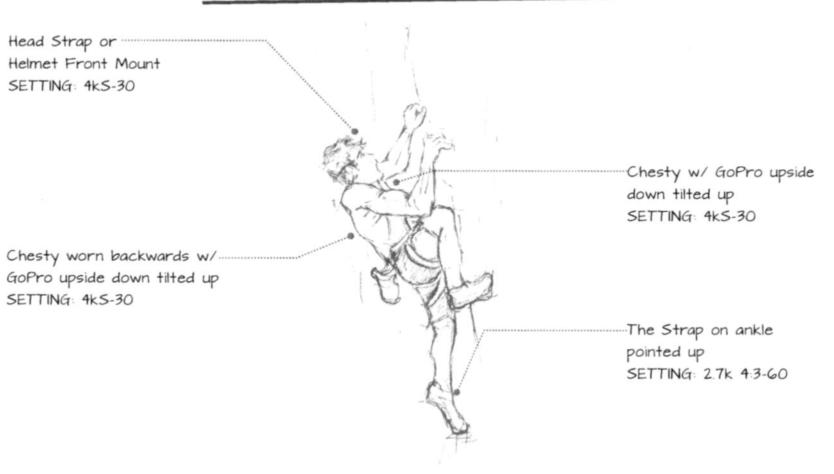
ROCK CLIMBING
Head Strap or Helmet Front Mount
SETTING: 4kS-30
Chesty w/ GoPro upside down tilted up
SETTING: 4kS-30
Chesty worn backwards w/ GoPro upside down tilted up
SETTING: 4kS-30
The Strap on ankle pointed up
SETTING: 2.7k 4:3-60

SNOW SPORTS

SKIING
Curved Adhesive Mount on top of helmet
SETTING: 4k-60
or 1080S-120
Handlebar Seatpost Mount on ski pole. Hold in front or behind you for selfie.
SETTING: 2.7k 4:3-60
or Time Lapse Photos @ 1 photo/.5 second
Helmet Front Mount OR Head Strap over helmet
SETTING: 2.7k 4:3-60
or 1080S-120 (looking forward)
The Strap around boot
SETTING: 1080-240
Chesty (with camera right side up)
SETTING: 4k-60
or 1080S-120

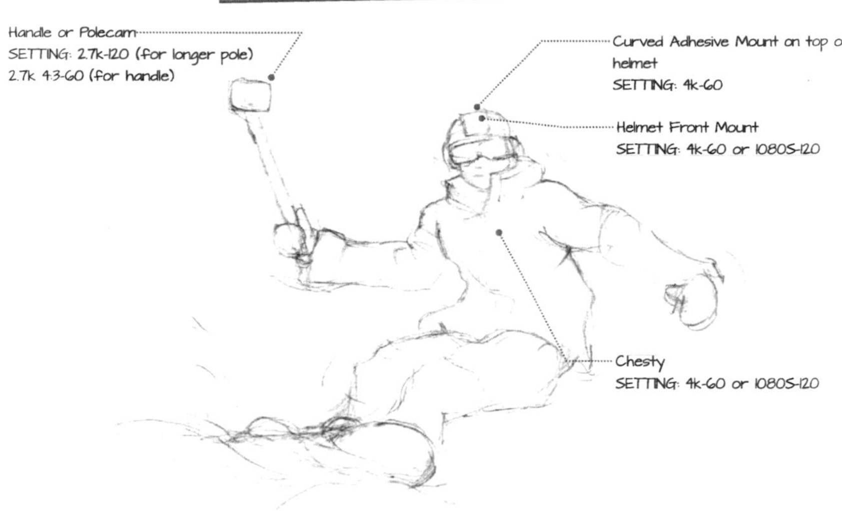

AIR SPORTS

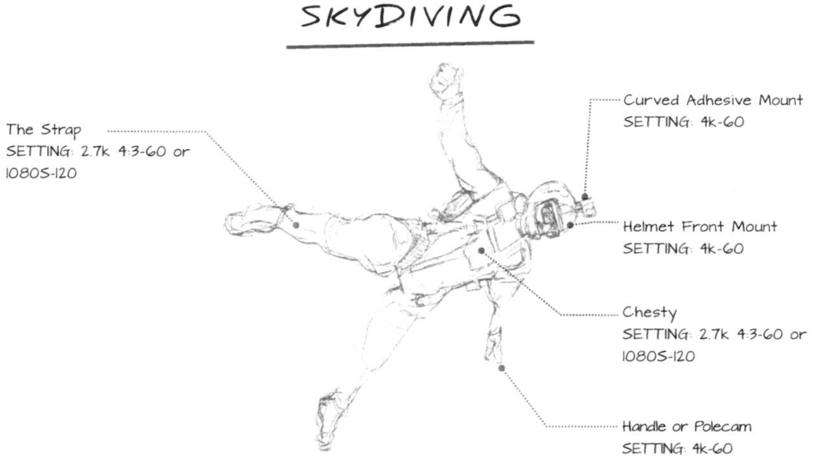

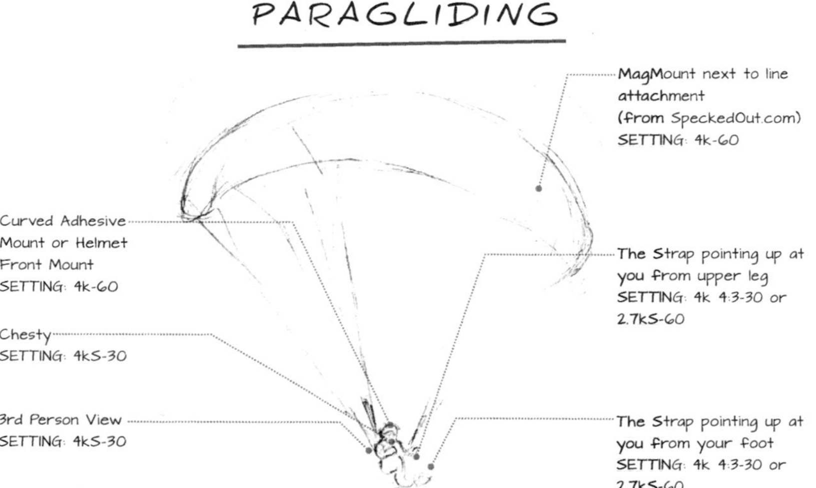

Now that you've got your camera mounted, you are ready to move onto Step 4 to learn some vital photography and cinematography knowledge!

STEP FOUR
CAPTURE YOUR ACTION

Learn These "Not-So-Secret" Photography Secrets & Get Results

Now that your camera is set up and ready, it's time to hit that record button. Whether you are shooting video or photos, there are a few important elements that are (almost) always part of a memorable photograph or video. The shooting tips in this step will help you capture the footage you know your HERO6 Black is capable of- the kind of immersive, exciting videos and photos that motivated you to get your camera in the first place.

TELL A STORY

When you are thinking about different shots for your video, remember that you want to tell a story. If you want to make a video that grabs your viewers' attention, **start thinking about your video before you are out there in the action**. The best GoPro videos inspire us and motivate us to go adventure by telling a story, showing the action, and leaving on a high note.

FILM THE PREP

Instead of just recording the main activity, film the preparation- show the beforehand when you are getting your gear ready for the adventure or a pulled back shot of you leaving for your destination. Film a zoomed in close-up when you are putting on your gear or prepping your important equipment.

RECORD THE ACTION

This is where you can record some or all of the angles shown in this book of the main activity. This is where you show off your skills with high action shots or beautiful scenery.

MAKE THE ANGLES A MYSTERY

When possible, try to film multiple angles of the same action without seeing any other cameras in the scene. This keeps the viewer involved in the action, not in the filming techniques.

CLOSE WITH A BANG

Close your video with a dramatic point of view shot that leaves your viewer wanting more, or better yet, wanting to go out there and do what you are doing- having fun!

LIGHTING

In the eyes of most photographers and videographers, lighting is everything. Sometimes the radical action captured with point of view cameras can overpower less than optimal lighting, but good lighting ALWAYS makes a shot look better.

Fortunately, the HERO6 Black is the best GoPro yet when it comes to producing high quality video in less than optimal light. The HERO6 Black uses a dynamic range (also known as global tone mapping), to automatically compensate for bright and dark areas. This results in more even-toned and vibrant videos straight out of the camera. But, not even the best GoPro can compensate completely.

Figuring out lighting with your mounted camera is especially tricky because you have to foresee how your lighting will be when you are filming. The way you see light in your footage changes dramatically depending on how you mount your camera and the angle you choose to shoot.

When you are preparing for your adventure, think about where the sun will be and what direction you will be facing during the most important times. Then consider what lighting scenario you want for your shot. When using GoPro® cameras, there are so many mounting techniques that there is almost always an angle that will capture the lighting you desire.

Wearable mounts offer the least amount of flexibility in regard to where you point your camera. A handheld polecam offers the most flexibility because you can adjust your angle to compensate for different lighting scenarios.

Here are some lighting situations you will come across:

THE GOLDEN HOUR (AKA THE MAGIC HOUR IN CINEMATOGRAPHY)

The Golden Hour refers to the hour around sunrise and sunset.

During this time, **lighting is softer and warmer**. Shadows are lighter and longer which can make for a dramatic effect. Sometimes, it can be difficult to keep your own shadow out of the shot during this time, but the results of shooting during these times usually pay off big time. Because the light is not as bright during the Golden Hour, follow the recommendations for "Low Light Situations" at the end of this Lighting section.

FRONT LIT LIGHTING

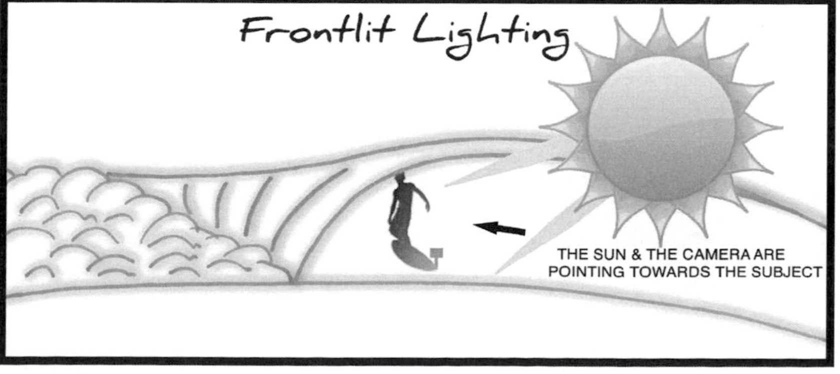

Front lit lighting is when **the light from the sun is on the subject's face** and the camera is between the sun and the subject. Front-lit lighting tends to make for the bluest skies and best scenic colors, but it also causes harsh shadows on people which can sometimes be less than flattering.

Front lit lighting is the rule that most of us have heard at least once and probably 100 times. "Have the sun behind you when you take a picture!" Front lit is one of the best ways to light a photograph. Depending on the orientation of your scene, front lit lighting can occur either through the morning or the evening hours.

BACKLIT LIGHTING

Backlit lighting is when the **sun is behind the subject**, usually causing the subject to be too dark against a bright background.

There are positive aspects of backlit lighting though. One is that there are no shadows on a person's face, which means a lot of portraits are taken during backlit conditions. Backlit photos in waves also bring out those green, moody photos where the light is shining through the water. This happens in the tube of the wave, so if you can get yourself in the right spot, the results can be beautiful.

The problem with filming in backlit lighting with a GoPro® camera is that the camera will take a "correct" exposure reading which often makes the subject too dark. To correct the exposure on your subject when backlit, you have to override the camera so that it overexposes the image (makes it brighter than the camera thinks it should be). See the next section on Exposure to learn how you can manually override your camera's exposure reading.

CLOUDY LIGHTING

Cloudy lighting is exactly like it sounds-capturing footage when there is no distinct angle of the sun because the **light is being diffused by the clouds**.

Especially when using a wide angle lens like the one on your HERO6 Black, filming when it is cloudy gives the footage a "white" look to it, so filming in cloudy conditions is not optimal. The footage won't have the same richness and color as a sunny day, but certain shots work well in cloudy conditions.

When filming in cloudy conditions, it's also helpful to zoom in for a narrower field of view to minimize the amount of sky in your frame.

Because cloudy lighting doesn't have shadows, you can still capture usable footage if you are filming an activity that would otherwise be going in and out of shadows, like skateboarding through a city or mountain biking through trees.

High thin clouds are A LOT different than grey clouds. High, thin clouds add nice texture in the sky without diminishing the light, so if there are high clouds in the sky, go for it!

MIDDAY LIGHTING

Midday Lighting is when **the sun is nearly directly overhead**, which happens for a relatively long period throughout the middle of the day.

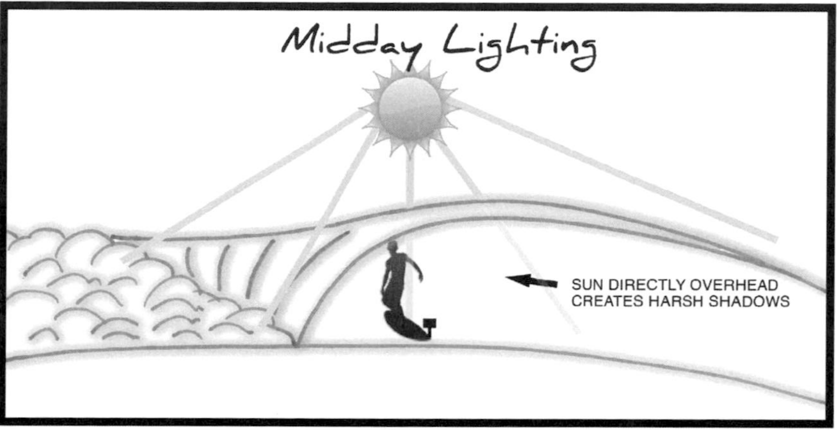

This is the worst option by almost all photographers' accounts. Harsh sun usually produces washed out colors and a lot of shadows. The best thing to do during midday lighting is to film in the shade. Or with a point of view camera, you can change the angle to minimize the harsh shadows of the midday sun. A helmet-mounted position looking down works well for midday lighting.

One exception is in the ocean where the water is really clear, like in Australia, the Caribbean or Hawaii. You can actually use the midday sun's rays to your advantage in clear water because those rays create some cool effects underwater and bring out the blue shades of the water.

FOR EXTRA DRAMATIC LIGHTING

When filming in shaded areas, for example under a canopy of trees or beneath tall buildings in the city, **look for light sources that sneak through to your lens periodically** in small amounts. These rays of light that come in and out of the trees or through gaps between buildings can add a lot of drama and mood to your video. For the best effect, compose your shots so the light comes toward your camera's lens. Also, a darker background creates more contrast. As you are filming, look for opportunities to let moody light enhance your scene.

When taking still photos, you can also use this type of lighting to enhance your composition. But with still photos, you can stop and let the light hit your lens in a more precise manner.

You can also add a similar effect in postproduction, using "light leak" overlays. Light leaks are slightly different, but they are commonly used as overlays to add drama to a scene. For some free light leak overlays, check out RocketStock's freebies (for Premiere Pro only). You can download the fully functional freebies from their website.

LOW LIGHT SITUATIONS

Filming in low light situations (early morning, evening, cloudy or shady), will often create blurry photos or videos.

For the best results when you are recording video **in low light situations, lower the frame rate to 24 or 30 frames per second**.

This lower frame rate allows your camera to take in more light for each frame, resulting in better quality footage. The higher frame rates (60FPS and higher) are better suited for normal daylight. You can also turn on Protune and **raise the ISO** anywhere from 1600-6400, but remember that a higher ISO results in video with more noise.

When taking photos, **avoid taking Burst Photos** in low light situations because your subject will often be blurred. In the other photo modes, try to keep your camera as stable as possible when you press the Shutter Button.

You can **use the low light to your advantage** to create a cool, blurred background effect. To obtain your subject in focus with a blurred background using Burst or Time Lapse photo modes, keep the primary subject stationary in relation to the camera and create movement in the background. For example, mount your camera to the front of a bike, pointing back at you so you and your camera move in unison. When you are recording in low light situations, the camera will not have enough light to keep the moving objects in focus. This will give your photos the blurred background effect. This technique works specifically well and looks really eye-catching for time lapse sequences and burst sequences.

EXPOSURE

Exposure refers to the amount of light that is let into your camera during recording. "Correct" exposure is usually a balance between overexposed (where there is a loss of detail in the bright, highlighted, areas) and underexposed (where there is a loss of details in the darker, shadowed areas). Getting correct exposure is easiest to capture in front-lit or sometimes cloudy conditions. If you are shooting in other lighting conditions, in most situations, you will want to adjust exposure in editing software after you film. For photos, using RAW or HDR will help capture detail in scenes with a lot of contrast.

By default, the HERO6 Black camera sets exposure automatically, however, there are **three ways you can affect the exposure**:

1) One way is to **use Exposure Control on the Touch Display** for tricky lighting conditions as mentioned in Step 2- Settings. Exposure Control enables you to adjust exposure for a specific area of the frame.

2) The second way to affect exposure is to use **Exposure Value Compensation** when Protune is turned on. You can adjust the exposure by telling the camera to make your video or photos up to two stops brighter (+2) or darker (-2). You can instantly see the effect of your changes on the Touch Display.

3) The third method is to use Shutter Speed and ISO lock to **manually set your exposure**, as you learned about in the Protune video and photo settings in Step 2. The Live View on your Touch Display is a great tool to determine to correct exposure.

ACTION

For GoPro® camera users, the action often speaks for itself. Unlike traditional photography, you've already chosen your angle by the way you mounted your camera. Now it's time for you to get some great action in front of your lens. The more intense the action, the better the results.

When filming, remember to **keep your camera steady and let the action create the movement**. With video shots, a steady camera helps create footage that is easy on the eyes- too much shaking in your hands and it becomes hard to watch.

When taking photos, a steady camera helps ensure that your photos will come out "sharp" and in-focus.

For editing purposes, it's easier to **turn the camera off in between "action" moments**. You can also **utilize HiLight Tagging** as described below. If it's too hard to reach your camera or your activity doesn't allow it, you can film continuously. It just means you will be searching through longer clips of footage later to find those "WOW" moments.

HILIGHT HILIGHT TAGGING

Finding your magic moments during a video clip can send you on a long search through your files. Taking advantage of a feature called HiLight Tag might just be your solution.

When something memorable happens while you are recording video or playing back video on the Touch Display, press the Mode Button on the side of your camera. Pressing this button will add a HiLight Tag. If you are using Voice Control, just say "GoPro HiLight", "Oh Sh*t", or "That was Sick".

Adding a HiLight Tag does not affect your video footage or add anything visible to the video.

You can also add HiLight Tags while recording with the GoPro App, Remo or the Smart WiFi Remote.

When you go to edit your video in Quik, GoPro Studio or the GoPro App, you can see the HiLight Tags on the video timeline so you know exactly where to go to find your magic moments.

FILMING TECHNIQUES

It's not really necessary for a recreational filmmaker to know the names of the various filming techniques, but an awareness of the various techniques will inspire you to add more flair to your videos. When you watch videos that inspire you, pay attention to what techniques the filmmaker used to make the video stand out and make an impression.

Since most recreational GoPro users don't have expensive filming equipment, it's best to make do with what you already have to mimic these techniques in the grassroots do-it-yourself GoPro style everyone loves. If you are interested in a gimbal, a gimbal makes all of these shots really smooth, eliminating the need for a tripod to film most of these shots.

TILT SHOT

This technique is like **looking up and then down** or vice versa. To film a tilt shot, point the camera up and then down by rotating it on its horizontal axis. This shot is typically filmed using a tripod. You can use the Tripod Mount to mount your HERO6 Black on a tripod if you are looking for a professional looking shot.

If you don't have a tripod or are on the go, you can **mimic a tilt shot** by holding your HERO6 Black camera with two hands and smoothly tilting the camera from top to bottom or vice versa.

PAN SHOT

A pan shot is similar to a tilt shot, except, instead of moving the camera up and down, a pan shot is **filmed in a side-to-side motion**, rotating the camera on its vertical axis from left to right or vice versa. This technique is like looking left and then right.

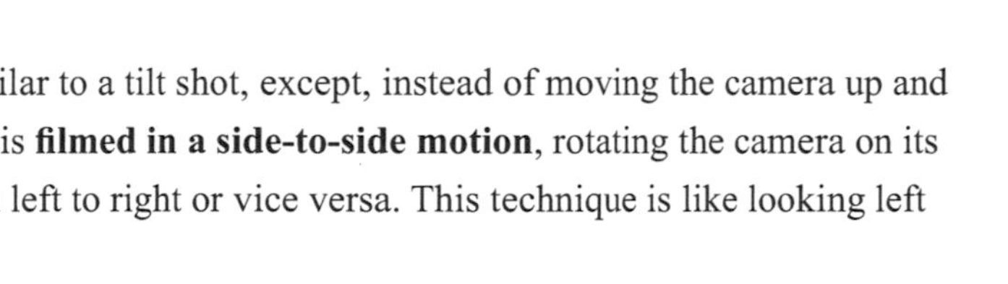

For eye-catching shots, rotate your camera from an empty scenic shot towards your subject, bringing your subject into the frame. Also, adding a panning motion to time lapses (using the Egg Timer) adds a nice touch of movement.

DOLLY

A dolly shot is typically filmed with the camera mounted on a camera dolly, **moving the camera towards or away from the subject**.

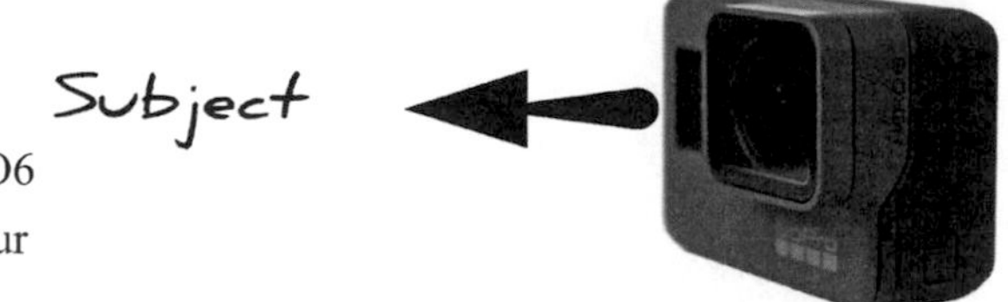

A gimbal makes this shot really easy without the use of a dolly. If you don't have a gimbal, you can mimic this technique by holding your HERO6 Black steady while moving your camera slowly towards or away from your subject. This filming technique looks great with stationary subjects for intros to a video.

TRACKING SHOT

In a tracking shot, the camera moves from left to right or vice versa, keeping the camera on the same axis to **move parallel with the subject**.

A great way to mimic this technique with your HERO6 is to hold the camera upside down on a pole or handle while riding a bike or skateboarding alongside your subject. The goal is to create smooth movement that moves with your subject. Include foreground objects in the shot for a real sense of movement.

FOLLOW SHOT

In a follow shot, the **camera physically follows the subject** at a (more or less) constant distance.

You can capture this angle of yourself by mounting your HERO6 on an extension to the back of your equipment, vehicle, etc. You can also ride behind someone on a skateboard, bike, snowboard or surfboard and follow your friend. For a steady shot, **use a polecam with your camera upside down** like shown in the Follow-Along Angle of the Handle / Polecam section.

CAPTURING AUDIO

The improved audio recording and controls on the HERO6 Black let you capture amazing high-quality footage with audio to match. The camera's internal audio recorder selects the best audio from the three microphones and compiles a stereo audio track.

Unlike previous GoPro cameras, which often had muffled audio, since the HERO6 Black doesn't require an external housing for waterproofing, the microphones are always open for clear audio.

After you go underwater, the microphone openings tend to hold some water. **Blow them off to remove the water** from the tiny holes to capture the clearest audio possible.

There are several options for recording audio, which were covered in Step 2- Settings, but here is a quick recap:

Manual Audio Control enables you to change settings for high wind or low wind situations, instead of letting the camera's internal recording system decide.

When you enable **RAW Audio**, which is found in Video Protune settings, your camera will record a separate .wav audio file, in addition to the video's audio file. You can choose how much internal processing you want for the audio- Low, Medium or High.

The in-camera audio quality on the HERO6 Black is really clear, but if audio quality is especially important to you- for an interview, YouTube clip, or whenever you need extra clear audio- consider using a pro-level **external microphone**. GoPro makes the Pro 3.5mm Mic Adapter that allows you to plug any 3.5mm microphone into your HERO6 camera. The connector plugs into the USB port so your camera is not waterproof when the external mic is attached, but you can access the port while it is mounted in the Frame with the door removed. Using a microphone is not possible while filming in the water.

UNDERSTAND YOUR LENS

The HERO6 Black comes with a built in Fisheye Wide Angle Lens. What does this mean? A fisheye lens is **an ultra wide-angle lens that allows more of the scene to be included in the frame**. Especially at the widest angle, fisheye lenses cause curvature of whatever is around the edges of the frame.

The linear field of view was created to minimize the fisheye effect, but you will find that Linear is not always the best option for your shots. The best thing to do is learn how to work with the fisheye lens.

A Fisheye Wide Angle Lens is perfect for a GoPro camera for several reasons:

1. The camera **can be mounted extremely close to you** and still capture you in the image.

2. The lens has a short depth of field, which means **everything that is about 12 inches from the camera and beyond will be in focus.** (See Step 7 for more about Macro Lenses if you want to film objects closer than 12 inches) This is great because you don't have to focus the camera.

It is important to understand the best techniques for using a fisheye lens because it is an art in itself.

Here are some vital tips:

1. GET CLOSE! If you aren't close to whatever you are filming, your subject will be very small in the frame. You know how some rear-view mirrors on cars say "Object May Be Closer Than They Appear". The same is true with fisheye lenses because they distort the perspective to make things look smaller than they look with the naked eye. Remember this and get closer to your subject than you think you would need to.

2. The middle of the frame has the least amount of distortion, so frame your images with the distortion in mind.

If the horizon is towards the top or bottom of the frame, it will have a curved appearance. You can remove the fisheye effect in postproduction, as you will learn in Step 5, but you also lose a bit of the content around the edges of your frame.

3. **Use the foreground to your advantage.**

By having some sort of object near the foreground, it will **give your image more depth.** Your arm, helmet, board, or foot make good foreground objects to create that sense of perspective. You can even create a cool look by "framing" your image with a foreground object.

4. Work with the sky, instead of against it.

Because wide angle lenses capture so much in the frame, high clouds and sunset colors in the sky add a lot of drama to a scene. When the sky is gray, try zooming in for a narrower FOV.

PUSHING THE SHUTTER

One last thing when it comes to capturing the action is that when shooting photos, the camera **beeps when the camera takes the photo**, which makes sense. **But if you are shooting RAW or HDR, the camera beeps again after the camera has processed the image**. Because of this many people understandably think that there is a delay.

In **Single Photo Mode and Time Lapse Mode**, your camera actually takes the photo **as soon as you press the Shutter Button**. In **Burst Mode**, there is about a **.5 second delay** between when you push the Shutter Button and when your camera begins taking photos. In **Night Photo and Night Lapse Mode**, there is about a **2 second delay** to reduce camera shake.

When shooting self-portrait action photos in the Burst Mode, the Smart WiFi Remote or Remo is especially useful. With video, you can record continuously during the action, but with self-portrait action photos, you need to push the Shutter Button at the exact right moment. The remote can also be used to continuously take photos in Single Photo Mode for as long as you hold down the Shutter Button (as long as HDR or RAW are disabled). For more WiFi Remote tips and ideas, see the WiFi Remote section in Step 7- Beyond the Basics!

ACTION SEQUENCE TIPS

An action sequence is made by **editing together multiple photos to show your subject moving across the photo**. When shooting a photo sequence with the goal of creating an action sequence, **set up your shot so that your subject moves across the frame**. Pull back your camera a bit from the subject so that your subject can enter the photo on one side of the frame and exit on the other side of the frame. You need to have enough side-to-side distance so that you can have a few different images of your subject without overlapping.

For the easiest editing, **set your camera up on a tripod** or propped up on the ground so that the scene remains the same and your subject is the only thing that moves.

In Burst Mode, there is about .5 second lag time between when you push the Shutter Button and when your camera takes the photo, so push the Shutter Button a little before the action to get your subject in the frame.

Even when you are recording fast action, such as running, jumping, skateboarding, biking, snowboarding, etc., you can usually **spread out the sequence to take 30 photos over 3 seconds**, unless the action is really fast.

For Burst Mode photos, you will need to **film in bright daylight** to give your camera enough light to take sharp photos. If you find that your photos are turning out blurry, the most common problem is that there is not enough light for your camera to shoot such a fast sequence without getting blurred shots.

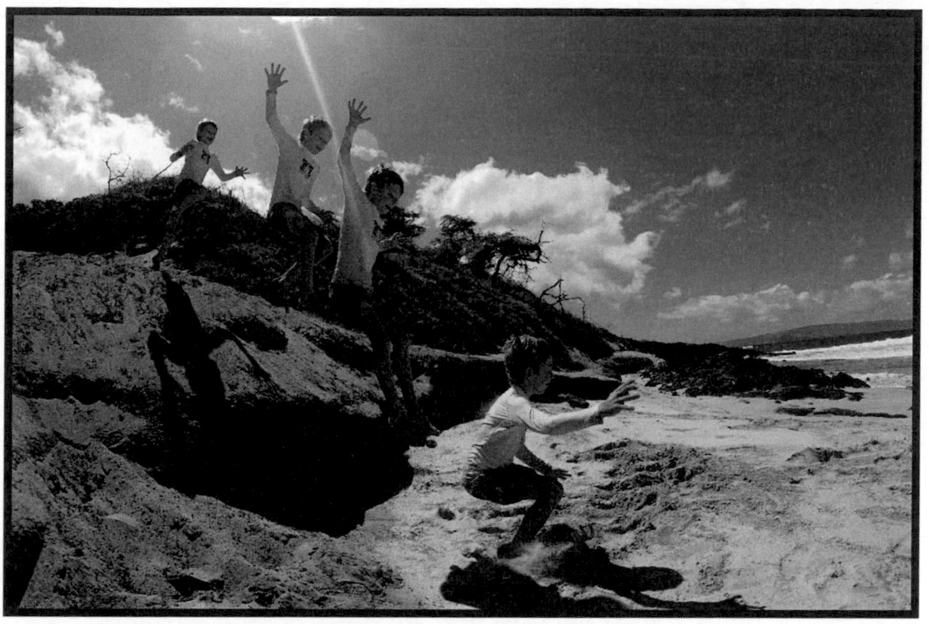

Photos taken on the HERO6 Black Edition in Burst Mode at a rate of 30 photos over 2 seconds at 100 ISO.

As an alternative to Burst Mode, you can **use 4k 4:3 @ 30 FPS to record video and pull still frames** as needed. This works especially well for self-portrait action clips so you don't have to worry about pressing the Shutter button right before the action.

For slower action, such as hiking, **set your camera on Time Lapse Mode** at one photo every .5 seconds. This will ensure that your camera continues shooting until your subject has completely crossed the frame.

See Step 5- Editing An Action Sequence for step-by-step instructions on how to put together your own action sequence.

MAKE YOUR TIME LAPSES STAND OUT

In addition to using Time Lapse Video or Photo Modes to create a time lapse video, you can also speed up regular video footage for time lapse clips. Speeding up regular speed video footage to create a time lapse effect takes up more computer memory during editing and fills up your video card faster so it is not ideal for long duration time lapses. However, it can be useful for short time lapse clips. See the tip at the end of editing a time lapse video in Step 5 to learn how you can make any video look like a time lapse.

Because time lapses are time-consuming to record, when possible, set up your time lapse shot using the Touch Display screen to preview the composition. If you are using an egg timer or camera slider (see below), look at the beginning shot, but also make sure the composition looks good at the end of the movement.

When recording extended time lapses, you can use an external power supply, like the Heavy Metal 5500 or GoPro's Portable Power Supply, which powers your camera through the USB cable. If using an external power supply with your camera mounted in the Frame, remove the side door for access to the USB port on your camera.

Although your camera should be mounted in a stable position when recording footage for a time lapse, adding movement gives time lapse shots a professional look. A few simple techniques can be used to create this slow-moving effect.

USE AN EGG TIMER

The Egg Timer Mount (as described in the Custom Mounts in Step 3 - Mounting) will give your time lapse shots a rotating movement that creates a cool effect.

USE A CAMERA SLIDER

A camera slider provides a smooth track to move your camera from left to right or vice versa during a time lapse.

You can make your own camera slider or buy one (they aren't cheap), but for a really good time lapse, you will need to add a mechanism for it to steadily and slowly move across the slider. For short time lapse shots, a string and some patience is one cheap and easy way to do this. Or you can use a gimbal, and more patience, to slowly and manually move your camera.

MORE TIME LAPSE IDEAS

• Record an artist making a drawing or a painting. Choose a relatively short interval depending on the predicted time of the project. 1 frame every 2 seconds would work well for a 45 min to 1 hour-long art project.

• Mount your camera to the back of a standup paddleboard for a downwind paddle or a bike for trail ride. Try to get a stationary object in the foreground, like the board or a bike seat so you don't make your viewers dizzy. The moving action in the background makes for an exciting action time lapse. Short intervals typically work well for action time lapses.

• Film the sunset at the beach or lake. Try to choose a day with scattered clouds, and it's even better if the clouds are moving quickly through the sky. The movement of the clouds, the reflections on the water and the dwindling light will create dramatic time lapse clips. Try to frame your shot so there is some movement close to the foreground, like breaking waves or trees blowing in the wind. Because of the wide-angle lens on the HERO6, movement that is far off in the distance won't make much of an impact.

• Stand out in a crowd. Film a crowded area with the subject standing still in the middle. Record in video mode with a slower shutter speed to create extra blur around the subject. When you speed it up, the subject will look like an island of calm in a sea of movement.

MAKE A HYPERLAPSE

A time lapse is typically filmed from one stationary position or with very slow, steady movement. A hyperlapse, on the other hand, is filmed by moving the camera's location between every frame. To film a hyperlapse, keep your camera fixed at a certain point or object as you move. A short interval of .5 or 1 second will allow you to move quickly and get a lot of shots in a short period of time. Remember, since each photo will be one frame in your video, you will need a lot of photos to make a short video clip.

TIPS TO EXTEND BATTERY LIFE

The HERO6 Black uses a built-in rechargeable 1220mAh lithium-ion battery that should give you about **1.5-2.5 hours of continuous recording time** depending on a few factors. See the chart below for approximate battery life of continuous recording in various video resolutions. Battery recording times will be less in cold weather.

VIDEO RESOLUTION	ESTIMATED RECORDING TIME
4k-60	1:10
4k-30	1:40
2.7k-120	1:00
1440-60	1:15
1080-240	1:00
1080-120	1:05
1080-60	1:40

The battery can be recharged by connecting your camera to a computer or USB-charging device via the included USB cable.

You can also use the GoPro Auto Charger or Wall Charger. If you decide to use your phone's charger, the HERO6 Black requires **a charger that outputs 5V and 1A** so check your charger before you connect it to your GoPro. Using the wrong charger could potentially damage your camera.

The Black is compatible with external USB power, so if you want to use an external USB power source like GoPro's Portable

Power Supply or the Heavy Metal 5500, you can run off external power for an extended amount of time.

Unlike NiCad batteries, Lithium batteries don't have a memory charge, so **recharging your battery even if it is not completely drained will not reduce the battery life**. Like all lithium-ion batteries, the battery in your HERO6 will eventually lose some capacity over time, so a fresh battery may be your best bet if you notice that your battery is not performing like it used to.

Follow these additional tips to preserve your battery's life:

• **Store your camera at a normal room temperature** when possible. Try to keep your battery out of extreme heat, especially when it is fully charged. Keeping your camera (with the battery in it) in a hot car will deteriorate your battery's capacity.

• If you need to store a spare battery for an extended period, use it until about 40% battery life remains and store the battery in sealed bag in the refrigerator.

There are several things you can do to preserve battery life while actively using your HERO6:

• If you know you won't be filming for a while, **turn your camera off to save battery**. Your camera will go into standby mode after about five minutes of inactivity. This standby mode greatly reduces the amount of battery that is being used. But if you know you won't be filming for a while, it's easy to hold down the side Mode button to turn off your camera or say "GoPro Turn Off" so that it doesn't use any of the battery life.

• **QuikCapture Mode reduces any standby time** by turning your camera on and recording with one push of the button. There is a delay however while you wait for your camera to turn on, so QuikCapture Mode doesn't work for all filming scenarios.

• **Turn off the WiFi if you are not using it**. The WiFi uses some battery power to create the wireless signal. Keeping the WiFi on is worth the reduction in battery life as long as you are using the WiFi Remote or the GoPro App. But, if you are not using either of those, turn off the WiFi in the Connect dialog found in the top tray on the Touch Display.

• The Touch Display uses up a good chunk of battery. If you are using the Touch Display often and don't need it to be so bright, you can reduce the screen brightness on the Preferences menu. If you are primarily using the Touch Display to set up your shots, **let the screen go to sleep after you have composed your angle** and tightened your camera in place.

Now that you have the knowledge to capture your footage, get out there and start filming! In Step 5, you will learn how to edit your photos, videos and time lapse clips!

STEP FIVE
CREATION

Now It's Time To Put It All Together

So, now you've got the footage! This should be the exciting part and with our help, it will be! There are so many fun, creative ways to edit your videos and photos! Creating your edited product is where a lot of GoPro® camera users get lost and this is why so many people have thousands of unedited photos and hours of uncut footage stored on their hard drives. But it should be where you get excited because this is where you get to create! Follow this advice and you will soon be able to show everyone how much fun you are having and encourage them to get out there too!

BEFORE YOU START EDITING

TRANSFERRING FOOTAGE TO YOUR COMPUTER

To begin viewing and editing your GoPro footage, you need to transfer your videos and photos from the microSD card in your camera to your computer. We will cover transferring and editing on your phone or tablet at the end of this video editing section.

The easiest way to transfer your GoPro files to a computer and keep them organized is to use the free Quik For Desktop.

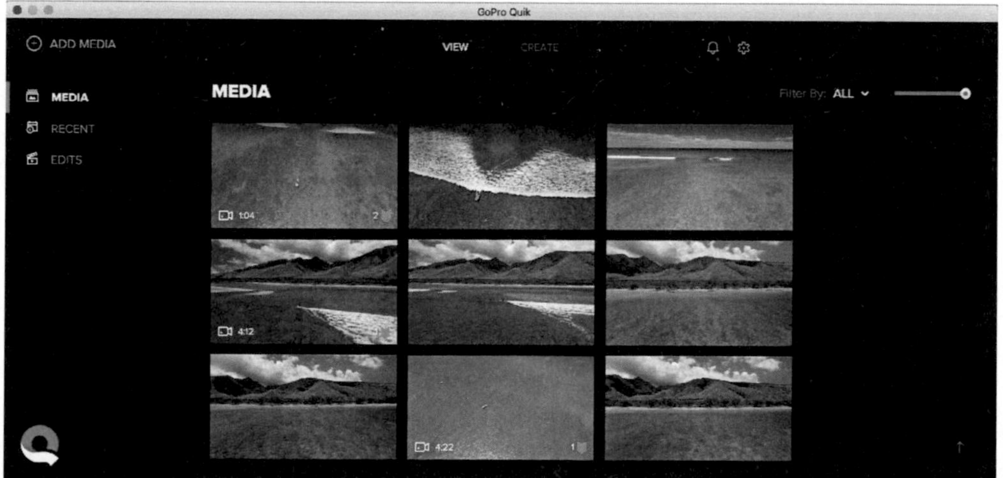

Quik for Desktop keeps your files grouped together the way you recorded them and organizes them by camera, which is useful if you own more than one GoPro. For example, if you took 500 photos in Time Lapse Mode, Quik for Desktop keeps them together as one file for organization purposes. You can still access each individual photo, but you don't have to sort through so many files to find the ones you want.

If you were to transfer these files without using the App, each photo would be shown as an individual file, creating an organizational headache.

You need to set up a free User account through GoPro (with a user name and password) to use Quik for Desktop. You can download Quik for Desktop from GoPro's website at gopro.com/shop under Apps. This software works for Mac and PC.

If you sign up for a GoPro Plus account, which is GoPro's subscription cloud service, you can access your files on any computer or device.

Make it easy on yourself and **follow the steps below** to utilize Quik for Desktop **to transfer your GoPro footage to your computer.**

Step 1: With your camera turned off, **connect your camera to your computer** with a USB cable. You will see a red LED light once it is connected.

Step 2: **Press the Power/Mode Button on the side of your camera** and Quik for Desktop should open automatically.

Important Note: If you are having problems locating your microSD card when your camera is connected to your computer, remove the card from your camera. Insert the card into the adapter and insert the adapter into the SD Card slot on your computer. Quik for Desktop will still recognize your files as GoPro files.

Step 3: An image of the HERO6 Black will show up on your screen. **Click Import Media** to import your files.

Step 4: **View your transferred pictures and videos.** The pictures and videos you just transferred will be organized by date in Quik for Desktop. You can also use the filters at the top right to only view videos, photos or HiLights. Double-click on a video or photo to view it. Be aware that Burst and Time Lapse photos won't preview in full resolution, but the actual files are high quality. (If you are experiencing choppy video playback, refer to the troubleshooting section at the end of this book for solutions.)

Step 5: **Now you are ready to start editing.**

TIP: Split Video Files. Be aware that your camera will automatically split long video files into multiple video files. On the Black, files will be split once the file size reaches 4GB, which is after about 8 or 9 minutes if you are recording at 4k-30. Lower resolution videos will record for a longer period before splitting. There is no interruption during recording and the time counter on your camera will show the total time recorded, regardless of how many files are created.

The reason for these split files is for compatibility with the FAT32 formatting usually used within the camera, which is limited to a 4GB maximum file size.

Split videos can be seamlessly stitched back together in GoPro Studio or any other video editing software and you won't lose any video time.

STORAGE

Your GoPro files are going to require a lot of storage space. You will probably want to **dedicate an external hard drive to your GoPro files** (or at least a big block of memory). How much storage you need really depends on how often you use your camera, but a portable 2TB hard drive is a good starting point. Go bigger if you can. An external hard drive is the easiest way to keep your full resolution files on hand. You can also use GoPro Plus cloud storage, but the video files stored on GoPro Plus are reduced to 1080p video resolution. And remember to always back up your files to cloud storage or another external hard drive because you don't want to lose all of your hard-earned memories.

TIP: Changing the import location for your files. If you choose to use Quik for Desktop to import your files, you can set the import location to your external hard drive by selecting the Settings (Gear) icon on the top right bar of Quik for Desktop. If you move your external hard drive around from computer to computer, the files will not automatically show up in your Quik media on a different computer. To add the files to your media, Click Settings in the top right and Scan the hard drive where the new files are located.

DELETING FILES

To prevent the accidental loss of files, your micro SD card is set as Read-Only. When your camera is plugged into the computer with a USB cable, you can copy your files from your camera into your computer's hard drive, but you do not have the ability to delete files from the micro SD card. Instead, if you want to format (erase all files) from the micro SD card, you can use one of the following options:

Use the Format SD Card Option on the Camera

1. After you have copied the files from your camera to your computer, swipe down on the Touch Display to bring up the Preferences Menu.
2. Scroll to the bottom of the Preferences until you see the Format SD Card option. Tap Format SD Card.
3. The screen will ask if you want to Delete all files. Tap Delete.

Use Quik for Desktop

When your camera is connected during import, under the Settings icon next to the image of the HERO6 Black, you can choose the option to "Automatically delete files from camera after importing".

Use the GoPro App

You can copy and delete files using your smartphone or tablet.

To erase individual files:

1. With your camera's WiFi enabled and your camera connected to the GoPro App, select the GoPro Media Icon (the grid) in the App.
2. When you select a video or photo file, tap the Trash Can Icon to erase that specific file. You can erase video files, a batch of Time Lapse or Burst photos, or individual photos from a Time Lapse or Burst sequence.

To format your camera's memory card (which erases all of the photos and videos) using the GoPro App:

1. With your camera's WiFi enabled and your camera connected to the GoPro App, select the Settings Icon.
2. In the Settings Menu, under the heading Delete, you can choose to Delete the Last File or Delete All Files from SD Card.

VIDEO EDITING

VIDEO EDITING SOFTWARE

The video-editing tutorials in this chapter, Editing Your Video, Editing a Time Lapse Video and Pulling Frame Grabs, use GoPro's free editing software called GoPro Studio. GoPro recently stopped providing support for GoPro Studio because they are planning to incorporate GoPro Studio's editing features into Quik for Desktop, but these changes are not available yet. Although GoPro stopped offering support for GoPro Studio, until they fully incorporate the editing tools into Quik for Desktop, **GoPro Studio still provides the best free editing option specifically for GoPro videos**.

You can **download GoPro Studio 2.5 for free** from third party websites. One good source for downloading GoPro Studio is TechSpot.com. Make sure to download version 2.5 for the most up-to-date editing tools.

GoPro Studio does have some problems with crashing, so the best way to utilize these GoPro-specific features is to **edit a few clips at a time, save often and export them**. If you have any problems running the software, or with the software crashing, make sure your computer meets the minimum operating requirements, is running the current operating system, and has plenty of hard drive space.

For alternative free editing software and assembling longer videos, try iMovie for Mac or VSDC for Windows.

GoPro also offers two free mobile editing apps- Splice and Quik- so you can produce videos straight from your phone or tablet. You will learn how to apply your new editing knowledge to these apps as well.

PRE-EDITING IN QUIK- Creating Clips and Adding GPS Gauge Overlays.

There are several "pre-editing" tools available in Quik for Desktop to prepare your files for editing. After you double click to preview a video clip, there are **four options** at the bottom of the Quik screen.

• Tap the Scissors Icon **to trim** a video clip from a longer clip. The slider allows you to custom trim a video to any length. This will create an additional video file with the new clip and won't affect the original. If you want to add GPS overlay gauges to your trimmed clip, turn on the gauges before exporting the clip.

• The circular arrows icon allows you to **rotate your videos** or photos if needed to correct the orientation.

• Tap the image icon to **pull a still image** from your video.

• The fourth icon **turns on gauges**, such as Info (distance, altitude, elevation gain and date/time), Speed, G-Force, and the path you traveled. GPS must have been enabled when the video was recorded to use this feature. All of the gauges can be resized and repositioned on your video.

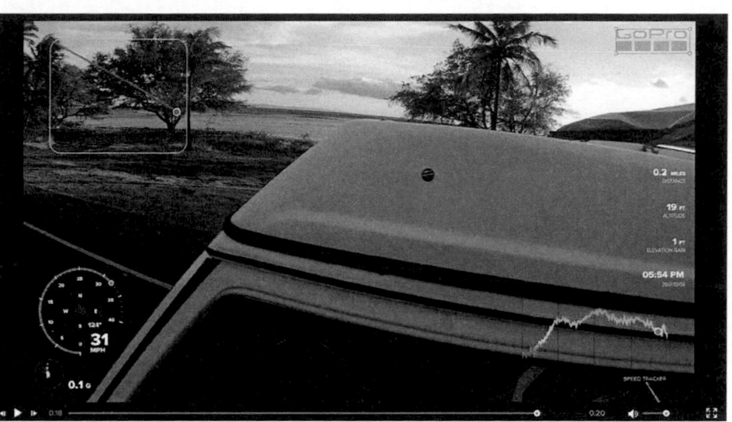

Use Quik to add GPS data overlays to your

TIP: IMPORTANT WORKAROUND FOR HEVC FILES: GoPro Studio does not support HEVC files. To edit an HEVC clip in GoPro Studio, trim the file first in the Quik for Desktop App. The newly created file can be opened in GoPro Studio.

EDITING YOUR VIDEO

This is one simple way to edit your footage. There are lots of options when it comes to video editing. But the goal of this section is to help you get your first edited clip of GoPro footage using FREE software and to understand the basics of video editing.

This video editing tutorial uses GoPro Studio because it gives you the most precise control when conforming your videos for smooth slow motion and allows you to combine clips, music and titles all within one program.

If you are using Premiere Pro CC or Final Cut Pro, similar editing techniques can be used and some tips for these programs will be offered throughout the editing section.

Here are some tips when you first start to think about how you are going to edit a clip:

• **Have a vision** for your finished product. If you plan to put together a video, create a storyboard or timeline to plan ahead and look for the pieces you need.

• **Bookmark** your edit worthy moments. If you weren't able to use the HERO6's HiLight Tagging feature while you were recording, you can add HiLights in Quik for Desktop as you view your videos. The HiLight tags should transfer all the way through to GoPro Studio. That way you won't have to look through hours of "in between" time for the clips you want to use.

• **Erase files as you go**. If you look through a video clip and see that there is nothing usable, erase it as you go. You will have lots of files to sort through, so the more you can thin out your library, the easier it will be to find your usable clips.

Follow these step-by-step instructions to create your first edited GoPro video:

#1- Select the Video Files To Use and Open Them in GoPro Studio

1. After transferring the GoPro files to your computer using Quik for Desktop, sort through your footage for two or three video clips you want to use for this tutorial. Hold Command (Mac) or Ctrl(PC) to select your desired clips.

2. With the clips highlighted, right click (Ctrl+Click-Mac) and select "Open in Studio".

#2- Select Desired Clip, File Size and Playback Speed

1. Save your project as you go along by clicking File>Save Project. Saving often will prevent you from losing any work if the program unexpectedly quits.

2. Click on the first clip you want to edit to bring it into the editing window.

3. If you recorded the clip upside down, you can push the Rotate/Flip box to automatically flip your footage right side up.

4. Search through the clip by pushing "Play," finding your HiLights (if you added any) or by sliding the timebar to find the "WOW" moment you want to extract.

5. Click on the "Mark In Point" below the video frame to choose where you want your clip to start. You can push pause at the exact frame you want to start with and then push the Mark In symbol. This will leave off anything before that selected point.

6. Play the clip or slide along the timebar and click on the "Mark Out Point" at the point where you want to end the clip. This will leave out everything after that point.

7. Click on "Advanced Settings" on the bottom left below the video clip.

8. Under "Advanced Settings", there are three settings you should adjust.

a. Choose Image Size (for now, you can leave it at the same size it was shot).

> **TIP:** If you change the image size, make sure to keep it in the same aspect ratio as it was filmed. Otherwise, GoPro Studio will stretch the video to make it conform to the other aspect ratio. If you prefer to crop your clip to a 16:9 Aspect Ratio, you can crop your clips in Step 2 of GoPro Studio (Read on to learn how to crop).

b. Frame Rate. If you want the clip to play at normal speed, you can keep it at the original frame rate. If you want the clip to play in slow motion, this is where you make it happen by choosing a slower frame rate than what you shot the footage at. If you recorded at a high frame rate and want your video to play in slow motion, try to avoid going below 24(23.98) FPS if possible. There are more advanced methods (like using Flux which you will learn about shortly) to produce super slow motion clips from footage recorded without a high frame per second rate.

TIP: You can also adjust the playback speed of the video in Step 2, under Video, but changing the frame rate in Step 1 is a more precise way of making sure your video is playing at 24 FPS.

c. Quality- Depending on how you plan to display your clip, you should choose Medium or High.

9. Save your new clip as a new file name in the empty white box below the frame.

10. Click the blue "Add Clip to Conversion List" at bottom right.

11. Repeat steps 2-8 with the other clips you want to put in your video.

12. Click "Convert" at the bottom right.

#3- Edit the Appearance of the Individual Clips

1. Click on "Proceed to Step 2".

2. When the program asks you to choose an edit template, choose "Blank Template" and click the blue "Create" button. "Step 2 Edit" on the top bar should now be highlighted.

3. In the box on the left, click on the first clip you just converted to bring it into the editing window. When you have the clip on the left highlighted, any edits you make will be to that clip. (Make sure the ProTune preset is turned off because it will oversaturate your video footage.)

4. Scroll down the tool bar on the right side and under Image, you can adjust Exposure, Contrast, Saturation and Sharpness. Be careful not to get too carried away because too much of these can make your image look doctored, especially when using the Saturation slider. You can also try out GoPro Studio's presets on the very bottom of the bar. If the colors look oversaturated to start with, under Presets choose "None" to make sure no presets were automatically applied.

5. Under "Framing Controls", you can adjust Zoom, Positioning and other options. Try these out for your knowledge and see if any of them improve the look of your clip, but be aware that zooming in can reduce the quality of your edited footage.

TIP: If you shot your footage in a 4:3 Aspect Ratio (4k 4:3, 2.7k 4:3, or 1440p), you can use the "4x3 to Wide" preset which will give your footage a similar look to a SuperView shot. This does not crop your clip, but rather scales and stretches it to make it fit into a Widescreen 16:9 Aspect Ratio. If you would prefer to crop your video to make it fit Widescreen without the distortion of the 4x3 to Wide preset, drag the clip to the storyboard to preview it in a Widescreen Aspect Ratio. Then, in the Framing dialog box, adjust the Vertical slider until you are happy with the cropping.

6. When finished editing the Appearance of your clip, move on to the next clip until you are happy with the appearance of the clips.

#4- Combine Clips, Add Music and Put Together your first Movie

1. To combine your clips, select each clip from the box on the left and drag the clips in the order you want them into the storyboard below. Drag them to the right of the video camera icon (where it says, "Drag Video Here"). You can rearrange the order by dragging the clips in the storyboard.

2. If you find the clips are too long or have unnecessary parts, you can fine tune the start and stop points for each clip from within the storyboard by using the Mark In and Mark Out Points button.

> **TIP: Multiple Speeds.** After dragging your clip into the storyboard, split the clip and speed back up certain parts to create more exciting action. Find a point of the clip where you want to speed back up the action and click on the "Split Clip at Current Position" button (to the left of the "Mark In Point" button) to split the clip. This will split the clip into two pieces. Then, click on the portion of the clip you want to speed back up, and in the Video dialogue on the right side, adjust the speed. The following percentages will bring your clip back to normal speed if you converted it to 24(23.98) FPS in Step 1. 250% for video shot at 60 FPS. 500% for video shot at 120 FPS. 1000% for video shot at 240 FPS. By speeding up certain parts, you can make the slow motion parts more dramatic and impactful.

> **TIP: Reverse Motion.** You can play your video in reverse by clicking on the "Reverse" box under the Video dialogue. To make it exciting, drag a clip into the storyboard twice and play the second one in reverse so the action plays back on itself.

3. Add transitions in between the action clips for a more professional look. Click on the "+" sign in between each clip to change it from a cut to a dissolve. (iMovie and Windows Live Movie Maker offer more transition options).

4. Add some titles to the beginning and end. Click the "+ Title" icon at the top of the left bar. When you click on the title "clip" that you just added in the bar to the left, you change the title text and appearance on the right side. Fill in the text in the preview box on the right to give it a title (Snowboarding Chile, e.g.). Once you are happy with the words and appearance, you can either: Drag the title "clip" onto the Video bar in the storyboard before the first clip for it to be a title screen on its own OR Drag it into the Title bar on the storyboard for it to show up over the video clip.

5. Add music to create the mood. At the top of the box to the left, click the Media icon to the left of the "+Title" icon. Add a song from your computer and drag the song into the Audio bar of the storyboard. You can adjust the length of the song by clicking on the song in the storyboard and dragging the end to match the end of your video clips. If you don't want the original audio from the video clips in the background along with the music, you can click on the audio icon that is on the video clip thumbnail in the storyboard to turn off the clip's audio.

6. Press the Spacebar to preview your edited movie and make any changes.

7. When you are happy with your edited video, click on Step 3: Export. This will bring up the export dialogue. If you edited a Widescreen 16:9 video, under the Presets, select HD 1080p or HD 720p and export the finished video. To export 4k video (best for footage filmed in 2.7k and 4k), select Custom and under Image Size, select 4k. To export video at a Standard 4:3 aspect ratio, under the Image Size tab, select Source. You now have your first GoPro® video clip!

> **TIP: Preparing Files For YouTube.** When producing videos for YouTube, you can upload either 1080p or 4k (called 2160p on YouTube) resolution videos. The YouTube uploader will automatically detect your video resolution and give viewers resolution options to suit their device.

TIP: If you want to get even deeper into how GoPro Studio Software works, go to GoPro.com and under the Support Tab>Product Manuals, you can access a pdf version of the GoPro Studio manual. The Studio Manual has tons of helpful information.

*After you become comfortable with GoPro Studio, you may want a program like Final Cut or Premiere that has more capabilities, but to begin with, GoPro Studio will give you a good intro into video editing.

MUSIC TIP: When you are putting together a video for YouTube, you must have permission to use music. There are a few sites that give you permission to use their songs for free (they usually ask that you give them song credits in exchange for the free music). Try out these sites which offer some free songs you can use for your videos if you plan to upload them to YouTube:

http://incompetech.com
http://www.melodyloops.com
http://freemusicarchive.org
YouTube also has a selection of free songs under Creator Studio>Create>Audio Library.
Or you can buy songs at stock sites like iStock.com (they also have a free download every week if you sign up for an account).

For sound effects, try:
https://www.freesound.org
http://soundbible.com/royalty-free-sounds-1.html

Go Deeper

Once you get comfortable with the basics of video editing, check out the options below for some extra effects.

Super Ultra Slow Motion Video Using Flux

As you learned previously, to achieve true slow motion, you are limited to the frames that were actually recorded in the original video. For example, when you conform video recorded at 120 FPS down to 24 FPS, you can only slow down the footage 5x to maintain smooth video footage. When using the Speed slider bar in Step 2 of GoPro Studio, that is 20% of the original speed.

With Flux, you can slow your footage down to 3%-10%, so you can achieve super ultra slow motion far slower than the original frame rate would allow. This creates an almost paused effect.

However, not all is perfect with the Flux option. To achieve super slow motion, Flux makes up frames that don't exist by analyzing the frame before and the frame after and filling in the space with digitally-created frames. For some scenes, this works really well, and for others, the results are far less than perfect.

Consider the following tips when you want to edit your clips into ultra slow motion:

• When possible, record at a high frame rate so that Flux doesn't have to create so many frames. The fewer frames that Flux has to digitally create, the better your chances for an effective result. However, Flux can be used with footage recorded at any frame rate.

• Choose the right scenes to apply Flux to. Clean backgrounds and simple scenes will work better because they are more predictable. Flux really works best when the subject is against a plain blue or grey sky. Busy scenes with lots of background elements, such as bushes or water, make it harder for Flux to imagine what the missing frames should have looked like. You can try Flux out with any clips, but if the results come out strange, the background could be the problem.

• Choose the right section of the clip to apply Flux. Flux is best applied when the subject is above the horizon, so split the clip when the subject goes above the horizon and split the clip again before the subject comes back down. The resulting section would be the best bet to slow down for a successful application of Flux.

• GoPro recommends slowing down the footage to 3%-10% for the ultra slow motion sections, but Flux can be applied to any video that has been slowed down using the Video Speed slider bar in Step 2 of GoPro Studio.

To Apply Flux:

1. In Step 2 of GoPro Studio, click on the thumbnail of clip you want to use in the section on the left side and drag the clip to the Storyboard.

2. Find a short section of the clip that you want to show in super slow motion. It's best to isolate a short 1-3 second clip because when you slow it way down, the clip will become a lot longer.

3. Split the clip before and after the section you want to slow down by dragging the slider to the points you want to clip and pressing the Split Clip icon on the left side above the Storyboard.

4. Make sure the clip you want to slow down is highlighted and under the Video tab on the right side, drag the Speed Slider to the left to reduce the speed of the video. When you drag the slider the Flux option will appear. Leave this box checked for the clip or clips where you want Flux applied.

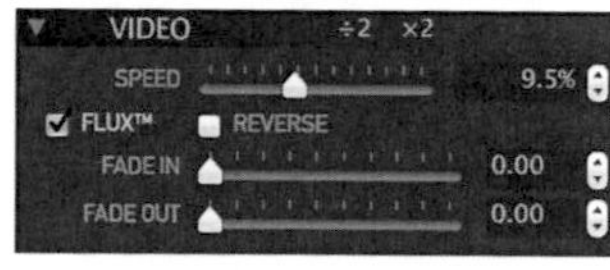

5. Export your video. On the export dialog, there is another option to Apply Flux. Leave this box checked to apply Flux and export your video.

NOTE: Exporting with Flux applied takes considerably longer because GoPro Studio has to analyze and create new frames, so make sure you only apply Flux to the clips that need the extra frames.

Remove The Fisheye Effect

The wide angle lens on the GoPro causes some curvature round the edges of the frame. Some people prefer to reduce the amount of fisheye effect in their videos. The best way to reduce the fisheye effect is to record video in Linear FOV. Unfortunately, since GoPro has stopped updating GoPro Studio, removing fisheye from HERO6 Black videos in GoPro Studio isn't as easy as it was for earlier camera models. However, there is still a way to remove the fisheye appearance from the wide angle lens using GoPro Studio.

The "Remove Fisheye" box in Step 1 of GoPro Studio will appear for files originally recorded in H.264 (not the High-performance Settings), but this won't fix your HERO6 Black videos.

Although it's not as effective as using advanced editing apps such as Final Cut Pro or Premiere Pro, the best way to remove fisheye from your videos in GoPro Studio is to use a combination of Framing controls. In the Framing dialog in Step 2 of GoPro Studio, there are three sliders you can use to reduce the fisheye effect. First, use the H.Zoom and H.Dynamic silders in combination to reduce the fisheye effect so that the fisheye effect is reduced. These will stretch out the center of the frame to reduce the "bubble" in the middle.

The original image is on the left. H.Zoom and H. Dynamic framing adjustments were applied to the image on the right.

If you want even more of a reduced fisheye effect and can spare losing some of the content around the edges of the frame, after adjusting your image using H.Zoom and H.Dynamic, use the Zoom slider to zoom in and crop out the edges of the frame. If you are editing to a lower resolution than the recorded video resolution, you have enough extra resolution to zoom in and still maintain high res video. If you filmed in 4k and are making a 1080p video, you can zoom in 200% without losing resolution. 2.7k zooms 140%. In GoPro Studio, these percentages need to be estimated because there is not a percentage marker in the Zoom slider.

TIP: ADVANCED EDITING: For more accurate fisheye removal, use advanced editing apps. In Premiere Pro, use Lens Distortion>Curvature in Effect Controls to reduce fisheye. In AfterEffects, use Optics Compensation. In Final Cut Pro, use the Fisheye filter, or the free Alex4d Wide Angle Fix plugin.

Use Keyframes To Add Effects

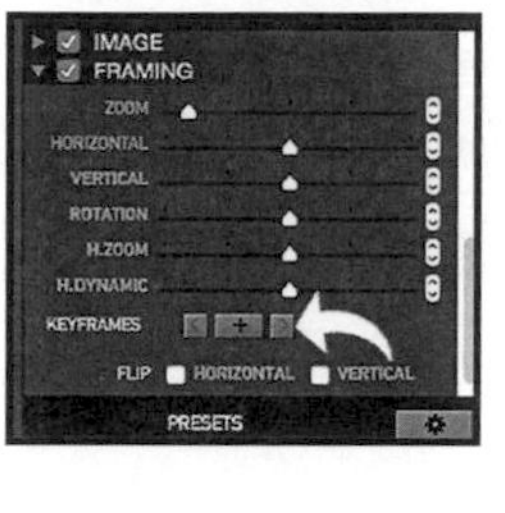

Use Keyframes to add changing visual effects within a video, or to create movement in a stationary scene, such as panning or zooming. A keyframe is used to make a marker of any of the visual settings, including, Saturation, Exposure, Contrast, etc. as well as Framing Controls like Zoom, Horizontal, Vertical, etc.

Keyframes buttons in GoPro Studio are located in the White Balance, Framing, and Image dialog boxes on the right side.

To add Keyframes to your video:

1. In Step 2 of GoPro Studio, drag your clip into the Storyboard.
2. In the Storyboard, move the Time Indicator to the beginning of the clip.
3. In the Image Settings>Framing, click the + button next to Keyframes. This will add a Keyframe at this point for adjustments made to that dialog box.
4. Make any visual adjustments you want to make at this Keyframe.
5. Move the Time Indicator to a point later in the clip.
6. Click the + button next to Keyframes. This will add a Keyframe at this point.
7. Make any visual adjustments you want to make at this Keyframe.
8. Play the video and watch the transition from the first Keyframe to the last.

For example, you can use keyframes to move across the frame of a scenic shot. To mimic a panning effect, first Zoom in on the scene. Use horizontal controls to add a Keyframe at the beginning of a time lapse clip that is viewing the left side of the frame. You can then add another Keyframe at the end of the time lapse that is viewing the right side of the frame. The video will then transition from the first keyframe to the last as the video plays, creating a panning effect.

Use keyframes to pan across an image, adding a sense of movement to a stationary shot.

You can also use keyframes to mimic a zoom shot. If you filmed in 4k or 2.7k, zoom in to an object such as a moonset over the ocean. Since your GoPro doesn't zoom, you can use keyframes to make it look like you zoomed in.

To mimic a zoom shot, add a Keyframe at the beginning of a full frame clip. Then add another Keyframe at the end of the clip that is zoomed in. The video will then transition from the first keyframe to the last as the video plays.

Create a Cinemagraph

Cinemagraphs are a relatively new media creation- basically a fusion between a photo and a video. In a cinemagraph, most of the scene appears stationary as you would see when viewing a photo. The magic of a cinemagraph is that a selected part of the image shows movement. Imagine a beautiful sunset photo, with all of its colors to appreciate, but in this scene just the ocean and one palm tree are moving in the breeze. These kinds of imaginative scenes can be created using a cinemagraph technique.

Cinemagraphs are generally short, with the moving areas set to "loop"- play over and over. Cinemagraphs can then be used on websites or social media.

There are two ways to make a cinemagraph- one you can create one manually using an advanced video editing app, such as Premiere Pro, Final Cut, or even Photoshop. There are several helpful tutorials on YouTube if you search for "Cinemagraph Tutorial". Once you learn the technique, you will be able to create these to your heart's content.

The second method is to use Flixel, which is easy, but requires a paid annual subscription. Flixel allows you to easily create cinemagraphs and also provides hosting so you can easily share the results.

Tips for Creating a Cinemagraph

- Use a tripod. A stationary shot will make it easier to expose the moving areas through the still image.
- Make sure some still areas are areas that would naturally contain movement, so the viewer can easily recognize the effect.
- When planning your cinemagraph, envision which area you will use for revealing movement.

EDITING A TIME LAPSE OR NIGHT LAPSE VIDEO

A time lapse is a fusion of photos and videos because you are capturing the scene through a long sequence of photos, but you display the scene as a movie. Time lapses are fun, creative additions to any video and they can give your viewers a great understanding of the overall scene. Night lapses and hyper lapses also use the same editing steps.

The easiest way to edit a time lapse, night lapse or hyper lapse is directly in GoPro Studio because of its simplicity and quality. Even if you choose to use another editing app for video editing, you may want to create your time lapses in GoPro Studio first.

Remember how you learned that 24 frames per second has the closest look to a movie. The goal here is to condense all of those time lapse photos into a video that plays at 24 frames per second so that each photo becomes a frame in the movie. You can play a time lapse at a faster or slower frame per second rate depending on the scene you recorded.

Editing Tips:

- If you recorded in Time Lapse Video Mode, your time lapse will automatically play as a video. If you used Time Lapse Photo Mode or Night Lapse Mode, editing a batch of time lapse photos into a time lapse video is easy. GoPro Studio combines them automatically for you. When you **click on the batch of photos in Quik for Desktop and open them in GoPro Studio**, GoPro Studio **automatically combines them into a video**. You can then convert the file as you would any other video and adjust it in Step 2.

- See **something you don't like** in one of the photos of the sequence? If you used one of the photo modes and something showed up in a frame, you can remove the photo from the batch before you import into GoPro Studio by right clicking over the thumbnail of the file in Quik for Desktop and selecting Show In Folder/Show In Folder and then removing the photo. You can also cut the frame out of the clip in GoPro Studio without noticing it in the edited video.

- In Step 2, you can **edit the appearance** of the time lapse video like you did in the Editing Your Video tutorial. You can adjust the speed, exposure and other settings using the dialogue boxes to the right.

- Work with the speed. **Try adjusting the speed** in the Speed slider on the right to get the look or length you are going for.

- As you learned earlier, you can **use keyframes to add extra movement,** such as panning or zooming, to your time lapse.

• Depending on your computer's speed, your time lapse probably will not play back smoothly until you export it. The preview doesn't show all of the frames, so it will look choppier than the final exported video. **Export your video to view the full effect of your time lapse**.

• If you want to scale the time lapse to Widescreen 16:9, use the 4x3 to Wide preset. If you would prefer to crop your time lapse to make it fit Widescreen without the distortion of the 4x3 to Wide preset, make sure the clip is in the storyboard and in the Framing box, adjust the Vertical slider until you are happy with the cropping.

> **TIP: Time Lapse From Video.** You can also simulate a time lapse look from a regular video clip using GoPro Studio. In Step 1 of GoPro Studio, click on Speed Up under Advanced Settings. When you click on Speed Up, a slider will appear with a box to insert a number, indicating how many frames you want to remove. A higher number will skip more frames and speed up the motion. You can also click on Motion Blur once Speed Up is checked to give your time lapse a blurred effect in between frames.

MOBILE EDITING APPS- SPLICE AND QUIK

Mobile editing is easy and convenient, but you will still probably want to use a computer for longer edits or high-res (2.7k and higher) footage. Transferring and editing files takes longer on a phone or tablet and the resolution output is generally lower, even if your phone records 4k video. But, it's still fun and convenient to edit and share your footage on the go!

GoPro offers two free mobile editing apps so you can easily make edits on your phone or tablet. The two apps are Quik and Splice. Splice is currently only available on iOS. Quik is available through the App Store (iOS) and Google Play (Android).

To edit your GoPro footage in Splice or Quik, the files you want to edit must be saved to your phone. You can save videos to your phone by using the GoPro App and downloading the files you want to use. You can also access files on your microSD card by using the Quik Key, which is a mobile card reader made by GoPro. If you are using an Android phone with a microSD card slot, you can insert your camera's card and access your files this way as well.

AUTO EDITS USING QUIKSTORIES

Quik Stories makes it even easier than ever to share your GoPro content. Quik Stories uses WiFi/Bluetooth to automatically transfer your recent photos and videos from your GoPro to your device and edits them into a short video with music. The video can then be instantly shared, or edited further.

• Footage captured **within two hours of each other** are edited into one Quik Story. Multiple Quik Stories may be automatically edited, depending on how much footage you filmed in the previous 72 hours.
• QuikStories will transfer videos, single photos and time lapse videos, but **not time lapse photos or burst photos**.
• All of the transferred footage will remain on your camera's memory card.
• Automatically transferred **files can be accessed in the Media section** of the GoPro App. After 7 days, those files will be deleted from the App unless you save them to your phone's media.
• If you are filming with the intention of making a QuikStory, **shorter clips at 1080p-60 will transfer much faster** than longer clips or higher resolution video. If the video resolution is incompatible with your device, the GoPro App will automatically convert files to a lower resolution.

How To Use Quik Stories

1. To make a QuikStory, make sure the camera has been connected to the App previously.
2. Turn on your GoPro's Wi-Fi and Bluetooth (turn on Wireless Connections under Connections from the top tray)

3. Launch the GoPro App and Swipe Down on the home screen of the App to search for photos or videos shot within the last 72 hours.
4. The GoPro App will automatically transfer recent files and edit them together. When your edited video is ready, the App will notify you that "Your QuikStory is ready!"
5. Tap "Get It" to go into Quik, which is GoPro's automated mobile video editing app.
6. Open Quik to preview your edited video. The edited video might turn out exactly how you want it, or it may just be a starting point for you to begin with.
7. For further editing, use the Quik editing tools that you will learn about next to remove unwanted clips and adjust highlights.
8. Once you are happy with the video, you can share your clip via apps (depending what apps you have on your device), messages, email, copy the link or add it to your photo library.

QUIK

Quik is just like the name says- **a great tool for making quick edits that are virtually automatic**. Quik doesn't offer a full toolbox of editing tools like Splice does, but if you want an easy way to combine videos and photos, add filters by theme and throw some music in there, Quik will get the job done for you. As you just learned Quik is used to edit your QuikStories. Quik can also put together an automatic weekly video of your footage.

Quik has the following tools to choose from:

• **Style**- Choose a video style based on Quik's pre-designed themes. The style can be changed instantly on your edit simply by selecting a different style.
• **Music**- Add music to your video. Choose from GoPro's library or add music from your phone's library.
• **Settings**- Choose the pace, which will change the speed of how fast elements are displayed one after the other. Choose the format, which can be Square or Widescreen. You can also delay the music to start later in the video.

But that's not it- there are more editing options available depending on what type of clip you are editing- either a Title slide, a video clip or a photo.

To edit title text slides, individual video clips, or photos, **Tap the screen and then the pen icon** to enter the editing dialogue.

When editing a **Title Slide**, the four editing options at the bottom of the screen are:
• **Text**- Edit the title text or add title slides.
• **Delete**- Delete a title slide.
• **Duration**- Adjust the length of the title slide.
• **Duplicate**- Duplicate the selected title slide.

When editing a **Video Clip**, the following tools are available:
• **Text**- Add a text overlay on your video.
• **Delete**- Delete the selected clip.
• **Trim**- Trim the beginning or end of the clip to select the area you want included
• **Speedometer** (IF GPS was enabled)- turn this on to display your speed.
• **Rotate**- Rotate videos if the orientation is off.
• **Volume**- Adjust the video's audio volume.
• **Speed**- Adjust the playback speed of your clip to Slow (if you filmed at >60 FPS), Regular or Fast.
• **Fit**- This will show the full view of the clip, which may create black bars at the top and bottom.
• **Duplicate**- Duplicate the selected video clip.

For **photo editing**, two additional options are available:
• **Focus**- Determine where you want to set the focus to add a filter to the photo.
• **Duration**- Set the video duration of the photo to Long, Regular or Short.

Once you have finished editing in Quik, save your video to your photo library or share it through Social Media outlets.

SPLICE

Splice is a mobile video editor that offers much of the freedom and creativity of a desktop video editing app.

Now that you know the basics of video editing, you can apply that knowledge to Splice. Using the editing techniques you just learned for GoPro Studio, you can make video and photo compilation edits with a variety of transitions, titles and audio.

Just select your media from your device's photo library and add them to the storyboard. You can also use files from your DropBox, Facebook, Google, Instagram or GoPro Plus. From the storyboard, you can edit the individual clips, add audio and titles, change the transitions and produce a quick and easy video of your event.

Splice has the following tools to choose from:

Trim/Cut- Trim the ends off your video or cut parts from the middle of your clip.

Wand Tool (Filters)- Apply filters to your videos or photos. Some examples include Warming, Blue, Noir (black and white), and Sepia.

Speed (for videos)- Adjust the playback speed for slow motion or speed up your videos. Remember what you learned about slow motion frame rates so you don't end up with choppy video. The same rules apply here!

Titles- Add title pages to your video or subtitles on your clips.

Motion- Crop your images or add a Ken Burns effect (slow pan and zoom) to your videos and photos.

Audio- Add voiceovers, music and soundtracks to your video. You can adjust your clip's audio, as well as add two tracks of music and a voiceover.

When you finish editing, there are a variety of ways to share your edited video directly from the app, including sharing a link, saving the video to your device or uploading it to your favorite social media.

> **TIP: More editing apps**. There are a few other mobile video editing apps you may find useful. Chromic has some nice color grading tools. Post Edit is similar to Splice but you can also overlay a drawing on the video or add sticker graphics. Adobe Premiere Clip is another full feature video editor with an option to auto generate a video like Quik or manually edit your videos. One of the best aspects of Adobe Clip is the large selection of filters to choose from.

Check out these tips to make your mobile videos more fun to watch:

- Combine GoPro clips with other videos taken on your phone. Any videos or photos in your Camera Roll can be used in the video.
- Add titles. Give your videos some character with titles or subtitles.
- Choose the music for the mood. If you don't like the selections available, you can also add your own music, but remember to be aware of not using copyrighted music without permission.
- With mobile videos, longer is not always better. You can often make the point in a short 60 second clip, which is the maximum length of an Instagram video.

PULLING FRAME GRABS

A frame grab is a **still image (photo) taken from a video clip**. With the improved video image quality on the HERO6 Black, a still image taken from 4k video (especially the HEVC high-performance resolutions) is about the same quality as an image taken in photo mode, so you can really utilize your video clips to extract amazing still images. The frame grab that you pull from video will have the same resolution as the video file, so a higher resolution video produces a larger still image. **Here are a couple of easy ways to pull a frame grab:**

In Quik for Desktop

With the video paused on the desired frame, click the Grab a Photo icon at the bottom of the screen. Quik for Desktop will add a new thumbnail with the extracted frame.

On the Camera's Touch Display

If your video file is still on the microSD card in your camera, play the video on the Touch Display. Tap the Image icon at the top of the screen. Then scroll to the frame you want to grab and click the check mark.

In GoPro Studio

1. In Step 2 in GoPro Studio, make any aesthetic adjustments to the video before exporting your frame grab.

2. When ready to export the frame grab, slide the time bar to scroll to the exact frame in your video that you want to export. You can also move forward or backwards frame by frame by using the buttons on either side of the play button.

3. In the top menu, click Share>Export Still

4. Name the file and if you want to export the file at full size, choose Native under the Size to Export dropdown menu. GoPro Studio will export a JPEG photo file to the location you chose on your computer.

After exporting a frame grab, you can adjust its appearance in a photo-editing app like you will learn about next.

PHOTO EDITING

When it comes to photography, there are lots of things you can do with a GoPro! There are tons of ways to edit photos and you will eventually find your own style. This section will help you give your photos or frame grabs that extra pizazz they need after coming straight from the camera.

Back in the days before digital, we selected our film based on its color and grain qualities. In the digital age, we give our photos a little more in postproduction. Images straight out of the camera can always use a little help looking better, so this section is written to help you process images to make them look their best.

There are also quite a few things that are lacking when compared to a traditional camera such as a DSLR. Editing is where you can take your GoPro photos and make them stand apart. With a few simple edits, you can boost the colors, improve your photos and even mimic quite a few of the looks you would capture using a DSLR.

Mobile Apps

Mobile photo-editing apps offer most of the functionality of desktop-editing apps on your full resolution photos. There are tons of apps available and you can easily do all of your photo editing on mostly free apps if you choose to. For these tutorials, editing techniques are shown using Lightroom Mobile and Snapseed.

Lightroom Mobile is one of the most popular apps for professional photographers, and once you learn the techniques on your device, you can easily replicate these adjustments on your desktop if you choose to. Since some of the features require a Creative Cloud membership (which costs $10/month), Snapseed is used as an alternate for those adjustments. Pixlr is another full-featured free app to look into that has a few features not available in Lightroom or Snapseed, although the free version is full of ads.

You may already have your favorite apps, so feel free to use the following editing tips to make similar adjustments. The recommended apps may not be the best since new apps are constantly being developed. However, at the time of publication, they are some of the best and are able to make the adjustments shown in these tutorials.

There are two downsides to editing photos on a device- 1) transferring large files (it can use a lot of data and take up storage), and 2) monitoring image quality on a smaller screen. However, the convenience and ease of editing photos on your device is enticing.

If you are editing your photos on your device, there are a couple of ways to access them:

#1 If your files are still on your microSD card, you can use the GoPro App to wirelessly download them to your device, or access the files on the Quik Key (a microSD card reader that can be inserted into your phone or tablet).

#2 If you have already downloaded your footage off of your card, you can email them to yourself from your computer and save them to your device's photo library.

#3 If you are a GoPro Plus subscriber, you can access your content on any device through the cloud.

 **Desktop Apps**

If you want to edit photos on your computer, Lightroom has all of the tools necessary to edit your photos like a pro- in fact, most pros use Lightroom. If you took RAW .grp photos, RAW files can be edited in Lightroom or Camera Raw. Photoshop is only needed for more complicated editing when multiple layers are needed.

If you don't have Photoshop or Lightroom, you can get full access to both for $10 a month, which also includes the full version of Lightroom Mobile and Photoshop Fix for your device. You can also get a fully functional free 30-day trial to see if you like their apps. The author of this book is not affiliated with Adobe- it's just the industry standard. Professional editing software will make your work a lot easier and give you better results.

If you would prefer to use a free desktop program, you can use Gimp, which is free. Gimp allows you to make most of these adjustments, but Gimp usually requires a few extra steps to achieve similar results.

Whether you choose to edit photos using your device or a computer often depends on the number of photos you are editing and your final use for them, so let's move on and learn how to work some magic on your GoPro photos.

This is just one recommended workflow for adjusting your photos- there are many ways you could go about doing this. For the most efficient photo editing workflow, follow these steps in order.

Note: If you already have your own editing workflow, you can move ahead to the section on Removing Fisheye.

BASIC EDITING

Let's start with the basic editing that should be done for any photo. These little adjustments will have a big impact. Although we are using Lightroom Mobile for this tutorial, similar adjustments can be made on most photo-editing programs, both desktop and mobile.

Import your photos
After you have transferred photos onto your phone, or have inserted the Quik Key, open Lightroom Mobile and select a photo you want to work with.

Applying Presets/Filters
Under the Presets option, you can scroll through the presets to see how they affect the appearance of your photos. This is like adding filters in other mobile editing apps. With experience, you will know your favorite go-to's. Or you may decide that you prefer to manually adjust the appearance of your photos.

Priime is another free mobile app with some amazing filters for your photos.

If you are using Lightroom or Photoshop on your computer, you may also want to add the Nik Collection, which is a collection of free plugins from Google. The Nik Collection contains, among other tools, a comprehensive set of filters for color correction. After you install it, access the color filters by clicking Photo>Edit In>Color Efex Pro.

Color Correction
Straight out of your camera, your photos may look a bit dull. It's easy to correct the appearance of your photos in a few simple steps to make your photos full of color and life. These adjustments are made using the Light and Color tools in Lightroom

Mobile, but every decent photo-editing app has similar features. In Snapseed, they are found in Develop for RAW files or Tune for JPEGs

1. Use the Light tool to adjust Exposure, Contrast, Whites and Blacks. Exposure and Contrast are typically the most impactful adjustments to fine tune the tone of your photo.

2. Using the Color tool, the Vibrance and Saturation adjustments will add more impact to your images. When adjusting Vibrance and Saturation, add color until it looks oversaturated and then back it down a bit so the image doesn't look over edited. You will rarely go beyond +25 for Saturation, depending on the photo. If you took the photo using a manual White Balance setting, you may need to adjust White Balance or Temperature. If you used Auto White Balance, these most likely won't need to be adjusted.

3. Lastly, after other adjustments are made, use the Clarity slider in the Effects tool if the image needs more contrast and punch. The Clarity slider boosts the midtones of a photo.

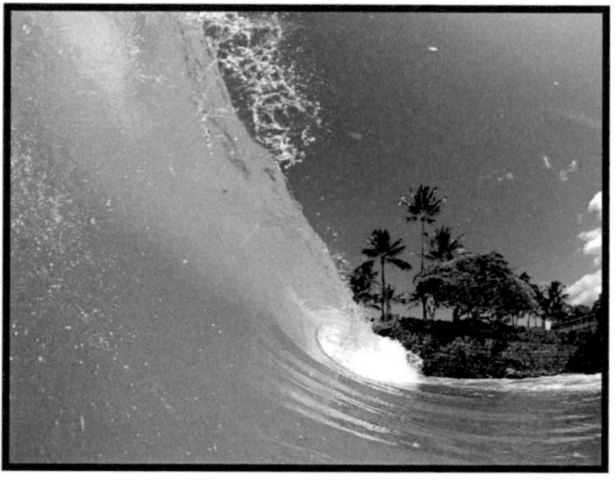

The Original photo is on the left. The image on the right was adjusted using the basic editing adjustments shown above. Here are the adjustments made: Exposure -.37, Contrast +30, Whites +15, Blacks -14, Vibrance +30, Saturation +14.

These same adjustments can also be made easily using the Develop Module in Lightroom.

REMOVING FISHEYE

You learned how to remove the fisheye effect for video, but there is also an easy way to correct the lens distortion in your photos if they need a more linear perspective.

Using the lens correction adjustment will cause some loss of the content around the edges of your photos, so make sure you don't lose anything that you feel is important to the composition. Also, keep an eye on objects around the edge of the photo to make sure they don't become too stretched out in appearance.

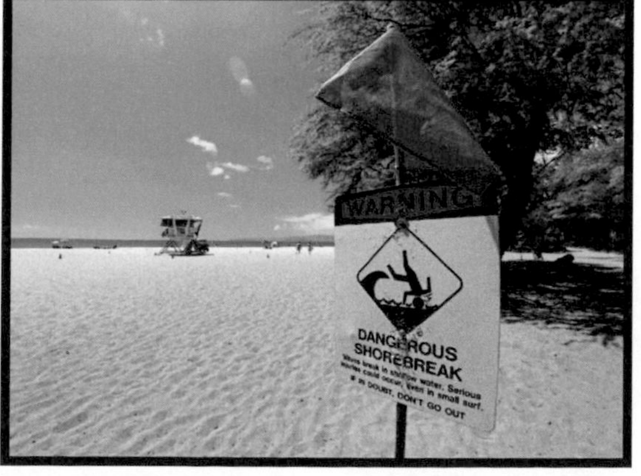

Lens corrections were made to the image on the right to remove the fisheye effect. Notice the straight lines on the sign pole and edges of the sign.

Since Lightroom Mobile typically takes a while for the lens profile to be added, here's how to remove the fisheye using SKRWT, which is a paid app (about $1.99US), but it's one of the best available:

1. Import your photo into SKRWT and select the curved edges icon on the bottom right.

2. Select the GoPro tab on the right. Slide the bottom bar to the positive numbers until you are happy with the results. Between 10-15 is typically a good range to remove fisheye from a photo taken in Wide FOV.

3. Save your image to your phone and make any additional edits using Lightroom Mobile or Snapseed.

Lightroom Mobile also has a lens profile tool to correct fisheye, but fisheye removal will not work until the HERO6 Black lens profile is added. After a new camera is released, there is a delay before the lens profile is added to the app.

If you make the Lens Correction adjustment using Lightroom on your computer, you can also fine tune the amount of distortion removed using the Distortion slider. You can also make this correction in Photoshop using Filter>Lens Correction and selecting your camera model. Make sure Geometric Distortion is checked.

CROPPING

Cropping is best done after you have decided whether you want to use the lens correction option or not since the lens correction will change your photo's content.

TIP: Cropping your photo is another technique you can use to remove the wide angle look of your photo. By cropping the edges of the frame and keeping the center of the image, you can remove the areas with the most distortion.

The 12 MP photos from the HERO6 Black Edition give you plenty of room to crop your image and still have a high-resolution photo. Cropping is a great way to affect the composition of your photo. This is where you can get closer and get creative. If you are using the photo for Instagram or other mobile media, you don't need much resolution so feel free to be bold.

The Original image (on the left) was cropped to fit a square (1:1) format.

Follow these steps to crop your photo in Lightroom Mobile:

1. Select the Crop Icon on the bottom toolbar at the right side of Lightroom Mobile.

2. Select your desired Aspect (square, original, etc. or you can enter custom dimensions). There are many aspect ratios to choose from when cropping depending on how you plan to use the image. Square (1:1) is obviously a common choice for social media such as Instagram. 4:3 will maintain the same proportions as your original GoPro photo.

3. If your photo is not straight, use the Angle slider to straighten your photo.

4. Under Orientation, you can rotate or flip the photo. Change the orientation to see if another orientation creates a more enticing perspective.

5. Drag the corners of the crop box to crop your image. You can also move your image inside the box to reposition it.

6. Click the check mark to apply the cropping.

CLONING

Removing unwanted objects is much easier in a photo than in a video. Cloning is especially useful to remove sun glare. Sunspots are common when using a GoPro in backlit lighting because the wide angle lens captures so much of the sky.

You will need to turn to another app besides Lightroom Mobile for cloning, or healing, as it is often called. Most of the mobile apps, including Snapseed or Photoshop Express let you clone out unwanted areas using the Healing Brush on your touch screen.

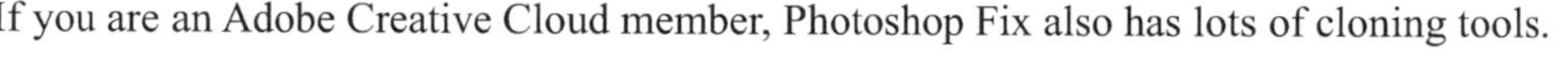

It can be tricky to fine-tune your cloning on your device, but when working in Snapseed or Photoshop Express, the more you zoom in, the patch becomes smaller and will give you better results.

If you are an Adobe Creative Cloud member, Photoshop Fix also has lots of cloning tools.

See the snorkelers in the image on the left? Thanks to the Healing tool in Snapseed, they are gone in the image on the right. Cloning/healing is a great way to remove unwanted elements in a photo.

SELECTIVE BLUR

When using a GoPro, everything beyond 1 foot of your camera will be in focus. This wide depth of field is great because you don't need to worry about focusing your camera.

For some photos though, you might want to mix it up by adding a shallow depth of field look that is often seen when using a DSLR. DSLR's have the option of changing aperture settings to achieve a shallow depth of field, which brings more attention to the area you want your viewers to focus on. You can easily mimic this technique using a number of free apps on your device.

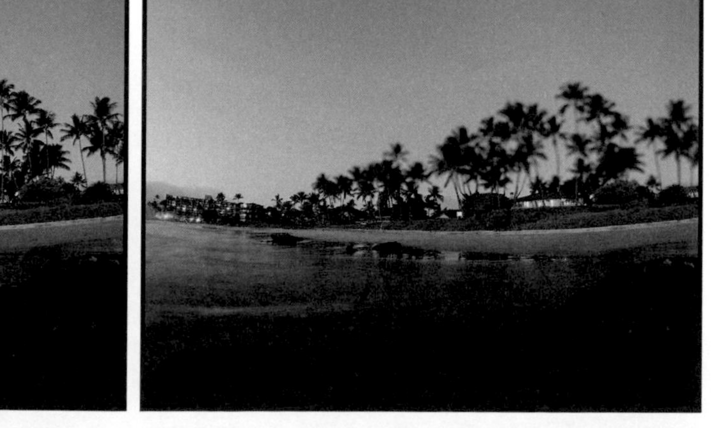

In the bottom photo, the foreground and background was blurred to create the effect of a shallow depth of field.

You can selectively blur areas of the photo, leaving your subject in focus. This can be done for free using the Selective tool in Lightroom Mobile. Make two selective edit areas and then in the Detail tool, reduce the Sharpness to create a blurred effect. Pixlr also offers simple blur effects by using the brush and eraser tools. Photo Focus is another free app with more blur options.

Try to keep objects in focus that are along the same plane to mimic the way a DSLR would naturally capture a shallow depth of field.

FINISH IT OFF

Once you have finished editing your photos, you can finish it off by adding a few final touches.

A vignette adds a dark area around the edges of the frame, or you can choose a stylish edge, such as a film emulsion. Lightroom Mobile has vignette controls. Snapseed and Photoshop Express both have some good edge and frame options.

You can also add some fun lighting effects. Lens Distortions and Pixlr are free apps with lens flares and other effects that are easy to preview and add to your photos.

This photo was edited into black and white using Lightroom Mobile. The Film Emulsion edge was added in Photoshop Express.

ADVANCED, BUT SUPER COOL PHOTO TIP

Make Your Photos Come To Life with the Parallax 2.5D Effect.

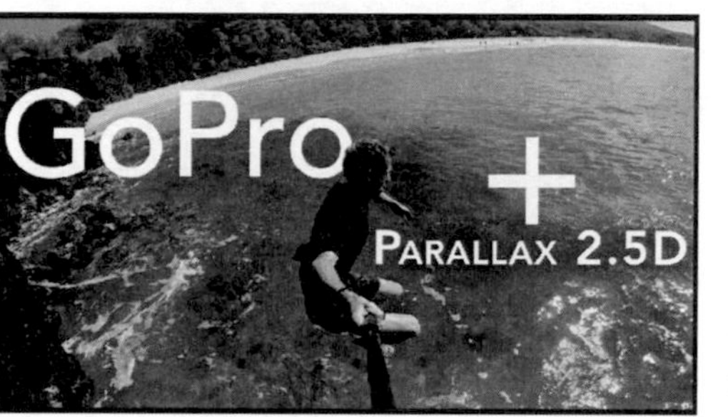

You may want to add some photos into your edited videos, but a still photo lacks movement. Adding a Ken Burns effect or using keyframes can create some movement to your photos, but if you really want the picture to come to life, check out the Parallax 2.5D effect.

Using this effect, the subject and background are edited onto separate layers. Each layer is then edited to zoom separately, creating the illusion that the subject is moving into the scene. Using Parallax 2.5D is a great way to integrate photos into your videos without them looking stale and stagnant.

If you are interested in adding a 2.5D Parallax Effect to your photos using Photoshop, you can watch a tutorial by the author of this book on YouTube at bit.ly/2lHsdzF.

RESIZING YOUR IMAGE

Your HERO6 Black camera produces high quality large images, but if you decide you want to print an image larger than the original file size (a 30"x40" print @ 300 DPI for example), it's best to increase the size (called upsampling) of your photo. The newest version of Photoshop does a great job of upsampling your photos.

If you are really going large (up to 1000% of the original) and want the best, there are also a few professional software options for resizing images that are even better than Photoshop. These are not free (cost is usually $100-200), but they are worth the investment if you plan to resize a bunch of images or print large wall art.

The two most popular resizing software for high quality large prints are:
Resize by OnOne Software (onOneSoftware.com)
Blow Up by Alien Skin Software (alienskin.com)

EDITING AN ACTION SEQUENCE

As you learned previously, an action sequence is a digitally composited blend of photos taken using Burst Mode or Time Lapse Mode with your HERO6. Tips for setting up this type of photo are provided in Step 4- Capture Your Action.

The most effective way to make an action sequence is using a desktop photo editing program. This cool looking effect can be done using Gimp or Photoshop. This tutorial shows you how to make an action sequence using Gimp, since it is free photo-editing software. The process seems complicated at first, but once you get the hang of it, you can make these images rather quickly.

Photos taken on the HERO6 Black Edition in Burst Mode at a rate of 30 photos over 2 seconds. As you can see, the subject is not completely sharp, which can result from taking Burst photos of fast action in low light situations.

On your device, you can use SeqPic ($.99 for the version that allows you to composite multiple images) to composite your images. SeqPic lacks some editing techniques available on a desktop app, but it does a decent job on most sequences.

Steps for Editing An Action Sequence

1. Select the batch of photos you want to use for the action sequence. Open the photos in their location on your computer and drag them into a new folder with easy access. If the subject ends up overlapping too much, you can turn off some of the photo layers when you are editing.

2. Open Gimp and open the first photo of the sequence by going to File>Open and select the first photo of the sequence. Click Open.

3. Add the rest of the photos to the file you are working with by clicking File>Open As Layers. Select the rest of the photos and click Add.

4. Reverse the order of the layers so that the first photo of the sequence is on top. Go to Layer>Stack>Reverse Layer Order.

5. Next add a layer mask to the top photo (layer). A layer mask lets you select which part of the photo you want to show up. Click on the top layer in the layer bar to the right. Go to Layer>Mask>Add Layer Mask. In the dialog box that appears, select Black (Full Transparency) and click Add. The first photo of the sequence will disappear from view.

6. Now you are going to bring back the pieces of the photo that you want to show up in your action sequence. Select the Paintbrush Tool.

7. On the left side below the tools, make sure the foreground color is set to White. Painting with white will paint away the Layer Mask, bringing back your subject. (If White is set as the background color, you can click the little arrow to switch White to foreground.)

8. Paint over the area where your subject was to bring your subject back onto the screen. If you need to adjust how much you painted, switch your foreground color to black. Black will cover back up the areas you painted white. Fine tune the layer mask until you are happy with the parts of the photo that are showing up.

9. If the subject in the layer below is too overlapping with the photo you are bringing back in to view, turn off layers until you see the layer you want to appear. Turn off layers by pressing the eye icon next to the layer on the layer bar to the right.

10. Repeat steps 5 through 9 for each photo (layer) that you want to show up, except for the bottom photo.

11. Finally, in the layers bar on the right, right click (Control + Click on Mac) and select Flatten Layers. You can now make any color adjustments like you learned in the previous section.

12. Export your file by clicking File>Export and save your file as your preferred file type.

If you prefer watching a tutorial video on how to do this, you can watch one of our video tutorials on YouTube that will walk you through the steps.
For the tutorial using Gimp, go to this address: http://bit.ly/1gJ3Ztf
For the tutorial using Photoshop, go to this address: http://bit.ly/GXoQv9

Now that you've edited your photos and videos, you are ready to move on to Step 6 and show them to people!

STEP SIX
SHARE IT

Get Your Vision Out There For People To See

You've made it this far, now it's time to share your masterpiece. Even if your first video or photos are not masterpieces, friends and family will be excited to finally see you in action.

GoPro has really put priority on making it easier to create your content and share it. Read on to find out the many ways you can share your photos and videos.

SHARING THROUGH THE GOPRO APP & QUIK

The GoPro App allows you to **share photos and videos directly from the App**. You can share files that are on your camera's microSD card or files you have downloaded to your device. If you want to view files when your camera is not connected, save them to My Media by clicking the small icon on the bottom left to download them to your device.

When saving files to your device or sharing them to social media/email, depending on file size, you may be given the option of a low resolution or high resolution file. The low-resolution file is best for posting to social media or emailing to friends since it is a smaller file for uploading and viewing on small devices. A high-resolution file is a better option if you want to save the original file to send to your computer for editing.

There is only limited editing directly available within the GoPro App, but you can trim a 5, 15 or 30 second clip to email to your friends or post to social media.

For more advanced editing options on your device, use Splice or Quik as you learned about in the previous section. You can also share to social media or directly to your friends via messages and email through Quik for Desktop, Splice and Quik.

SENDING LARGE FILES

If you were out filming and captured some great video footage of your friend or even a stranger who was out there shredding, you might be struggling to figure out how to share your video files. Even a short video file is too big for most email services, so you need to find a better way to share files. You can use one of the old school ways of sharing files such as putting the file on a USB flash drive and loading it onto your friend's computer.

If you don't have the convenience of physically sharing the file, there are a few free ways to send large files. (These are the current size limits at the time of publication.)

WeTransfer lets you share files up to 2GB as often as you like without signing up for any plans. All you need to do is to enter your email and the recipient's email address and link the file.

Hightail (formerly YouSendIt) offers a free plan that lets you send files up to 250MB, which isn't much if you are sharing 4k files, but it could be sufficient for short clips depending on the resolution. You can send much larger files with the paid plans.

DropBox has a free basic plan that lets you store up to 2GB that you can share with anyone you invite. When editing videos on your mobile device using Splice, you can also access your DropBox files for editing.

SOCIAL MEDIA

Social Media and Online Sharing Sites are great ways to get your experience out into the world. Social Media has undoubtedly contributed to the explosion in popularity of GoPro cameras. Many GoPro camera users are extremely active in social media communities. After you edit your videos and photos, here are a few FREE ways to get them out there for people to see.

Video-Sharing Sites:

You Tube - Most popular

You can create a channel and upload your videos for private or public viewing. YouTube is by far the most popular video sharing website so far, and with Google's backing, will continue to be. With a basic account, you can upload videos smaller than 2GB and less than 15 minutes in length. You can upload as many videos as you like. You can even earn some extra cash from your videos if you enable ads and one of the videos goes viral.

Vimeo - Creative/Non-commercial Videos

With a free basic account, you can upload 500MB of video per week. The content must be original and non-commercial. You also have the option of making your videos private with password protection, which is convenient if you want to share selected videos with a limited crew.

Metacafe - Huge Audience, Revenue-Sharing

Metacafe is one of the largest online video entertainment sites. You can upload your content and share it with friends, get Facebook comments or just let the world find it. If you get enough views, you may earn a little side cash too.

Dailymotion - Huge Global Audience

This video-sharing site allows you to earn revenue from your videos and offers a free membership with unlimited uploads.

Photo-Sharing Sites:

Below are a few favorites out of the plethora of free photo-sharing websites available. Every one of the sites below has free accounts, but many of them are restrictive unless you upgrade your account. Check out these sites and see which one best serves your sharing needs.

Flickr, 500px, Webshots, Photobucket, and Fotolog are some of the most useful photo sharing sites.

Social Media:

And of course, there are the Social Media sites we use to share our lives. Most of them allow us to upload photos and videos, or links to videos.

Facebook - Post photos & videos (either through links or natively).

Instagram - Easily share photos and short videos (currently up to 60 seconds) with a variety of fun filters and basic editing tools, as well as share links to your videos.

Pinterest - Pinterest is the perfect place to share ideas and pick up new tips on using your GoPro camera

Path - A more personal way to post photos & videos

Twitter - Post photos & links to videos

MySpace - Post photos & videos

Google+ - Share photos & videos

PHOTO PRINTING

The HERO6 Black takes high-resolution photos that allow for a wide variety of printing options. If you use the resizing software recommended in Step 5, you can use your GoPro® camera to make almost any size print you want.

With the plethora of creative photo printing options available, here are a few of the best:

Acrylic Face Mounts
The printed photograph is mounted behind a thin layer of acrylic and usually comes with a hanger mounted to the back, so it is ready to hang. Acrylic Face Mounting creates a modern look for wall art.

It's a tricky process, but Bumblejax or BayPhoto are two labs that can produce these eye-popping prints for you.

Metal Prints
This printing process actually prints your photo directly onto aluminum, creating a unique modern display, with lots of shine and realism.

Google "Metal Prints" or check out BayPhoto, Costco or Bumblejax.

Wood Prints
Photos printed on wood have a very organic feel and create an instant art piece. If you print without a white under layer, the wood grain shows through your image, giving it a unique texture that is perfect for adding a personal touch to your photography.

Check out Woodsnap.com or Google "Wood Photo Prints" to find a printer who can print your photos on wood.

Gallery Wraps/Giclees
Make your photo look like a traditional wrapped piece of art by printing it on a gallery wrap. Choose Metallic Photo Paper for extra vibrancy in your photo.

Google "Gallery Wraps" or check out BayPhoto for printing options.

GATHERINGS

Use your footage as a reason to gather friends together and have a party. You are the filmmaker so have a pseudo premiere. But don't be greedy. Set your friends up to film them (if they don't have their own cameras). Edit your footage together into a mini flick and let everyone hoot and holler over the results. Here are a few ways to display your videos and photos.

Big Screen TV
Showing your videos on the Big Screen is an impressive way to watch your creation up close and personal. 4k Monitors, HD DVD Players and BluRay Players are currently the highest quality. If you are viewing your footage on a 4k television, see the 4k section in Step 7- Beyond the Basics.

Digital Projector
Pop up a white movie screen and watch your footage outdoors for a truly impressive display. Digital Projectors vary in quality (usually from 720p up to 4k) and price, of course.

Computer
Computer monitors are not the most social way to show your videos, but they are usually high quality and most of them display 1080p. Some monitors display 2.7k and even 5k.

Congratulations, you now have the knowledge and power to create and share your experiences with the world! In Step 7, you will learn more tricks to take your GoPro footage to the next level.

STEP SEVEN

BEYOND THE BASICS

Take It Further

Once you have mastered the basics of using your HERO6 camera and see how much fun these cameras can be, you will probably want to add more flair and style to your videos and photos. When you are ready to add some extra features to your camera setup, these additional tips and accessories will help you get even better shots.

The list of accessories and extras that are available for your GoPro goes on and on, but in this step, we will break it down to the accessories that will make the biggest impact on your footage and on your filming experience.

4K

As you have learned, the HERO6 Black records video footage at 4k resolution. While 4k gives you clear video and lots of freedom when it comes to editing, the high resolution is still being integrated into some of our technology.

4k is also known as Ultra High Definition (UHD) or 2160p (since other resolutions are defined by the line height and 4k refers to the width). 4k is 4x the resolution of 1080p, which means there are 4x as many pixels in the footage. What this means for anyone watching 4k footage on a 4k monitor is incredibly clear, realistic-looking video that looks like you can jump right in. The difference can really be seen the closer you get to the screen.

If you want to watch your HERO6 Black footage in 4k, it's best to record your footage in 4k. The HERO6 Black records 4k at 60 frames per second, which makes it possible to film almost everything you need in 4k.

Although it is lower resolution, you can record in 2.7k and then upsize to 4k when you edit. The results are surprisingly clear and 2.7k opens up the possibilities for an even higher frame rate and more field of view options.

Because of the high resolution, 4k is incredibly demanding in terms of computer performance. If you are playing back your footage through your computer connected to a 4k monitor, your computer must also be 4k compatible or the footage will most likely play back choppy. Editing long clips also requires a lot of memory. If you are having trouble editing 4k, you probably need to upgrade your computer to make it compatible for 4k playback. A flash hard drive (aka SSD), enough RAM and a good graphics card will greatly improve your computer's performance when editing in 4k.

If you want to watch your 4k content from your camera directly to your TV, some TV's are capable of 4k playback with a USB card reader or USB drive. Check with your TV manufacturer to check compatibility.

These accessories will instantly improve the quality of your videos and photos:

GIMBAL / STABILIZER

Although it's an expensive add on, the mount/accessory that will make the most impact on your videos is a gimbal, also known as a stabilizer. No other accessory will have as big of an impact as a high-quality gimbal. Mounting your GoPro to a gimbal will eliminate unsightly camera shake or rocky videos. In case you don't know, a gimbal keeps the horizon straight and absorbs shock from your movements keeping the video footage smooth even when your filming technique isn't. The result is Hollywood style videos for a fraction of the cost (and much simpler for a one-person film crew like you may be).

Even if you correct your videos using post-processing stabilization techniques, they still won't match the quality you would capture using a high-quality gimbal. And even though the GoPro Hero 6 has integrated electronic video stabilization (EIS), the result is still not as buttery smooth as a good gimbal.

There are basically two types of gimbals- a handheld gimbal or a mountable/wearable gimbal. Some double as both.

The GoPro Karma Grip is the most obvious choice because it's made by GoPro and typically native hardware is the most compatible. When GoPro updates the camera's firmware, they also update the Karma Grip's firmware if needed.

The Karma Grip features a detachable gimbal so it can be used in the handle as a handheld gimbal, or mounted when used with the additional purchase of the Karma Extension Cable. The Karma Grip can also be mounted to your body or gear with the handle attached, but most often, it's too large to be functional.

The Karma Grip is included with the Karma drone and is also sold separately. Unfortunately, the Karma Grip is not waterproof, so if you want a waterproof setup, check out the following options. For a mountable gimbal that is waterproof (it can go underwater to 3'), check out the FeiyuTech WG2. For a strictly handheld splashproof (not waterproof) gimbal, check out the FeiyuTech G5 or Removu S1.

The downsides of a gimbal

• Most gimbals are not waterproof, so this limits their use in certain water activities or extreme weather conditions.

• Gimbals are sensitive electronic devices- meaning they can break! They are pretty tough, but not tough enough for many of the activities a GoPro is used from filming.

• Audio can be a problem. Some gimbals have a tendency to block one or more of the GoPro's microphones. Others emit a small electronic noise that can be heard on your videos. It really depends on how important your audio is.

Tips for using a gimbal

• When using a gimbal, turn off your camera's Stabilization (EIS). Since the gimbal will take care of stabilizing your shots, you can film at the highest resolution settings (4k-60, 2.7k-120, etc.).

• A gimbal will compensate for a lot of your erratic movements, but if you try to film using stable filming techniques (using some filming techniques from Step 4) along with a gimbal, your footage will be amazingly smooth.

• The Karma Grip can be mounted as a wearable gimbal using the mounting ring. The Extension Cable allows you to separate the gimbal from the grip, allowing you more flexibility for mounting positions.

• Don't subject your gimbal to sudden changes in wind- for example, sticking it out of the window in a moving vehicle. It is a sensitive electronic device that can be damaged rather easily.

FILTERS

Backscatter, GoPro, Sandmarc, and Polar Pro offer a variety of filters to enhance the colors and quality of your photos and videos. There are two types of filters available: some fit directly on your HERO6 Black while others are made for the SuperSuit. Make sure you select the right type before you make your purchase. Also, because the HERO6 is the same size as the HERO5 Black, filters designed for the HERO5 Black will work with the HERO6 Black. Here are some of the filters that will make the biggest impact on your footage.

POLARIZER

A polarizer filter is probably the most important filter because it filters out glare, which your camera can't do.

The Sandmarc Circular Polarizer filter mounted on the HERO6 Black.

In the photo on the right, the Polarizer reduced glare on the water, adding a variety of tones to the ocean. You can also see increased contrast between the clouds and sky.

For bright sunny days with lots of glare, use a polarizer filter to reduce glare and light. A polarizer filter reduces reflections from the water, enhances water clarity, and makes the sky appear darker blue. Sandmarc makes a circular polarizer which rotates to adjust the intensity of the polarizer effect.

NEUTRAL DENSITY (ND)

A neutral density filter reduces the amount of light that makes it to your camera's lens. A neutral density filter can be used to slow down the shutter speed on bright days, giving your footage a motion blur effect. This can work well, for example, if your camera is mounted to your car and you want the car to be in focus, but the passing scenery to have a blurred effect.

A neutral density filter is also useful for using Night Photo Mode (even when it's not totally dark) to use a longer Shutter time for a more pronounced blur effect. Neutral density filters can be purchased in a variety of grades- a higher number means more light will be filtered out. Most of the ND filters come in a set (anywhere from ND4 to ND32) so you can select the right one for the lighting conditions.

• In Bright Full Sun, try an ND16 filter at 1/60 sec @ 100 ISO.

• When using an ND filter, if it's too dark at the slowest shutter speed available (1/30 or 1/60), use a brighter filter *ND4 or ND8), or raise the ISO until you have the correct exposure. To darken the exposure, adjust the shutter speed to a faster shutter (1/120 or 1/240) and lower the ISO to 100.

UNDERWATER DIVE FILTERS

The HERO6 Black features automatic toning adjustments for underwater filming, so a dive filter is not as important as it was with previous GoPro cameras. If you decide you want to add some dive filters anyways, there are several colors to choose from. A red filter works best in tropical blue water, while a magenta filter is the best choice for green water. Dive filters work best as you get deeper underwater (about 10 feet below the surface and below) where the colors of the spectrum fade away.

MACRO LENSES

With the HERO6, anything further than 12 inches away from your lens will be in focus. If you want to film close-ups closer than 12 inches away, a macro lens allows you to film up to 3 inches away and capture great in-focus close ups. A macro lens is a specialty lens used specifically for close-up macro shots and is not for general shooting. PolarPro offers an easy to use snap on option. Backscatter makes a macro lens for underwater use that works with their Flip filter system.

PORTABLE LIGHTING

Most of your daytime lighting will come from the sun, but using an external light can extend your filming time or even just fill in light when the sunlight is not bright enough.

There are a variety of external lights that can be mounted directly to your GoPro or placed in a scene for spot lighting. Lume Cubes are small cube-shaped portable lights and are one of the best options because they are waterproof to 100 feet. Just one Lume Cube can put out up to 1500 lumens (that's bright).

For Night Video

Mount your light to your GoPro for night filming. Most of the portable light manufacturers make a mount that allows you to mount your GoPro camera alongside their light. Most night video (without artificial lighting) requires using a high ISO setting resulting in lots of "noise". The use of a light allows you to bring your ISO back down, improve the view of the scene and continue GoPro'ing into the night.

As a Fill Light

In low light settings, such as under a canopy of trees or on a cloudy day, external lights work well for filling in shadowed areas. Place the light up against a subject or one of the key landscape areas for highlighting. Or place the light behind a translucent object for backlighting.

Underwater

Light disappears quickly as its filtered through water. As you dive down under water, an external light fills back in the light, restoring color to a dull underwater scene. And if you are diving deep where it gets even darker, your own light source will be the only source of any real usable light.

Light Painting

As you learned in the Night Photo section, you can use a variety of light sources for light painting, and an external light is an obvious choice. Hold it in your hand or shine light onto a scene to "start painting."

DOME PORTS

The GoPole Dome Port is one of the most economical options. The Dome Port pushes water away from the lens, creating a clear line between above and below the surface. Frame grab from video recorded at 4k @ 60 FPS.

A dome port is the perfect photography tool for water lovers. Even without a dome port, your GoPro will capture amazing water photos, but a dome port adds another dimension. A dome port is a large curved piece of acrylic that mounts onto the lens. This dome pushes water away from lens, making it possible to take photos right at the surface with objects above and below the water both in focus. Filming with a dome port is a specialized art. It's best done on a calm day so you can position your camera halfway above and halfway below the surface. Shoot with the sun at your back and use a high frame rate for video, or burst photos to increase the chances of capturing a unique perspective. You can also use it completely underwater, or above the water, but the results won't be as dramatic.

Some dome ports mount to the SuperSuit for deeper dives, while other mount directly to the camera without a housing for shallower surfaces. A port that mounts directly to the camera makes it easier to change settings on the fly, whereas the dome ports that require a housing allow for deeper dives. The Knekt KSD6SS is the best quality dome (and most expensive) and requires the SuperSuit. GoPole, Split and PolarPro also offer affordable dome port options.

TAKE IT TO THE SKY

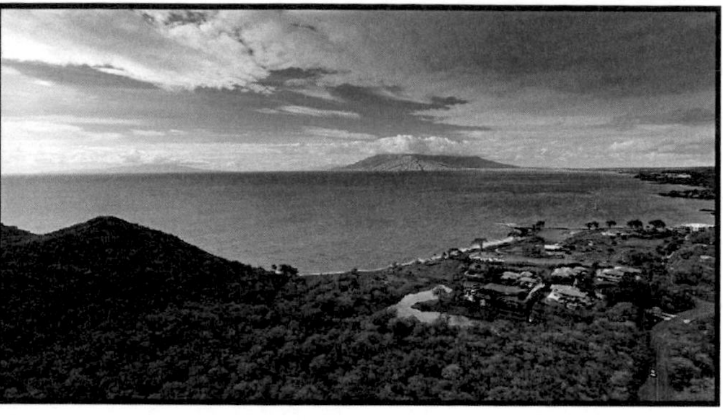

The HERO6 Black mounted in the Karma drone and a photo taken from the air, showing the potential of new perspectives. Shot in Single Photo Mode at 12MP Wide.

If you are looking for a new perspective, a drone is your answer. Drones are not for everyone, but if you are interested in drones, GoPro's Karma can take your HERO6 Black into the sky. The screen on the controller gives you a live view of what your HERO6 Black sees, as well as the ability to change all of the modes and settings in-flight. The gimbal produces super smooth footage and is removable, which enables you to use the same gimbal for handheld shots, as we covered in the Gimbal section. For all of the tips, tricks and info you need about Karma and aerial cinematography, check out the *GoPro: How To Use GoPro Karma* book, also by Jordan Hetrick.

REPLACEABLE LENS COVER

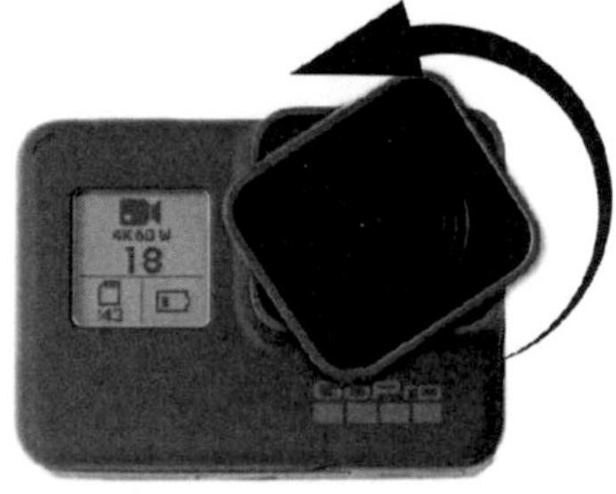
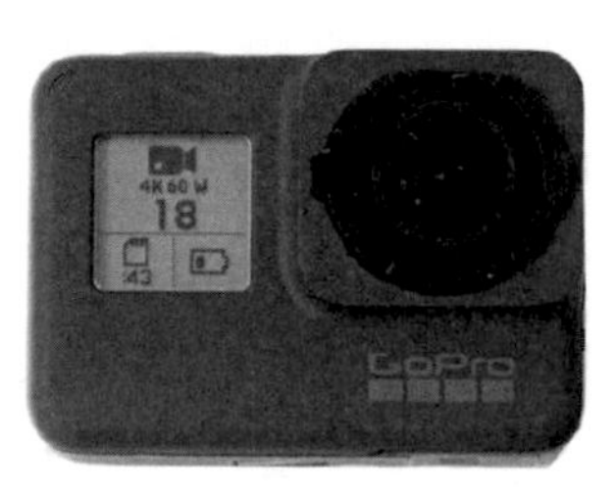

The glass lens cover is the one element of your HERO6 Black that can be easily replaced. If you scratch or break the glass cover in front of the lens, GoPro sells a replacement kit. The kit comes with everything you need to replace the lens cover, as well as an extra replacement. It's easy to pop off the lens cover (just pull and turn counterclockwise) to install a nice new piece of glass over your lens, but be careful to keep it clean beneath the glass.

Now that you know which accessories will improve the look of your footage, check out these tools to enhance your filming experience.

REMOTE CONTROL

There are two remotes available for the HERO6 Black- the Smart WiFi Remote and Remo, which is a voice activated remote. The ability to control your camera from a distance really opens up the possibilities for different shots.

Remo- Voice Activated Remote

Remo is essentially an extension of the Voice Control feature on the HERO6 Black. Remo allows you to use Voice Control from up to 33' (10m) away and is waterproof up to 16'. As long as the WiFi is still enabled on your camera, you can even turn your camera on and off using Voice Control. The remote also has a big Shutter Button on it, so you can press the shutter remotely. The drawback of Remo is that it only works for a relatively short distance and only in certain conditions (wind and noise interfere with Voice Control).

The Smart WiFi Remote

The Smart WiFi Remote is waterproof up to 33' (10m) deep and can control your camera from up to 600'/180m away in the right

conditions away so you could even have a friend on the beach push the shutter button for you. When using the WiFi Remote with one camera, the LCD Screen on the remote mimics the camera status screen on your camera, and you can instantly control your camera from a distance.

The WiFi Remote can control up to 50 cameras at once, so if you get more than one WiFi-enabled GoPro® camera, you can control all of them at the same time. When more than one camera is connected to the WiFi Remote, the remote LCD display will tell you the number of cameras connected, the recording mode and the remote's battery status.

The WiFi signal does not work underwater and will lose the connection within a few inches from the surface. The camera should automatically reconnect to the remote once you bring your camera back to the surface of the water.

Try out these uses for a Remote:

Action Self-Portrait Photos
When your camera is mounted to your equipment and is unreachable, use the remote for action photos in Burst Mode to get a great sequence at just the right moment. Carry the remote in your hand (or even better, attach it to your wrist with the Velcro strap that comes with the remote) and push the Shutter Button (the Red Circle) when you want to start the sequence.

Inaccessible Angles
If your camera is mounted somewhere inaccessible, like on the wing of an airplane or the side of your truck while you are off-roading to some remote camping spot, use the remote to start and stop the video during the exciting parts of the ride.

Undercover Angles
If you are trying to record footage without anyone noticing, set your camera in the right spot and start recording or taking photos as soon as the action starts. This works great for nature shots because animals are more likely to approach your camera when no one is around.

Polecam
If you have a polecam setup, use the remote to shoot Burst photos or to start and stop recording video without having to reach your camera. By using the remote, you still have access to push the shutter button when your camera is out of reach. Strap the WiFi Remote around the base of your pole using a piece of Velcro and shoot away. Some premade poles (like the GoScope and Remote Pole by SP-Gadgets) have mounting spots for the Smart WiFi remote.

MORE FREE APPS

Check out these free apps to do even more with your HERO6 Black!

Periscope
Stream live video from your HERO6 Black (GoPro streaming available on iOS only)

Periscope lets you use your GoPro camera to broadcast live directly to Periscope on your iPhone. If you have a need or desire to broadcast yourself or an event live, Periscope makes it possible.
It's simple to connect- Just turn your GoPro on in video mode and connect to your GoPro's WiFi. Then open Periscope on your iPhone and tap the broadcast button. The GoPro button will be highlighted. Give your broadcast a title and go live.

These tips will help you produce a more successful Periscope broadcast:

• You can also double tap to switch between your GoPro and iPhone camera to broadcast from multiple angles. While broadcasting, use the on-screen Periscope lock to prevent accidentally double tapping and switching camera views.

• Since viewers are mostly watching your broadcasts on their devices, use a 4:3 standard aspect ratio for broadcasts to show as much of the scenery as possible. Go with 1440-30 and your viewers will get the most out of your shots. If you choose to film in a Widescreen resolution, don't forget about using Touch Zoom when you need a "zoomed in" view.

• When broadcasting, your GoPro acts like an eye and can be used without recording. Make sure to press record on your camera to save your video onto your memory card. Periscopes are only accessible for 24 hours, so if you didn't save the recorded video, it's gone after that.

If you aren't into Periscope, the Livestream App (also for iOS only) is another option for live video from your GoPro.

Younity

Access your GoPro videos and photos anywhere (iPhone, iPad, Windows, Mac)

If you are not a GoPro Plus subscriber, the GoPro App only allows you to view content that is currently on your camera's microSD card or media files that you have downloaded to your phone/tablet through the GoPro App. You can download files from your camera to your phone/tablet, but unfortunately, the amount of storage required for your GoPro files will quickly outgrow your device's capacity.

But, with the Younity App, you do not need to worry about formatting your camera's memory card even though you have not posted your photos or videos yet. The Younity app allows you to stream your GoPro content from your computer to your phone or tablet. Younity automatically finds any GoPro videos and photos on your computer so you can view them when you are away from your computer.

Just install the App on your phone and computer. If you are using an external hard drive to store your files, make sure to add that location too. The App will look for all of your GoPro files and allow you to access to them from your device.

Trace

Auto Edits and Stats for Surfing, Snowboarding or Skiing (iPhone, Android)

The app is free, but to make use of it, you need to buy the device (costs around $200) to mount to your equipment. This device records stats about your riding. Then, after your session, the App automatically edits your highlights, corrects color and overlays the stats onto your video. It's kind of like what the GoPro App does, but in a much more detailed manner.

This device and app is specifically designed for surfing, snowboarding, or skiing, which is useful if you are really into your riding and want to get better by trying to improve your stats. The most useful aspect, however, is that the app sorts through your footage and auto-edits your video for you.

OFF THE GRID HERO6 SETUP

GoPro camera enthusiasts live outside of the box. With these accessories, you can step away from your computer for days or weeks and still be able to record your adventures:

Portable Battery Charger

Out of the box, the only way to charge your HERO6 is to plug it into your computer and wait for the batteries to refill. The GoPro Auto Charger or Wall Charger lets you recharge with a wall socket or your vehicle's lighter socket giving you the freedom to get out there and disconnect. A portable power bank, like GoPro's Portable Power Pack, also comes in handy for a few charges when you are totally out there.

Portable Data Storage

If you know you are going to be capturing lots of footage without being able to offload onto a computer, the best option is to bring a few high capacity (128GB) microSD cards. When you fill one up, swap it out for a new one and keep it in a safe spot. Another option is to use a portable memory card backup device to store your photos and videos when you are away from your computer. Digital Foci makes a couple of models with at least 500GB storage capacity and a built-in MicroSD card reader that will read the MicroSD cards from your HERO6. This will give you plenty of storage so you can empty your memory card onto this device and keep filming.

TIP: Thanks for reading! If you purchased this print book new through your account, you can pick up a free digital copy of this book through the sales page where you bought it. It's part of the Matchbook program and offered for free by the author so you can also keep a copy of this book on your device.

Now get out there and have fun!

TROUBLESHOOTING

These are some of the most common problems GoPro users run into. If you encounter any of these problems, try these solutions first. You can always contact GoPro's customer support via telephone and they will troubleshoot any problems with you right away. See GoPro's website for their customer service contact info for your country.

CAMERA MALFUNCTIONS

If you experience any of the following problems: first try the solution offered. If the problem happens repeatedly, reinstall your camera's firmware by performing an update through GoPro's website, through the GoPro App or through GoPro Studio. It's possible that the firmware did not install properly during the initial installation. If the problem persists, contact GoPro's customer support.

Problem: The camera heats up when recording.
Solution: This is normal, especially when filming at high resolutions or frame rates. If you continue to experience overheating, turn off the WiFi or temporarily turn off your camera to let it cool down. Also, recording in short stints will reduce the strain on your camera.

Problem: The camera freezes up and stops responding.
Solution: This is not normal and could indicate a problem with the installation of the firmware. To unfreeze your camera, remove and reinsert the battery. If it continues to happen, try manually reinstalling the firmware through the Support page on GoPro's website.

Problem: When recording, the video splits in the middle and half of the screen stops recording or loops.
Solution: This was a firmware issue in version 1.51 and sometimes happens in 4k with Stabilization enabled. Make sure your camera's firmware is updated to resolve this issue.

PLAYBACK ISSUES

Problem: Your computer is not recognizing the memory card when your camera is connected to your computer.
Solution: Make sure your computer is running the current operating system.

For Mac Users: Some programs may interfere with the communication between your camera and computer. Usually you can import the footage using Image Capture, which is located in your Applications.

Alternatively, if your computer has an SD Card slot, remove the microSD card and use the microSD card adapter to transfer your files.

Problem: Your video plays in fast forward after transferring it to your computer.
Solution: Import the video to GoPro Studio. Convert the frame rate in GoPro Studio. If this does not solve the problem, reinstall the firmware on your camera.

Problem: There is only audio and no picture.
Solution: Reinstall your camera's firmware by performing an update through GoPro's website, through the GoPro App or through GoPro Studio. If the problem continues, contact GoPro's customer support. You may need to get a replacement camera.

Problem: Choppy video playback. Some users experience choppy video playback. This is mainly due to the highly-compressed video files that require a lot of work from your computer. GoPro cameras use a very complex compression codec called h.264 to store a lot of video footage in a relatively small amount of memory. Your computer will most likely have the most trouble playing high resolution or high frame rate files. The good news is that your files are recorded properly. The not-so-good news is that your computer may not be able to handle the large video files.
Solution: First make sure you transfer your files to a folder on your computer before attempting to view them.

Next, import your video into GoPro Studio and convert the portions of the clips you want to watch. In Step 2: Edit of GoPro Studio, if your video is still playing choppy, set the playback quality to Better (Half Resolution) or even Good (Quarter Resolution) if you are still experiencing choppy playback. This will allow most computers to play the video footage smoothly, as it should be seen.

If you are still experiencing choppy playback, check to make sure your computer meets the minimum system requirements as shown in the User Manual. If your computer does not meet these requirements, you may need to update your computer.

If you are experiencing any other issues with your HERO6 Black or any of GoPro's other products, contact their Support team.

"Photography to me is catching a moment which is passing, and which is true."

~Photograher Jaques Henri-Lartigue

GoPro®

HOW TO USE

THE GoPro® HERO 6 BLACK

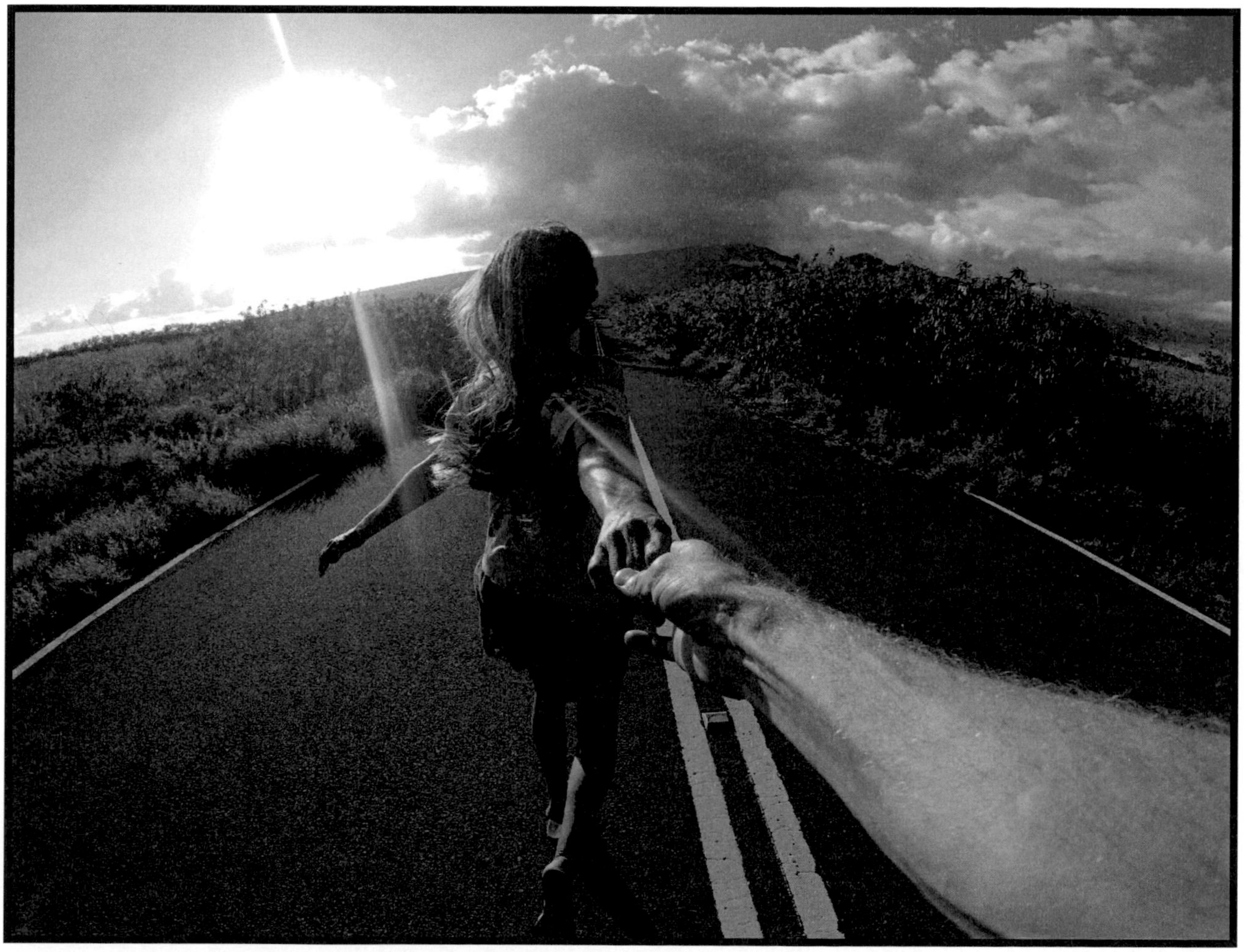

The Book for Your Camera- The Hero 6 Black

by Jordan Hetrick

14. THE *MARY ROSE*

Discovered on the seabed on which she sank, and raised to the surface over 400 years later, the *Mary Rose* has become one of the world's best-known preserved warships. This large and powerful English galleon, weighing 600 tons and armed with eighty guns, had been built in 1509 for King Henry VIII's Royal Navy. Named for Henry's younger sister Mary and the Tudor emblem, a rose, she was the first warship to carry siege artillery on deck. In July 1545, while departing the English coast at Portsmouth on the way to do battle with the French fleet, she keeled over in a gust of wind, took in water through her lower deck ports, and quickly sank. The *Mary Rose* had been built for a crew of about 400, but on this—her last voyage—she carried between 600–700 men, and only about forty survived. Many scholars believe that the ship's demise was, in fact, due to her being overloaded. The remains of the *Mary Rose* were found by divers in 1965, but it wasn't until 1982 that her hull was brought to the surface and restored for display at a museum in Portsmouth.

15. THE *HENRY GRÂCE À DIEU (GREAT HARRY)*

Launched in Kent, England, in June 1514, the *Henri Grâce à Dieu* was in its time the largest warship in the world. Also known as the *Great Harry,* she was built on the orders of King Henry VIII. She weighed in at 1,000–1,500 tons, and had a crew of approximately 700 men. Originally equipped with 184 guns on two gun decks, between 1536 and 1539 she was rebuilt and fitted with 21 heavy bronze guns, 130 iron guns, and about 100 hand-held anti-personnel guns called "murderers." Formerly, battles between ships had to be at close proximity, and usually the greatest harm came to the human adversaries. But with gunports cut in the hull, the *Great Harry* became the first "ship-killer," able to inflict significant damage on enemy boats from a distance. For special state occasions, the *Great Harry* was decked out in sails that looked like cloths of gold; in fact, she was built to be Henry VIII's diplomatic showpiece, and saw relatively little battle action. Unfortunately, this great vessel was accidentally destroyed by fire in August 1553. However, a likeness of her exists in the "Anthony Roll," a pictorial survey circa 1545 of the ships in Henry VIII's Royal Navy drawn by Anthony Anthony, a clerk in the ordnance office. This priceless illustrated record is currently housed in the Pepys Library at Magdalene College, Cambridge.

16. MAGELLAN'S FLAGSHIP *TRINIDAD*

The ongoing quest to explore the world and discover new trade routes spurred explorers to ever greater achievements. The development of such ships as the caravel facilitated longer voyages, so that by the early 1500s circumnavigation of the globe became possible for the first time. Working for the Spanish, the Portuguese explorer Ferdinand Magellan set sail in September 1519 with a fleet of five ships and about 270 men. His flagship was the *Trinidad,* and his plan was to find a route to the Spice Islands (Moluccas) by sailing westward through the newly discovered South Sea. After befriending an island king in the Philippines, Magellan became involved in the tribal warfare of the natives and was killed in a battle there. But another ship in the original fleet, the eighty-five-ton caravel *Vittoria* (pictured here in the background) continued onwards under the command of Juan Sebastián del Cano, and became the first ship to sail around the world when she arrived back in Spain in September 1522—almost three years from the day her journey began.

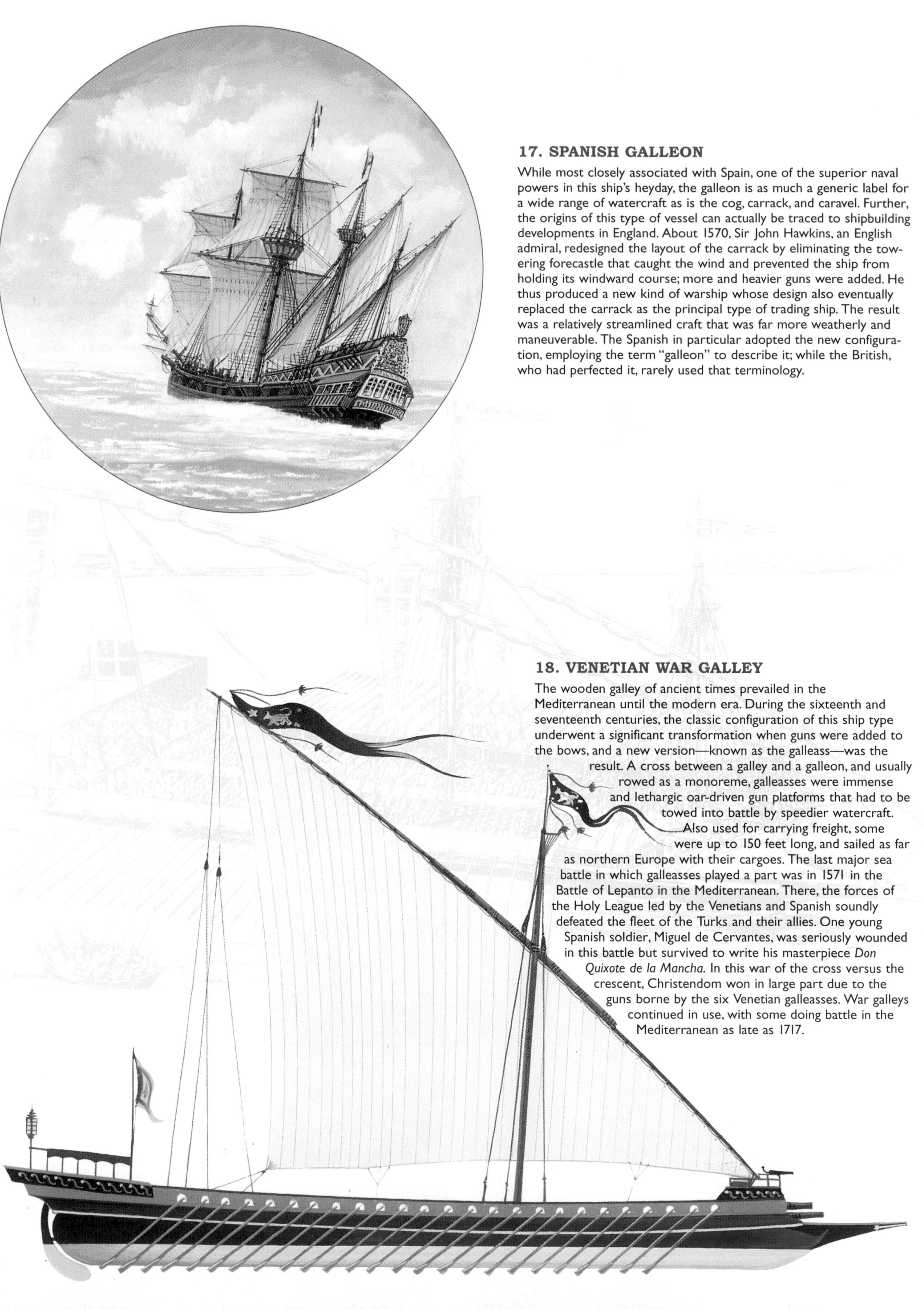

17. SPANISH GALLEON

While most closely associated with Spain, one of the superior naval powers in this ship's heyday, the galleon is as much a generic label for a wide range of watercraft as is the cog, carrack, and caravel. Further, the origins of this type of vessel can actually be traced to shipbuilding developments in England. About 1570, Sir John Hawkins, an English admiral, redesigned the layout of the carrack by eliminating the towering forecastle that caught the wind and prevented the ship from holding its windward course; more and heavier guns were added. He thus produced a new kind of warship whose design also eventually replaced the carrack as the principal type of trading ship. The result was a relatively streamlined craft that was far more weatherly and maneuverable. The Spanish in particular adopted the new configuration, employing the term "galleon" to describe it; while the British, who had perfected it, rarely used that terminology.

18. VENETIAN WAR GALLEY

The wooden galley of ancient times prevailed in the Mediterranean until the modern era. During the sixteenth and seventeenth centuries, the classic configuration of this ship type underwent a significant transformation when guns were added to the bows, and a new version—known as the galleass—was the result. A cross between a galley and a galleon, and usually rowed as a monoreme, galleasses were immense and lethargic oar-driven gun platforms that had to be towed into battle by speedier watercraft. Also used for carrying freight, some were up to 150 feet long, and sailed as far as northern Europe with their cargoes. The last major sea battle in which galleasses played a part was in 1571 in the Battle of Lepanto in the Mediterranean. There, the forces of the Holy League led by the Venetians and Spanish soundly defeated the fleet of the Turks and their allies. One young Spanish soldier, Miguel de Cervantes, was seriously wounded in this battle but survived to write his masterpiece *Don Quixote de la Mancha.* In this war of the cross versus the crescent, Christendom won in large part due to the guns borne by the six Venetian galleasses. War galleys continued in use, with some doing battle in the Mediterranean as late as 1717.

19. THE *GOLDEN HIND*

Sir Francis Drake was one of England's great naval heroes, as well as a visionary explorer and daring privateer. His fame rests primarily on two achievements: he was the first Englishman to circumnavigate the globe on his historic voyage in the *Golden Hind,* 1577–1580; and he was admiral of the fleet that defeated the great Spanish Armada in 1588. In December of 1577, Drake departed for his perilous 36,000-mile sojourn with five ships, including his flagship the *Pelican*—later renamed the *Golden Hind.* This sturdy vessel weighed in at between 100 and 120 tons. In the course of his travels, Drake raided and pillaged the Spanish colonies along the western coast of the Americas, returning with booty worth between £300,000 and £500,000, including perhaps as much as twenty-six tons of silver. Of the five ships that began the expedition, only the *Golden Hind* survived to make the return trip in September 1580. For his achievement, which marked the beginning of the rise of England as a major maritime power, Drake was knighted by Queen Elizabeth I. The *Golden Hind* is depicted in the painting on the left, and also in the background sketch below, where she is shown off the coast of British Columbia.

20. THE DEFEAT OF THE SPANISH ARMADA

The defeat of the Spanish Armada in 1588 is one of the key events in English history, and its broader implications eventually affected all of Europe. The battle took place over a period of days between July 28 and August 12, and ultimately led to the defeat of the Spanish who were forced to abandon their plan to invade Britain. Sir Francis Drake was the vice-admiral of the English fleet, and the *Revenge* was his flagship. Regarded as one of the finest galleons in the world, she was built in 1577 by the leading shipwright of the day, Matthew Baker of Deptford. The *Revenge* was one of the first of the new "race-built" vessels to grace the English fleet, relatively small in scale, weighing something under 500 tons (half the size of the *Great Harry*), with forty-six guns along the two sides of her gun deck. She is shown here engaging the *El Gran Grifón,* a supply ship under the command of the Duke of Medina Sedonia, the admiral-in-chief of the Armada. The Spanish vessel was badly damaged in the battle which ensued on August 3, 1588, and she was ultimately shipwrecked on Fair Isle in the Shetland Islands in September of the same year.

21. THE *HOORN*

In 1602, a confederation of Dutch merchants formed the Dutch East India Company (*Vereenigde Oostindische Companie,* or V.O.C.), whose charter specifically prohibited the use of "its" spice trade routes—the Cape of Good Hope around Africa and the Strait of Magellan in South America—by nonmembers. But the imperious Isaac Le Maire, a wealthy and powerful Amsterdam merchant, refused to be daunted by the V.O.C. monopoly, and launched an expedition whose primary goal was to chart a new course to the Pacific that would bypass the V.O.C. restrictions. He chose his son Jakob, the eldest of his twenty-two children, to head the entire undertaking. Willem Schouten, an experienced mariner, took charge of the larger ship, the 220-ton *Eendracht* ("Unity"), while Willem's younger brother Jan skippered the 110-ton *Hoorn* ("Horn"). The expenses were shared equally by Isaac Le Maire and the citizens of Hoorn, Schouten's hometown. With two sparse crews totaling a mere eighty-seven, the explorers departed on June 14, 1615. Unfortunately, the *Hoorn* caught fire about six months later while ashore in Porto Desire on the coast of Patagonia, when her hull was being scorched clean of weeds. The *Eendracht* sailed on successfully to round the southernmost tip of South America, circumventing the Strait of Magellan, thereby founding a new trade route to the Pacific. Often lashed by bad weather, this remote and desolate part of the Americas was named Cape Horn after the town that had helped sponsor the expedition.

22. THE *MAYFLOWER*

The *Mayflower* attained her special place in history when she successfully transported 102 Pilgrims from Plymouth, England to Massachusetts, to found the first permanent European colony in New England. This brave band of pioneers consisted mostly of members of the Separatist Church, dissenters who sought to purify the Church of England of all Catholic influence. Setting sail on September 16, 1620 with Christopher Jones as her captain, the *Mayflower* withstood a solitary and turbulent crossing of the North Atlantic to navigate safely around Cape Cod, anchoring in the harbor at Provincetown. After several weeks there, the group eventually set sail for Plymouth harbor, just a few miles away, where they made their historic landing on December 21, 1620. The 180-ton *Mayflower* was modeled on the design of a fluyt (or "fly-boat" in English), a flat-bottomed merchant ship of Dutch origin.

23. TASMAN'S *HEEMSKERCK*

At a time when the Dutch East India Company was extending its trading empire in the Pacific, Abel Janszoon Tasman was already one of the company's leading navigators. He had distinguished himself by venturing 1,000 miles beyond his predecessors into the uncharted regions of the North Pacific. In 1642, he embarked upon a voyage of discovery to the area we now know as Australia; to be precise, according to his official instructions, the expedition was "destined for the exploration of the Unknown and Discovered South Land, the South-East Coast of New-Guinea, with the Islands lying round about." His ships were the *Heemskerck*, a Dutch war yacht named after a famous sixteenth-century Dutch admiral and explorer, and the *Zeehaen*. By circumnavigating Australia, Tasman's route proved it to be a vast island continent, and not part of a southern landmass connected to the South Pole. His discovery of Van Diemen's Land—renamed Tasmania in his honor—and his exploration of New Zealand, were further revelations that led cosmographers of his day to redraw the map of the world, and paved the way for future explorers.

24. THE *VASA*

Sweden was once a proud and mighty military power. In the 1620s, her great king Gustavus Adolphus ordered the construction of a mighty warship named the *Vasa*. This magnificent vessel was intended to demonstrate the might and prestige of the Swedish nation, and to compete against the forces of the Holy Roman Empire who were Sweden's enemies. Built in Stockholm from the finest oak, the *Vasa* was approximately 214 feet in overall length and weighed about 1,400 tons. She was heavily armed with sixty-four guns made of bronze. Great ceremony attended her maiden voyage on August 10, 1628, and huge crowds gathered to see her off. Unfortunately, disaster struck. Only moments after she set sail, the great ship heeled over, took on water through her lower gunports, and sank; at least thirty people died in the catastrophe. In 1956, the wreck of the *Vasa* was located on a seabed in the Baltic. Items found with the vessel included many of its art treasures (about 700 sculptures and ornaments adorned it), twenty skeletons, six sails, cutlery, a pewter mug, and even some personal belongings of the crew. The ship is now on display at the Vasa Museum in Stockholm. (See page 48 for a drawing of the stern decoration of the *Vasa*.)

25. ARMED YACHT *ROYAL CAROLINE*

Launched from the shipyards of Deptford in 1749, this stately vessel resembled a small warship and was run strictly according to naval rules and regulations. It was used primarily for transport across the English Channel or to review the fleet. There were many ships of this type, of all sizes and rigs, owned by the royal houses of Europe. King George III inherited the *Royal Caroline* in 1760 when he attained the English throne, and he rechristened her the *Royal Charlotte* in 1761 when he sent her to Germany to fetch his future wife, Princess Charlotte of Mecklenberg–Strelitz. With her elegant lines and magnificent gilt "gingerbread" carvings, this particular craft was a splendid example of her type. She served the English royal family until 1805 and was dismantled in 1820, making her the royal yacht with the longest service record.

26. H.M.S. *ENDEAVOUR*

Originally named the *Earl of Pembroke* and constructed in the Fishburn shipyard of Whitby as a "cat"-built collier, the *Endeavour* came of humble beginnings. Yet the 368-ton vessel became one of the most famous exploration ships of all time under the command of Captain James Cook, perhaps the greatest mariner of them all. Cook favored these Whitby cats of shallow draught* because they could "safely sail near enough to land with time to turn away from warning sights, smells, and sounds; if at the worst they took ground, they could sit on it a while without much fear of a fatal capsize." When the ship foundered on the Great Barrier Reef in June 1769, Cook's wisdom was borne out; after extensive repairs, she was practically as good as new to continue the voyage, and eventually returned to England in 1771 relatively intact.

With a crew of ninety-four, the *Endeavour* set sail in August 1768 from Plymouth, England. The expedition was under the joint auspices of the Royal Society (the oldest scientific organization in England, founded in 1660) and the British Admiralty. The primary purpose of the voyage was to observe the transit of Venus in order to help scientists calculate the distance of the earth from the sun. This task Cook easily accomplished ahead of time. He was also instructed to locate the great, fabled southern landmass of *Terra Australis Incognita,* and possibly gain a colony or two for England. While Abel Tasman was the first to explore New Zealand and Australia (then called New Holland), the Dutch had neglected their development. An expert hydrographer, Cook accurately charted a map of New Zealand's coastline, and reached the southeastern corner of the island-continent of Australia, naming the area New South Wales. Cook's achievement was to bring these regions fully into the world picture, and pave the way for European expansion there. Today, he is as great an historical figure in Australasia as he is in England.

*the depth of water a ship draws

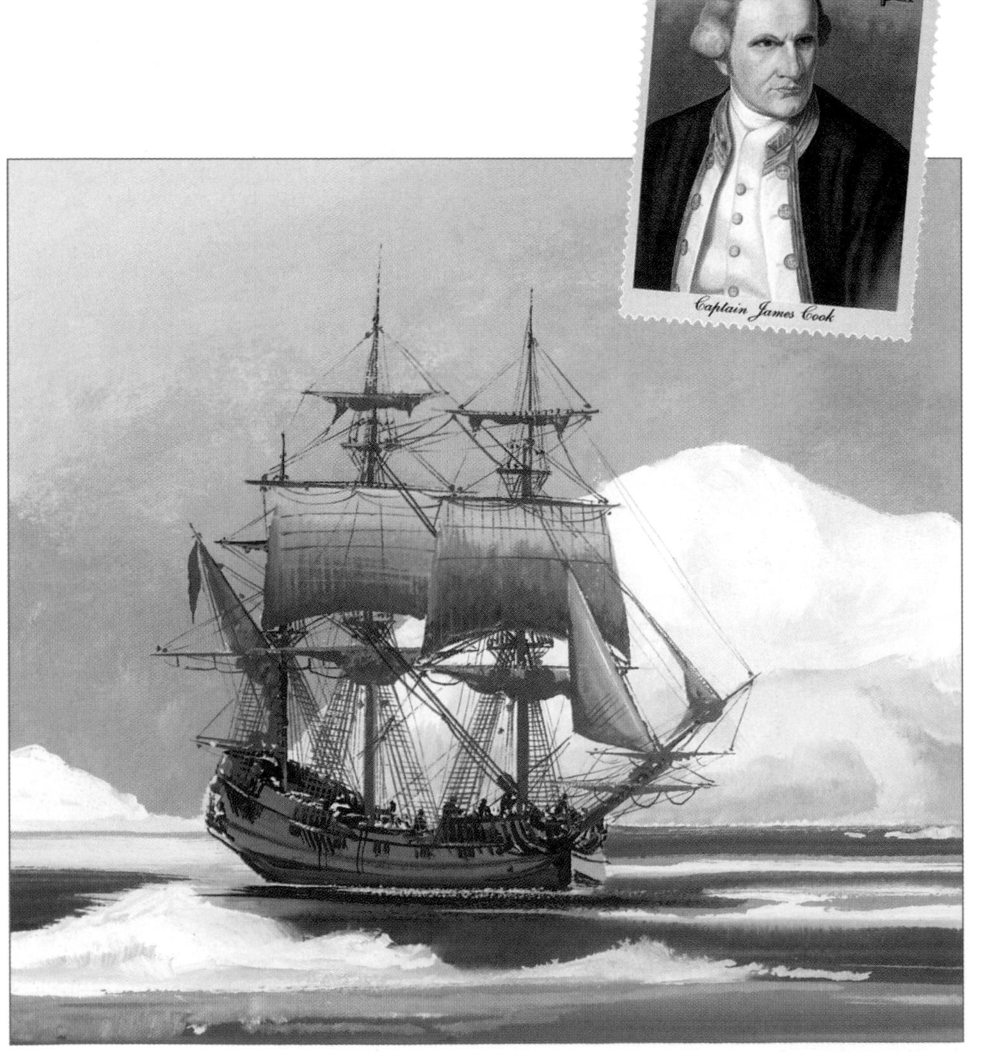

27. H.M.S. *RESOLUTION*

Acknowledging the outstanding accomplishments of his first expedition to the Pacific, the Admiralty commissioned Captain Cook for another voyage and, as it happened to be his ship of choice, in another converted collier. Formerly known as the *Marquis of Granby,* the *Resolution* had also been built by Thomas Fishburn of Whitby, although she weighed about 100 tons more than the *Endeavour*. Cook's second voyage, from 1772 to 1775, took the *Resolution* and her sister ship the *Adventure* (another refitted Whitby collier) into the southern Pacific, where the *Resolution* became the first ship to cross the Antarctic circle, thus disproving once and for all the existence of the fabled *Terra Australis Incognita.* Impenetrable ice prevented the expedition from discovering the continent of Antarctica, so the vessels turned southward to warmer waters for further exploration of the Pacific.

Cook embarked on a third voyage (1776–1779), also with the *Resolution,* this time in search of a Pacific entrance to the supposed Northwest Passage. His failure to find it seemed definitively to disprove its existence. In January 1778, Cook and his crew became the first Europeans to lay eyes on the Hawaiian islands, naming them the Sandwich Islands after the Earl of Sandwich, First Lord of the Admiralty (and inventor of the sandwich). The Hawaiians were at first friendly to their English guests, but later, relations turned unexpectedly hostile, and Cook was beaten to death in a skirmish on the beach in February 1779.

28. PIRATE BRIGANTINE

Usually the greatest challenges faced by ships on the high seas were the result of inclement weather and the vicissitudes of war. Yet through the ages, sailors faced another grave and not so obvious threat in the form of pirates who could be just as deadly as a naval attack or a sudden squall. Often flying their signature skull-and-crossbones flag—also known as the Jolly Roger—armed pirate ships would attack vessels of all kinds to steal their cargoes and weapons, and enslave or kill their crews. Sometimes referred to as the world's second oldest profession, piracy dates from ancient times where it is mentioned as early as the fifth century B.C. by the great Greek historian Thucydides. Certain parts of the world were especially plagued by pirates—e.g., the Mediterranean, the West Indies, the Gulf of Mexico, the Far East, and parts of South America. Starting with the Crusades in the eleventh century and extending into the early nineteenth century, Muslim pirates were notorious for their exploits along the Mediterranean coast bordering the North African states of Tripoli, Tunis, Morocco, and Algiers. Under President Thomas Jefferson, the United States launched an unconventional war against these so-called Barbary pirates that eventually brought an end to this centuries-old scourge. In general, the powerful and organized naval response to piracy by seafaring nations caused its decline after the eighteenth century. Even so, there are still many instances of piracy today, especially in the Far East and South America. In this picture, a brigantine (a versatile combat vessel particularly favored by pirates) flying the Jolly Roger, her decks crowded with armed men, attacks a small merchant ship.

The above illustration is reproduced by kind permission of Mr. and Mrs. G. Bannerman, Vancouver, British Columbia.

29. THE *HECTOR*

Like the Pilgrims of the *Mayflower,* the emigrants aboard the *Hector* risked the Atlantic crossing in the hope of making better lives for themselves in the New World. In the summer of 1773, the *Hector* sailed to Canada from Loch Broom in the western Highlands of Scotland with about 200 onboard. This small and sturdy 200-ton cargo vessel—with not even the barest amenities of a passenger ship—managed to carry this courageous band of Scots to a safe landing in Pictou harbor. The arrival of these settlers marked the beginning of a steady stream of Highland emigration to the area that became known as Nova Scotia (New Scotland) on Canada's Atlantic coast. A full-size replica of the *Hector* is now being built to sail once again in the waters around northeastern Nova Scotia.

30. U.S.S. *RANGER*

John Paul Jones was one of America's first great naval heroes, and it was as commander of the *Ranger* that he first attained celebrity. The 308-ton U.S.S. *Ranger* was built in Portsmouth, New Hampshire, and was an eighteen-gun sloop—sometimes known as a Continental corvette. During the Revolutionary War, while a captain in the Continental Navy, Jones sailed to France in the *Ranger* carrying word of General Burgoyne's historic surrender at Saratoga. As his ship entered Quiberon Bay on February 14, 1778, Jones fired thirteen guns and received in return a rousing salute from the French fleet marking the first time that the new American flag—the Stars and Stripes—was officially acknowledged by a foreign power. It was also aboard the *Ranger,* later the same year, that Jones launched the series of bold sea raids along the British coast that earned him his distinguished reputation as a fearless seaman.

31. THE *PYROSCAPHE* AND THE ARRIVAL OF THE STEAM ENGINE

For many centuries, ship designers and builders had sought a viable alternative to the traditional forms of propulsion used by ships. Sail power depends on the wind; vessels propelled by oars rely on the stamina and fitness of the men pulling them. It wasn't until the 1780s that the steam engine had gotten far enough along in its development to be used to propel waterborne vessels. The first to successfully utilize this new technology was the French paddleboat, the *Pyroscaphe,* designed by the Marquis Claude de Jouffroy d'Abbans. In June 1783, the 140-foot long, 150-ton steamer sailed for a full fifteen minutes at six miles per hour against the current of the River Saône near Lyon in central France. From these modest beginnings, steam navigation would become a vital means of propulsion for many types of ships within a matter of decades.

32. THE *CHARLOTTE DUNDAS*

The *Charlotte Dundas* was the first vessel ever to use steam propulsion for commercial purposes. She was a small wooden paddle steamer about fifty-six feet in length fitted with a Symington steam engine. This ten-horsepower engine drove a single paddle wheel recessed in the stern within a drum structure. The *Charlotte Dundas* was built under the patronage of Thomas, Lord Dundas, of Kerse for use on the Forth and Clyde Canal in Scotland. Making her debut in March 1802, she demonstrated the value of steam by pulling two 70-ton lighters (barges) 19½ miles along the canal, a passage that took six hours. Unfortunately, her career came to an abrupt end because of concern that the wake of repeated voyages would erode the canal banks.

33. U.S.S. *TURTLE*

Regarded in many quarters as the first experimental submarine, the U.S.S. *Turtle* was a small egg-shaped wooden structure that could be operated underwater to attach a gunpowder charge—the world's first torpedo—to the hull of an enemy warship. She was designed by an American inventor named David Bushnell, who is justly considered one of the fathers of the modern submarine. The *Turtle* was equipped with a large handle which, when turned, would force water from the submarine's ballast tank to make the craft rise to the surface. The propeller was also hand-cranked by her single, very strong, crewman. She was used during the War of Independence in September 1776 near Bedloe's (Liberty) Island in New York harbor to attack a British warship, the H.M.S. *Eagle.* The operation was unsuccessful because the *Turtle*'s gunpowder torpedo could not be screwed to the strong copper-clad hull of the enemy vessel. Nonetheless, the mission marked the first use of a submarine in warfare.

34. 38-GUN BRITISH FRIGATE

Frigates were introduced into the fleets of many navies as relatively small, fast ships, often with just one gun deck. They evolved to perform a wide array of roles that were not feasible for the larger men-of-war. As "the eyes of the fleet," frigates were protected from attack by a tacit understanding that line-of-battle ships would fire only on their counterparts. And by being situated at a relative remove from the smoke of gunfire, with a less obstructed view of a battle's progress, frigates could assist disabled ships and collect casualties. Civilian duties included the policing of trade routes, and the protection and escort of merchantmen. A special class of 44-gun frigates was introduced by the British Navy during the Napoleonic Wars against France (circa 1792–1815), with guns mounted on two gun decks. Built to outrun what they couldn't outgun, they were not particularly effective. The term frigate remains in use today for smaller warships able to perform antisubmarine, anti-aircraft, and general fleet duties.

35. U.S.S. *CONSTITUTION*

Launched in 1797, the U.S.S. *Constitution* is the oldest commissioned U.S. Navy ship still afloat. In fact, she is nearly as old as the document she is named after. In 1794, Congress authorized six warships to be built to combat the Barbary pirates, who at that time routinely and mercilessly plundered ships that sailed the Mediterranean. A 44-gun frigate fashioned from the oak of more than 1,500 trees, the *Constitution* was much larger and better-armed than the 44-gun frigates of the British Navy. She was 175-feet long and had a displacement of 2,200 tons. Her British-made guns were of a heavier caliber than those carried by her British counterparts.

The long and glorious career of the *Constitution* included the defeat of the British frigate *Guerrière* during the War of 1812, which represented a shining moment in the history of the new navy. British fire from extremely close range failed to penetrate the *Constitution*'s hull, leading to her nickname of "Old Ironsides." Oliver Wendell Holmes' poem of the same name aroused public sentiment for her preservation after her retirement, and she is now permanently berthed at the Charlestown Navy Yard in Boston harbor.

36. H.M.S. *VICTORY*

In 1805, Britain found herself once more at war with France and its ruler, the military genius Napoleon Bonaparte. While there were many significant naval engagements during the Napoleonic Wars, there was none so crucial historically as the Battle of Trafalgar on October 21, 1805, with British forces under the command of Vice Admiral Horatio Nelson in his flagship H.M.S. *Victory*. The resounding defeat of the combined French and Spanish fleets spelled the end of Napoleon's planned invasion of Britain, and marked the beginning of British supremacy on the seas.

The H.M.S. *Victory* was built between 1759 and 1765 as a "first-rate" ship of the line at Chatham Dockyard in southeast England. Warships of this era were categorized into six "rates" determined by the number of guns and size of their crews, the first rates being the largest and most powerful. Just over 226 feet long and with a weight of approximately 2,162 tons, the *Victory* had a crew of about 850 men. She was equipped with twenty-seven miles of rigging and four acres of sails, and over 2,000 mature trees were felled for her construction. At the Battle at Trafalgar, she was armed with 104 guns of several types on three gun decks. The *Victory* is enshrined in dry dock at Portsmouth Naval Base, and is currently undergoing restoration by the Royal Navy to match her 1805 condition in time for the bicentennial celebration of the Battle of Trafalgar in 2005.

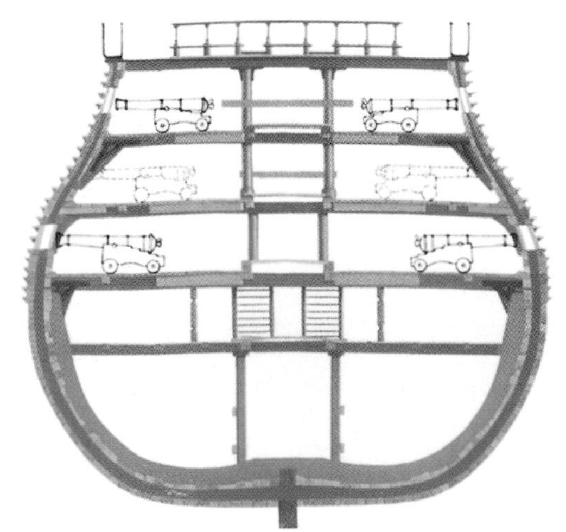

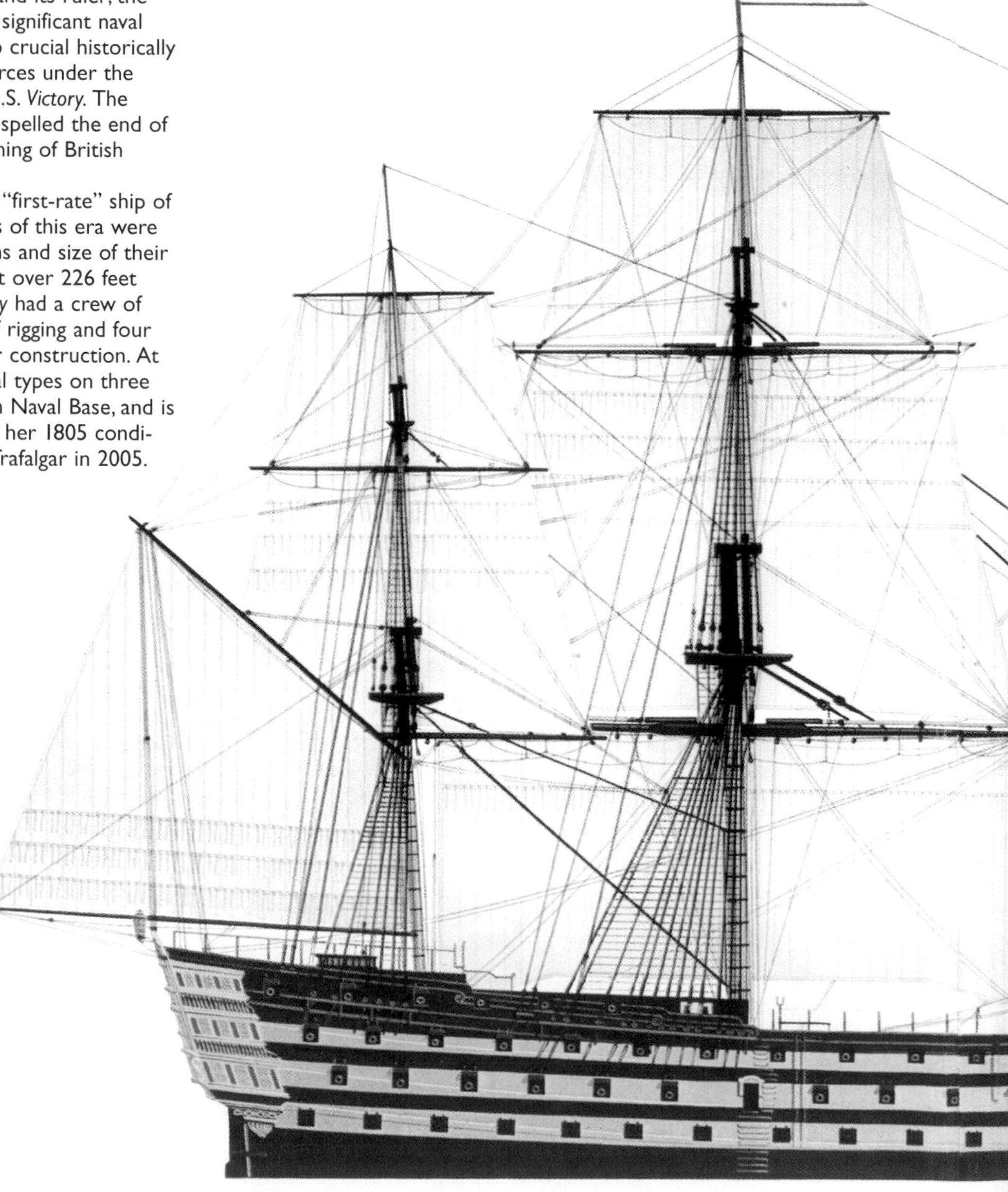

37. CHARLES DARWIN AND THE H.M.S. *BEAGLE*

The H.M.S. *Beagle* was the survey ship in which the English naturalist Charles Darwin made the voyage of discovery that would inspire a revolutionary change in human thought, eventually embodied in his book *Origin of Species* (1859). A small, ten-gun sloop of 235 tons launched in 1820, the *Beagle* journeyed from 1831–1836 to many previously unexplored regions in the southern Pacific, including the Galapagos Islands, located just below the equator. There Darwin's observations on the geology, and especially the flora and fauna, of the islands sparked his thinking on the subject of evolution and natural selection. In 1848, another English naturalist, Alfred Russel Wallace, made his own expedition to South America and the Amazon basin that led him to draw conclusions very similar to Darwin's. In 1858, the two published their findings simultaneously in a joint paper in the *Journal of the Linnean Society* entitled "On the Tendency of Species to form Varieties; and on the Perpetuation of Varieties and Species by Natural Means of Selection."

38. EAST INDIAMAN

The East Indiamen were the stately and frequently ornate trading ships operated by the East India companies of various European nations—particularly Holland and England—that sailed along the trade routes to India, the East Indies, and the Far East. From the 1600s to the early 1800s, their mercantile empires flourished and expanded due to the burgeoning demand for products like sugar, spices, furs, silk, porcelain, and precious stones, retrieved from the far reaches of the globe. These ships were the best specimens of any type produced in their heyday, and were often constructed and equipped in the private shipyards of the East India companies themselves. They generated huge support industries not only to build them, but also to maintain and supply them. In order to protect the East Indiamen against pirates and the warships of other countries, they were always armed, and the British versions (especially) resembled large frigates. By 1820, the largest vessel still in use weighed approximately 1,200 tons, like the one depicted just above in the drawing. The Dutch East India Company was in serious decline by 1795, while its English counterpart eventually ceased operations in 1858.

39. PADDLE STEAMER *SIRIUS*

The first ship ever to cross the Atlantic under continuous steam power, the *Sirius* was a wooden cross-channel side-wheel paddle steamer originally intended for service between London and Cork in Ireland. Built in 1837 at the shipyards of Leith, Scotland, and measuring only 200 feet in length, the 700-ton *Sirius* sailed the Atlantic from Cork in April 1838 with about forty passengers on board. Making an average speed of 6.7 knots, she arrived at Sandy Hook, New Jersey, at the entrance of New York harbor, after a voyage of just over eighteen days. Detained by a storm at sea that consumed her entire store of coal, the crew had to break up some of the ship's internal fittings and furniture for fuel to keep up the steam in her boiler. The *Sirius*' achievement marked the beginning of regular transatlantic steamship service, heralding the era of the ocean liner.

40. S.S. *GREAT BRITAIN*

Designed by the brilliant British engineer and architect Isambard Kingdom Brunel and launched in 1843, the *Great Britain* was by far the largest ship in the world at that time. At 322-feet long and with a displacement of 3,270 tons, she was the world's first steamship with a hull made of iron rather than wood. Instead of side paddle-wheels propelling her through the water, she had a screw propeller fitted in the center below the stern. Today, a screw propeller is the usual fitting for ships with engines, but for a large ship in the 1840s, it was a revolutionary advance. The hull of the *Great Britain* was divided into watertight compartments for safety, another innovation that has become standard today. The vessel made her first transatlantic voyage to New York in 1845, thus becoming the first propeller-driven ship to achieve the Atlantic crossing. The *Great Britain* later became a luxurious emigrant clipper, nicknamed the "greyhound of the seas," eventually carrying over 16,000 immigrants from England to Australia. After the mid-1880s, this famous vessel was retired and used as a moored storage hulk in the Falkland Islands off South America. In 1970, the *Great Britain* was returned to her birthplace at the Great Western Dockyard in Bristol where she is on display while undergoing a complete restoration.

41. PADDLE STEAMER *CENTRAL AMERICA*

Built in 1852 by William H. Webb at his New York shipyard on the East River, with two oscillating engines from the Morgan Ironworks of New York, the *Central America* was an elegant side-wheel wooden paddle steamer that transported cargo and passengers. She served on the Panama route, carrying many tons of gold from the California gold fields to the east coast of the United States. Sailing from Havana in September 1857, at the height of the hurricane season, she met with a violent storm and sank with a great loss of life. Over 400 people and about $2 million in gold were lost in the disaster. In 1989, the wreck of the *Central America* was recovered (about 200 miles off the coast of the Carolinas) in a high-tech diving operation, along with her cargo of gold—whose value had ballooned over the course of more than a century to nearly a billion dollars.

42. JUNK

Different regions of the world have their own special types of waterborne transport, uniquely adapted to local conditions. Found only in East Asia where it is associated especially with China, the junk is one of the best known of these craft. It reaches farther back in history than any other type of ship, and its exact origins are thus obscured by the mists of time. In 1298, Marco Polo described the junk in detail in his account of his travels to China, a description that still applies to the vessels that are a familiar sight in the Orient today—a tribute to their early technical perfection. While these craft may take different forms, they are usually wooden-built with keel-less flat bottoms, square bows, and a high stern. Their most striking common feature is the sail—sometimes called a lugsail—with very obvious bamboo battens mounted across its width to stiffen it. Some trading junks were built to the enormous size (for a junk) of up to 3,000 tons for long-distance voyages on the Pacific and Indian oceans. At one time, junks were the backbone of Chinese war fleets. A pole junk is depicted here.

43. AMERICAN WHALER

Because of the great demand for such products as whale oil, spermaceti, and baleen (whalebone), to name a few, the whale has been hunted relentlessly for centuries. Major whaling centers developed and flourished all over the world, while a wide variety of boats and ships evolved for use as whalers. During the 1800s, New England was at the hub of an important whaling industry. Still celebrated among the many whaling vessels built there is the *Charles W. Morgan.* Weighing 313 tons and with a length of 106 feet, she hailed from the Hillman yard in New Bedford, Massachusetts, and was launched in 1841. She was named after her owner, a Quaker whaling merchant. The *Morgan* made thirty-seven voyages in eighty years, and covered more miles than any other American whaler. After a long and productive career, she made her last voyage in 1921. America's last surviving wooden whaler, she has since been fully restored and is currently on display at the Mystic Seaport in Connecticut.

44. THE *GREAT EASTERN*

Isambard Kingdom Brunel's towering achievement with the mighty *Great Britain* led to the design and construction of an even larger ship. It was hoped that this undertaking would prove to be a significant financial success, since despite Brunel's visionary genius as a designer and builder, his projects were often plagued by severe financial problems. The massive *Great Eastern,* or "Great Iron Ship," was a huge 692-foot-long vessel with planned accommodations for 4,000 passengers and 6,000 tons of cargo. She weighed around 27,400 tons fully loaded. This leviathan was by far the biggest ship in the world when launched in 1858. Possessing side paddle-wheels as well as a stern propeller, her iron structure was immensely strong, with double iron plating from the keel to the waterline—the first time this now well-established construction method was used in a major ship's design. Unfortunately, the *Great Eastern* was not successful as a passenger ship—bankrupting both her builder and her owners—but she was nevertheless the forerunner of the great liners of the future. Eventually, in 1865, she found gainful employment when she was hired to lay the first transatlantic telegraph cable on the seabed between Europe and the United States.

45. *GLOIRE*

The launch of the *Gloire* in 1859 proved to be a milestone in the development of the warship. Prior to that time, fighting ships had been made of wood. But great advances in the manufacture and implementation of metals meant that, sooner or later, wood would no longer be used as the primary building material for military ships. Already, commercial ships such as the *Great Britain* demonstrated the viability of iron in their construction. The French *Gloire* was thus the first of a new breed. While her hull was made of oak, her sides were fortified with a belt of iron armor plate almost five inches thick. This reinforcement qualified her as an "ironclad," and was in direct response to the threat posed to all-wood ships by technological advances in naval weaponry, including the use of explosive shells instead of solid cannon balls. The vessel's extra armor plate, together with her steam power plant and screw propeller, made her the most advanced man-of-war in the world at that time. Despite the *Gloire*'s heavy iron armor, she could steam at a respectable 13.5 knots, while her armament consisted of a single deck of guns of a new 66-pounder design.

46. H.M.S. *WARRIOR*

The British reaction to the French *Gloire* in this nineteenth-century arms race was the rapid construction of an iron warship to counter the new French ironclad. The result was the H.M.S. *Warrior*—the pride of Queen Victoria—which was launched in 1860. The hull of the *Warrior* was constructed entirely of iron—a first for a warship. Three-hundred-eighty-feet long, she was also "encased with Wrought Iron Plates" along the vital central section of her hull. Like the *Gloire,* she was classed as a frigate, but at 9,210 tons, she was much heavier than her French rival. The steam-powered *Warrior* sported another major innovation in the form of an armored citadel that housed most of her guns. In 1887, the *Warrior* was reclassified as an armored screw battleship, and ultimately she was more important as an icon of naval history than for any actual wartime service. She was eventually restored in the 1980s, and is permanently moored at Portsmouth Navy Yard in England where she is on view to the public.

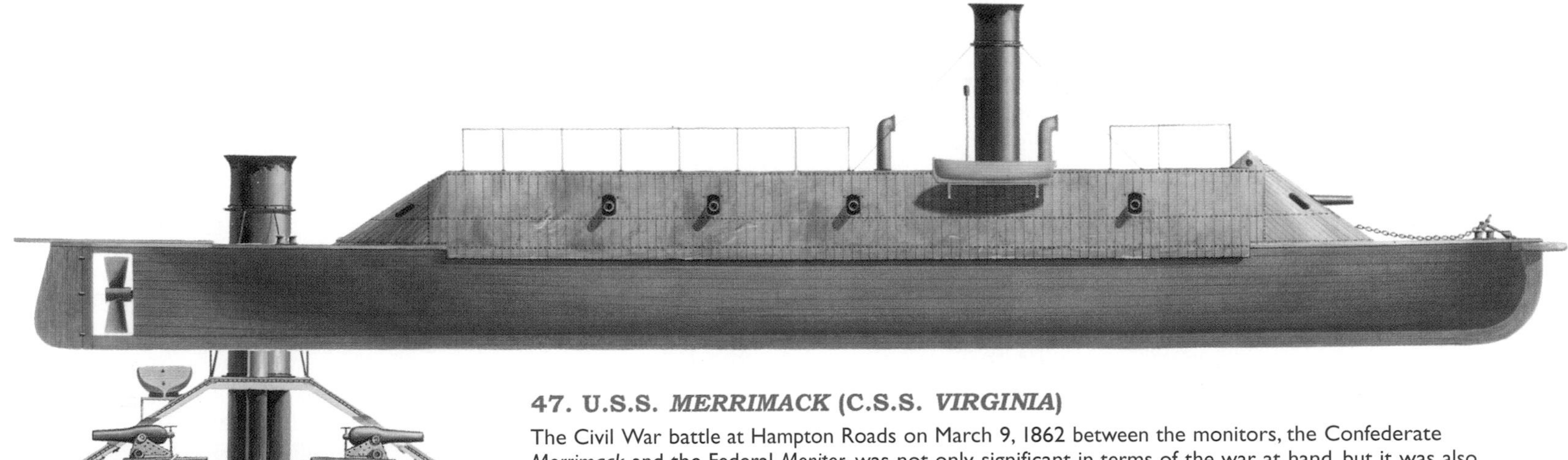

47. U.S.S. *MERRIMACK* (C.S.S. *VIRGINIA*)

The Civil War battle at Hampton Roads on March 9, 1862 between the monitors, the Confederate *Merrimack* and the Federal *Monitor,* was not only significant in terms of the war at hand, but it was also the first "Battle of the Ironclads." Monitors are long, flat warships, and these two were the very first of this type. The *Merrimack* was modeled on the U.S.S. *Merrimack,* a steam frigate built in the 1850s. She had been scuttled and set on fire early in the Civil War by her northern crew. However, in 1861, the Confederate States Navy rebuilt her with a new superstructure—mounting a number of fixed guns at her front, sides and rear—and renamed her the C.S.S. *Virginia.* She was also equipped with a ram at the bow, a throwback to the ram-armed war galleys of the past. The Hampton Roads skirmish represented the triumph of industrial age warfare, and helped to accelerate ironclad construction programs already underway in both Europe and America.

48. C.S.S. *ALABAMA*

One of the most significant of the few naval actions of the Civil War took place not in American waters, but off the coast of France. The combatants were the C.S.S. *Alabama,* an armed cruiser of the Confederate Navy, and the "screw sloop" U.S.S. *Kearsarge* of the Federal Navy. The *Alabama* was built in 1862 in Liverpool, England for the Confederacy, and under the able command of Captain Raphael Semmes, she was the scourge of Yankee shipping for nearly two years. In need of repair after a long series of successful raids (all told, her damage to Federal shipping amounted to about $6 million), the *Alabama* stopped at the port of Cherbourg on the French coast in June 1864. There she was blockaded by the U.S.S *Kearsarge* under the leadership of Captain John Winslow until the overhaul was completed. On June 19, the *Alabama* emerged from Cherbourg harbor to challenge the Federal sloop and a major battle ensued. After just over an hour of fierce combat, the *Alabama* suffered critical damage and started sinking. At the news of her demise, which spelled the end of her reign of terror on the high seas, the North was jubilant.

49. U.S.S. *MONITOR*

The clash of the *Monitor* and the *Merrimack* (*Virginia*) in March 1862 represented a turning point in naval history not only because it was the first battle of the ironclads, but also because it was the first time that a revolving gun turret—now a commonplace feature of warships—was used on a military ship. Designed by Swedish-born American inventor John Ericsson, the U.S.S. *Monitor* was equipped with a rotating turret on the deck in which the vessels' two 11-inch Dahlgren cannons were mounted. Most of the ship lay below the water line, making her a difficult enemy target at best. The controversial craft, which was very flat and narrow, had a length of 172 feet, and was sometimes referred to as "a tin can on a shingle." She was completed in a record 101 days at the Continental Iron Works in Greenpoint, New York (now part of Brooklyn) where her various parts were assembled from eight different foundries.

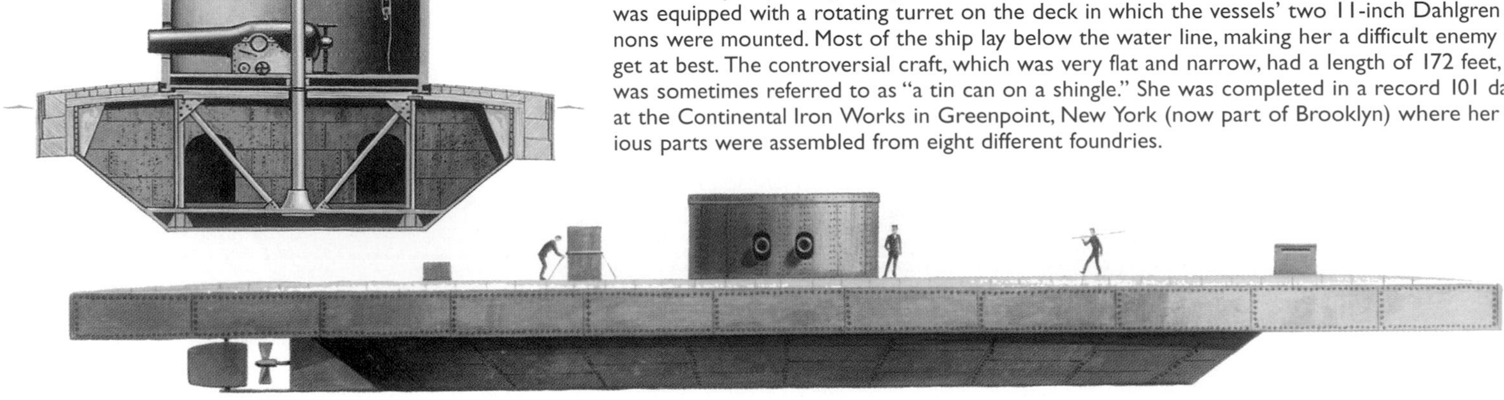

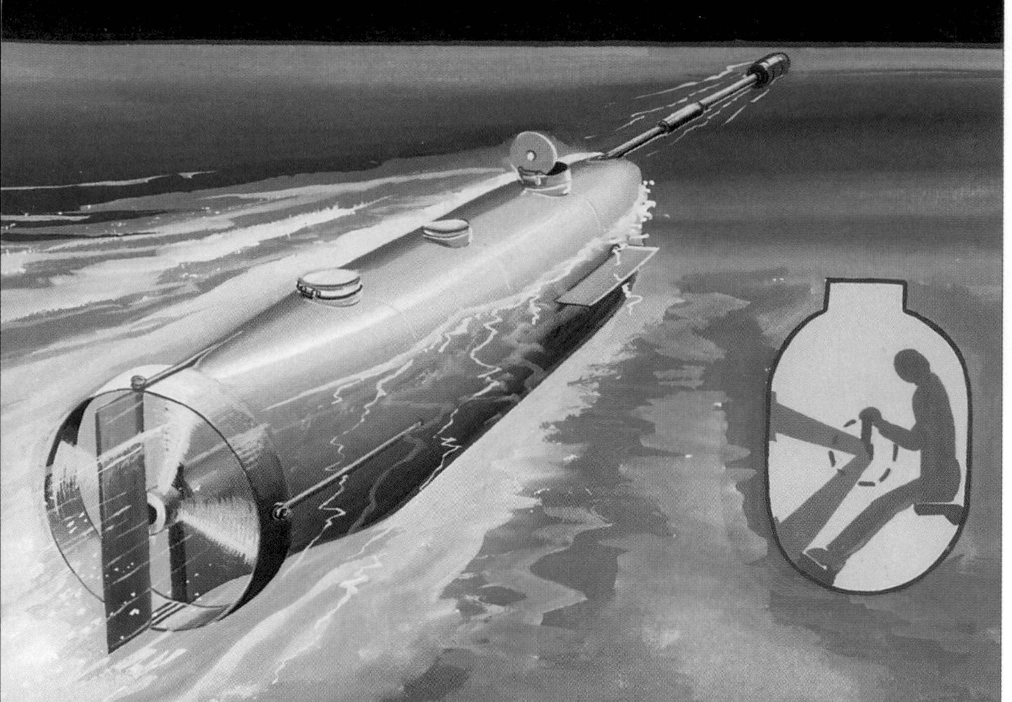

50. C.S.S. *HUNLEY*

The Civil War naval battle of February 17, 1864 marked another historic occasion in the development of maritime warfare. For the first time ever, a submarine sank a ship during wartime. The place was the outer reaches of Charleston harbor off the South Carolina coast, where the submarine C.S.S. *Hunley* engaged and sank the Federal frigate U.S.S. *Housatonic*. Named after her designer, H. L. Hunley, the vessel was a nearly forty-foot-long contraption fashioned from a cylindrical iron steam boiler, with a crew of nine men. Eight men were required to hand-crank the propeller, while one man was needed to steer and navigate. With its primitive ballast system, the craft could not really dive and was trimmed to move semi-submerged. The bow of the *Hunley* was armed with a twenty-two-foot wooden spar, tipped with a 135-pound explosive charge. In the Charleston battle, the submarine went into action and blew a hole in the 1,800-ton *Housatonic*. Unfortunately, the ensuing explosion also sank the *Hunley,* and all on board were lost. It would still be some time before submarines would work well under water, and be made safe for their crews. For over 130 years, the wreck of the *Hunley* lay undiscovered, until 1995, when best-selling author Clive Cussler and his diving team found her after a fifteen-year search; her subsequent excavation and restoration is still in progress, and there are plans underway to build a museum in her honor on the Charleston waterfront.

51. *CUTTY SARK*

The only clipper ship of her era that has been preserved, the *Cutty Sark* is one of the most renowned and beloved of all British ships, perhaps second only to Nelson's H.M.S. *Victory.* With 32,000 square feet of sail, she was one of the fastest of her kind, and could attain a speed of over seventeen knots—equivalent to a 3,000-horsepower engine. Her Scots owner, "Old White Hat" Jock Willis (so-called because he was always seen in a tall white top hat), spared no expense in her design and construction. He had high hopes that she would take first place in the annual tea race from China to London. Weighing in at 963 gross tons, the *Cutty Sark* was composite-built with a light iron frame overlaid by wooden planking. She was about 212 feet long and sported three masts that were all square-rigged. As destiny would have it, 1869—the year she was launched—coincided with the opening of the Suez Canal, an event that sounded the death knell for the tea clippers. With the distances shortened, steamships could now make the trip east quicker via this new passage that was inaccessible to sailing ships. The clippers eventually moved on to the wool trade between Australia and Britain. The *Cutty Sark* sailed this route between 1885 and 1895 under the command of the venerable Captain Richard Woodget, a superb mariner and a hero to his crew. Man and ship were perfectly matched, and the vessel made her best times with him at her helm. The *Cutty Sark* is now on display in dry dock at Britain's National Maritime Museum in Greenwich.

52. MISSISSIPPI STERNWHEELER

Since the development of steam propulsion for ships, paddle steamers of many types and sizes proliferated. Some were made for oceangoing, some for river traffic, while others were built simply for pleasure. In the United States, the best known are those that plied such great rivers as the Mississippi. River-going paddle steamers had two general classifications: "sternwheelers," equipped with a single paddle-wheel at the stern in the center; and "side-wheelers," furnished with a large wheel amidships on each side. On the Mississippi River, both kinds abounded. Luxury models served as floating gambling casinos where thousands of dollars could be won or lost on a short one-day cruise. Others qualified for the popular inland-river racing competitions during the 1870s, like the one between the paddle steamers *Robert E. Lee* and the *Natchez* from New Orleans to St. Louis. The *Natchez* was a large craft, about 307-feet long and 43-feet wide. Not long after this historic race, river-steamer passenger transport gave way to the era of the railroad. The painting here depicts a truly grand Mississippi stern-wheeler—one of the veritable "palaces on paddle wheels."

53. PADDLE STEAMER *MOUNT WASHINGTON*

Used in many parts of the world, small paddle steamers were a familiar sight along inland waterways for many decades from the mid-nineteenth century onwards. Some side-wheel paddle steamers had very prominent walking beam mechanisms atop their superstructures which were a part of the apparatus that turned the paddle wheels. The illustration here shows the *Mount Washington,* a classic example of this type.

54. THE *PREUSSEN*

Often regarded as the biggest sailing ship ever built, the magnificent *Preussen* was launched in 1902. She was one of several huge sailing ships built in Europe between 1890 and 1921, at a time when the breed was being all but replaced by ships with engines and no sails. Almost 408-feet long and with a displacement of 11,150 tons, the *Preussen* was a steel ship able to carry up to 8,000 tons of cargo. She had five masts, all square-rigged, which made her the only five-masted full-rigger in the world. While she had forty-eight sails in total, it took only forty-five men to sail her because deck-mounted steam engines did some of the work, such as cargo winching and anchor-hoisting. The vessel was built for and operated by the "Flying P" ship line of F. Laeisz & Son of Hamburg, Germany to carry nitrate around Cape Horn from Chile, which she did for eight years. Unfortunately, her thirteenth voyage was her last. Passing through the English Channel in November 1910, she collided with a cross-channel ferry, and was wrecked by a storm on the English coast near Dover before she could be repaired.

55. DRIFTER

Fishing boats have taken many forms, from small craft to huge ships, with the size and type often depending on local marine conditions and the kind of fish being caught. One especially wide-ranging prototypical fishing boat is known as the "drifter." Once propelled by sail, today these craft are usually powered by engines. They were (and still are) designed to catch fish that swim in shoals near the surface by casting drift nets. Herring are usually the main catch of drifters. At their height, drifters were predominant in the North Sea between England and Norway, and around the coasts of Ireland and Scotland where herring could be caught in large numbers. At the time of the Industrial Revolution in Great Britain, drifters provided food for the rapidly expanding populations of the industrial towns, where the growing network of railway lines moved the fish swiftly to their destinations.

56. THE HOLLAND SUBMARINE

The true father of the modern submarine is the Irish-born American John Philip Holland. By the end of the nineteenth century, many of the devices necessary to make a workable submarine had at last been invented, and Holland was able to combine them to launch the world's first successful production submarines. Among these technological innovations were the gasoline engine for surface propulsion and the storage battery for underwater cruising. Similarly, the invention of torpedoes that could be aimed and fired for long distances underwater represented another important step forward, since they afforded the vessel an opportunity to attack its target from afar without the danger of being blown up in the resulting detonation. The vexing problems of how to make the submarine submerge and then rise to the surface safely, and how to control it when it was submerged, were also adequately solved. Holland experimented with a number of test submarines which carried his name, and production models were eventually commissioned in the early 1900s by several countries, including the United States, Great Britain, and Japan.

57. THE *TURBINIA*

The development of the steam engine revolutionized the way ships were propelled, eventually eliminating the need for sails on larger ships. This was soon followed by another major advance, the more efficient and powerful steam turbine engine, invented by the British marine engineer Charles A. Parsons. It worked by directing steam under pressure onto the blades within a drum connected to a propeller shaft. The high-velocity jets of steam acting on the blades drove the drum around, which in turn spun the propeller shaft and its propellers at optimum speed. For years, Parsons tried to interest Britain's shipbuilders and the Royal Navy in his invention—always without success. So he built a motor yacht named the *Turbinia* in which he fitted three of his steam turbine engines, making it the world's first steam turbine-powered vessel. In a brazen move, Parsons debuted his revolutionary craft in 1897 by arriving uninvited at the Spithead Naval Review for Queen Victoria's Diamond Jubilee. The crowd was aghast as he maneuvered the *Turbinia* with great dexterity between two rows of cumbersome warships, while patrol boats were unable to stop what was—at a speed of over thirty knots—the fastest boat in the world. Soon, warships and ocean liners were being built with this type of propulsion system.

58. SCHOONER *THOMAS W. LAWSON*

Although the schooner was a very successful type of sailing ship, increasing competition from steam-powered merchant vessels prompted a number of design changes to its traditional types. One set of modifications was represented by the fore-and-aft schooner, and many of those constructed were equipped with more than the traditional two masts. The grandest of this new design was the enormous seven-masted fore-and-aft schooner the *Thomas W. Lawson,* named after a millionaire yachtsman and stockbroker of Boston. Built in Quincy, Massachusetts, she was one of several large American-built multi-masted schooners. A steel-hulled vessel of the incredible weight (for a schooner) of 5,128 gross tons, the ship sought to cut operating costs by having a crew of only sixteen, and used steam winches for managing her approximately one acre of sails. Completed in 1902, she was said to handle like "a beached whale" and was unsuccessful in service as a coal cargo ship. Refitted as an oil tanker later in her career, the *Thomas W. Lawson* was lost when the vessel foundered off Britain's Scilly Isles in 1907.

59. U.S.S. *PENNSYLVANIA*— THE FIRST LANDING

Crew members sought every possible vantage point to watch Eugene Ely land an aircraft on a specially constructed deck, 120-feet long, over the stern of the U.S.S. *Pennsylvania.* The deck had twenty-two ropes stretched across its width to act as arrester gear. Each rope was kept taut by fifty-pound sandbags. For the flight, Ely wore a football helmet, as well as bicycle inner tubes for flotation in the event of a sea crash. Swimmers and lifeboats stood by along Ely's approach to the ship. The date was January 18, 1911 and the place was San Francisco Bay. Ely successfully landed his Curtiss Model D-IV "Pusher" biplane on the deck of the *Pennsylvania,* and after forty-five minutes, took off again and landed ashore two miles away. This momentous event, demonstrating that ships could serve as floating airfields, marked the beginning of naval aviation.

60. H.M.S. *DREADNOUGHT*

In the early years of the twentieth century, Great Britain initiated a major naval arms race under the leadership of First Sea Lord John Fisher. Incorporating many of the best technological advances of the previous fifty years, the new warships produced rendered all preceding models obsolete.

The first of Britain's new super battleships was the H.M.S. *Dreadnought.* Completed in just fourteen months and launched in early 1906, she was a remarkable "all-big-gun" ship that gave Britain a clear edge over other nations in warship design. With a displacement of 17,900 tons, the 527-foot-long vessel was powered by Parsons steam-turbine engines and could attain over twenty-one knots. Her armament was state-of-the-art, with five revolving gun turrets—three on the ship's centerline—each with two 12-inch guns. The turrets had 11-inch armor plating, and the belt armor on the ship's sides had the same thickness. The appearance of the *Dreadnought*—the first modern twentieth-century battleship—attracted international attention, and she was the first of many to follow from Britain's shipyards. It was not long before other countries, such as the United States, Germany, and Japan, were building similar ships to rival those of the British; and all of them would come to be called "dreadnought," as her name became generic.

61. *VATERLAND*

The best known of several German transatlantic ships on the North Atlantic route was the Hamburg–America Line's *Vaterland*—Germany's answer to Great Britain's White Star Line of Olympic class steamers. Built in 1913, her maiden voyage was in May 1914, just prior to the start of the First World War. At that time, she was the largest liner afloat, 950-feet long and weighing in at 54,282 gross tons. The *Vaterland* could carry about 3,909 passengers plus 1,180 crew members, and steamed at twenty-three knots. Her luxurious interiors included a gymnasium and pool complex, several shops, and even a bank. She was also equipped with special safety features—like a twenty-four-hour wireless telegraph system and a large searchlight on the foremast—conceived as a result of the *Titanic* tragedy. Moored in New York harbor when World War I broke out, the *Vaterland,* unable to return to Germany, became the center of local German society and the site of many gala pro-German fund-raising events. Then in 1917, when the United States entered the conflict, she was seized by the American authorities. When she sailed again, it would be as an American troopship with a new name—the *Leviathan.*

62. R.M.S. *TITANIC*

The most famous tragedy of the seas is the sinking of the great ocean liner *Titanic* in April 1912. The *Titanic* was one of three sister ships ordered by the White Star Line, a British company in competition with the Cunard Line for the lucrative passenger trade across the North Atlantic. The *Titanic* had the reputation of being "unsinkable," and had been built to a very high standard with watertight compartments which were supposed to save her if she was holed in an accident. According to her original specifications, she was "11 stories high and four city blocks long. . . . Her interior fittings were sumptuous." A mighty ship of 46,329 tons, she sailed from Southampton, England on April 10, 1912, on her first transatlantic voyage to New York. She never arrived. Four days into her maiden voyage, she struck an iceberg and sank. Although it took over two hours before she finally slid beneath the waves, well over 1,400 of those on board were killed. It was later found that the vessel had only enough lifeboats for about half the total number of passengers and crew, while many who stayed on board simply could not believe this "unsinkable" ship would actually go down. The 712 survivors were rescued by the Cunard liner *Carpathia,* which later arrived on the scene of the disaster that made headlines around the world. As a result of the *Titanic* incident, new safety measures were mandated for ocean liners to prevent such a catastrophe from happening again.

63. H.M.S. *ARGUS*

The H.M.S. *Argus* attained her place in history as the first true aircraft carrier, with a flight deck for her aircraft running unobstructed from above the bows to the stern. Built in Glasgow, Scotland, she had been converted from the unfinished Italian ocean liner *Conte Rosso.* Operated by Britain's Royal Navy, the *Argus* first embarked torpedo-carrying aircraft in October 1918, but she was too late for operational service in the First World War. Her bridge and chart house were in a retractable housing, so that her 550-foot-long by 68-foot-wide flight deck would be free from obstructions when aircraft were operating from her deck. She could carry up to twenty aircraft, and her exhaust gases were exited through ducts in her stern.

64. BATTLESHIP *POTEMKIN*

The pre-dreadnought battleship *Potemkin* is historically important for the famous naval mutiny that took place aboard her in 1905. This revolt was the first of several key incidents leading to the Russian Revolution, the overthrow of Tsar Nicholas II, and finally, to the establishment of a Communist government in 1917. The *Potemkin* was a battleship of the Imperial Russian Black Sea Fleet. In June 1905, conflicts between the officers and crew led to mutiny, incited by revolutionaries among the sailors. The captain was killed and the crew took command of the ship. When the *Potemkin* returned to port at Odessa, rioting broke out on shore in support of the crew. The much publicized incident helped spread revolutionary fervor throughout the land. Eventually, the ship was scuttled—deliberately sunk—by her crew. Some time later, she was brought to the surface, refitted, and served as a warship during World War I. The vessel was finally scrapped after the war ended. In 1925, the great Russian director Sergei Eisenstein made the classic film *Potemkin* to memorialize these events.

65. R.M.S. *LUSITANIA*

Just as the sinking of the *Titanic* was a massive peacetime tragedy, the destruction of the *Lusitania* was of nearly equal magnitude as a disaster during a time of war. An ocean liner of the Cunard Line, the *Lusitania*—advertised as "Queen of the Seas"—weighed over 31,500 tons. She was built in Clydebank, Scotland between 1904–1906. In October 1907, she recaptured the famous Blue Riband award for Great Britain from Germany for the fastest Atlantic crossing by an ocean liner. Operating on the Liverpool-to-New York route, she continued making ocean crossings even after the outbreak of the First World War. In May 1915, upon returning to Great Britain from New York, she was torpedoed without warning and sunk by a German U-boat off the coast of Ireland. She sank to the bottom in eighteen minutes. 1,198 passengers and crew were killed in what was regarded as an unjustified attack on an unarmed civilian passenger ship. Of those lost, 128 were Americans. At the time, the United States was not yet a participant in the war, but the sinking of the *Lusitania* became a significant provocation for American involvement in the conflict nearly two years later.

66. COLLIER

Cargo ships that specialize in carrying particular kinds of loads have existed for many centuries. Sometimes these vessels only travel in the vicinity of their local coastlines, in which case they are usually called coasters; others are seagoing and can carry their cargoes over greater distances. The collier, dating from the seventeenth and eighteenth centuries, was designed specifically to carry coal—sometimes as much as 400 tons or more—and possessed a notably sturdy construction. Sail-equipped colliers were sometimes known as "cat"-built colliers. It was this sort of ship that Captain James Cook favored for his voyages of discovery from 1768 onwards, a fact testifying to their strength and endurance. Although colliers continued to be used well into the twentieth century, the decreasing demand for coal has led to a corresponding decline in the use of this type of vessel.

67. THE *AMERIGO VESPUCCI*

This elegant old-style Italian sailing ship, one of the most renowned of today's "tall ships," was named after the same sixteenth-century explorer whose name was given to the two continents of the New World. A welcome visitor at many OpSail events in the United States and Europe, the *Amerigo Vespucci* is a three-masted full-rigged frigate that bears a closer resemblance to Nelson's *Victory* than to any of her modern-day counterparts. The vessel was built in Italy in 1930–1931 for the Italian Royal Shipyard, and is today the training vessel of the Livorno Naval Academy. She is just over 331-feet long and has a crew of 355 when fully manned.

68. THE SCHOONER *BLUENOSE*

The term "schooner" came into widespread use in New England for a new type of sailing vessel that originated in 1713 at Gloucester, Massachusetts. Schooners have come in a variety of forms and sizes, but are traditionally fore-and-aft rigged two-masted sailing ships of a streamlined design. Their characteristics include a fore (front) mast that is shorter than the mainmast, as well as very specific arrangements for their various kinds of sails. Schooners are nearly always very fine sailing vessels and are often fast. They have fulfilled many roles, serving as cargo carriers and in fishing fleets.

The most famous schooner of all time is the Canadian schooner *Bluenose*. This beloved vessel won the annual International Fishermen's Trophy race for Canada numerous times in the period between the two world wars. Launched in 1921, she was a 285-ton vessel with a hull length of 143 feet. In addition to her racing prowess, she also worked the Atlantic Banks in the Lunenburg, Nova Scotia fishing fleet. The *Bluenose*'s days were ended when she was wrecked on a reef near Haiti in 1946. However, in 1963, the *Bluenose II* was born, a perfect replica built from the same plans and in the same yard as her predecessor. Today, she holds a place of honor in the maritime heritage of Nova Scotia.

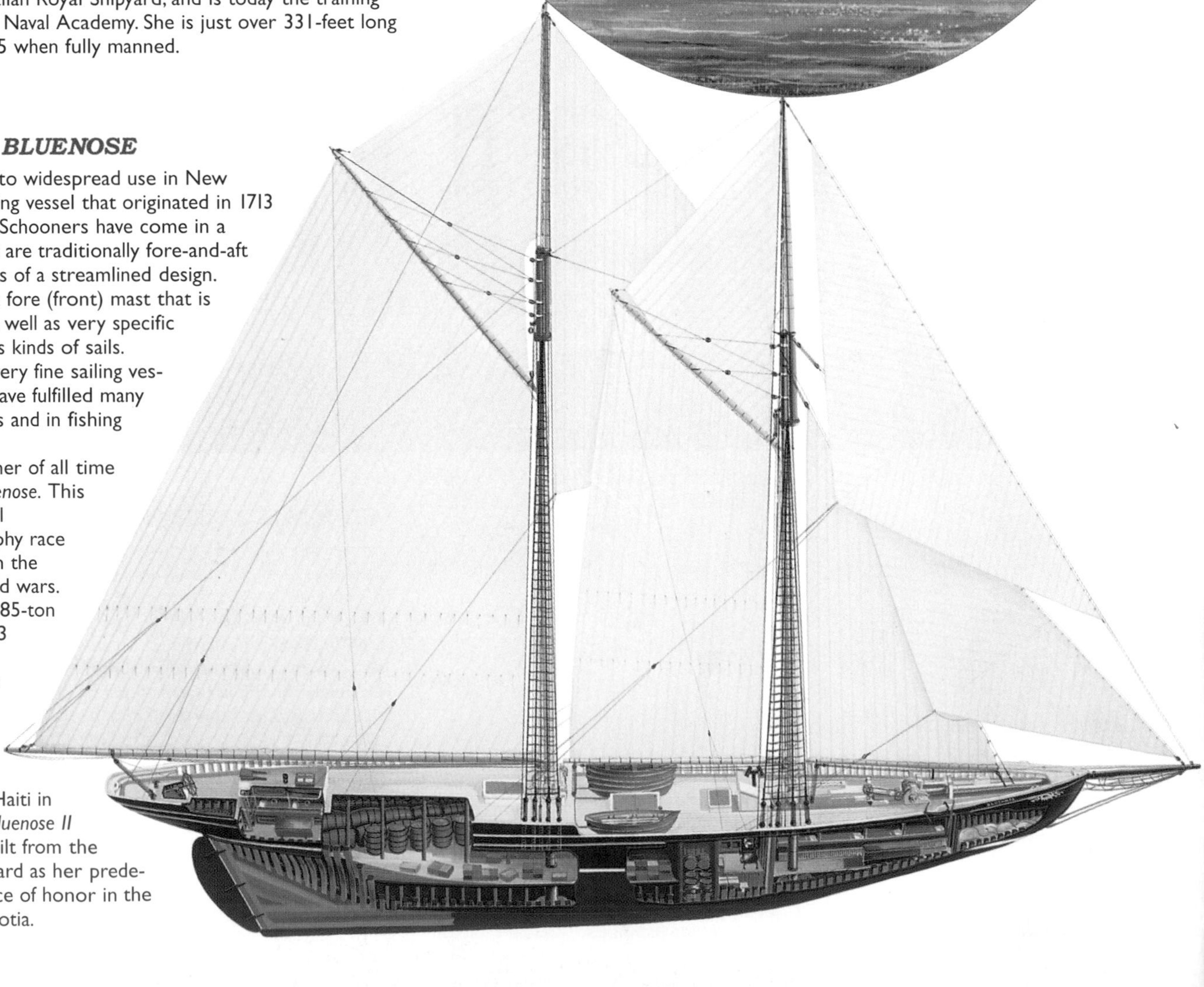

69. THE *ÎLE-DE-FRANCE*

Another of the great luxury ocean liners that steamed along the Atlantic route in the 1920s and 1930s, the *Île-de-France* was launched in 1926 by the French Line. Her bars were very popular at sea, especially with American passengers who were unable to (legally) obtain alcohol on land during Prohibition. The liner was considered a landmark of sorts because of her stunning Art Deco-style interior design. Capable of carrying over 1,500 passengers at a speed of twenty-four knots, the *Île-de-France*'s service was interrupted by the Second World War. Like other prewar ocean liners, she returned to normal operations after the war, making a celebrated comeback in 1949. In 1956, the *Île-de-France* suddenly made headlines around the world for a very different reason. On July 25 of that year, the liners *Stockholm* and *Andrea Doria* collided on the sea approaches to New York. The *Île-de-France* had just sailed from New York, and was on hand to pick up 753 survivors from the sinking *Andrea Doria.*

70. R.M.S. *QUEEN MARY*

Launched in 1934 by her namesake, and making her first transatlantic voyage in May 1936, the Cunard–White Star Line's *Queen Mary* was the ultimate among pre-World War II ocean liners in terms of both luxury and speed. In 1938, she was the final prewar winner of the Blue Riband for the fastest transatlantic crossing, and her record was bested only by the American steamship the *United States* in 1952. Weighing in at 81,237 tons, the *Queen Mary* was just over 1,019 feet long, and she could carry up to 1,939 passengers in addition to a crew of 1,174. She was the only large liner of her time to turn a profit. During the Second World War, the *Queen Mary* and her "half-sister" ship, the *Queen Elizabeth* (the *Mary* had three funnels and she had two), served as troop transports. Originally based in Sydney, Australia, she later served on the dangerous North Atlantic run, carrying up to 15,000 troops at a time on her summer crossings. Many of the American troops and airmen who were brought to Great Britain to fight the Germans were conveyed there by the *Queen Mary*. After the war, she became a civilian passenger liner once more.

71. BRITISH TUG

The first craft ever to be powered by an engine, the *Charlotte Dundas* of 1802, was a tugboat. As early as 1735, it was realized that a tug would be a valuable craft for helping larger vessels into port and guiding them to their berths. These versatile little ships have been vital to the operations of harbors and ports for over 200 years. They have taken many forms—from the smallest port and harbor tugs and tractors, to the giant oceangoing tugs that bring in badly damaged vessels in times of war to save them from a watery grave. The painting here shows a typical British in-shore tug built in 1939. Weighing 260 tons, it is over 114 feet long and comes equipped with a 1,000-horsepower engine.

72. OCEAN LINER *NORMANDIE*

Yet another of the magnificent steamships built to serve the North Atlantic passenger trade between Europe and the United States, the *Normandie* was an opulent French liner of the 1930s. Launched in 1932 after being christened with the world's largest bottle of champagne, she captured the Blue Riband from an Italian rival for the fastest transatlantic crossing by a passenger liner on her maiden voyage in 1935. The *Normandie* could carry up to 2,170 passengers, her crew numbered 1,345, and she weighed in at about 80,744 gross tons. At a colossal 1,029 feet, she was touted as the first ship ever completed to exceed 1,000 feet in length. Her sumptuous accommodations included a first-class dining salon longer than the Hall of Mirrors at Versailles, Lalique lighting fixtures, museum-quality paintings and sculpture, as well as an indoor swimming pool. Unfortunately, the *Normandie* met her end in a spectacular calamity. In the process of being converted into a troopship (and renamed the U.S.S. *Lafayette*) during World War II, she caught fire while moored at Pier 88 in New York and was totally lost.

73. REFRIGERATED CARGO SHIP—M.V. *BRISBANE STAR*

Refrigerator ships, or reefers, are specialized cargo vessels used for transporting food such as fruit, fish, meat, and dairy products. The holds of these ships are insulated, and are wholly or partially cooled to the appropriate temperature for keeping their perishable cargo fresh. These craft are usually known for their speed, a crucial factor in bringing the goods swiftly to their destinations. During the twentieth century, as the evolving technologies refined the capabilities of these cargo vessels, they played an ever more important role in international food transport. Refrigerator ships have also helped to ease the suffering caused by critical food shortages in wartime by delivering goods to nations in need, World War II being an early case in point. The painting here shows the *Brisbane Star,* a typical refrigerator ship, which was built in 1936.

74. H.M.C.S. *COLLINGWOOD* "FLOWER" CLASS CORVETTE

One of the most prominent types of warships in Britain's Royal Navy in the long fight against German U-boats during World War II was the "Flower" class corvette. These small ships with comparatively light armament took the fight to the enemy, hunting the deadly U-boats in the farthest reaches of the Atlantic in all kinds of weather. The design of the "Flower" class derived from commercial whaling boats, and although some were constructed in Great Britain, the majority were built in Canada. Serving with the Royal Navy and the Royal Canadian Navy, these diminutive warships had a length of 205 feet and a displacement of more than 925 tons, and carried a crew of about 85 men. They were equipped with listening apparatus for detecting submerged submarines, and were armed with single 4-inch or 6-inch guns, and light anti-aircraft armament for self-protection; they also carried depth charges for attacking submarines. Later in the war, larger and more heavily-armed ships were introduced for antisubmarine duties. The painting here illustrates the first corvette in the Royal Canadian Navy, the H.M.C.S. *Collingwood,* commissioned at Collingwood, Ontario.

The above is reproduced by kind permission of Collingwood School of West Vancouver, British Columbia, Canada.

75. "V" AND "W" CLASS DESTROYERS

Great Britain's "V" and "W" class of lightly-armed fleet destroyers were important warships that participated in both world wars. All class members had names starting with "V" or "W," like the H.M.S. *Volunteer.* There were several production runs of these gun- and torpedo-armed ships, and they first saw action in the later stages of the First World War as flotilla leaders. Thanks to a farsighted maintenance policy during their inactive periods, fifty-eight of them were available for service at the start of the Second World War. Updated with modern weapons and systems, they escorted convoys of cargo ships during the war, and attacked German and Italian submarines. Powered by geared steam turbine engines, these vessels were fast ships capable of a top speed of thirty-four knots, and each had a crew of about 134 men. They served with distinction, and successfully sank around thirty-nine German U-boats during the Second World War.

76. "GATO" CLASS SUBMARINE

During World War II, the U.S. Navy's submarine fleet was transformed into a highly effective force, a worthy predecessor to its contemporary counterpart. There were several classes of submarines that were especially crucial to military operations during World War II, including the "Gato" class. The vessels in this class played a significant role in the Pacific theater against the Japanese. The U.S.S. *Barb* is officially credited with sinking seventeen enemy vessels totaling 96,628 tons. This class was succeeded by the "Balao" and "Tench" class submarines, also built during the war years. The main difference between the "Gato" and "Balao" classes was the improved pressure hull of the latter, enabling the vessel to dive to even greater depths. One especially well-known "Balao" class submarine is the U.S.S. *Bowfin*—nicknamed the "Pearl Harbor Avenger"—which is on public display at the U.S.S. *Bowfin* Museum and Park in Honolulu.

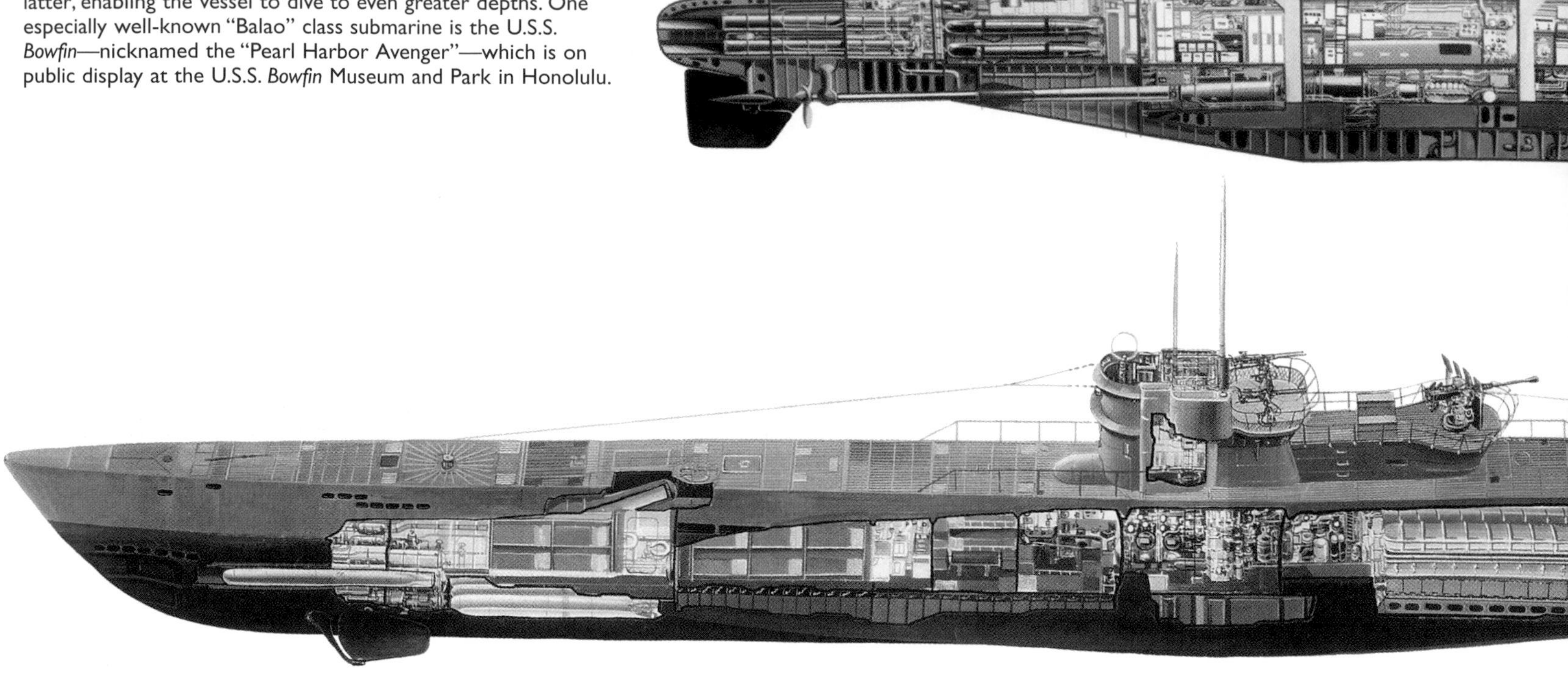

77. GERMAN TYPE IX U-BOAT

After the German conquest of most of northern Europe in the early years of World War II, merchant ships carrying supplies across the North Atlantic were a vital lifeline for the British. The greatest single threat to the survival of Britain during the early war years came from the German Navy U-boat (*Unterseeboot* in German). These heavily-armed submarines were sinking merchant ships in the Atlantic at an alarming rate, even after the cargo vessels grouped together in escorted convoys for protection. The U-boats had developed their own strategy in response to the convoy tactic, assembling themselves in patrol lines known as "wolfpacks." To oppose and sink the U-boats in what came to be known as the Battle of the Atlantic (1943–1945), special antisubmarine warships were developed for use by Britain and her allies. Long-range maritime patrol aircraft were also implemented for the same purpose. The Germans developed many different models of U-boats, some of the best-known being the Type VII and Type IX series. The Type XXI series was one of the most advanced kinds of submarine produced during the war, but it was completed in 1944—too late to see much active service. Eventually, the Allies were able to defeat the German U-boats during the later stages of the war, but it was a very closely-fought battle.

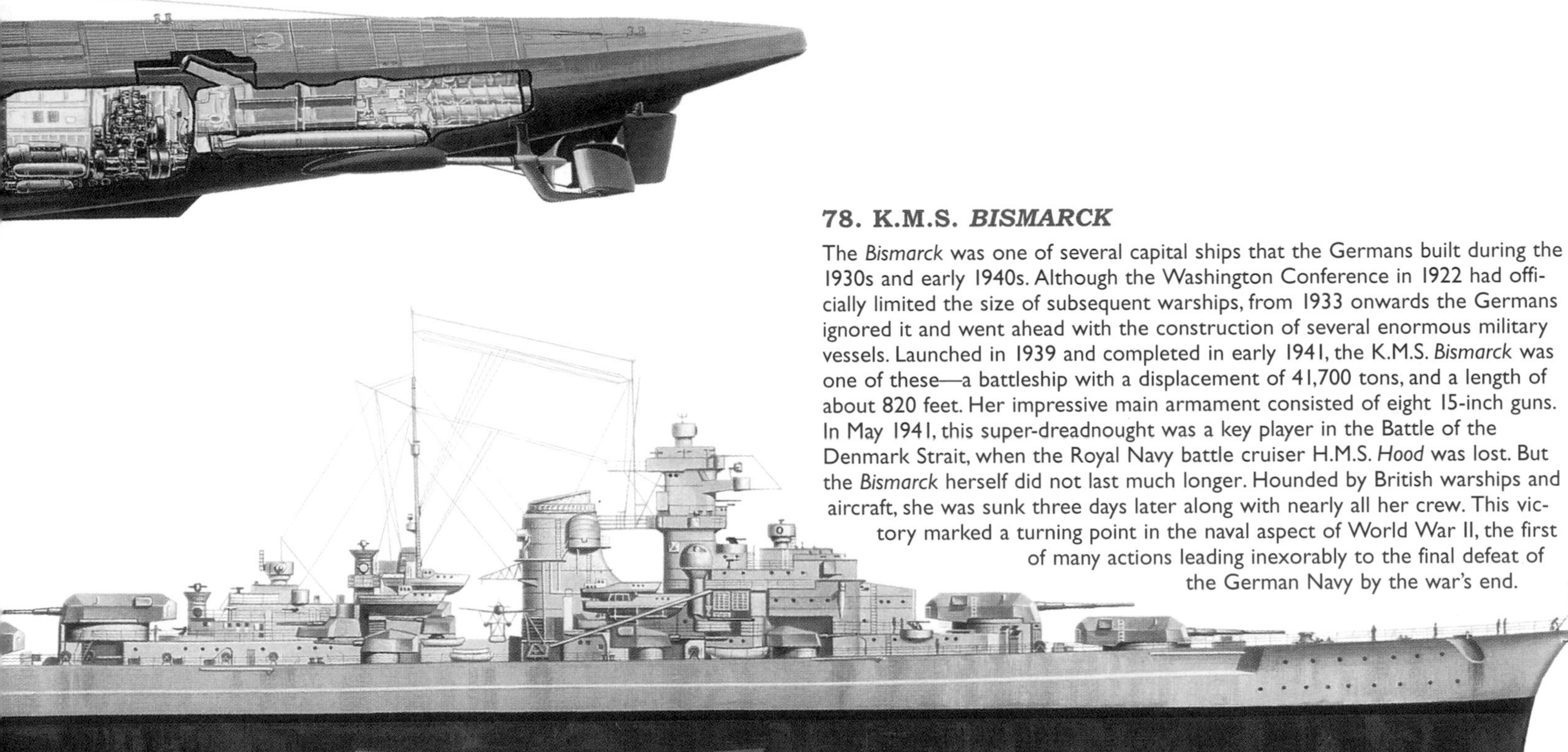

78. K.M.S. *BISMARCK*

The *Bismarck* was one of several capital ships that the Germans built during the 1930s and early 1940s. Although the Washington Conference in 1922 had officially limited the size of subsequent warships, from 1933 onwards the Germans ignored it and went ahead with the construction of several enormous military vessels. Launched in 1939 and completed in early 1941, the K.M.S. *Bismarck* was one of these—a battleship with a displacement of 41,700 tons, and a length of about 820 feet. Her impressive main armament consisted of eight 15-inch guns. In May 1941, this super-dreadnought was a key player in the Battle of the Denmark Strait, when the Royal Navy battle cruiser H.M.S. *Hood* was lost. But the *Bismarck* herself did not last much longer. Hounded by British warships and aircraft, she was sunk three days later along with nearly all her crew. This victory marked a turning point in the naval aspect of World War II, the first of many actions leading inexorably to the final defeat of the German Navy by the war's end.

79. H.M.S. *HOOD*

In the 1920s, this magnificent battle cruiser was the largest and most powerful warship in the world. Construction began in 1916, during the First World War, and she was completed in 1920. This capital ship measured 860 feet long and had a displacement of 41,200 tons. Her main armament was impressive, comprising eight 15-inch guns, as well as a variety of smaller guns, together with six 21-inch torpedo tubes. She carried a complement of about 1,477 men. Despite her immense size, she was able to attain a high speed of thirty-one knots. The H.M.S. *Hood* was the pride of Britain's Royal Navy at the start of World War II. Unfortunately, this first-class fighting unit met with a catastrophic end. In May 1941, she became engaged in a sea battle in the Denmark Strait between Iceland and Greenland with the German ships *Bismarck* and *Prinz Eugen*. During this action, she was hit by an accurate and deadly salvo of shells from the *Bismarck* and exploded. Almost everyone on board perished.

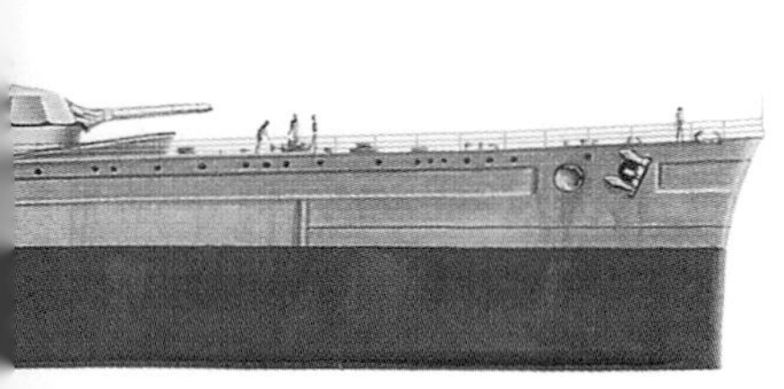

80. ROYAL NAVY M.T.B.

Following the development of modern underwater self-propelled torpedoes in the 1860s and 1870s, many of the world's navies started building small, fast torpedo boats that could utilize their striking power. Because these craft were especially swift and highly maneuverable, they presented difficult targets for lumbering cruisers and battleships. As a countermeasure, torpedo boat destroyers were introduced. Larger than torpedo boats, but rivaling the speed of the smaller craft and armed with guns and torpedoes, these gradually evolved into the destroyer of today.

In the early years of the twentieth century, a new type of fast torpedo-armed craft, the motor torpedo boat, was brought into service. Usually powered by conventional gasoline engines, these vessels looked like armed speed boats. They saw a good deal of action in the Second World War; in particular, the British with their M.T.B. or Motor Torpedo boat, the Americans with their P.T. or Patrol Torpedo boat, the Germans with their *Schnellboote* or E-boat, and the Italians with their MAS boat. Built in a variety of shapes and sizes, they were also equipped with a wide assortment and number of weapons. Usually, but not always, they stayed inshore, and their primary role was to attack enemy shipping with torpedoes and gunfire. British M.T.B.'s were on average around seventy feet in length, with the most powerful three-engined models able to reach about forty knots at top speed, making them one of the fastest naval craft.

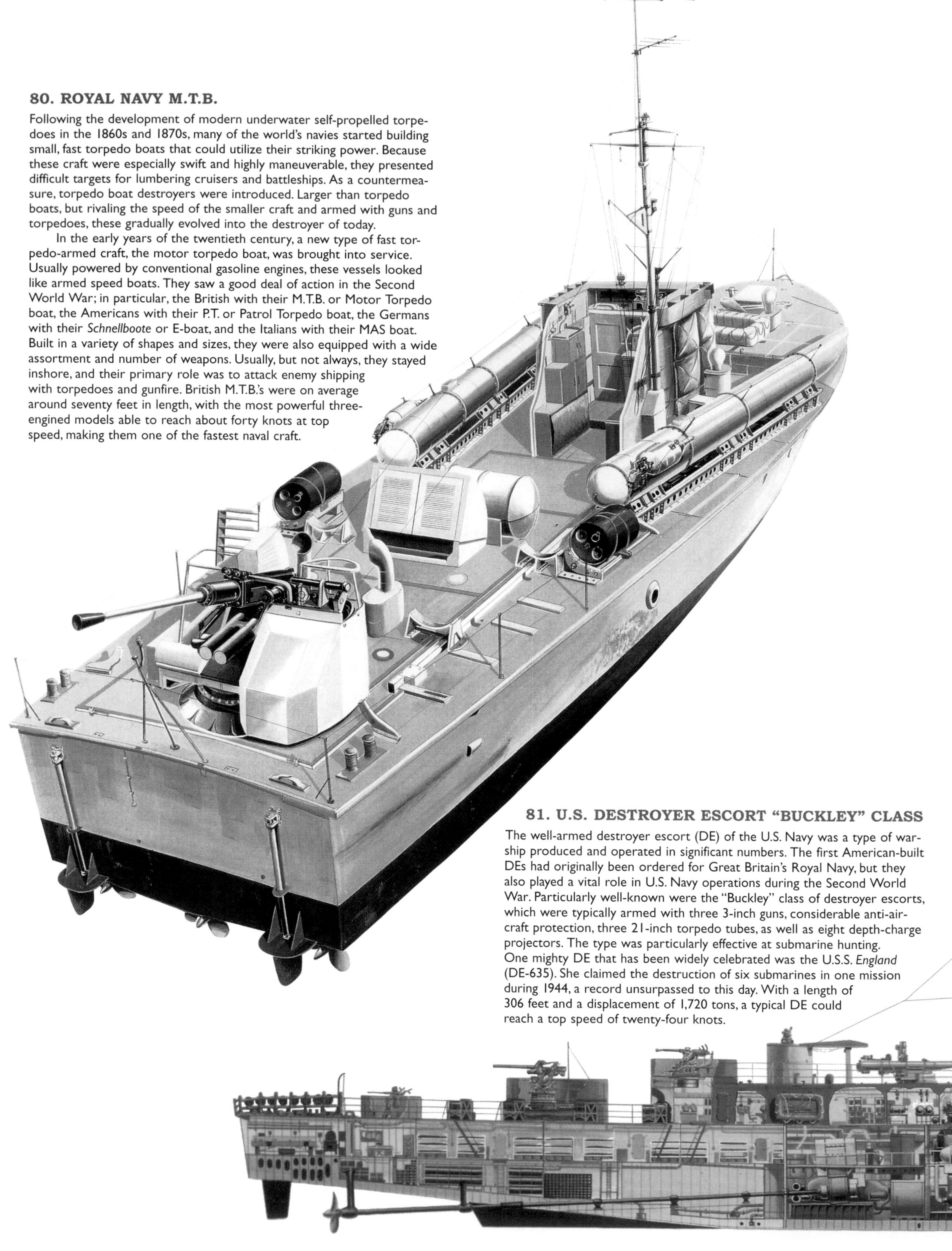

81. U.S. DESTROYER ESCORT "BUCKLEY" CLASS

The well-armed destroyer escort (DE) of the U.S. Navy was a type of warship produced and operated in significant numbers. The first American-built DEs had originally been ordered for Great Britain's Royal Navy, but they also played a vital role in U.S. Navy operations during the Second World War. Particularly well-known were the "Buckley" class of destroyer escorts, which were typically armed with three 3-inch guns, considerable anti-aircraft protection, three 21-inch torpedo tubes, as well as eight depth-charge projectors. The type was particularly effective at submarine hunting. One mighty DE that has been widely celebrated was the U.S.S. *England* (DE-635). She claimed the destruction of six submarines in one mission during 1944, a record unsurpassed to this day. With a length of 306 feet and a displacement of 1,720 tons, a typical DE could reach a top speed of twenty-four knots.

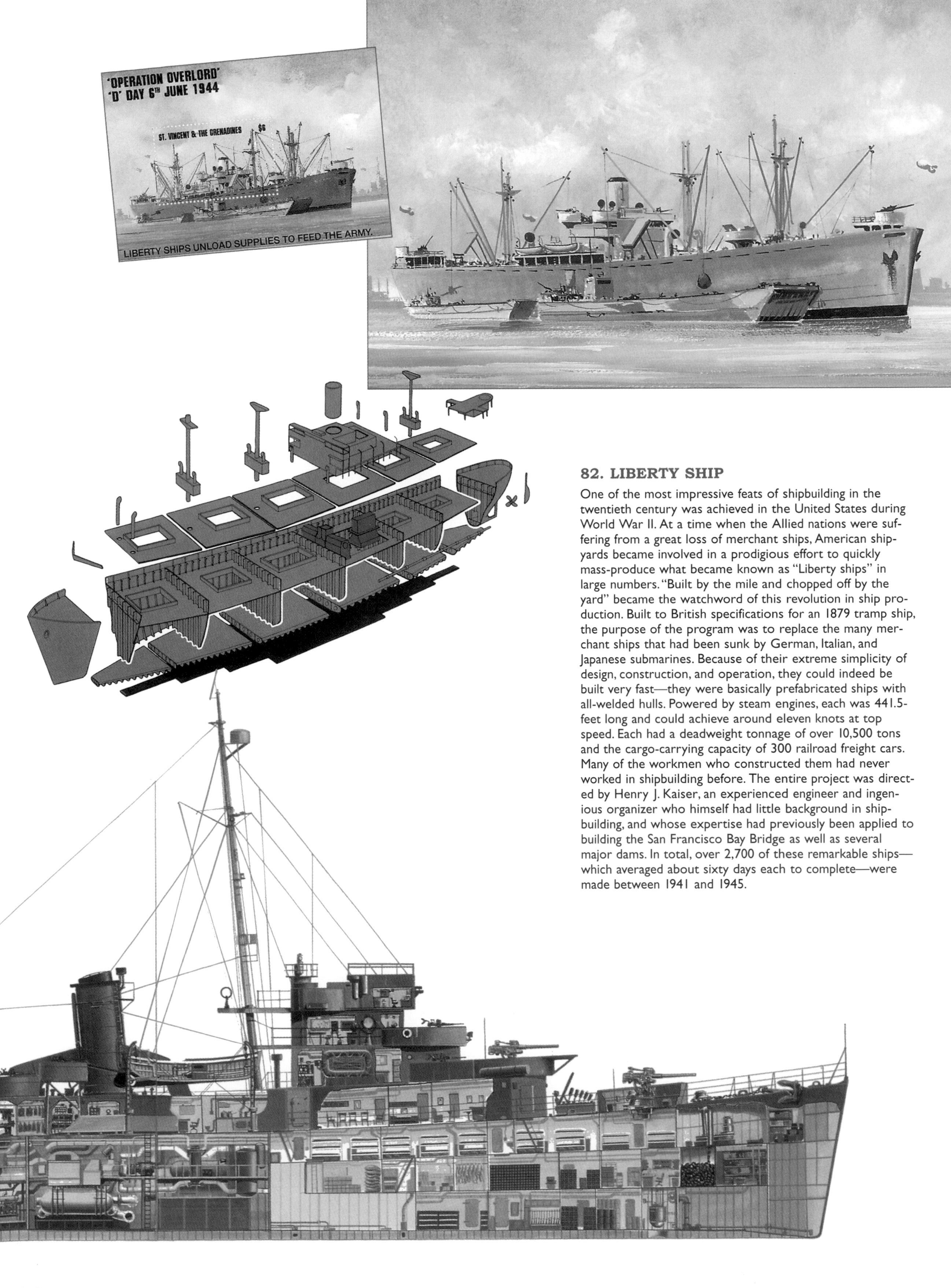

82. LIBERTY SHIP

One of the most impressive feats of shipbuilding in the twentieth century was achieved in the United States during World War II. At a time when the Allied nations were suffering from a great loss of merchant ships, American shipyards became involved in a prodigious effort to quickly mass-produce what became known as "Liberty ships" in large numbers. "Built by the mile and chopped off by the yard" became the watchword of this revolution in ship production. Built to British specifications for an 1879 tramp ship, the purpose of the program was to replace the many merchant ships that had been sunk by German, Italian, and Japanese submarines. Because of their extreme simplicity of design, construction, and operation, they could indeed be built very fast—they were basically prefabricated ships with all-welded hulls. Powered by steam engines, each was 441.5-feet long and could achieve around eleven knots at top speed. Each had a deadweight tonnage of over 10,500 tons and the cargo-carrying capacity of 300 railroad freight cars. Many of the workmen who constructed them had never worked in shipbuilding before. The entire project was directed by Henry J. Kaiser, an experienced engineer and ingenious organizer who himself had little background in shipbuilding, and whose expertise had previously been applied to building the San Francisco Bay Bridge as well as several major dams. In total, over 2,700 of these remarkable ships—which averaged about sixty days each to complete—were made between 1941 and 1945.

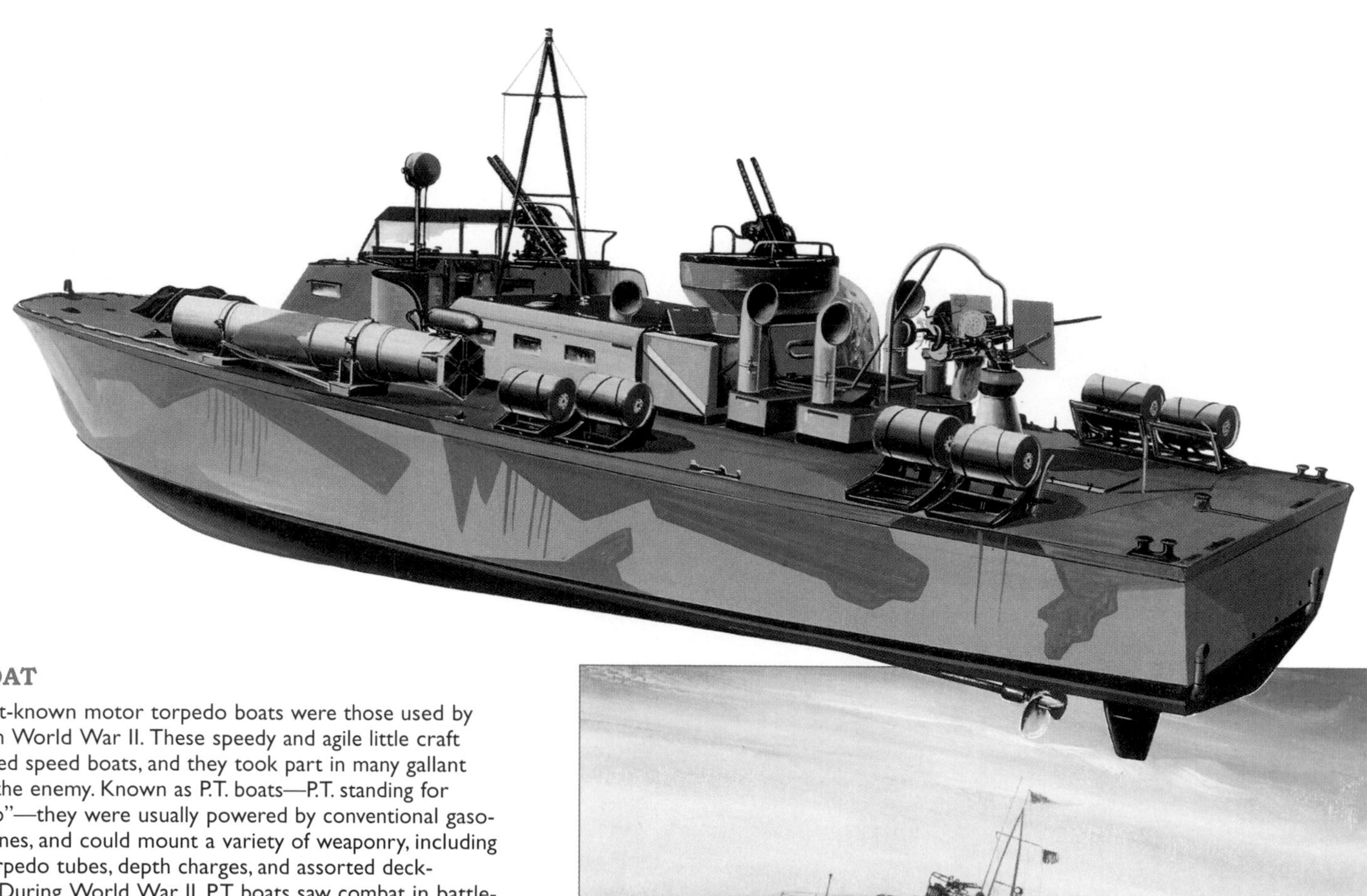

83. P.T. BOAT

Among the best-known motor torpedo boats were those used by the U.S. Navy in World War II. These speedy and agile little craft resembled armed speed boats, and they took part in many gallant efforts against the enemy. Known as P.T. boats—P.T. standing for "patrol torpedo"—they were usually powered by conventional gasoline-driven engines, and could mount a variety of weaponry, including two or four torpedo tubes, depth charges, and assorted deck-mounted guns. During World War II, P.T. boats saw combat in battlegrounds around the world, epecially in the Pacific against Japanese barges and in the Mediterranean against German MFPs and Italian warships. One of these vessels—P.T. 109—became famous because of the heroic actions of its commander, John F. Kennedy, during the Second World War.

84. THE *YAMATO*

The largest battleships with the largest guns in history were the *Yamato* and her sister ship, the *Musashi,* both built for the Imperial Japanese Navy during the Second World War. Ultimately, they would prove to have lacklustre wartime careers. Launched in 1940, the *Yamato* entered service in December 1941—the month of Pearl Harbor. She weighed in at a huge 72,809 tons (fully loaded). She was designed to mount no less than nine 18-inch guns, capable of firing 3,200-pound projectiles with a range of 22.5 miles. The vessel was also furnished with many smaller weapons, including anti-aircraft guns. Some of the smaller armament was mounted amidships in a unique set of turrets and mountings. The *Yamato* was sunk off the Japanese coast in April 1945 by a barrage of American aerial attacks due to inadequate air cover—with a loss of 2,400 lives. The *Musashi* had been destroyed earlier in the war in the Battle of the Leyte Gulf in October 1944.

85. "FLETCHER" CLASS DESTROYER

The "Fletcher" class of destroyers was a numerous class of warship, with no fewer than 175 examples being built in eleven different shipyards. These illustrious vessels formed the backbone of the U.S. Navy's massive effort in the Pacific theater. With a length of 376.5 feet and a standard displacement of 2,900 tons fully loaded, the "Fletcher" class destroyers were significantly larger than any of their predecessors. They could attain a swift thirty-eight knots, and mounted five 5-inch guns, a variety of anti-aircraft weapons, and ten 21-inch torpedo tubes. The first destroyer of this class to be commissioned was the U.S.S. *Nicholas* in June 1942; the last in 1945. They served with great distinction, and their success resulted in some continuing in service with the U.S. Navy until the 1970s, while others were sold off to foreign navies after the war.

86. U.S.S. *MISSOURI*

The largest and most destructive war in history came to an end on the decks of this mighty ship. On September 2, 1945, officials from the Empire of Japan boarded the U.S.S. *Missouri* in Tokyo Bay to sign the instruments of surrender that brought World War II to a close. It was very fitting that this momentous event took place aboard the *Missouri,* one of the most distinguished ships in the recent history of the U.S. Navy, and one of the most successful battleships ever built. This historic ship has fought in a total of three wars.

Commissioned in June 1944, after having been constructed as an "Iowa" class battleship in the New York Navy Yard in Brooklyn, the U.S.S. *Missouri* arrived in the Pacific theater early in 1945. She played a key role in some of the most crucial battles and campaigns there, including the Iwo Jima invasion. Next came the Korean conflict in the early 1950s when, in the course of those hostilities, she made two combat deployments to the western Pacific. Laid up in reserve from the mid-1950s onwards, she was recommissioned after refitting in May 1986. Then in 1991, the *Missouri* was sent to the Persian Gulf to provide massive firepower against Iraq-held targets during Operation Desert Storm. In 1995, the "Mighty Mo" was removed from the naval register; and in 1999, she was opened as a memorial and museum along Battleship Row in Pearl Harbor, Hawaii.

A true leviathan of a warship, the *Missouri* is just over 887-feet long, with an unloaded weight of 45,000 tons (about 58,000 tons fully loaded). At "full speed ahead," she could sail at over thirty knots. In World War II, her personnel numbered 2,534, and she was fitted with nine 16-inch guns in three gun turrets and twenty 5-inch guns. Her more recent armament included Tomahawk cruise missiles, which were used effectively in the Gulf War.

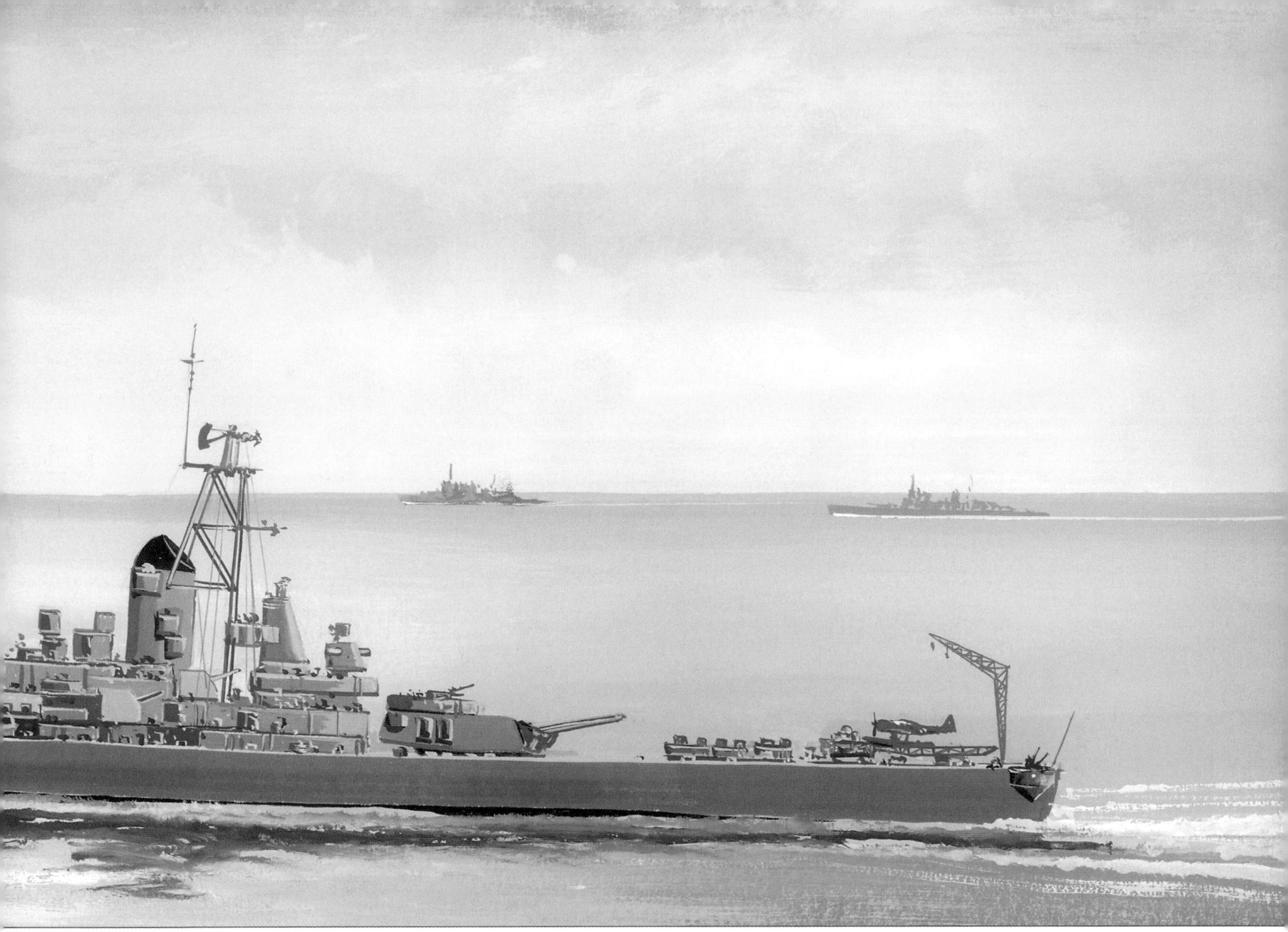

87. H.M.S. *VANGUARD*

The experiences of World War II proved that the mighty battleship is valuable in war only if it has friendly air cover and can work well as a team with other warships in the fleet. Because these vessels are so expensive to build and operate, their cost has become prohibitive for most countries. These factors have combined to spell an end to the ascendancy of the battleship as a centerpiece of naval combat. The H.M.S. *Vanguard* was both the largest and the last of her type to be built by Great Britain. She was begun in 1941 and completed in 1946, at a cost of £9 million—a great deal of money even for 1946, and this despite the fact that she used secondhand guns and turrets from other ships. In 1960, she was finally broken up, and the tradition of big warships in Britain's Royal Navy came to a close.

88. R.M.S. *QUEEN ELIZABETH*

One of the most distinguished of the British superliners of the twentieth century, the Cunard Line's *Queen Elizabeth* was launched in September 1938, but was almost immediately converted for use as a troopship in World War II. Serving six years in this capacity, she could carry up to 8,200 troops. After the war, the *Queen Elizabeth* entered service as a commercial ocean liner, and made her first postwar cruise in October 1946 on a transatlantic voyage from Southampton to New York. After twenty-three years of successful operation, she was retired in 1969 and replaced by the *Queen Elizabeth 2* (*QE2*). Instead of being scrapped, the first *Queen Elizabeth* was moved to Hong Kong in the early 1970s for refitting as a floating university. Unfortunately, soon after, the ship caught fire and the resulting damage was so extensive she eventually had to be scrapped. She is shown here as she looked in 1950.

89. THE *EXODUS*

The ship *Exodus* gained worldwide renown just after the close of World War II, when much of Europe was still in the throes of the destruction and dislocation the war had wrought. Many of the Jews who survived the horrors of the Nazi holocaust had become DPs (or displaced persons), and sought to emigrate to Palestine—which under a League of Nations mandate was administered by Great Britain. Despite British emigration restrictions to this area, refugee ships such as the *Exodus* attempted to reach Palestine with the help of underground Zionist organizations like the Hagana. The *Exodus* was formerly a Chesapeake Bay pleasure steamer, and then a Royal Navy troop and supply ship, prior to her purchase by the Hagana for bringing Jews to Palestine. As the vessel neared the coast of that nation in the summer of 1947, the British sent their destroyers to ram the ship and prevent the debarkation of its 4,515 refugees. A violent struggle broke out on board as the immigrants tried to defend themselves; three Jews were killed and about thirty were wounded. The passengers were subsequently treated like prisoners and returned to Germany—to British-occupied Hamburg. An international outcry was raised against Britain's actions in the incident, which led to the partitioning of Palestine and the establishment of the Jewish state of Israel in 1948.

90. U.S.S. *UNITED STATES*

In the days when the Atlantic super-liners had to possess both luxury and speed, there existed a fierce rivalry among them for the prize known as the Blue Riband. The course was between Ambrose Lightship in the United States and Bishop's Rock in England—2,800 nautical miles. The ship that made the passage the fastest was awarded a highly coveted trophy and also gained the substantial prestige associated with it. Many of the great ocean liners of the past have held this trophy at different times, including the *Queen Mary,* the *Mauretania,* and the *Normandie,* but fastest of all was the United States. This fleet and beautiful American ocean liner achieved the remarkable speed of 35.59 knots in 1952, cutting the Atlantic crossing time to only three days, ten hours and forty minutes. At 990 feet long, the mighty *United States* could accommodate 2,008 passengers. Eventually, the arrival in service of jet airliners able to fly the Atlantic in a matter of hours led to the end of the Blue Riband competition, since speed then lost its importance as an essential asset for ocean liners. In 1999, the *United States* was placed on the National Register of Historic Places, and today can be viewed in Philadelphia, just two miles from the Liberty Bell.

91. R.M.S. *QUEEN ELIZABETH 2*

In service now for more than three decades, the *Queen Elizabeth 2*—or the *QE2* as she is usually known—is the most celebrated of Great Britain's postwar ocean liners. Launched in 1967, she weighs in at 65,864 gross tons, can attain a speed of 28.5 knots, and spans 963 feet. During her time in operation, the concept of ocean travel has undergone a major transformation, so that today sumptuous accommodations and a variety of exotic destinations are paramount—not a quick trip across the Atlantic. By 1965, the airlines were handling ninety-five percent of all transatlantic travel, so that by the 1970s the *QE2* took primarily to pleasure cruising. Her name became synonymous with seagoing luxury. Unexpectedly, her commercial service was interrupted briefly in 1982 for troop transport operations during the Falkland Islands War. The Cunard Line currently has plans to replace her with a super cruise liner in the near future.

92. S.S. *NORWAY*

The *Norway* is yet another example of how the requirement for rapid ocean transit has given way to a new contemporary standard of long and lavish cruises. The trip is now an end in itself, rather than just the means, with exotic locations visited at a leisurely pace as much a selling point as the ultimate destination. The *Norway* began her life as the *France,* operated by the French Line. Launched in 1960, this elegant liner capable of thirty-five knots at top speed was, with her prominent winged funnels, distinctive from the start. Taken out of service in 1974, the ship languished in a harbor south of Le Havre for several years. Eventually, she was bought by a Norwegian shipping magnate, who spent about $80 million reconditioning her for service with the Norwegian Caribbean Lines. Renamed the *Norway,* and with her maximum speed reduced, she resumed operation in 1980 much to the envy of her competitors. Adding a new dimension to the experience of cruising, the *Norway* became a true floating resort with many lavish appointments, including a huge theater featuring Las Vegas cabaret acts as well as Broadway shows.

93. CONTAINER SHIP

The container ship is functionally the modern equivalent of the cargo ships of the past. These huge vessels are built to carry special containers in which freight is pre-packed before loading onto the ship. Each container is built to a specific standard size, and has a maximum capacity of eighteen tons. The standardization of the containers means the ships that carry them can be built to very specific dimensions, so the containers can fit neatly and precisely in the ships' holds or on deck. On older cargo vessels, freight could shift dangerously during bad weather; on modern container ships this danger is greatly reduced. Designated areas in ports are reserved for the storage of these containers after they have been unloaded or are not in use, with cranes required to load and unload them. When the containers are off-loaded at their destination, they are placed onto specially-designed trucks to continue the journey to their final destinations. The ship pictured here was built about 1999.

94. N.S. *SAVANNAH*

The American ship *Savannah* was the world's first nuclear-powered merchant ship. Constructed in 1958–1959 with a displacement of 21,840 tons, the vessel was built mainly to demonstrate the value of nuclear power for commercial cargo ships, but in practice it was not very successful. Nuclear-powered vessels are still relatively scarce, except for those in military service. The *Savannah* was named after the first steamship to cross the Atlantic, in 1819.

95. SUPERTANKER

The largest type of cargo ship in the world is the supertanker. These huge ships come in various sizes tailored to their respective roles, but the one quality they have in common is that they are all really big. Supertankers are designed to carry liquid cargoes—usually oil, but sometimes other products like liquefied natural gas. The vessel is a twentieth-century invention that evolved because of the huge demand for oil. Supertankers possess a very distinctive long, wide, and flat shape because their hulls contain huge storage tanks or containers in which the crude oil is carried. As the demand for oil around the world grew, so did their size. Eventually, Very Large Crude Carriers (V.L.C.C.) of 250,000 tons were built, but even those were soon outgrown by a new generation of Ultra Large Crude Carriers (U.L.C.C.), which reached up to and beyond 400,000 tons. Special refineries have been built at the water's edge in many parts of the world to receive the cargoes from these massive ships, and to refine the oil into the gasoline and other products that are used by people everywhere.

96. "OLIVER HAZARD PERRY" CLASS GUIDED-MISSILE FRIGATE

Named after the American naval officer who emerged victorious from the Battle of Lake Erie during the War of 1812, the "Oliver Hazard Perry" class of guided-missile frigates has served as a key component of American sea power for over two decades. Intended for area defense of surface forces against attacking aircraft and cruise missiles, these ships also fulfil a crucial antisubmarine mission; with a helicopter pad standard at the stern of these ships, each can embark up to two antisubmarine helicopters. With a displacement of around 4,100 tons (full load) and a crew of approximately 215, a top speed of twenty-nine knots is attainable. Fifty-one of these vessels were built for the U.S. Navy, and the first was launched in 1978. Although their American naval service is now in the process of winding down, some are still in operation with the navies of such countries as Australia, and more will enter service with foreign navies in the future.

97. NUCLEAR SUBMARINE U.S.S. *SEAWOLF*

Submarine technology has made tremendous advances since the days of the U.S.S. *Turtle*. Today's nuclear-powered submarines are among the most deadly and powerful warships ever built. One of these is the U.S.S. *Seawolf,* the pride of the U.S. Navy's underwater fleet. At 353-feet long and 40-feet wide, she is a large and impressive underwater boat powered by a pressurized-water nuclear reactor, and home to a crew of 133 submariners. She can carry a wide array of weapons, including up to fifty-two torpedoes, Harpoon anti-ship missiles, Tomahawk cruise missiles, as well as mines—and possibly, Poseidon nuclear missiles. Weighing up to 9,150 tons when submerged, this superb example of state-of-the-art technology can remain underwater for days on end and cruise to any part of the world. Officially, she can dive to depths of 800 feet, but the real figure is likely to be double that.

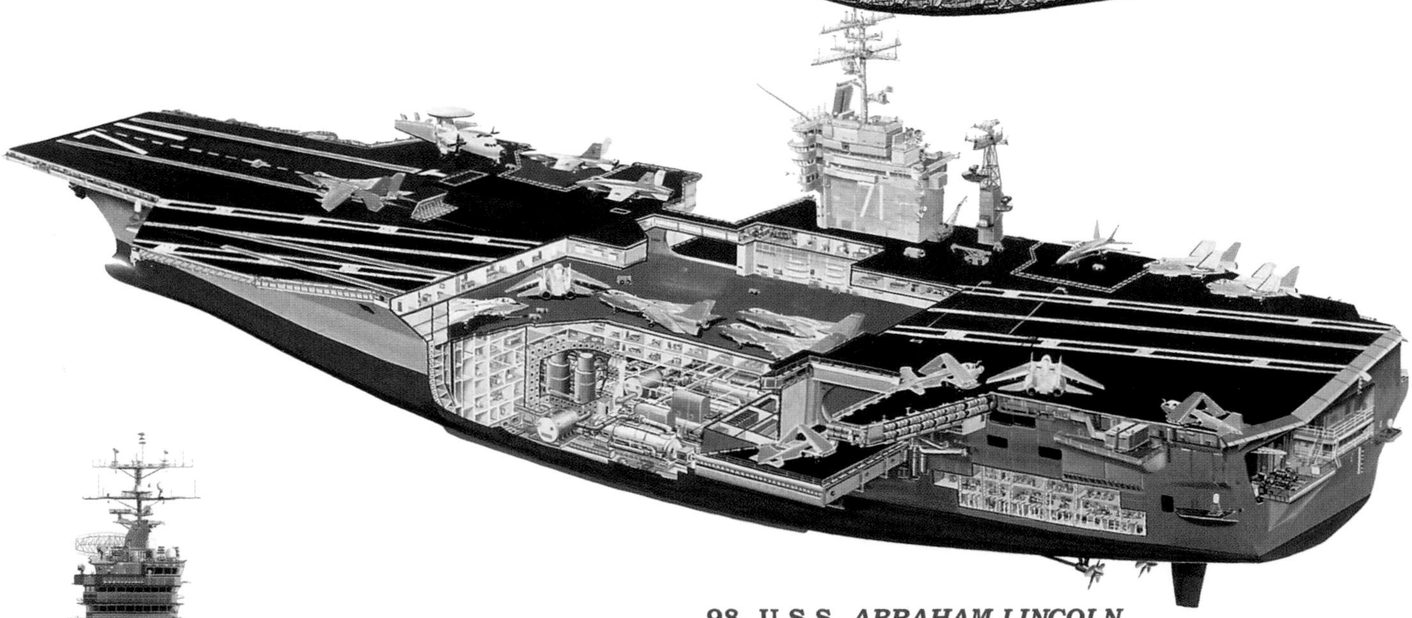

98. U.S.S. *ABRAHAM LINCOLN*

The value of the aircraft carrier was proven during World War II, and today this type of ship is a vital component of all the best navies in the world. Among the finest carriers afloat is the U.S. Navy's *Abraham Lincoln* of the "Nimitz" class. This magnificent floating airfield was launched in February 1988. Her crew comprises over 5,500 men and women, and she is a staggering 1,092-feet long. Her nuclear propulsion system gives her a top speed of over thirty knots, and her displacement totals around 100,000 tons. Most important of all are her aircraft, which includes the most cutting-edge and capable—the F-14 Tomcat fighter and the F/A-18 Hornet multipurpose combat aircraft. All together, she has an air group consisting of around eighty combat and support aircraft. When not in use, they are housed below the flight deck in hangars, where they can be worked on by their ground crews. When at sea, the carrier operates as one member of a battle group consisting of several types of warships.

The illustration below is reproduced by kind permission of British Columbia Ferries.

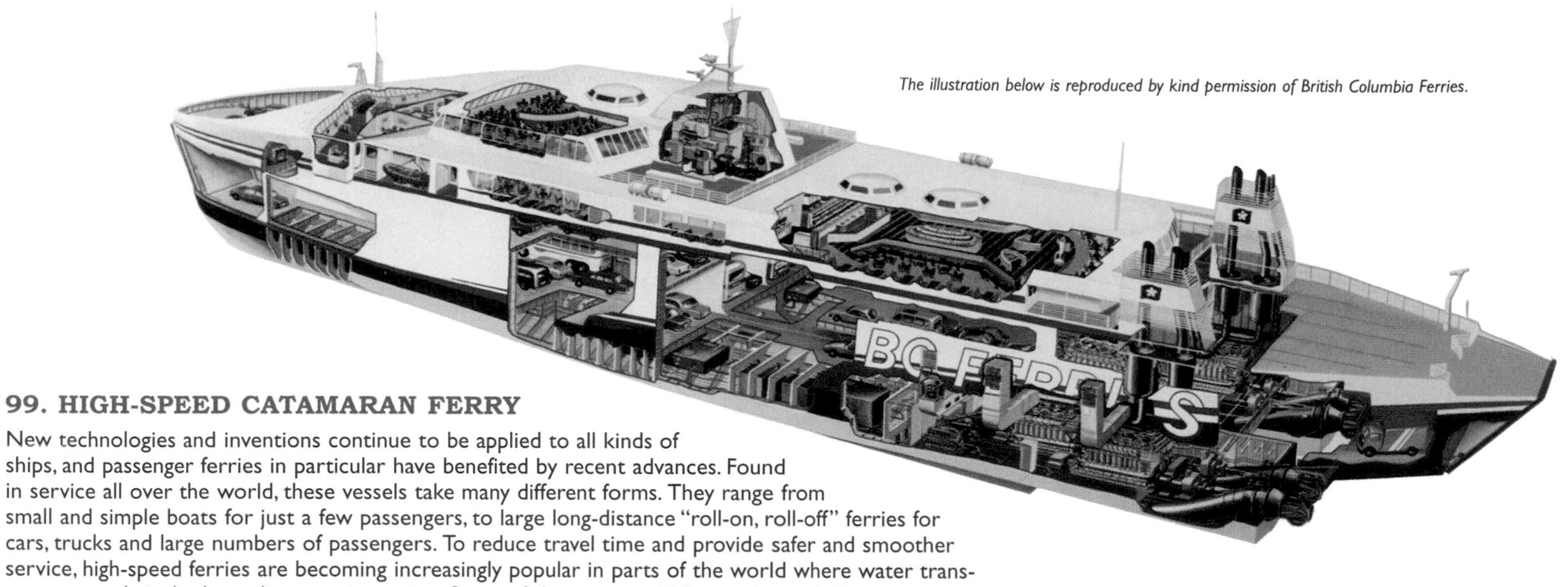

99. HIGH-SPEED CATAMARAN FERRY

New technologies and inventions continue to be applied to all kinds of ships, and passenger ferries in particular have benefited by recent advances. Found in service all over the world, these vessels take many different forms. They range from small and simple boats for just a few passengers, to large long-distance "roll-on, roll-off" ferries for cars, trucks and large numbers of passengers. To reduce travel time and provide safer and smoother service, high-speed ferries are becoming increasingly popular in parts of the world where water transport over relatively short distances is routine. Some of these newer high-speed vessels have a catamaran (or twin-hulled) design, and are notable for a comfortable ride in well-appointed surroundings; they are also equipped with the latest developments in navigational and safety equipment. The illustration shows one of the finest of these new high-speed catamaran ferries, in service with BC Ferries in Canada. The *Spirit of British Columbia,* another notable ferry in its sizeable fleet, is 560-feet long—the equivalent of two football fields back-to-back—with a total capacity of 2,100 people plus 470 vehicles; it was built in 1993.

100. SUPERSHIP *FREEDOM*

As the technologies available for the design and construction of oceangoing ships continue to evolve, there are plans in the works for superships of the future unlike anything that has gone before. The most ambitious of these is the *Freedom,* envisioned as a self-contained floating city. She is projected to be a massive 4,320-feet long, weighing in at 2.7 million tons, and with a superstructure twenty-five stories high. There will be as many as 50,000 people living on board, plus 15,000 employees for the many on-board shops and services. The *Freedom* will sail around the world, visiting the warmest regions with the best weather as she goes. She will be equipped with a flight deck on top similar to an aircraft-carrier platform for the landing and take-off of light aircraft, jets, and helicopters; and she will even have her own marina attached at the stern for small boats. Only the future can tell if this extraordinary vision will ever become a reality.

Index

(The number following the name of each ship refers to its caption number in the book.)

Background Illustration: Stern decoration of *Vasa* (#24), Rigsarkivet, Copenhagen, Denmark